This engraving by William Blake, c. 1796, was plate LXXX in John G. Stedman, *Narrative of a Five Years' Expedition, Against the Revolted Negroes of Surinam in Guiana, on the Wild Coast of South America, from the Year 1772 to 1777* (London, 1796). While one hand of Europe limply holds the rope that links the three continents, the other more rigorously clasps the hand of Africa in sisterly equality. This was a dramatic innovation in the concept of the relationship between the continents, reflecting Blake's abolitionist perspective.

CAPITALISM AND ANTISLAVERY

Also published by Macmillan

John Iliffe, THE EMERGENCE OF AFRICAN CAPITALISM
(The First Anstey Memorial Lectures in the
University of Kent at Canterbury, 1982)

Other books by Seymour Drescher

ECONOCIDE: British Slavery in the Era of Abolition
ANTI-SLAVERY, RELIGION AND REFORM
(*with Christine Bolt*)

CAPITALISM AND ANTISLAVERY

British Mobilization in Comparative Perspective

The Second Anstey Memorial
Lectures in the University of Kent at Canterbury, 1984

Seymour Drescher
Professor of History, University of Pittsburgh

Foreword by Christine Bolt
Professor of History, University of Kent at Canterbury

M
MACMILLAN
PRESS

First published 1986

Published by
THE MACMILLAN PRESS LTD
Houndmills, Basingstoke, Hampshire RG21 2XS
and London
Companies and representatives
throughout the world

Printed in the United States of America

British Library Cataloguing in Publication Data
Drescher, Seymour
Capitalism and antislavery: British
mobilization in comparative perspective.
(The second Anstey memorial lectures in
the University of Kent at Canterbury; 1984)
1. Slavery—Emancipation   2. Abolitionists
I. Title   II. Series
322.4'4'09034   HT1025
ISBN 0–333–36209–8

To my mother and father

Contents

Foreword by Christine Bolt   viii
Preface   x
A Chronology of Emancipation, 1771–1851   xiii

1 The Foundations of Slavery and Antislavery   1
2 Border Skirmish: Neither Wages nor the Whip   25
3 The Distinctiveness of British Abolitionist Mobilization   50
4 The Breakthrough 1787–92   67
5 The Impact of Popular Mobilization in Britain and the
   Caribbean   89
6 God's Work: Antislavery and Religious Mobilization   111
7 Class Conflict, Hegemony and the Costs of Antislavery   135
8 Antislavery and Capitalism   162

Notes and References   167
Bibliography   269
Index   292

Foreword

The Anstey Memorial Lectures, to be given and published biennially, were established in 1982 to honour Roger Anstey, the first Professor of Modern History in the University of Kent at Canterbury. Before his premature death in 1979, Roger Anstey was working on a sequel to his acclaimed study of *The Atlantic Slave Trade and British Abolition, 1760–1810*. This work was the culmination of a scholarly career which had included teaching appointments at the Universities of Durham and Ibadan; books on *Britain and the Congo in the Nineteenth Century*, and *King Leopold's Legacy: The Congo Under Belgian Rule*; and many articles in collaborative volumes and academic journals. Roger's scholarship is remembered and his company is missed by his colleagues at Kent, especially those in the History school which he helped to build up.

In 1982 the first series of Anstey Memorial Lectures was delivered by John Iliffe of St John's College, Cambridge, on *The Emergence of African Capitalism*, and they were published a year later by Macmillan. Seymour Drescher of the University of Pittsburgh gave the second set of Lectures in 1984, and they have been expanded into this book. Patrick Collinson, who has recently moved from the University of Kent to the University of Sheffield, will give the third series in 1986, on the general theme of religion in history.

The topics covered by these three lecturers clearly relate to Roger Anstey's major intellectual interests, with *Capitalism and Antislavery* addressing an issue which was the principal preoccupation of his last years. Seymour Drescher and Roger Anstey were excellent friends and intellectual sparring partners throughout that time. In one sense rivals in an exacting field of research, they none the less exemplified the generous exchange of ideas and information which is the best side of academic life. It is therefore peculiarly fitting that Seymour Drescher has been able to undertake this volume, and no one would have appreciated more keenly than Roger its freshness in terms of material and interpretation. *Capitalism and Antislavery* focuses on a critical but hitherto neglected aspect of antislavery: the role of popular mobilization. It sheds new light on the Somerset Case and the ending of slavery in Britain. It makes us think again about the composition, methods, regional strengths and distinctiveness of British antislavery, and reexamines its impact on other reform movements, the reactions of the campaign's opponents, and the connection with antislavery of the slave communities themselves. From this deeply felt study, reform re-emerges as reform, rather than capitalist dominance or elite reaction in disguise. There are findings here that should influence the course of the debate on British antislavery for many years to come.

University of Kent at Canterbury CHRISTINE BOLT

Preface

When Thomas Clarkson published his *Essay on the Slavery and Commerce of the Human Species* exactly two centuries ago, personal bondage was the prevailing form of labour in most of the world. For those, like Adam Smith, who were endowed with a long historical perspective and a global vision it seemed unlikely that slavery would ever be generally abolished. Freedom, not slavery, was the peculiar institution. Yet, just over a century after Clarkson's book appeared chattel slavery had been abolished in the Americas and international machinery was in place to facilitate its demise in Africa. However ambiguous were the long-term consequences of that historical process for the welfare of the affected populations, chattel slavery had itself become a peculiar and vanishing institution. Even in the longer perspective of two centuries it remains one of the most remarkable events in modern history, the first and, in a narrow sense, the most successful human rights movement.

A briefer version of what follows was presented as the Roger T. Anstey Memorial Lectures in May 1984. This book is intended as the fleshing out of an approach to British abolitionism first suggested in my earlier book, *Econocide*. At every stage I have been indebted to the international scholarly community. A period of intensive research, provided by a Guggenheim Foundation fellowship in 1977–8, was supplemented by a Huntington Library fellowship in 1982 and an American Philosophical Society grant in 1985. Two exploratory essays on British popular mobilization were written during a residency at Bellagio in the summer of 1980. Both the Anstey Memorial Lectures and the first draft of the present study were written during a Fellowship year at the Woodrow Wilson International Center for Scholars in Washington. The final version was completed while I was the first Secretary of the Center's European Program in 1984–85.

The gathering of materials was eased at every stage by archivists and librarians in Bedford, Brussels, Cambridge, Dublin, Duke University, Gloucester, Liverpool, Manchester, Norwich, New York, Oxford, Shrewsbury and Washington. For more extended demands on their service, I am grateful to the staffs of Friends House Library in London, Rhodes House Library in Oxford, the Bibliothèque Nationale and the Archives Nationales in Paris, the Henry E. Huntington Library in San Marino and the Hillman Library at the University of Pittsburgh. Debbie Nye at the Wilson Center and Faye Schneider at Pitt ably demonstrated the prowess of the word processor in taking on innumerable revisions.

Colleagues and friends have offered me an abundance of opportunities to explore various lines of argument along the way. My deeply missed companion, Roger Anstey, provided an international forum for the comparative analysis of antislavery at a Bellagio conference in 1978. Robert Fogel and David Landes enabled me to present one aspect of my thoughts on abolitionist mobilization at a Harvard seminar in 1980. Duncan Rice brought me to Hamilton College to present some soundings on the relationship between the ideologies of antislavery and industrial reform. The Woodrow Wilson Center offered an unprecedent mass of critical interlocutors from every field in the humanities and social sciences, as well as the opportunity for a formal colloquium on British popular mobilization, with Stanley Engerman and Robert Fogel as commentators. Finally, the Anstey lectures' audience constituted a lively and challenging mixture of scholars and nonspecialists.

A glimpse at the notes amply reveals how much my own analysis involves interchanges with a host of contemporary scholars. Some, above all David Eltis and Robert Fogel, have generously furnished me with unpublished drafts of essays or books in progress. Others, like David Brion Davis, James Walvin and James Epstein brought new data and essays to my attention. In return, I hope that I have fairly summarized the views of others. Fellow scholars will recognize interrogation as the sincerest form of flattery.

I have been fortunate in having colleagues prepared to flatter my own ideas in just that spirit. Van Beck Hall, Mary Turner and Lawrence Lipking provided valuable advice on various points of substance and presentation. Howard Temperley offered judicious comments on an early draft. Stanley Engerman, to whom I am already indebted for having read two drafts of *Econocide*, performed a similar service for all three drafts of this study. His enthusiasm and incredibly rapid responses stand in clear defiance of the scholarly laws of supply and demand.

I am grateful for the warm hospitality extended to me during the past decade by the Anstey family, Serge Daget, Margo Lieberman,

Brian and Andrea Levy, David Richardson, Margaret Stocks, Howard Temperley, James Walvin and Richard Weiss. The burdens of hospitality were not borne only by friends and colleagues. Each week for eighteen months my resourceful wife dissolved the monotonal rhythm of commuter marriage in the counterpoint of weekend honeymoons.

Finally, I would like to thank Christine and Ian Bolt for lavishly offering me their home in Kent and their indefatigable support during the Anstey lectures at Canterbury. They and the sponsors of those lectures allowed me to resume a discourse on the history of slavery only a few yards from the spot where I so often exchanged ideas with Roger himself. As I wrote in *Econocide*, whatever divergences of interpretation are apparent in our works, his impact will still be evident.

SEYMOUR DRESCHER

A Chronology of Emancipation, 1772–1851

1772   Chief Justice Mansfield rules that slavery is not supported by English law.

1774   The English Society of Friends votes to expel members engaged in the slave trade. The US Continental Congress bans slave importations.

1776   The Societies of Friends in England and Pennsylvania require members to free their slaves or face expulsion.

1777   The Vermont Constitution prohibits slavery.

1780   Pennsylvania adopts a policy of gradual emancipation.

1783   A Massachusetts judicial decision interprets the state Constitution as having abolished slavery. British Quakers petition Parliament against the slave trade.

1784   Rhode Island and Connecticut pass gradual emancipation laws.

1787   Sierra Leone Colony is founded. An anti-slave trade society is formed in London. Manchester launches the first petition campaign.

1788   A *Société des Amis des Noirs* is formed in France. Four Northern US States make the slave trade illegal.

1791   Slave Revolution breaks out in in St Domingue

1792   Second abolitionist campaign in England. The House of Commons resolves on gradual abolition. A Danish ordinance decrees gradual slave trade abolition. Sierra Leone is re-settled.

1793   Upper Canada enacts gradual emancipation. Abolitionist activity in Britain declines.

1794   The French National Convention abolishes slavery in the French colonies, a law which is repealed by Napoleon in 1802. The British occupy some French colonies, restoring slavery.

1795 Revolutionary warfare spreads in the Caribbean, including British colonies.

1796–7 British Caribbean slave territory expands through conquest.

1799 New York passes a gradual emancipation law.

1804 Haiti wins its independence.

1806–8 Popular abolition societies revive in Britain. Britain and the USA prohibit the slave trade.

1811 Slave trading is made a felony in Britain.

1813 Gradual emancipation is adopted in Argentina.

1814 A public campaign is launched against the revival of the French slave trade under terms of the Anglo–French peace treaty. The Netherlands prohibits slave trading. Gradual emancipation begins in Colombia.

1815 Napoleon decrees French slave trade abolition. The Congress of Vienna condemns the slave trade. A Parliamentary campaign begins for British slave registration.

1816 Blacks begin to win emancipation in the Latin American wars of Independence. A slave uprising occurs in Barbados.

1817 Portugal prohibits slave trading north of the equator.

1819 Britain establishes an anti-slave trade squadron on the Coast of Africa. The USA also authorizes an African naval patrol.

1820 The USA makes slave trading piracy.

1823 A London Anti-Slavery Committee is formed. Another petition campaign is launched. Slavery is abolished in Chile. A slave uprising occurs in Demerara.

1824 Slavery is abolished in Central America.

1829 Slavery is abolished in Mexico.

1831 Slavery is abolished in Bolivia. A British petition is launched for the immediate emancipation of British colonial slaves. The 'Baptist War' breaks out in Jamaica. The French again abolish their slave trade.

1833 The British again petition for immediate emancipation. An Emancipation Act is passed.

1834 British slavery is transformed in the colonies into Negro apprenticeship. A new French Society for the Abolition of Slavery is formed.

1838 After another petition campaign Negro Apprenticeship is abolished.

1839 The Papacy condemns the slave trade.

1840 An international anti-slavery conference is held in London.

1841   A multi-power Treaty is signed in Europe, guaranteeing mutual rights to search vessels for slaves. France refuses to ratify it.

1842   Slavery is abolished in Uruguay.

1844   French workers petition the Chamber of Deputies for slave emancipation.

1847   A second petition for slave emancipation is sent to the French Chambers.

1848   Slavery is abolished in the French and Danish colonies.

1851   Slavery is abolished in Ecuador. The slave trade to Brazil is ended.

1 The Foundations of Slavery and Antislavery

For almost a century and a half the history of British antislavery was the story of its leaders. Abolitionist historiography remained serenely ensconced within the framework of Thomas Clarkson's first narrative of the movement in 1808. Overcoming an entrenched economic interest, the abolitionist 'Saints' won a series of victories for humanity over brutal materialism and exploitation. Antislavery was the quintessential example of the Whig interpretation of history: a progressive political narrative more closely interwoven with religious than with economic or social development.

Roger Anstey's *The Atlantic Slave Trade and British Abolition* clearly stands as the most recent representative of the Clarksonian tradition. David Brion Davis aptly noted that Anstey was a kind of reborn abolitionist. In all of Anstey's writings, abolition was the political achievement of men inspired by a profoundly dynamic theology over ruthless sectional and commercial interests. For him, as for the 'Saints' and the nation which followed them, the destruction of the slave trade and of slavery was the modern era's most tangible evidence of human progress and divine providence.[1]

Anstey's work, however, could not be written with quite the serene assurance which had characterized the historiography of abolition for a century before him. He felt impelled to come to grips with a critical interpretation of abolition most closely associated with Eric Williams's *Capitalism and Slavery*. Appearing in 1944, Williams's work drew strength from a second stream of abolitionist historiography, the Marxian perspective of C. L. R. James and others. For Williams the rise of the Atlantic slave system fitted with extraordinary precision into the world market forces of the early modern period. Nowhere in history did men seem to have been more attuned to market incentives, to the possibilities of maximizing labour discipline and proprietary rights, or to openings for vast networks of credit-and-production. Williams simply proposed to carry forward the same process to explain slavery's demise with an analogous compound of economic forces and political economy. What made Williams's paradigm all the more intuitively compelling was that British abolition seemed to coincide with the very moment in British history when its society was being fully attuned to the forces of the world market.

Williams was also able to draw on two venerable critical readings of British abolition. From the outset British abolitionism had been viewed as a Machiavellian ploy by many foreign political observers. Whether Britain intended to destroy the slave trade to shore up its lagging West Indian colonies or to destroy all slavery in the Americas in the interests of an Indian monopoly, foreigners saw only a new version of perfidious Albion beneath the cloak of humanity. Moreover, domestic critics of the abolitionists saw in abolition a new form of ideological humbug, designed to divert attention from evils and social conflicts closer to home. Both groups rejected the manifest content of antislavery in favour of some less obvious motive or function.[2] This critical tradition flowed through and beyond Williams's work, affecting even Anstey's approach and assessment: as the latter wrote, almost wistfully, in older simpler days he would not have had to assess the relative importance of religious enthusiasm, national interest and political circumstance.[3]

Even if most of the specifics of Williams's economic argument have since been undermined, there remains the historian's residual hunch that somehow it is 'surely no accident' that abolition coincided with Britain's industrial revolution. Just what the nature of that connection was has proven more elusive than Williams imagined it to be.[4] What almost all recent historical works on British abolition have in common (including those of David Davis, David Eltis, Howard Temperley and James Walvin) is an attempt to understand abolitionism by expanding the older frame of reference beyond the linear narrative of abolitionist initiatives and a succession of Parliamentary debates and manoeuvres.[5] During the last 40 years it is this search for the ecology of British antislavery, its general social and imperial context, which has generated the most fruitful and most intense controversy.

I propose to approach the subject from two angles. First, British slavery was only one of a number of analogous systems formed by Europe's trading and settler diasporas in the three centuries after the first explorations of America. The British polity was also one of a number of analogous polities which legislated the termination of their respective slave systems between the 1780s and the 1880s. One may learn something of the significant variables by viewing the destruction process in a comparative context.

Second, the movement against slavery was only one of a number of simultaneous changes occurring within Britain itself during a period of dramatic social and political upheaval. What I will call the age of British abolitionism may be dated with fair precision. It began in 1787–8 with the first mass campaign against the slave trade and ended just half a century later in 1838 with a mass petition campaign against Negro Apprenticeship. I will focus attention on this period when popular pressure was effectively deployed as a means of altering national policy. There were echoes of popular abolitionism after 1840, but in historical perspective they have the quality of aftershocks in the wake of a fundamental shift.[6] I will therefore attempt to look a little more closely at those fault lines in British society which seem to have partly determined the timing and intensity of abolition.

In one respect historians are at a disadvantage in attempting such a probe. The great flood of petitions that flowed into Parliament between 1788 and 1838 has left only scattered manuscript remains and a residue of printed summaries and aggregate figures. It will therefore often be necessary for me to approach the question of popular abolitionism using more indirect indicators of popular behaviour than are often available to scholars. It is clearly possible that I have been led by the nature of my documents to make errors of judgment, great and small. But the evidence at hand is not insignificant. It indicates, at the very least, that an important and underexploited frontier remains accessible to students of both British antislavery and early industrial society.

One can best approach antislavery through slavery. This is not only because of the inevitable dialectic between any institution and its enemies, but because historiographically antislavery is now the weaker sister. During the past generation historians have been able to measure with ever growing precision and assurance the economic mechanisms governing trends in the Atlantic slave system. In one very important sense slavery was by no means a 'peculiar institution'. Gemery and Hogendorn's recent designation of the slave trade as the 'uncommon market' was appropriate only to the extent that its commodities were human beings, not because the buyers, sellers or users of slaves behaved differently from those in other markets. As economic men their actions and their profits were far more 'normal' than the post–abolitionist generation deemed morally acceptable.[7]

Quite naturally an economic model which could account so well for the establishment of slave systems and for the flow of slaves to the New World tempts one to explain the destruction process by economic forces operating in reverse. Eric Williams sought such an explanation in terms of a continuous secular decline in British slavery's imperial significance as a trading partner after 1776. This decline supposedly triggered the rise of hostile capitalist interests. Williams put it trenchantly and symmetrically: 'the capitalists had first encouraged slavery and then helped to destroy it'. Abolition was fundamentally a form of capitalist euthanasia. Subsequent research has failed to sustain his timing or particular complex of economic forces. Instead, if one considers the economic mix which stimulated the system – the American advantages in land and climate, the European advantages in capital development and international trading and the African advantages in supplying deracinated labour – the world economy as a whole seems to have been as optimal for expanding the Atlantic slave system at the end of British slavery in the 1830s as it was at the beginning of popular abolitionism in the 1780s, or at any time during the so-called 'golden age' of the mid-eighteenth century. As David Eltis notes, despite Britain's withdrawal from slavery and its creation of a powerful military–diplomatic complex, the Atlantic slave economy entered what was probably the most dynamic and profitable period in its existence in the 40 years after 1820.[8]

At every major juncture in the history of abolition British policy was undertaken in the teeth of a world economic context which placed a premium on the expansion of slavery. This was as much the case in 1792 when the House of Commons resolved to abolish gradually the slave trade as in 1799 when Parliament voted to tighten the conditions for carrying slaves, or in 1805–7 when Parliament finally prohibited British slave trading to both foreign and imperial areas. It was true after 1814, when Britain accelerated diplomatic and financial pressure on the other European powers to abolish their respective slave trades. It was true when Parliament resolved on the amelioration of slavery in 1823 and on immediate emancipation in 1833. It was still true when West Indian Negro Apprenticeship was abolished in 1838 and when British Indian slavery was abolished in the early 1840s. It was as true by mercantilist principles when a mercantilist British government unilaterally restricted the carrying capacity of its own ships in 1788, as it was when a laissez-faire British government unilaterally interdicted the slave trade in Brazilian coastal waters in 1850. Indeed, from John Bright's laissez–faire perspective of the 1840s every British anti-slave trade action after abolition in restraint of international trade had been an exercise in irrationality.[9] The real economic paradox of abolition is that in one major region after another – the British colonies, the American South, Cuba and Brazil – *political* power had to intervene to constrict or to abolish major slave systems whose economic advantages remained intact until well after the transformation of British abolitionism into a world human rights movement.

The key to the timing of slavery's ultimate demise in the Western economy lies not in its economic functioning but in its social peculiarity. In contrast with other slave systems, Atlantic slavery was a highly differentiated intercontinental system. Africa, the New World and Europe not only contributed separate components of labour, land and capital; they could remain relatively autonomous in their development for three centuries.[10]

In comparative perspective, which of the components of the Atlantic slave system underwent the greatest structural change prior to or during Britain's age of abolition? An enormous amount of recent research on the history of Africa has shown that continent as undergoing dynamic and complex patterns of change in relation to European and internal pressures, both to increase and to restrict the slave trade and slavery.[11] Yet it still seems to be clear that throughout the period up to British emancipation, Africa presented no structural impediment to the continuity of the Atlantic slave system either through a constraint on its supply of slaves or the evolution of products competitive with New World staples. Patrick Manning's recent summary indicates that slave exports from Africa were at or near all-time peaks in the age of British abolition. The supply-side capacity continued through and beyond British emancipation. Indeed, as many or more slaves were apparently exported from Africa in each decade of the period 1750–1840 than in any before or after (see Table 1.1). Moreover the average purchase price of slaves in West Africa seems to have fallen fairly steadily relative to prices of slaves in importing areas until long after British emancipation in 1833.[12] Barring political restraints, there was little in the volume or price trends to encourage a shift in the allocation of European capital away from the purchase of slave labour during the peak half-century of British abolitionism after 1788. The outstanding long-term characteristic of the African segment of Atlantic slavery seems to have been its extraordinary continuity as a support system of the slave trade.

It can be argued that what changed in Europe's relation to Africa

TABLE 1.1   *Atlantic slave trade (per annum) 1721–1850*

Period	Slaves (thousands)
1721–30	39.8
1731–40	52.2
1741–50	53.6
1751–60	52.9
1761–70	63.5
1771–80	58.0
1781–90	88.8
1791–1800	76.4
1801–10	61.7
1811–20	53.6
1821–30	64.6
1831–40	54.6
1841–50	43.3

SOURCE   Paul E. Lovejoy, 'The Volume of the Atlantic Slave Trade: A Synthesis', *Journal of African History*, 23 (1982), 473–501, Tables IV, VI; 1791–1810, ibid., as corrected by the unpublished estimates of D. Richardson; 1811–20, ibid.; 1821–40 from D. Eltis 'Free and Coerced Transatlantic Migrations', *American Historical Review* 88:2, Table 1.

towards the end of the eighteenth century was a suddenly expanded sense of the potential rapidity of social change to 'free labour' and rising consumption in Africa. But at best this was a perception of potential within Britain. Moreover the moment of high expectations diminished rapidly around 1800 with the devaluation of hopes in the Sierra Leone experiment.[13] There is little evidence of a sustained revaluation of the likelihood of rapid internal social transformation by Europeans during the age of popular abolition. Towards the end of the seventeenth century Blome's geography of the world allotted all of Africa about 3 per cent of its space. The proportion did not alter appreciably during the next 150 years: neither did the perception of West African backwardness. A popular geography which was reprinted throughout the age of abolition felt no need to alter its brief introduction to a static Africa by a *single* sentence from the 1770s to the 1820s.[14] As Anthony Barker said in summarizing the era of agitation against the British slave trade, the latter's days might seem numbered, but the association of Africa with cultural and economic degradation remained entrenched.[15] Until long after British emancipation even the radicals of Europe assumed that any major transformation of traditional society in Africa needed to be initiated from without, though not necessarily or even preferably through political domination.[16]

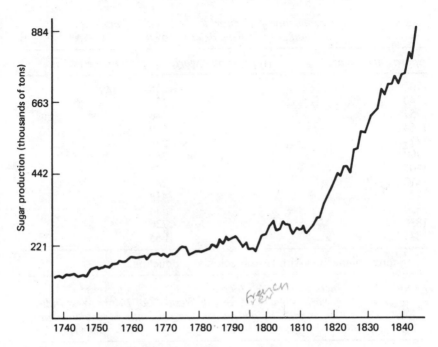

FIGURE 1.1   *World sugar production, 1740–1840*

SOURCE N. Deerr, *The History of Sugar*, 2 vols (London, 1949–50), passim. Estimates based on recorded figures and interpolations from these figures, with
no allowance for clayed conversion. (See S. Drescher *Econocide: British
Slavery in the Era of Abolition* (Pittsburgh, 1977), appendix II, 193 ff.)

The second link in Atlantic slavery, the Americas, was also a
clearly expanding sector of the system from well before the emergence
of British political abolitionism until long after emancipation. By
1750 a vast area between the Chesapeake and the Rio de la Plata in
South America provided an enormous frontier for slave systems
which were expanding far more rapidly than many areas in Europe,
whether based on bound or free labour.[17] In terms of major staples,
slave production of sugar, coffee, and cotton for the North Atlantic
increased after 1750. As Figure 1.1 shows, after drops caused by the
American and French revolutionary wars, sugar production increased at a far greater rate until 1840 than during any three decades
prior to the advent of abolitionism. As for cotton, slave labour
already provided 70 per cent of Britain's booming cotton industry at
the beginning of the age of abolitionism in 1787. That proportion
reached nine-tenths by the end of apprenticeship in 1838.[18]

TABLE 1.2   *Sugar production for export to the North Atlantic and comparison with British growth*

Approximate year	Approximate world metric tonnage (000s)
1700	58
1740	126
1754	156
1764	189
1774	220
1790	262
1807	271
1812	281
1821	438
1830	584
1836	726
1845	1063

Long-term comparison with British colonial production:

Period	Increase (%) of world sugar (per yr)*	Increase (%) of British West Indian sugar (per yr)	Increase (%) of British West Indies and Mauritian sugar (per yr)
1700–54	+1.8	+1.3	—
1740–90	+1.5	+1.7	—
1764–1812	+0.8	+2.0	—
1807–47	+3.5	−0.3	+0.5
1805/6–1837/8†	+2.8	−0.3	+0.2

* using nominal figures (excluding clayed conversion)
† using clayed conversion figures for 1805/06

SOURCES   (a) for 1700 R. S. Dunn, *Sugar and Slaves: The Rise of the Planter Class in the English West Indies 1624–1713* (Chapel Hill, 1972), 234; for 1740–1845 (world figures), N. Deerr, *The History of Sugar*, 2 vols (London, 1949–50), passim; for British sugar 1700–90, *Report from the East India Company* (1792), 23; for British sugar 1790–1847, *Parliamentary Papers 1847–8*, 58 (400); for world production† 1805/06, S. Drescher, *Econocide: British Slavery in the Era of Abolition* (Pittsburgh, 1977), 78.

As with Africa, this does not mean that there were not considerable and even dramatic changes within or between regions from the mid-eighteenth to the mid-nineteenth centuries. The leading tropical producers of 1770, French St Domingue and British Jamaica, had by 1840 been supplanted by Cuba and Brazil. Table 1.2 illustrates how British slave production of sugar became relatively stagnant as the

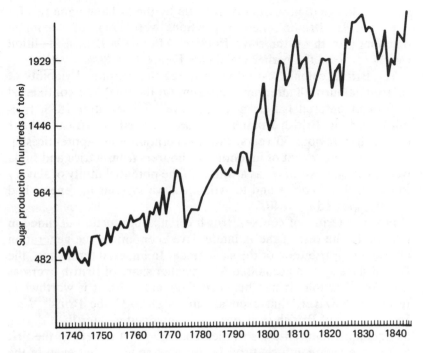

FIGURE 1.2 *British colonial sugar production 1740–1840*

SOURCE N. Deerr, *The History of Sugar, passim*, British colony figures plus interpolations (no allowance for clayed conversion).

abolition of the slave trade took hold during the second, third and fourth decades of the nineteenth century.

In the world economy, however, there was no competitive alternative to slave-grown cotton or sugar during the age of British abolitionism. On the eve of British emancipation slave labour still produced well over nine-tenths of the Atlantic economy's sugar. At their peak during the Napoleonic wars non-slave Eastern sugars constituted less than 4 per cent of the North Atlantic market.[19] Heavily protected free-labour competitors like beet sugar did not contribute markedly to the world market until well after British emancipation. I have elsewhere argued that the British slave sector of the Atlantic economy was curtailed by the abolition of the slave trade in 1807 after a period of dynamic growth. By the turn of the nineteenth century the British colonies produced over half the Atlantic economy's sugar. Before slave-trade abolition British capitalists had grabbed the lion's share of the windfall market opened up by the St Domingue revolution of 1791. Britain's new acquisitions were areas of maximum potential growth on the slave frontier. After 1808 British abolition clearly reversed the earlier trend (see Figure 1.2).[20]

The British colonial case demonstrated the continued viability of coerced labour well after emancipation. Of the total intercontinental flow of indentured labourers to ex-slave colonies after 1838, two-thirds went to British frontier colonies deprived of African labour during the previous 30 years. For a generation after apprenticeship more than 95 per cent of indentured labourers from Africa and India went to ex-slave colonies as a whole.[21] The potential utility of slavery to the British colonies and to Atlantic slave systems in general had not disappeared by 1840.

In world terms, of course, British colonial production declined in relation to the rest of the Atlantic slave economy in the generation after the redistribution of the slave trade. In imperial terms, too, the British·slave system accounted for a smaller share of British overseas trade by 1830 than it had between 1760 and 1820. It is worthwhile recalling, however, that even as late as 1828–32 the British West Indian share of British overseas trade remained greater than during any quinquennium in the so-called golden age of slavery in the first half of the eighteenth century. It also now appears that even in the last years of slavery the British slave plantations were still profitable and viable. According to J. R. Ward, the returns to planters were still as good as those on equivalent investments elsewhere.[22]

Taken as a whole, then, the economic relationship of the American colonial societies to Atlantic slavery remained stable and positive. As in Africa, regional sectors rose and fell but, until British abolitionism intervened, only one major staple region destroyed the institution: Haiti, for whose rulers after 1804 the level of staple exportation was insignificant compared with the fear of reconquest or re-enslavement. During or shortly after their struggles for independence the largely non-plantation societies of North and Latin America abolished the slave trade and, more slowly and hesitantly, slavery itself. In almost all areas which produced tropical and subtropical export staples the emancipation process was prolonged and, as in the French case, sometimes reversed.

It is the third geographical zone of the Atlantic slave system which underwent the greatest economic change between 1780 and 1840, with Britain clearly in the lead. In this sense Eric Williams and others have appropriately suggested that any structural change underlying the destruction of slavery is likely to be found in a Britain transformed by capitalist industrialization. However, one must not assume that industrialization somehow generated a technology which undermined coercive labour systems. We need only recall that a pre-industrial France both decreed emancipation in 1794 and the restoration of slavery wherever its military forces could prevail in 1802. France reached the same level of industrialization by 1840 that Britain had attained in 1760 without having generated a broad-based abolitionist movement. Finally the Soviet Union stood at the same level of industrialization in 1920 as Britain had more than a century before; yet whereas Britain dismantled its slave island system during the generation after 1810, the Soviet state created a forced labour archipelago at its frontiers and the Nazis reintroduced forced labour at a much higher level of industrialization in the 1940s.

Explanations deriving from demographic models for both the rise and fall of slavery will founder on the same anomalies as those which have undermined analogous economic models. William McNeill posits a fundamental change in world and European demographic patterns to account for the rise of antislavery attitudes in Europe in the 'great watershed' of 1760–90: 'Abundant, and overabundant, population makes resort to legal compulsion of labor unnecessary; and the abhorrence of slavery that flourished so mightily in the British Isles in the later 18th and 19th centuries co-incided with an unexampled growth of British population that strained job opportunities to the limit.' A population with accompanying labour shortage at home surely 'would have sustained a different climate of opinion'.

However, there was no fundamental change of demographic pattern in the tropical world beyond Europe in the 'watershed' period of 1760–90. Except at its temperate fringe, the tropical and sub-tropical Americas were still overwhelmingly European slave 'frontiers', attracting few free men as labourers in the late eighteenth century. As for the correlation between metropolitan overabundance and antislavery in the British Isles, McNeill's paradigm does not square with the evidence. One reasonable indicator of 'overabundance' and Malthusian pressure is the 'net rate' of migration from England between 1541 and 1871. Wrigley and Schofield show that the English established their overseas slave system during the very decades when their net migration rate reached a three-century peak (1641–61). At the other end of the process, British abolitionism 'took off' exactly when the net migration rate sank to its tricentennial *low* (1771–91).[23]

The outcome is the opposite of that predicted by the NcNeill–Malthusian model. Regional differentiation within England makes the pattern even more anomalous. Mass antislavery was born precisely where and when the economy was growing fastest, where real wages were rising, and where the local labour shortage was most acute during the last third of the eighteenth century. This is exactly the situation in which McNeill's demographic model calls for a non-abolitionist 'climate of opinion'. Those areas of Southern England or Ireland with their more than abundant and underemployed agricultural populations were drawn into the national abolitionist movement least and last during the nineteenth century.

Since world slavery was generally complementary to European economic and demographic patterns during the generations before 1790, we must look to indirect effects of the economic development of slavery to explain the timing and intensity of British abolition. Neither prices nor population patterns offer us evidence analogous to that which accounts for the rise of slavery.

BEYOND THE LINE

Within its overseas economic patterns, then, there was no general shift which forced or encouraged a radical redirection of European resources away from Atlantic slavery. Even European regions without footholds in America were still forming ventures into the slave economy as late as the end of the eighteenth century.[24] Yet, less than halfway into this peak century of transoceanic slavery (1750–1850), collective pressures emerged to destroy the pattern of plantation labour with which the South Atlantic had functioned for centuries.

Atlantic slavery was institutionally and economically the direct heir of medieval slavery. Both the Christian and Moslem dominated areas of the Mediterranean drew on the Roman model. Historians have carefully detailed the movement of slave-grown sugar and the plantation system from the Levant through Cyprus, Crete, Sicily, Italy, Spain and the African-Atlantic islands. The Iberian pioneers drew on both their Roman Law traditions and Mediterranean technology and capital in transporting the institution of slavery to the New World. As the centre of sugar production moved westwards the source of slaves also shifted. The North–eastern source of Mediterranean slaves was interrupted by Ottoman expansion in the mid-fifteenth century and Africa became the dominant source of Mediterranean slaves. Charles

Verlinden has demonstrated that what we have come to regard as the distinguishing features of New World slavery had evolved in the Mediterranean decades before the first Spanish encounter with America.[25] The historical continuity and depth of institutional slavery in the Mediterranean therefore allowed for the smooth development of institutionally analogous metropolitan and overseas Iberian slave systems.

Since Atlantic slavery remained congruent with Iberian institutions before the age of abolition, and since economic behaviour was not 'irrational' anywhere within the Atlantic system, we must look elsewhere to explain its demise. The key, I think, lies in the fact that the slave systems of North-western European states were indeed 'peculiar' institutions in relation to the metropolitan societies. From the beginning they were economically, socially and geographically anomalous. What then constituted the nexus of North–western European overseas slave systems? It was not their juridical or ideological continuity with the classical Mediterranean systems but a recognition that beyond the European world maximum economic benefits could be achieved only by encouraging the full development of institutions overseas which were not sanctioned at home. The result was an existential rather than a theological or philosophical dualism, which constituted the bedrock of the British slave system. The same ocean which linked complementary economic systems separated divergent social systems.

North–western Europe's staple export colonies were originally no more than specialized fragments of the metropolis embedded in a special environment. From its beginning the British involvement in the slave system differed from that of Iberian predecessors. It was not, as Eugene Genovese and Elizabeth Fox-Genovese argue for Europe as a whole, rooted primarily in the values created by the crusading aristocracies of the Mediterranean and the habits and territorial ambitions of feudal nobilities.[26] Its merchants did not follow royal banners or the cross to Africa and the Americas. Many of the slave-trading and colonial ventures were established primarily by charters to private investors, endowed from the outset with quasi-public privileges in whatever commercial or territorial foothold they could themselves establish beyond the line. As for the cross, it was most conspicuous in the English colonies only where, as in Massachusetts and Pennsylvania, it was distinctly not the royal version. Two centuries after settlement the Established Church had no Bishop beyond the line and a stillborn programme for conversion of the slaves in the plantation colonies. Secular latitudinarianism was a cornerstone of British slavery.

Given both the difficulty of expensive labour and the lure of comparative environmental advantage, North-western European rulers sustained the formation of social systems which to a greater or lesser extent differed from those in Europe. The character of slavery in the European-dominated areas of South-east Asia also owed more to the regional environment than to inherited European legal ideas.[27] Whatever the economic similarities and differences between New World plantation slavery and both its Mediterranean and African prototypes, there appears to have been a clearer idea north of the Mediterranean of slavery as an institution designed primarily for the colonial area. France, with its partial Mediterranean orientation, went furthest in attempting to incorporate non-European slaves into its metropolis.[28] But none of the three major North-western slave powers – France, Britain, and the Netherlands – actually incorporated slave law into their own social systems.

For North–western Europeans slavery was a specialized instrument designed to encourage the rapid development of their transoceanic trade and production. On the American side of the line the choice for and proportion of slaves in the labour force was equally pragmatic. In the experimental period of the sixteenth and seventeenth centuries severe labour shortages were experienced in every settlement from Canada to South America. The inhabitants of French Canada and New England purchased relatively few slaves and definitive trends waited on the balance between the prices of labour and staples. In 1670 Virginia's proportion of blacks was less than Rhode Island's a century later. As late as the early eighteenth century the proportion of slaves in New York and New Jersey was greater than in North Carolina. David Brion Davis rightly emphasizes the willingness of every early American colony to use Africans as a solution to its labour problem.[29]

Despite this circumstantial accommodation to slavery in the New World on the European side of the Atlantic there seems to have been a greater determination north of Iberia to confine slavery, as an institution, to colonial areas. In the early sixteenth century thousands of African slaves were imported into Lisbon and placed in southern Portugal, Spain and other parts of the Western Mediterranean. Even in Portugal, when the first boatload of Africans was marketed in Lagos in 1444, the crowd was so moved by the sight of families being separated and sold that they intervened. Thereafter, however, the institutional continuity and economic incentives of slavery overcame this initial reaction.[30] Slavery remained firmly implanted in Iberia. In sixteenth-century Europe the 'underground railroad' ran across the Pyrenees to Toulouse. When an enterprising Dutch slaver brought his cargo to the city of Middleburg in the Netherlands in 1596 the citizens declared the slaves free. Thereafter Dutch slavers delivered their cargoes to the Americas or dropped their Barbary captives at Mediterranean ports.[31] During the early seventeenth century, when the Dutch seafarers were accumulating more slaves than they could deliver to their own colonies, they looked to the other American islands even at the cost of developing the colonies of their rivals.[32] The Janus-faced French, with both Atlantic and Mediterranean interests, briefly experimented with African galley slaves in the seventeenth century. They later made provision to allow black slaves to reside temporarily in France without losing their slave status, but the French were also clearly disturbed by the sight of men being bartered in public on the streets of Paris.[33]

Apparently no attempt was ever made to import whole boatloads of African slaves into Britain. Nor were exceptional slave laws promulgated in England, a situation which was ultimately to generate the first clash between slave-holders and their antagonists in eighteenth-century Britain. The buying and selling of human beings in batches remained an integral part of the culture-shock which faced metropolitans beyond the line. An early eighteenth-century English admiral, in his first letter from Jamaica, disgustedly described the 'shoal of buyers' flocking on board a slaver to pick over the 'poor Fellows . . . as if they had been so many horses.'[34] We will consider the British case in greater detail, but we may note that one of the strongest images evoked in Mansfield's crowded courtroom during the famous Somerset case of 1772 was the threat of people being brought to England to be sold in lots like cattle.

In any event North-western European states were clearly not anxious to give the same encouragement to the flow of cheap black slaves to the metropolis as to the colonies. However receptive Iberia had been to black labour when Portugal developed the African slave trade in the fifteenth century, the Anglo-Dutch economies had an abundant domestic labour force on hand when they systematically entered the trade two centuries later. At the end of the sixteenth century the English government was more anxious to restrict than to encourage black immigration and made an attempt to expel those who had already settled in the country.[35] Demographic conditions in

England were then quite different from those in Iberia at the dawn of the Atlantic slave trade. Moreover, by the end of the sixteenth century certain customary restrictions about treating fellow Christians as chattels had become too deeply rooted in the metropolis to be easily violated. When the Barbadian planters were shifting towards an African labour supply Parliament was outraged at the news of Britons being sold like cattle in the markets of Barbados.[36] The issue was not, of course, harsh treatment. The same Parliament had few qualms about the most ruthless deportation of Irish resisters to the West Indies as bound labour.[37]

It might be plausible to explain the ease of introduction of racial slavery into British America as just one more degree of dependency placed at the bottom of the colonial social ladder beneath indentured servitude. However, it seems clear that both masters who bought and servants who sold their labour were aware of the discontinuity between servants and slaves which made for crucial differences in the willingness of servants to bond and masters to buy bonded labour. Where the proportion of black slaves to white servants remained very low the slave status did tend to become just another rung of domestic dependency with many avenues of entry and assimilation into Euro-American society. In the plantation zone, where the proportions were reversed, the treatment of white servants tended to diverge in time from the conditions of imported Africans.

Alexis de Tocqueville pointed out that the great democratic revolution which overtook France in 1789 occurred in that part of Continental Europe where the peasantry was already least encumbered by personal servitude. In another illustration of the paradox, it was in just those areas of the British empire where the condition of blacks most closely approximated that of free whites that the institution of slavery first came under attack. In the areas of most intensive African settlement not only was the production system more clearly differentiated from that of the metropolis but slavery was more consciously articulated as something alien to the Euro-American heritage.[38]

For eighteenth-century Americans slavery was a social and economic fact which had become a racial fact. For eighteenth-century Britons, slavery remained far more a geographically than racially conceived system. British metropolitans were told endlessly that slavery was especially repugnant to their constitution. An attempt to reintroduce even temporary slavery for white Englishmen in the mid-sixteenth century had failed because of popular reluctance to enforce such a statute.[39] Throughout the entire period when Britons were expanding New World slavery, British pamphleteers, jurists, newspaper editors and geographers presented England as an island of liberty in a world filled with slaves. Anyone who read accounts of voyages, popular geographies or newspaper accounts of foreign social systems knew that if Britons were not slaves, almost everyone else was. There were Polish and Russian peasants who were 'mere slaves'. There were beautiful white Caucasian slaves.There were Christian slaves of the Ottoman Empire, who were sold by other Christians, even by members of their own families. There were, of course, galley slaves in France, and European (even British) slaves in North Africa. The most casual readers always had to make their way through a dozen varieties of Eurasian bondage before they came to Guinea or Negroland.[40]

Geographers, journalists and publicists served up an endless array of slaveries beyond the control of either British subjects or statesmen. In 1772 Arthur Young, who counted everything in (or out of) sight for eighteenth-century Britons, offered a political arithmetician's birds'-eye survey of slavery with quantitative precision. Of the estimated 775 million on the face of the earth Young allotted 33 million to freedom. All of Asia, Africa, most of the Americas, Southern and Eastern Europe were consigned to slavery. If a British reader could take comfort in the thought that one free person in every three on the globe was a subject of His Britannic Majesty, he or she was simultaneously reminded that 19 out of 20 human beings were unfree. To this grim statistic Adam Smith added that the unfree were likely to remain so for ages to come.[41] On the very eve of the age of abolition, to be enlightened was to be impressed with the vastness of unfreedom. Mercantile handbooks cautioned the aspiring British merchant to follow foreign customs when in foreign lands. North–west Europeans who entered the Atlantic slave system in the wake of the Iberians usually approached slavery as part of a world they had not made.[42]

This was the fundamental context of British overseas slavery. On the one hand it was treated as a stain from which British-born subjects were forever free, unless captured by men beyond the range of British law or power. On the other hand it was an overriding world-historical social fact. A good illustration of this dual attitude can be drawn from one of the most beautifully packaged atlases published in eighteenth-century Britain, long before the enlightenment could have made its mark. Appearing in 1728, the atlas had more élite subscribers than any of the dozens of others I have reviewed at the wonderful Goldsmiths' Library collection at the University of London. The section on the African trade began with a violent diatribe against its practitioners, that is the _Africans_, who sold their own people instead of developing more worthy items of trade.[43]

Even projected beyond the line slavery polluted, and an edge of contempt often carried over from descriptions of Africans selling each other into descriptions of Europeans in the Caribbean. On the one hand it was recognized that slavery was a social and economic response to peculiarities of climate or production. On the other hand many metropolitans contemptuously concluded that the quality of their fellow Britons clearly degenerated as one moved beyond the line. Adam Smith implied it was the jailbirds and flotsam of European society who became the masters of slaves.[44]

Despite the sale of redemptioners and Scots and Irish bondsmen on Philadelphia's streets, Pennsylvania sustained a reputation as 'the best poor man's country'. Who in the eighteenth century would have so described Jamaica or Barbados? Long before abolitionism American slaves were the ultimate term of reference for political economists who wished to emphasize the extremities of subordination in some British industries.[45] The phenomenon of absenteeism was of course one of the more obvious signs that the slave islands were not the best rich man's country either. Those who resided for some time in Africa and the slave colonies tended to 'suspend' patterns of customary behaviour. Even if extensive allowance was made for economic practices, the prevailing plantation pattern of concubinage and sexual exploitation in the islands identified slavery as somehow polluting and polluted.[46]

This tension between economic utility and social distaste was present early in the development of the British slave colonies. Such attitudes appeared far too soon to attribute the phenomenon to the enlightenment. The condemnation of the slave trade as un-Christian and inhuman was distilled even into mid-eighteenth-century children's literature. Nor did slavery appear to be an institution for achieving a rapid cultural transformation of Africans into Europeans. Before the stirrings of public abolitionism neither planters, traders nor pamphleteers took any pains to refer to African barracoons, slave ships or plantations as schools of Christianity or civilization. When West Indians returned enriched and inserted themselves into the highest echelons of British society, antagonists could always hark back to that inescapable whiff of pollution. West Indians were always outsiders, corrupted by ruling slaves and then enslaving electorates with not-too-well-gotten gains. Like the nabobs of the East India Company, West Indians were designated as carriers of despotic habits. Their very success beyond the line was at once their excuse and their flaw.[47]

While both enlightenment and early evangelical thought was still ambivalent or passive towards slavery, and long before any fundamental change in the European image of black Africa, this bifurcated world lay at the heart of the problem of slavery for European society.[48] On the eve of political abolitionism in 1785, William Playfair's commercial survey continued to exhibit the dualism between social distaste and economic fatalism. On the one hand, trade was disgraced by traffic in human beings. On the other hand, some areas, like the East and West Indies, seemed to 'court the yoke', and the tropics in general were seen as exceptional cases.[49] As long as the political economists' proverbial two hands pointed in the usual opposite directions, the slave system was hardly in dire danger from that quarter.

In geographical commentaries the sense of alienation clustered around differences in climate, disease environment or any number of social customs, religious practices, dress, diet, social structure and political institutions. However, the most significant way in which slavery itself was rationalized, even in racial terms, was through its linkage with economic requirements. Regarding slave labour, the belief that only Africans could work effectively and continuously in tropical heat was widely promulgated in British popular literature. Anthony Barker notes that there was a general lack of interest in racial differences beyond the rationalization of cheap tropical labour.[50]

On the other hand, market acumen was considered to be a significant characteristic of Africans. Whatever aspersions might be made on their cultures or habits, their 'cunning' as economic men, especially in slave trading, was emphasized.[51] This is hardly surprising. It was most often as competing and interdependent traders that the Europeans, Afro-Europeans and Africans came into continuous contact.[52] Since each culture was mediated for the others so largely through market behaviour, it was as market-men that they knew each other best. And precisely because of its basis in exchange there was never any analogue in the British Parliament to the famous debate, between Las Casas and Sepulveda at Valladolid in mid-sixteenth-century Spain, on the legitimacy of Indian slavery. That debate had centred on the legitimacy of enslavement in just wars. Trade, not war, was the sanction for British Atlantic slavery.

This perspective was congruent with what was the hard-core justification of the slave trade from beginning to end. If the sense of distance allowed for the tolerance accorded to overseas slavery, the incentive of individual and collective wealth manifestly underlay its positive encouragement. Capitalism provided the principal motives and the ideological underpinnings of British Atlantic slavery. When they were first alarmed by the opening salvos of the abolitionist attack, the defenders of the system tested out rationalizations of slavery on the basis of racial inferiority and biblical sanction.[53] Quite significantly, however, neither line of argument was sustained in either polemical or Parliamentary debate.

On the one hand, the more rigorously one argued the case for racial inferiority on grounds tending towards the separation of species, the more one threatened the established ideology of Christian social thought. In eighteenth-century Britain, racial materialism was far too heterodox, society too institutionally Christian and black slaves too remote a social force to generate a receptive audience for an ideology of slavery based on race. If Edward Long's affirmation of black inferiority was not 'totally unrepresentative of his time'[54] any defence of slavery which relied on it was. His works were more often cited by abolitionists than by slave apologists and 'the debate over slavery never developed into a debate over the nature of the Negro'.[55] There is abundant evidence of racial disparagement of black people in eighteenth-century English literature, but antislavery proved to be far more potent than anti-black sentiments in Britain during the age of mass abolitionism.

On the more orthodox side, the more strenuously one argued in favour of the biblical sanction for slavery the more one threatened the relevance of the Bible as a sanction for British liberty. Both the racial and biblical lines of argument were burdened by an implicit delegitimization of contemporary metropolitan norms. Racial, biblical and classical Aristotelian proslavery arguments occupied a very subordinate place in British political discourse during the eighteenth and early nineteenth centuries.

The essential rationale for British-sponsored slavery, from first to last, was its apparent contribution to the collective wealth and power of the empire. There is every reason to take at face value the terms of Royal Charters for the African company, and the preambles of eighteenth-century sustaining legislation for slavery. The first Charter gave a group of British investors the sole right of bartering '*for* or *with* any negroes, slaves, goods, wares, merchandises whatsoever'.[56]

Other preambles forthrightly proclaimed this trade and the plantations it served to be in the interest of Britain. Under political attack it was to this bastion that the slave interests quickly repaired and took their stand. They demanded only an adherence to the traditional sanctity of the market. To them this entailed the 'extension of internal manufactures and the freedom of exporting those manufactures to every state or power whether neighboring or distant that offered an advantageous market, without attempting to set any limits to the enterprising genius of the people', whether in Africa or America.[57] It was within this frame of reference that millions of pounds were deployed and accumulated for over 150 years in the Atlantic slave economy.

On the other hand, whilst capitalism depended upon racial slavery at the periphery, at the core and at least in part of the periphery, too, a labour force emerged which was socially, legally and vociferously distinct from capital. And during the third quarter of the eighteenth century at least one community, the Quakers, slowly withdrew itself from the slave system.[58] It is possible that it was the capitalists' intensive involvement with the market *per se* which produced the conditions for their withdrawal. As a result of immersion in the market, with its combination of calculation, trust and interdependence, human sensibility expanded within the capitalist ethic. One must be cautious about placing too much reliance upon the 'sensibility' generated by the market mechanism, however. Historians may identify whole groups, like the Quakers, as the very embodiment of eighteenth-century capitalist mentality and as 'vanguards' of industrialism,[59] but a broader look at the Atlantic market raises some doubts. Anstey, Curtin and other students of African history and the Atlantic slave trade demonstrate that there were no more complex chains of trust, interlocking trade diasporas, long-term lines of credit, discounting mechanisms and other recipes for economic transaction than in the world of the slave trade.[60] Were the slave traders of eighteenth-century London and Liverpool less cognitively aware of the long-term consequences of slave dealing than the Quaker brewers and bankers? If it is true that capitalist relationships increased the demand for unfettered relationships with all human agents, including workers, the evidence should probably be sought not within the boundaries of a marginal religious group but in the general impact of market relationships in Britain. It was the role of labour, not of the entrepreneur, however sophisticated, that was crucial.

In contrast to most Continental European societies, although not perhaps to the Netherlands, the major elements of a market society were in place in Britain by the early eighteenth century. One of the basic springboards for a future attack on slavery was already in place in the form of a widening trust in the beneficent operation of a free labour market. Moreover British society was moving towards a consensus at home based on that market experience. All human beings, including those palpably resistant to market incentives would, in the long run, exceed the capacities of coerced labour.[61]

As regards *overseas* slavery, however, the market was passive. It hardly impelled members of British society to take action on behalf of particular groups within the empire. The separation of labour as a marketable commodity from the labourer, and the market's role as a regulator of human activity, were extolled in Britain just while it was constructing its overseas slave system. Many of those who exulted in the possibilities of the market society were quite forward in maximizing the opportunities to expand British slavery.[62] A peculiar historical conjuncture would be necessary to thrust the African trade to the top of the British political agenda at the end of the eighteenth century.

In regard to capitalism, then, British slavery arose as a result of a peculiar correlation between the European core and the Afro-Caribbean peripheries of the Atlantic economies. New World capitalist slavery easily overcame the costs of coerced labour transported thousands of miles because of the continually demonstrated inefficiencies of non-coerced labour in both Africa and the Americas. There is no doubt that if freely-contracted labour could have been induced to produce rice, sugar, coffee and cotton at competitive world prices, European capitalists would have forgone the arduous and dangerous task of transporting unprecedented numbers of human chattels to inhospitable frontiers with high rates of mortality. For three centuries after 1500, Europeans continuously experimented with the backward-bending supply curve for the Indians and Europeans in America, and for Africans in Africa, trying to find a competitive substitute for transplanted slave labour. It was only when the supply or coercion of slaves was restricted by political intervention that tropical planters turned to other forms of labour or went out of staple production altogether.[63]

The integration of this economic system was aided by a correspondingly 'narrow' social chain of instrumental relationships. Very few individuals actually understood or experienced the full range of human relationships embodied in the Atlantic economies. People like the African Olaudah Equiano (Gustavus Vassa) who passed through the full cycle from capture in Africa through slavery in the Americas to freedom, intermarriage and ultimately into abolitionism in England were quite exceptional.[64] None of the beneficiaries of such an extended system, from enslavers in the African interior to consumers in Britain, had to look at the system comprehensively and personally. The slave merchants of Africa were apparently unconcerned with the alterations of lives produced by their exchanges. The European merchants and planters received a group of captives and judicial offenders who were simply offered to them for sale in indiscriminate lots. Their economic activity was sanctioned by the rulers at both ends of the chain.

Before the late eighteenth century most of those who expressed dismay and anger about slavery bent before this massive systemic fact. From Las Casas to the early Quakers and evangelicals, reformers turned their efforts to improving conditions rather than demanding root-and-branch political prohibitions of the slave trade and slavery. As Thomas Clarkson looked down at the vast array of ships in Bristol harbour at the beginning of his first tour in 1787 he was only the last to experience a sense of awe at the unfathomable distance between individual denunciation and effective action.[65]

My answer to the question as to why slavery was allowed to grow undisturbed for so long is therefore a combination of economics and geography. New World slavery everywhere raised and quickly buried doubts about the legitimacy of slave trading. But since racial slavery represented a continuing and palpable departure from North-west European social patterns, its relation to the metropolis was not a matter of just adding on one more nuance of dependency. Socially, rather than theologically, slavery was rationalized by an implicit and very convincing experience of distance and impotence, just as seventeenth-century piracy was be viewed as more 'normal' in the Caribbean or the Mediterranean than along the coasts of Northern Europe. A 'Braudelian' sense about the difficulty of overcoming spatial distance is as necessary to understanding the smooth functioning of the slave system as is its economic viability.

The early modern European world was also not one in which slavery was generally rationalized as a foundation of human progress.[66] Even its mercantile ideology, affirming the harmony of sweet trade against predatory cultures of violence, could hardly incorporate slavery as an affirmation of its moral effects.[67] While John Locke was subscribing to the Royal African Company and prescribing slavery for the constitution of Carolina, he pronounced slavery so vile an estate that no Englishman would plead for it. And surely it remained vile, for Englishmen. By the mid-seventeenth century, when English subjects began systematically to buy and sell other human beings on a large scale, neither chattel slavery nor inherited bondage existed any longer within the boundaries of their own land. The language of antislavery ran through their rhetoric, their rituals and their riots throughout the eighteenth century. A 'libertarian heritage' was 'the dominant political ideology in the eighteenth century, to which all groups subscribed'.[68] The world was therefore no longer as safe for slavery as in Roman times by simple reference to the 'law of nations', because it was no longer ubiquitous or central to certain powerful societies.[69] The world was made safe for North-west European colonial slavery by the tyranny of distance rather than by universal principles. As long as it remained spatially confined to a periphery slavery could thrive;[70] but as long as it remained so its most powerful overseas beneficiaries could not ultimately control their fate.

2 Border Skirmish: Neither Wages nor the Whip

I have been insisting on a sharp differentiation of social relations between metropolitan Britain and the frontier colonies during the first century of the British Atlantic slave system. Yet some recent historians of black people in Britain would insist that black slavery was in fact an institution in England itself and remained legal, with qualifications, until the Emancipation Act of 1833. There is no dearth of evidence that blacks were being bought and sold in the metropolis. Advertisements for runaways insisted on their status as the property of their masters and were accompanied by warnings of prosecution for any who dared to harbour them. They were collared like dogs. Couples were separated by indifferent or petulant masters.[1]

Yet it was precisely this transfer of social relationships from the slave colonies of the New World to the metropolis which first converted the latent social contradiction between slavery and freedom in Britain into a public issue. Insofar as boundaries are exercises in power the frontier between slavery and freedom was a flashpoint of private tension long before abolition became a legislative issue. The flow of slaves into Britain was a direct consequence of economic success. The burgeoning plantation economy sent a steady stream of successful slave traders and colonists back to Britain to savour the fruits of capitalism and the pleasant amenities and trappings provided by the centre of the empire. The most successful British slave–owners therefore first breached the line by their individual decisions to enjoy the use of servile domestics in Britain.

There is little evidence to indicate that British merchants and politicians experienced any difficulty in adjusting to the requirements of seventeenth-century colonial development. While colonists experimentally evolved their slave laws in America, sanctioned with very little modification by the imperial government, the latter quickly decided that African Negroes 'ought to be esteemed goods and commodities within the Acts of Trade and Navigation'. It was also said of Negroes that they, 'being usually bought and sold among Merchants, so Merchandise'.[2] However, it is important not to make the mistake of assuming that blacks or Africans *per se* were thereby 'reduced' from 'humanity' to 'commodity' by such declarations.[3] In the first place the very terms of the Royal African Company's charter and all the slave traders recognized that they were trading with as well as for Africans, so the reduction of blacks to merchandise referred only to those Africans who had been purchased. Contemporaries were quite aware that not all Africans or all blacks were commodities. Even as regards the black slaves, the seventeenth-century British colonists had no more difficulty in dealing with property at once defined as human and as property than had societies for over 2000 years before. Orlando Patterson aptly notes that the implication of 'inherent' contradiction is a problematic intrusion of a philosophical concept into a socially-defined institution.[4] The ascription of property rights in human beings to others was only the transference of certain rights in human beings into the hands of merchants and planters. The tensions which arose over slavery in Britain were historically induced.

In North–west European societies there was an inherent social tension. Slaves, human beings in whom property rights were sanctioned by law, came into societies without other individuals over whom such a complex of rights was exercised. Indeed, popularizations of British law claimed that its 'air was too free for a slave to breathe'.[5] When blacks were brought to England the question was not whether they were or became human beings after having been merchandise; it was whether or to what extent they retained their status and their masters retained their proprietary rights within Britain. Nor was it clear whether, even in the free air of England, at least some rights in their person still belonged to their masters.

At the beginning the tension was isolated and muted. The intrusion of blacks claimed as slaves into the metropolis was what Bernard Bailyn has termed a 'latent event', a cumulative process which was only dimly recognized for decades as a social problem and therefore never sufficiently measured or controlled to gauge its impact on the system as a whole.[6] Blacks entered Britain in a variety of ways. Some were brought as personal trade allotments or servants by captains completing the triangular voyage of the slave trade. Others, attached to élites on the West African coast, were brought to England for education: still others formed part of transoceanic crews. But most of those who remained or who resided for long periods were brought by ships' captains, colonial slave-owners and absentee planters.

Almost at once it was clear that slaves in Britain were socially and legally anomalous. There were no statutes in Britain sanctioning the institution. As one early legal decision aptly put it, 'the law took no notice of a negro.'[7] This was as true of the 'commodity' status established on the African coast as of the slave law elaborated in the colonies. The customs officers in Britain, unlike those in the colonies, took no notice of blacks. Had the British government really intended to recognize Negroes as goods and commodities in England, as well as in Afro-America, they would have duly appeared on the lists of enumerated goods entering British ports. None of the collections of British customs regulations for the metropolis published in the eighteenth century seems to indicate that blacks coming to Britain were ever enumerated as imports. Duties were never levied on entry, or exit, as they were in the colonial ports.[8] Slaves appear on the great customs ledgers and in the annual enumerations of the value of trade and navigation of Great Britain only as colonial commodities. In every sense blacks were invisible in the British commercial and tax structure. Labour law was no more attentive than commercial law. Eighteenth-century handbooks for English Justices of the Peace offered magistrates the relevant statutes for dealing with gypsies, apprentices, agricultural labourers, and the poor in general. They offered no hint whatsoever on how to deal with blacks, either as slaves, as free subjects or as some intermediate alien status with its own peculiar bundle of rights, obligations and discipline.[9] That the law literally 'took no notice of Negroes' was not just a legal nicety.

In this respect we should also note that race as such played no role in the legal decisions concerning the status of black slaves in England. In Britain there were essentially two and only two justifications for black slavery: religious and commercial. The religious justification was used only in very early legal opinions. It allowed that Negroes could be enslaved because they were heathens. The major and more enduring justification for proprietary claims was the right ultimately conferred by purchase or inheritance. In the British courts it was the only recognized evidence for the claims of slave-owners.

The most obvious evidence that we are dealing with a latent social problem is that the British in the eighteenth century had no idea of the number of 'slaves' in Britain. Until well over a century after the beginnings of a steady flow of colonials to the metropolis no one even thought to estimate the number of blacks in Britain. Only after 1760 did estimates occasionally begin to be made, infrequently, and without any indication whatsoever of the mode of calculation. One writer in 1763 guessed 20 000. Another in 1765 raised the figure by half to

30 000. In the heat of the famous Somerset case the West Indian Edward Long reduced that figure in a pamphlet by 90 per cent to 3000. This was startling in view of the fact that he wished to maximize the dangers of the black presence and the capital at risk. While the work was in proof the figure of 14 000–15 000 was given out at the Somerset hearings. So Edward Long promptly quintupled his estimate in a postscript. As the abolitionist movement got under way at the end of the following decade, a West Indian raised the metropolitan black population estimate to a minimum of 40 000.

As a check, but only as a general check, I have attempted to calculate the number of blacks in Britain around the time of the Somerset case (1772), using the official figure for black movement out of Jamaica. I agree with the estimate of F.O. Shyllon and Howard Temperley that there were about 10 000 blacks in Britain at that time on whom *any* claims could have been made. Significantly, the official source comes from colonial, not metropolitan, records.[10] However, 10 000 must be considered a maximum figure for 'slaves', as are other estimates drawn from contemporary sources. All of these, including the 'Somerset' figure of 15 000, were estimates of blacks, not slaves, in Britain. Some proportion of those blacks, and it may have been considerable, were not claimed as property. Some had been dismissed or abandoned by their owners. Others were apprentices, indentured servants, sailors, runaways, or were descendants of free blacks.[11] Therefore we know even less about the number of masterless blacks than of the population as a whole.

Based on a study of London parish registers Stephen Braidwood has reached a similar maximum estimate.[12] Blacks were concentrated in the three major ports with West Indian links. In nine parish registers in London only 168 baptized persons were listed as black between 1783 and 1787. Even in the most densely populated parish, St George's in the East, they accounted for only 3 per cent of all baptisms, suggesting a very small national presence. The principal point is that few were stimulated to estimate the number of blacks in Britain, and no British official sought to make a census of either blacks or 'slaves' at any point before or during the age of abolition.

From a survey of London 'places wanted' advertisements over a period of 20 years I also conclude that the black population was overwhelmingly male. This conclusion is reaffirmed by the survey of London parish baptism records which yielded a ratio of four black males to every black female. The black population, much less those claimed as slaves, was not capable of reproducing itself. The black demographic profile lowered pressure on the British to conceive of slavery as an inherited status in Britain. One of the major divisions between New World slavery and indentured servitude was minimized.

The very ephemerality of our data about blacks in England also tells us much about their salience in British as opposed to colonial slave societies. This is especially significant in determining the degree of institutional similarity or difference in the status of blacks on both sides of the Atlantic. Most contemporary accounts and almost all subsequent histories of slavery have placed major emphasis on the fact that there were 'slaves' in England, despite the 'free air' phrase that wafted from text to text throughout the seventeenth and eighteenth centuries. As in the New World they were publicly advertised for sale, and packed on board ships and returned to the West Indies just as they had been brought to Britain.[13]

On the other hand, blacks formed a more substantial part of the population even in New England than in Britain, where they represented less than 0.2 per cent of the total (see Table 2.1). The difference in numbers was reflected by a difference in social classification. Everywhere in the New World colonial slaves were clearly a separate order. There were specific statutes designed to control their behaviour as slaves and sometimes as a class of free men. As instruments of production they could be bought on credit and used as collateral. They were the principal element of both capital and labour in many colonies where they were dutiable and taxable.[14] In Britain blacks lacked economic and legal visibility as well as the racial salience they had in the New World. It was not in the colonies but in Britain that blacks were almost invisible men.

Besides gross numbers we lack some of the most significant tools for the analysis of slavery elsewhere. We have no firm idea of their geographical or temporal distribution, and only the most anecdotal evidence of prices paid for sales in Britain.[15] There are certainly no price series for comparing valuations by sex, age or skill. We have no idea how often blacks in Britain were disposed of at public auction in payment of debts. In other words, in contrast to the colonies, we are unable to determine whether a 'market' for blacks developed over time, or when it began or ended. If there were as many as 10 000 'slaves' in Britain at the beginning of the reign of George III, we should have a substantial record of estate inventories listing blacks as assets with their valuations.[16] In other words, the whole argument that New World slavery was analogous within the line is, to this moment, based on inferences from newspaper advertisements for

TABLE 2.1   *Percentages of Blacks in Britain, New England, and
Pennsylvania on the eve of their respective 'abolitions'*

	Year*	Percentage of blacks
Great Britain	1771	0.09–0.2†
Massachusetts	1780	1.8
Connecticut	1780	2.9
Rhode Island	1780	5.1
Pennsylvania	1780	2.4

* Decennial years on the eve of abolitions
† the lower percentage is based on an estimate of 10 000 blacks in Britain (see
above), the higher on the 14 000 at the Somerset hearings.

SOURCES Population of Great Britain: B. R. Mitchell and Phyllis Deane, *Abstract of
British Historical Statistics* (Cambridge, 1962), as modified by E. A. Wrig-
ley anbd R. S. Schofield, *Population History of England 1541–1871: A
Reconstruction* (Cambridge, 1982) 209, Table 7.8.
North American Colonies, *Historical Statistics of the United States*, 2 vols
(Washington, 1975) II, 1168, z 1–19, 'Estimated Population of American
Colonies: 1610 to 1780'.

sales and runaways. Even such advertisements are not always what
they seem. An advertisement for a black runaway could often have
been for someone legally apprenticed, indentured or otherwise con-
tractually bound. Advertisements for the disposal of minors might
fall into a different category from that of adults, and so be more
comparable to the parish orphans sent northwards to Lancashire in
the 1780s.

There is a tendency to assimilate the social situation of eighteenth-
century blacks in England to that of the New World. Blacks were, of
course, usually recognizable because of their colour. They were
socially stereotyped because of their concentration in domestic service and shipping. In London they were sufficiently numerous and
mobile to elicit a proclamation prohibiting their entry into the lucrative trades as apprentices. But one must recognize that other groups
were also quite distinguishable by their accents and dress and social
roles in eighteenth-century England. George Packwood's famous
advertisements for his strop razors featured a stereotypical dialogue
between a merchant and his black servant for his razor strops:
however, other groups were also parodied and often more feared.[17]

An extensive survey of many years of London newspaper letters
from the early 1760s to the early 1790s reveals far more complaints
about Scottish, Irish, Jewish and other European intruders than

about blacks. Even at critical public moments in the history of British slavery, such as the years 1772 or 1787, there were far more demands in the London newspapers for a census and social control of Jews than of blacks. Nor was there any pattern of crowd action against blacks as there was against other minorities.[18] The very paucity of official information and public attention given to blacks, measured against either their colonial counterparts or other metropolitan minorities, implies a relative lack of social 'tracking'. Their high colour visibility was not matched by a correspondingly high social tension.

Yet, however indistinctly, the stage was set for a special kind of class struggle. Blacks did not arrive in Britain like the Scots, Irish, Jews and other minorities. They arrived with masters who claimed them as slaves and who, within limits, tried to retain that bundle of rights they had claimed with full public sanction in the colonies. They tried to retain the options to buy, to rent, to recapture, to bequeath and to discipline their black servants. If masters avoided shackles, colonial-style public floggings and mutilations, they likewise avoided paying wages for services. In this too, the law was clearly not against them, taking no notice of a Negro. For newly-arrived blacks, with no links to the outside world, it was at best a case of neither wages nor the whip.

The evolution of black slaves' status in England has usually concentrated on a handful of laconic legal decisions. At the beginning of the eighteenth century some court decisions clearly indicated the most favourable possible interpretation of black freedom in Britain. Other legal opinions favoured the planters' proprietary claims. This was especially evident in the famous 'after dinner' opinion of Yorke and Talbot in 1729. In response to a West Indian petition it held that the master lost none of his property rights in his slaves in Britain, that baptism was irrelevant and that masters could compel the return of their slaves to the colonies. In 1749, Yorke, now Lord Chancellor Hardwicke, had an opportunity to read his after-dinner discourse into a legal decision. For this reason, argues James Walvin, during the two decades after 1729 'the overwhelming majority of the people' accepted slavery as legal in England.[19] Blacks could only avail themselves of the mechanism of flight into the safety of the black underworld.

The use of less than a dozen law cases scattered over a century is really too sparse to describe any clear ebb and flow of the status of blacks in the period before 1770. There were sales and occasional estate auctions of blacks, but they were also rare enough to elicit letters of surprise in the press.[20] Counsel for Somerset used the image of human cattle auctions as one of the horrible possibilities of a decision against his client. What was far more frequent, as we gather from eighteenth-century accounts, were a relatively large number of private transactions in which a person was sold from one master to another without recourse to public institutions. The world of captains, merchants, planters and aristocrats, all linked to the slave world, offered a sufficiently developed network of supply and demand to form a private market. The moment when slavery appears to have come closest to full legal recognition in English courts was under the auspices of judges such as Lord Chancellor Hardwicke and Chief Justice Mansfield who sought to harmonize the commercial customs of the burgeoning mercantile community of the mid-eighteenth century with its increasingly extra-European linkages.[21]

Law cases arose only when one or another of the parties – the buyer, the seller, or the bought – interfered with the process. And it was here that the cosy world of the slave–holders ultimately broke down. To capture the tensions of this world it is necessary to move outside the law courts and their frustratingly brief list of cases and decisions. The popular world of Britain also had norms of which the courts might take little notice. They were linked to its own experiences. It is difficult to reconstruct but these popular attitudes created enough 'static' within the slave dealers' world continually to threaten and ultimately undermine their claims. Before abolitionism popular opinion was divided and fragmented. Yet even without collective action it upset the world the slave–holders were attempting to create.

One may begin by first considering those early legal decisions which seemed to confirm the validity of slavery abroad, but threatened it root and branch at home. Holt's unequivocal decision that English soil freed should have allowed no room whatever for a slave status. Nevertheless, his early decision was almost completely insulated even from the legal world, let alone the public. None of the fundamental statements favourable to blacks in Britain seems to have been linked together as a set of precedents until Granville Sharp ferreted them out for his dramatic campaign against English slavery in the late 1760s. The slave–owners, on the other hand, saw to it that the Yorke-Talbot opinion was bruited about.

Yet there was a parallel set of popular beliefs which continued to challenge the masters' claims from beginning to end. One was the long-standing belief that Negroes were enslavable because they were infidels.[22] Hence they would also be enfranchised on becoming Christians. The British planters seem to have carried this belief with them to the islands. The linkage of baptism to freedom sometimes extended to the colonies as well, e.g. to Jamaica until 1717, and to St Helena. Under the rules of the East India Company baptism conferred freedom. In one case in England a court ordered a master for whom a baptized black had worked for seven years to pay wages. 'This directive released the black from his slave status.'[23]

Planters took the precaution of nullifying baptism by colonial statute. Nevertheless the belief continued to flourish in England. From the accounts of Morgan Godwyn in the 1680s to Clarkson more than a century later it is clear that this popular belief persisted. The first move of a runaway slave might be to locate a clergyman or sponsors who would baptize him and might thereafter risk legal suits to keep his master at bay. Godwyn described the awful dramas of masters prohibiting or even interrupting baptism ceremonies, dragging off their black servants before a stunned but hesitant minister. There is no way of knowing whether the Yorke-Talbot Manifesto of 1729 diminished the number of those seeking escape from servitude through baptism, but the violence of *baptismus interruptus* was still being enacted in the 1760s. Horrified newspaper correspondents were still asking whether masters could prevent baptism and whether baptism entailed freedom.[24]

A second mode of *de facto* change of status was apparently more effective. Historians such as Walvin, Shyllon and Freyer have uncovered extensive evidence of the free black community in London. They conclude that the black community provided a haven for runaways in the face of general white hostility based on racial fears of miscegenation, competition, and so on. However, the evidence from Sir John Fielding, a London magistrate, indicates that both the poor and the magistrates refused to take action to restore runaways to their masters on grounds that no act against the peace or felony had been committed. At the critical point where they needed public aid in the metropolis masters simply could not count on the help of either the white citizenry or the magistracy to enforce their claims in persons. In the absence of any instructions about slaves or Negroes in their handbooks, metropolitan law officers, with popular support, were free to make their own decisions. That they generally refused to act certainly does not bespeak an attitude dominated by fear of an uncontrolled black presence in London.[25]

The apparent ease with which runaways could sustain themselves in London reinforces the idea that the British community did not act out of notions of racial solidarity. Even the concept of miscegenation, which enabled West Indians in the eighteenth century to treat inter-racial unions as a form of social pollution, at least within the metro-polis, was not widely shared. The public calmly accepted the well publicized celebration of Gustavus Vassa's marriage to a white woman and of less notable intermarriages as well.[26] William Cobbett, usually regarded as having his hand on the pulse of popular opinion, makes a fine hostile witness in this respect. Cobbett was outraged by the insufficient racial consciousness of his fellow Englishmen, who felt no alarm whatever at blacks taking whites not only as servants but as marriage partners.[27] British fear of miscegenation was cer-tainly below the level required to make English crowds turn blacks over to masters.

The behaviour of the West Indians shows how fragile was their hold on 'property' which was determined to get away from owners in Britain. The very circumstances of the Yorke-Talbot decision of 1729 demonstrate the position of British masters. It was obviously made in response to an unsatisfactory situation in which planters were having difficulty keeping baptized, that is, acculturated blacks, in servi-tude.[28] Historians have concluded that the Yorke-Talbot opinion was affirmed in court by Yorke, now Lord Hardwicke, in *Pearne* v. *Lisle*. But *Pearne* v. *Lisle* was not an action between a master and a servant. A master had rented out the services of his servants to a defaulting purchaser. Hardwicke upheld the master's right to payment for the service. Hardwicke simply took the opportunity to repeat his opinion of 1729 on the nullity of baptism. The case did not directly involve conflicting claims of master and servant, but of monetary compen-sation between masters.

The most telling piece of evidence on the difficulties of masters on the European side of the Atlantic lies in the third part of the Yorke-Talbot opinion. The masters were particularly anxious to get the right of forced return on the record. Their servants were working without wages in a world of wage–earners. The most intense moment of psychological pressure to escape would come when return to the slave colonies was imminent. Lacking slave legislation in Britain, the owner's chief disciplinary weapon was the ship, not the whip.

This is why forced return was so crucial in the maintenance of the masters' social control. The slaves were fully aware of the difference between being on English soil and on a vessel bound for the colonies. Sometimes advertisements posting rewards for black runaways would stipulate that the claimant had to get him on board a specific ship leaving for America. Olaudah Equiano, the most famous black in eighteenth-century England, served in the colonies, on the high seas, and in England. Long before the Somerset case he had been told by English lawyers that on British soil he could claim his freedom. On returning to London from a voyage his master therefore made a special effort to keep him on board and to transship him out of Britain. The master made no appeal to the magistrates to constrain his slave. He simply hired individuals to transfer Equiano to a West Indian vessel by force. Both men behaved as though being in or out of England made a decisive difference in their power to affect the outcome.[29] This confrontation occurred at the height of the 'Hardwicke era' and before Lord Chancellor Henley's 1762 decision, which casually referred to the *common* application of *habeas corpus* in favour of black servants in such conflicts.[30]

How can we best describe what was going on? It was not the functioning of slavery, in the colonial sense, and under the rule of law. It was a private class war, with masters hiring enforcers to drag blacks on to departing ships. If magistrates were not enforcing masters' rights they were only haphazardly enforcing servants' personal rights against kidnapping. This private war on the streets and docks of London was the equivalent of the struggle over black baptism in the churches. It was a deadly game of hide-and-seek, and the same public which would not intervene to protect the masters' claims would not always intervene to protect the servant.

This anomalous situation also helps to explain why many domestics did not run away, even in the more porous environment of urban Britain. Service, even without wages, did provide a welfare exchange for those who had only uncertain chances in the free market. The very young, the very old, the unacculturated, those with families overseas, even some of the robust, must have hesitated to take the leap unless they were brutally abused.[31] Moreover, if the common law took no notice of a Negro neither did the poor law. One Londoner described a horrible scene in which a gangrenous black man was dumped from a vehicle just beyond his parish line to save the parish the cost of a pauper burial. The first reaction of some bystanders was to suggest getting another vehicle to repeat the process while the black still breathed. Only the determined intervention of a bystander allowed him to reach a hospital bed.[32] A free black, like all other aliens, had to take his chances without the safety net of poor relief. The welfare function of even wageless service might often have been for eighteenth-century blacks what it was for Russian slaves.[33]

Among the servants the terms clearly favoured the most able-bodied runaways. The game of hide-and-seek had to be paid for by the master who could act only if he could locate his slave. One master used the newspaper to rail against an insolent piece of property who simply refused to return to the colonies.[34] Notices like this help to explain why the masters finally felt that the *status quo* was against them. The failure rate or the costs of private recovery were high enough for them to wager all collectively, in 1772, in the case of James Somerset, in hopes of a ruling which might finally induce the courts to become active agents of slave control. A West Indian later recalled that because of judicial indifference, slavery was collapsing in England even before Mansfield's decision.

In this context one can reappraise the significance of the Somerset case. The traditional view emphasized the dramatic finality of Mansfield's decision as a reaffirmation of the principle that 'every slave, as soon as he touched English ground, acquired his freedom'.[35] This was presented as a turning point: either that all slaves were freed by a single court decision, or that the principle of freedom, which had been momentarily clouded by planter pressure, was finally reaffirmed.[36] For a half-century, however, most historians of slavery have tended to take a different tack. A close study of Mansfield's behaviour and language clearly shows that he was more interested in avoiding than in reaching a decision and in narrowing rather than broadening its impact.[37] His concerns were not in the maximum extension of liberty but in social and damage control. In another case, before Somerset was forced on him, he said, 'I would have all masters think them free, and all Negroes think they were not, because then they would both behave better'. In the Somerset case itself, he emphasized that 'the setting of 14 000 or 15 000 men at once loose by a solemn opinion, is very disagreeable in the effects it threatens'. At £50 per capita, Mansfield implied that hundreds of thousands of pounds and untold difficulties of control were at stake.[38]

Of course he had little idea of the size of the black population, and even less of how many of them were actually claimed as slaves in England by masters. He may also have been daunted, as his later decisions show, by the fact that the courts might have to do even more damage to West Indians who placed their faith in the Yorke-Talbot decision when black servants began to sue for back wages. It is hardly likely that a Chief Justice who made his legal reputation by moulding common law principles to fit the needs of Britain's burgeoning commercial classes relished the idea of depriving a portion of them of their property rights.[39] The very first item he noted in rendering his Somerset decision was the trust that West Indians had placed in the Yorke-Talbot opinion in bringing their servants to the metropolis.[40]

In any event, all recent historians agree that Mansfield did his best to avoid a broad decision. He slipped out from under a previous case on a technicality. He advised an out-of-court settlement. Before bringing Somerset's case to a decision he actually advised the planters to appeal to Parliament for legislation. He finally did not issue a decision on the broader question of English soil at all but on the narrower one of whether *habeas corpus* applied to the forcible transportation of blacks from England. Mansfield clearly stated only that English law did not allow the master to seize his servant to be sold abroad, 'and therefore the man must be discharged'.[41]

Historians have concluded as a result that some contemporary commentators were right; that Mansfield had not abolished the slave status in England at all. He only placed one limitation on the slave-owners' bundle of rights. The blow was symbolic, not decisive. Dependency continued without wages and provided for qualified servitude.[42] Slaves continued to be bought and sold. Mansfield had merely brokered away the single right of forced deportation. Many blacks were held in virtual slavery. Some were still forcibly deported in violation of the decision. The legal condition of slaves coming to England was actually worsened by future recourse to indenture. Slavery, slightly modified, continued until British colonial emancipation in 1833. So, with the partial exception of Peter Fryer, runs the main thread of recent assessments.[43]

Let us look first at what the Somerset case clearly did not do. It did not, as has been pointed out, ensure that all British slaves on touching English soil were forever free. As late as 1826 the decision of Lord Stowell on the slave, 'Grace Jones', was that a black reverted to slave status if he or she returned to the slave colonies, even after the most prolonged residence in Britain. This, however, had little to do with slavery in Britain itself. It merely reaffirmed the supremacy of 'municipal' law. English law applied in England, colonial law in the colonies.[44]

What of the fate of the overwhelming majority, that is, those blacks who did not return to the colonies after 1772? It seems clear that legal claims on their involuntary services no longer existed. That much follows from Mansfield's decision. Somerset was not deported. He was not remanded to his original owner. He was not remanded to the one who had attempted to force him to leave. He was simply discharged without qualification. There was no implied contract whatever in slavery, as Mansfield had pointedly ruled early in the trial. The great expounder of contract law was not about to becloud the clarity of contract even for the West Indian interest. All blacks in England, unless they were voluntarily indentured, were henceforth in a similar circumstance. Deportation was still possible[45] but not with legal sanction. Thus capital in slaves brought to England was indeed effectively abolished, even though it took some years for behaviour to conform to the law. The popular interpretation was correct, belatedly, but long before 1834.

Third, historians present indisputable evidence to show that Mansfield disallowed all claims for back wages in later cases which came before him.[46] This is relevant as part of his strategy for damage control. Just as he did not allow Somerset's master to claim any further service by an 'implicit' contract, so too he denied any back wages on the other side. 'No contract' cut both ways. The law still took no special notice of a Negro. But if I understand Mansfield correctly, this held only for back wages. No blacks could be constrained to work after 1772 without a contract. It amounted to this: if blacks had been working without contract it was too bad for them; if they refused to do so any longer it was too bad for the master.

It is, therefore, hard to agree with Walvin's contention that Mansfield's decision 'led to a worsening of the legal position of freshly imported slaves'.[47] If they were imported without contract they were no longer under any constraint. If they came under contract they were no longer slaves. If, as Walvin states, they were obliged to sign indentures under constraint they might appeal to the courts that they were neither under contract nor constraint. We shall see that the courts took the constraint provision quite seriously.

Thus Mansfield's decision, however limited in scope, clearly doomed the slave status in England. No black in Britain in 1772 was any longer under any general constraint by virtue of previous condition of servitude to stay either in service or to return to the colonies. Only if they voluntarily did so did they revert to slave status. Blacks, like whites, were not entitled to the benefits of the poor law unless they had been born in an English parish or had otherwise qualified.[48] All blacks brought to England as slaves before 1772, however, were off the coercive legal hook, even if ignorance, age or fear of poverty might diminish their effective choices. Paradoxically, the soil of England did not free forever, but the air of England was indeed too free for a slave to breathe.

The Somerset case delivered a deadly blow to slavery in Britain by refusing to uphold the master's right to disciplinary deportation. But most recent historians of blacks in Britain have developed the argument that so many elements of the masters' rights were kept in being by the courts after 1772 that Mansfield's decision left blacks in a state of dependency amounting to slavery until 1833. These historians cite the counter-evidence of forced deportations of blacks even after the Mansfield decision.

I would contend that there was a shift in the balance of power in the class struggle between masters and black servants, which was signaled by the Somerset case. Because it did not abolish all the owners' bundle of rights at once or unequivocally, Mansfield's decision did not directly abolish the residual rights of masters in Britain. Here, the more recent historiographical tradition is technically right. But because Mansfield failed to uphold the slave-holders' most important disciplinary tool – exportation to slave law beyond the line – he doomed the attempt to transfer slavery to Britain. The limited success of the West Indians in the early eighteenth century had not been due to the fact that they had the law or its interpreters fully on their side; they clearly did not. They succeeded to the extent that they were more fully mobilized than the public at large. As in the case of baptism, potential friends of the blacks were unsure where their legal rights to intervene began or ended. Those who sympathized with the blacks were unorganized individuals. They risked substantial costs with no hope of compensation even if they were successful. Their responses were therefore diffuse and uncertain.

When the issue was first joined over the withholding of baptism at the turn of the eighteenth century, the isolated Anglican clergyman Morgan Godwyn already understood that the force which might ultimately affect the planters' behaviour was public opinion. Godwyn proposed that every Anglican minister be directed to sermonize against planter behaviour. The latter, anxious to be received as respectable Englishmen, would no longer resist offering baptism.[49] In the absence of such a mechanism of mobilization, the metropolis remained open to the filtering of social standards from beyond the line.

Granville Sharp's campaign gave the distaste for claims to property in persons an opportunity to crystallize. The year before the Somerset case Sharp had secured a warrant for the arrest of a master who had attempted to drag a slave to a waiting boat on the Thames. Within a week the grand jury of Middlesex, undeterred by proprietary considerations, indicted the master and his accomplices. Lord Mansfield opened the subsequent proceedings by noting that he himself had always respected the rights of property in slaves. This made no impression on the jury. Mansfield deliberately restricted his charge to the jury to a determination of whether or not the evidence of ownership was conclusive, but the jury made their own feelings known. When the foreman announced that they did not find the servant to be the defendant's property, the jury collectively shouted 'No property, no property!'[50]

In terms of popular mobilization the difference between the Somerset case and all previous ones lay in its notoriety. None of the earlier libertarian decisions of Justices Holt or Henley had been widely publicized. The Somerset hearings were as widely reported in Britain as the decision. Mansfield, by recessing the case from one session to another, actually enhanced its impact. Newspapers published extensive excerpts and summaries of the legal arguments. Mansfield's initially broad interpretation of the high stakes involved ensured that the contest would be inflated to its highest level of abstraction: property versus liberty. The newspaper public was treated to disquisitions on medieval villeinage, higher law theory, contract theory, baptismal liberation theory, brief histories of slavery, excerpts from the writings of Anthony Benezet and speculations about the imperial impact of the case. West Indian observers openly acknowledged that opinion was hostile to their cause. John Dunning, Counsel for Somerset's master, felt constrained to begin with an apology for taking up the unpopular cause and closed by hoping aloud 'that he had not transgressed his duty to humanity'.[51]

As a result of its public notoriety the Somerset case emerged with two interpretations. The first, emphasized by Mansfield, some West Indians, and some newspapers, was that only one right, the unrestricted deportation of blacks, had been withdrawn from the master's bundle of rights in Britain. The broader and more widely heralded opinion was that British slavery within Britain had been repudiated *in toto*.[52] Why did Mansfield not set the record straight in the final two decades of his life? It was because his Somerset decision continued to give him the best of both worlds. It was *'Fiat justicia, ruat coleum'*, ('Let justice be done, though the heavens fall') but the heavens were allowed to fall only just so far. Before the Somerset case Mansfield had clearly said that uncertainty had always been his aim concerning the status of blacks in Britain. In the late 1760s, his protege, William Blackstone, weakened the 'free soil' passage in his *Commentaries* as it applied to Negroes. From the Somerset decision Mansfield salvaged what ambiguity he could.[53]

Mansfield saw to it that, in his court, no back wages were ever paid for unremunerated service.[54] He thus paid 'due attention' to Yorke-Talbot's pledge to the masters, as he had said in opening his decision, by refusing to pay 'due wages' to the servants. The master suffered no *ex post facto* losses for having conducted his or her domestic economy under the Yorke-Talbot dispensation. Subsequently the eighteenth-century courts continued to refuse to consider slavery as an implicit contract for hiring. They never decided that a black brought to England was under any obligation to continue to serve a master without an explicit contract and they would not validate any indenture for life.[55] This was consistent with indentures of Europeans going in the other direction. It meant that on conclusion of the indenture, even if the ex-slave were back in the colonies, he or she was free of obligation. The limitation of service obligations brought black servants into alignment with white servants.

In such circumstances it is difficult to see how in any situation, except that of an unindentured black servant returning to the colonies, the law was in any way different from that affecting a British subject. Walvin points out that runaway black sailors could not return to the slave colonies without risking recapture,[56] but this would also have applied to a white European making his escape from a North African or a French galley ship. Ineligibilities for parish relief also merely placed them in the category of other foreign-born aliens. By 1795 court reporters rightly concluded that English law enforced no distinctive element of slave law in England.[57]

Legally, after Somerset, either slaves had to be freed *before* coming to Britain under indenture or they were free to depart from service once reaching the metropolis. So much for their status *de jure* as far as one can determine. What of their status *de facto*? Historians of blacks in Britain have cited incidents of deportations as evidence against the idea that Mansfield's decision freed the slaves. Only one year after the Somerset decision a black died aboard a London vessel bound for the West Indies while efforts were being made to get a writ of *habeas corpus* on his behalf. In 1790 a black girl was hunted in the streets of Bristol and temporarily forced on board a ship.[58] In 1779 a Liverpool ship-owner advertised a boy for public auction. In 1785 Granville Sharp was still having to advise enquirers that no price had to be paid to masters to redeem runaways. And as late as 1788 a Swedish abolitionist in London, as a precautionary measure, paid a master £20 to redeem the kidnapped son of an African prince. The signatories were two leading abolitionists, Clarkson and Ramsay. 'Behind every slave whose situation was subjected to legal scrutiny and public attention,' concludes Walvin, 'there marched a silent army of anonymous Negroes who had to look to themselves and to their friends, rather than to an English court, for justice.'[59] On these grounds, concludes Shyllon of slaves in Britain, 'it was not until 1834 that it can truly be said that black slaves in Britain were emancipated, as were their brothers and sisters in British Colonies in the West Indies'.[60]

Shyllon, Walvin and Fryer are quite right to point to an advertisement of a slave for sale and the instances of coerced returns as attempts to ignore the Somerset decision. Private deportations and attempted deportations did not end on 22 June 1772. One must prod the evidence a little further, however. Of the repeatedly cited cases the significance of the two final incidents of deportation is unclear. In both cases the victims were under-age girls. One was released by judicial proceedings. The story of the attempted London deportation of 1773 includes the fact that the black died while a writ of *habeas corpus* was being obtained. Others were obviously more fortunate.[61] Assuming, however, that all these deportation cases were violations of the Somerset decision, it is important to note, from our perspective, that the very last incident of deportation is dated 1792. The single cited instance of an offer for sale is obviously well before 1792. Thereafter the historical record on both sales or forced deportation is apparently silent. There is a clear inference to be drawn from this clustering of all overt violations before, and none after, 1792. The final moment when Mansfield's 'narrow' interpretation seems to have yielded totally to the broader interpretation precisely coincides with the first popular mobilization against the slave trade in 1788–92. In retrospect that mobilization in both confirmed and mythologized the import of the Mansfield decision.[62]

There were two groups in Britain who help to confirm this. The black community and the West Indians would have been especially sensitive to the persistence of any property claims exercised over blacks at the end of the eighteenth century, yet black writers spoke as axiomatically of the absence of slavery in Britain as the most self-congratulatory correspondents in the popular press.[63] The West Indians also had both individual and collective incentives to emphasize the continuity of rights in their slaves. Their instinctive response to the abolitionist offensives of 1788–92 was to highlight every possible unsavoury analogue to colonial slavery in the metropolis: the poverty of the British 'peasantry', the flogging of soldiers and sailors, the atrocious working conditions of chimney sweeps, and so on. The official Jamaican response was to insist on the existence of a host of 'slaves' of one kind or another in the metropolis. Yet, despite a search for counter-examples as intense as desperate ingenuity could devise, nothing was made of Mansfield's narrow decision to argue that there were black slaves *even* in Britain in 1788. On the contrary, West Indians acknowledged that the control of black servants in England had been crumbling even before the Somerset decision.

There are other indications that, by the 1780s, it was generally assumed that slaves arriving in Britain were free. The largest single wave of blacks arriving in Britain after 1772 came in the wake of the American revolution.[64] Many had fled to the British in response to a promise of emancipation. Others left America with Loyalist masters. Yet the post-war Loyalist compensation commission took it for granted that all blacks automatically elevated their status on coming to Britain, even though any Loyalist who took his black slaves to the West Indian islands could sell them there.[65]

The popular view, that there were no slaves in Britain, was therefore undisputed by 1792, both among the abolitionists and their opponents. But what of Mansfield, the crusty old Lord Chief Justice himself, who had minimized the import of his decision at every opportunity after 1772? As late as 1786, on the eve of popular abolitionism, Mansfield was still diligently denying to blacks both back wages and the status of having been employed in Britain for the purpose of qualifying for relief. The great jurist of contract law was as consistent as ever. No contract meant no employee status. Only *after* the wave of popular abolitionism, in 1793, did Mansfield acknowledge in the presence of his old radical nemesis, Granville Sharp, that English law had undermined slavery in Britain.[66] Something more than just the law was involved. Eighteenth-century Justices could also follow the petition returns.

By the early nineteenth century we can do more than cite a cascade of sermons, letters and public discourse to show how far the 'free air' ideology had prevailed in Britain without any further generalization in the courts. In September of 1810 broadsides and advertisements appeared in London announcing the exhibition of a 'Hottentot Venus' at Piccadilly in London. It was swiftly followed by an outraged letter from 'an Englishman' to the *Morning Chronicle*. This 'friend to liberty' appealed for an investigation of 'the wretched object publicly shown for money'. He noted that the African's 'master', to get her to dance, held a stick up to her like 'the wild beast keepers'. Since British air frees, why was such indecency, such 'slavery', allowed? The stick-holder replied the very next day, denouncing the accusation. He claimed possession of passports from the British Governor of the Cape Colony. The Hottentot had as much right to exhibit herself as a giant or a dwarf.

The subsequent newspaper accounts of the argument showed how far things had come since the days before abolitionism. The attorney-general and the Court of King's Bench quickly became involved. The proprietor of the 'Liverpool museum' claimed that the Hottentot was exhibiting herself under a two-year contract. This was met by an objection that the original contractor had sold his rights to the present one. Therefore the African had been offered for 'sale' and was not a free agent.

To resolve the issue the legal authorities found it necessary to communicate with the Hottentot, Saartjie Baartman, to discover whether she felt that she was acting under duress. Since she spoke no English, a translator had to be appointed for the interview. Two translators finally appeared at the meeting, one for each side, along with a master of the Crown Office. To allow Baartman to speak quite freely, the African Institution undertook to provide for her if she chose neither to return to the Cape nor to remain with her manager. It turned out that the performer was in fact the nurse of her exhibitor. She had come to England of her own accord, had two servants, and received half the profits by contract. For our purposes there are some striking features of the affair. First, a network was in place which would quickly involve the public, courts and the government in cases of suspected servitude; that is, newspapers, court officers, a special private institution for Africans, an attorney-general, two translators and a guarantee of support if she chose to stay in Britain.[67]

Who in England could fail to see the distance between the unprotected fugitives described in the advertisements for runaways 50 years before and the mobilized legal niceties surrounding the investigation of the 'Hottentot Venus'? Her legal situation was clearly better than if the Somerset decision had never been made. Even the existence of a 'contract' did not mean that Baartman was without legal recourse. Had she indicated that she had not consented to a transfer of her contract she would have been entitled to its nullification.

Was the 'Hottentot Venus' affair just a *cause célèbre*, a public figure at the centre of fashionable London with all the mobilized eyes of the capital ensuring a surfeit of justice? Or was the 'army of anonymous blacks' in Britain still unprotected by any machinery beyond the harsh glare of London's African Institution? A year before the 'Hottentot Venus' episode, nine blacks reported to be slaves on a Portuguese ship were rescued from a Liverpool prison where they had been incarcerated 'for debt' pending the departure of their ship. Especially remarkable was the attitude of their fellow white prisoners in what had only two years before been the world's slave-trading capital. In a show of solidarity the white prisoners prevented the Portuguese ship's captain from taking possession of the blacks until the abolitionists arrived.[68]

Peter Fryer comes closest to my own conclusion in dating the virtual disappearance of slaves in England in the mid-1790s. He conceives of the process, however, as a continuous 'withering away' from the 1740s to the 1790s. The blacks simply 'voted with their feet' in a self-emancipation of flight from their owners. This reflects a historiographical frame of reference which assumes that there were only two major potential variables in abolition, the courts and the blacks. The overwhelming majority of Britons are at best assigned an auxiliary role.[69] This approach, however, leaves two major problems unresolved. How did this form of self-emancipation virtually abolish slavery in England, and why by the mid-1790s? Flight from masters was, after all, ubiquitous in England, France, the Americas and Asia for generations before 1790 without producing a corresponding 'withering away' of the estate.

My reading of the process is somewhat different. There had been a haemorrhage of the able-bodied from wageless servitude dating from well before the 1740s. For this group the Mansfield decision probably confirmed and accelerated the process. There may even have been a 'take-off' into wage service. From January to December 1772 the ratio of advertisements for 'places wanted' by blacks to runaways in London's *Gazetteer* was 10:7. By the period of March to June 1775, the ratio was 5:1 in the same newspaper, and for the first six months of each year in the *Morning Herald* of 1787 and 1788 the ratios were 8:0 and 6:0 respectively, indicating the virtual disappearance of runaways by the end of the 1780s.

The critical new variable of the 1780s was the level of abolitionist mobilization and enforcement. It generated networks to help just those blacks who had always been least capable of voting with their feet, the aging, the newly arrived, foreigners and children. The eighteenth-century black group which was always at greatest risk for being treated as property was children. To judge from the news-papers, most blacks sold in London before Somerset were children, as was that last, most famous, Liverpool offer of 1779. They were therefore probably overrepresented as claimed chattels. By the early nineteenth century not only were black adults free to walk away from their masters, but abolitionists were free to rescue black children from concealed incarceration or from ships in British ports.[70]

As popular awareness expanded, even the intervention of élite abolitionist patrons became unnecessary. The dockside of Waterford in Ireland probably offers as good a case of the provincial mentality as any place in Britain. Early in 1833 a vessel arrived at Waterford from Fayal, in the Azores. An enslaved African came ashore and spoke in broken English to a few bystanders on the dock. They directly informed him that having set his foot on British ground he was free, 'which information threw the poor fellow into the greatest ecstasy and he capered and danced about the quay for several minutes. An Irish chimney sweep in the group insisted on treating his sable brother to a glass of the native, after which he conducted him to the Mayor's office.' The Mayor 'told the black he was free and at liberty to go where he pleased'. The black and the Irish chimney sweep then left the office arm in arm. The black's choice not to return to the Azores cost the ship's captain the $300 surety he had posted with the owner.[71]

When an Irish chimney sweep and a provincial Mayor could re-enact the five-year drama of Granville Sharp and Lord Mansfield in the course of a single day, with time out for a liberty libation, what shred of the bundle of property rights in persons remained? It is therefore unreasonable to maintain that slavery persisted in Britain until the Act of Emancipation went into effect on 1 August 1834. Other than servants who remained with masters out of fear or affection, or who returned to the islands in total ignorance of the law, it is difficult to see in what sense slavery remained in being in Britain during the 40 years before British colonial slave emancipation.[72]

One final consideration weighs against any continuation of prop-erty rights in persons in Britain until 1834. The Emancipation Act of 1833 povided compensation for owners of all slaves. A payments schedule was set up according to the value of slaves in each area. Britain was not listed in the schedule. It seems that no master claimed, much less received, a single pound for any black servant in Britain in 1833. Parliament's assessment of property claims in per-sons residing in the metropolis appears to have been congruent with that of the Irish chimney sweep. If 'slavery' still existed in Britain as late as 1834 it would be true only in the sense that 'villeinage' existed. It was at best another case of villeinage without villeins. Unlike even villeinage, however, slavery in Britain was never an institution whose relationships had gradually disappeared. It was a relationship which had never been institutionalized. Once the 'slaves' disappeared not even a legal shadow remained.

In attempting to measure the impact of public opinion before mobilization I have had to link a series of scattered events. Only by combining episodes which reveal the fears of slave-owners, the hopes of slaves and the ambivalence of the community in which they both lived, has it been possible to suggest the balance of forces and numbers which determined the status of black slaves in England in the eighteenth century.

The Somerset decision left intact the distinction between slaves abroad and servants at home. The ideological momentum, however, had now shifted. As late as 1772, British society still seemed susceptible to transfers of claims to property in persons from beyond the line. Slave–owners felt comfortable in asking how the sanctity of such property could lose its force in Britain. Did slave property lose its vigour with every degree of longitude or latitude as it approached the British Isles? Were rights one thing in Grenada and another in Greenwich? Just such a troublesome question had induced the eighteenth-century French government to suspend its 'free soil' principle in favour of colonists whose servants temporarily accompanied them to France (on condition of incarceration and repatriation). With the Somerset decision British courts moved in the opposite direction, re-emphasizing the dichotomy by suspending the full use of legal claims for repatriation beyond the line. From Somerset on it was the abolitionists who began to invoke the old West Indian 'salt water' rhetoric in favour of universality. Did an ex-slave, sailing from Britain to the Caribbean, become a bit more of a slave with each changing degree of latitude or temperature, landing in the West Indies as a piece of livestock? Each wave of popular mobilization pushed the 'degrees' of freedom further offshore. In 1824 the Court of King's Bench unanimously held that the moment fugitive slaves, *even of a British subject*, 'put their feet on board of a British man of war, those persons who before had been slaves, were free'.[73] Well before emancipation, freedom had expanded from the water's edge of Britain to the shores of the colonies.

Independently of colonial emancipation, the victory over slavery was so complete in England itself that the venue of decision-making could move from the Court of King's Bench to Piccadilly, from London to Waterford and from Chief Justices to chimney sweeps with no loss of legal efficacy. It could also now move from polemics to parodies.

A contemporary stanza on the 'Hottentot Venus' affair told the whole tale:

> That in this land of libertie
> Where freedom groweth still
> No one can shew another's tail
> Against the owner's will.[74]

The first definitive defeat for British slavery occurred where the two sharply contrasting patterns of imperial capitalism clashed head on. In Britain, economic development had evolved within a social and ideological context which made the separation between property and people, labourer and labour, an axiom of social relations. In plantation America the fusion of property and people had also been carried to its most extreme elaboration. Its credit system depended heavily on slave property. The entire value of some colonies was invariably calculated simply as a function of their slave capital.

At the point of first engagement the imbalance of forces proved to be overwhelming. In 1772 planters in England and Lord Mansfield himself might speak gravely of the £800 000 at risk, multiplying the number of blacks in Britain by their plantation price in the colonies, but this argument was inherently far from compelling. All blacks in Britain were not claimed by masters. No one maintained, even before Somerset, that the whole bundle of rights available to owners in America was secured in Britain. It was precisely the indeterminate and diminishing value of their claims which drove masters to seek in Mansfield's authority what they could secure neither from Parliament, the magistrates, nor the crowd.[75]

Elsewhere in Anglo-America those areas which were least dependent upon slavery also moved to dismantle the institution in the generation after the Somerset case. In Britain the resolution was simplest. By any reckoning it involved proportionately less property, and a smaller slave labour force. Britain was also less encumbered by the heritage of formal racial controls and collective attitudes which paved the way for legal discrimination in America long after emancipation.[76]

Regarding popular antislavery, however, the Somerset case was a skirmish, not a battle. Both Mansfield and Somerset's lawyers emphasized the difference between the formal sanctions of slavery in the colonies and the absence of statutory support in England.[77] If the historical revisionists underestimate the legal significance of the decision, they have accurately portrayed the clear continuity of master behaviour for sometime after 1772. Until the early 1790s there were incidents of blacks being forced on board outward–bound ships. Popular mobilization therefore provides the crucial link between the legal impediment to masters in Britain and the breakthrough to transatlantic abolition. In Marc Bloch's sense, the Somerset case was a harbinger, not the origin, of the age of British abolitionism.

3 The Distinctiveness of British Abolitionist Mobilization

Having alluded to the final defeat of eighteenth-century attempts to transfer the transatlantic slave system to the metropolis in terms of law and popular opinion one may turn to the attack on the overseas system itself. Historians of Atlantic slavery disagree about many elements in the history of its abolition. Most, however, date the beginning of the political destruction process at some point in the last third of the eighteenth century. In 1770 the slave trade and slavery were sanctioned from Canada to the southernmost settlements of Spanish South America. The African slave trade was encouraged by every maritime power in the North Atlantic. By the end of the next century every new World society had abolished it and both the slave trade and slavery were rapidly declining in their Afro-Asian strongholds. In international terms the process was not uniform. Especially during the era of British abolitionism centres of the slave trade and slavery shifted from one region to another so rapidly that the quantitative decline of the Atlantic slave system, in economic and demographic terms, was drawn out for over half-a-century after British emancipation.

As a political issue colonial slavery was not a problem of Western culture in general. The coexistence of substantial slave and free labour systems under one administration was a prerequisite of significant abolitionist concern. Germans, whose states were not involved with Atlantic slavery, did produce an antislavery organization consisting of a handful of professionals for a few weeks on the eve of the revolutions of 1848. It has left only a trace of its existence in the archives.[1] Again, in 1857, a single liberal celebrity like Alexander von Humboldt could prod his king into promulgating a law that any slave would become free if he stepped on Prussian soil.[2] Fortunately for slaves there were less circuitous itineraries on the underground railroad.

Even a *bona fide* slave colony might be too insignificant to engage the attention of its metropolis. The Swedish ambassador to France was simply unaware of slavery on Swedish St Bartholomew until British abolitionists brought it to his notice.[3] Public inattention to slavery was indeed characteristic of most of the Continent. British abolitionists would prod mainland satellites into existence and stiffen their resolve with a flow of information and missionaries while British governments prodded their rulers. In this sense, abolitionism was colonized on the continent of Europe as slavery was in America.[4] It was often more difficult to rouse the natives of Denmark and the Netherlands to sustained abolitionist fervour than it was to convert the heathen beyond the line.

If overseas slavery was one of the requisites of abolitionism, a highly articulated political life in the metropolis was another. The Swedish abolition society held a meeting and rejected public petitioning in favour of a private appeal to the King. Abolitionists in the Netherlands and Denmark were almost equally modest. Denmark might appear to be an exception to the linkage outlined here. Without either peaceful or revolutionary mobilization in the metropolis its government resolved in 1792 on the gradual abolition of the Danish slave trade after ten years. However, the Danish decision was made, as Green-Pedersen notes, with reference to contemporary British (not Danish) popular mobilization and in anticipation of a proximate British abolition. The abolitionist ideology of the Danish commission was 'a foreign import' referring explicitly to British abolitionists and British Parliamentary proceedings.[5] Second, Danish involvement in the slave trade did not end in 1792, nor even in 1802. The Danish West Indies continued to be an entrepôt for the 're-export' trade, shipping Africans to neighbouring islands under the Danish flag. The government had phased out only the least lucrative branch of their slave trade. Danish participation ended only with the British conquest of their islands in 1807.[6] Finally, the 56 years between the decision to abolish the Danish African slave trade in 1792 and the emancipation of the Danish Caribbean slaves in 1848 was the longest interval between these two phases in any colonial sector of Northern Europe. In the Danish case extra-metropolitan stimuli clearly took precedence over internal pressures. Emancipation came in response to a slave uprising.[7] An alternative hypothesis such as that which links Danish abolitionist action against its transatlantic system with the emancipation of the Danish peasantry in the late eighteenth century[8] must take account not only of the framework of the Danish

Commission of 1792, but the persistence of Danish Caribbean slavery for well over half-a-century after the abolition of Danish serfdom.

The Netherlands, as Pieter Emmer has put it, was a case of 'abolition without reform', following a stolid path to emancipation 30 years after the British initiative. As Emmer comments in a line ascribed to Heinrich Heine: 'If the world were to come to an end, I would go to Holland, where everything happens fifty years later.'[9] So the Dutch may actually have come in 20 years ahead of schedule. Slow-growing metropolises with dynamic slave sectors delayed even longer in conforming to the British example. The Spanish government resisted rigorous enforcement of laws passed (under British pressure) for the abolition of the Atlantic slave trade for almost two generations. British hegemony over Portugal in the early nineteenth century did not extent to the actual elimination of slavery in Portuguese Africa.

The Iberian cases remind us that the plantation slave sector of an empire was not always peripheral to and more backward than the metropolis, nor even the more 'dependent' sector of the European–American relationship. Historians who address the question as ultimately one of a military and political balance of power between free and slave zones must consider that the Brazilian plantocracy was demonstrably strong enough and flexible enough to ensure both its own existence as a ruling class and national independence from Portugal in the early nineteenth century.[10] On the West African coast the Portuguese presence also existed on the sufferance of powerful local rulers. There was no Portuguese 'power' in Guinea in the usual sense of colonial domination as portrayed in nineteenth-century writings; Portuguese traders and Luso–African intermediaries served the commercial needs of the region. Imperial powers could not all act like the Anglo-American ones. It was ultimately the British metropolis which played the role of secondary abolitionist metropolis to Brazil.[11]

In most metropolitan cases a low level of abolitionism seemed to be linked to a generally low level of political mobilization. France provided another variant, in which general metropolitan mobilization in two revolutionary surges was never channeled in the direction of sustained abolitionism. Revolutionary France was the first metropolitan area to abandon the colonial slave system with its emancipation decree of 1794. But France also had the distinction of restoring slavery and the slave trade in 1802 and again in 1814. France's definitive termination of the slave trade did not occur until a generation after Britain's, and the second French emancipation was not decreed until 1848, 15 years after the British decision. Each major French forward thrust came in the wake of revolution, and all came with little abolitionist mobilization in the metropolis.[12]

If the Netherlands experienced abolition without reform, France experienced revolution without abolitionism. Between revolutionary decrees its antislavery coteries were small élites which neither sought nor encouraged a broad following. French slave emancipation in 1794 came in response to the successful slave revolt in St Domingue and the imminent prospect of British conquest of the French colonies. Napoleon's abolition of the recently restored French slave trade during his final hundred days in 1815 was an appeasing gesture to the British in a moment of international weakness. And if metropolitan revolutionaries took the initiative in decreeing the second and final slave emancipation in 1848, a slave uprising just before the decree reached the islands ensured that it would not be postponed or rescinded.

Victor Schoelcher, the author of the 1848 emancipation, was acutely aware that French abolitionism had no popular national base comparable to that in Britain. The universal manhood suffrage elections of April 1848 for the Constituent Assembly produced a body which clearly threatened to be every bit as stringent in its expenditures for social reform as its restricted suffrage predecessor. Schoelcher's executive decree therefore preempted a postponement of emancipation on grounds of fiscal constraints. Given the Assembly's immediate action against the National Workshops of Paris, Schoelcher may well have been right.The Second French Republic and its Napoleonic successor did act to constrict the impact of emancipation. The Second Empire, with no internal abolitionist opposition, was even able to restore a 'slave trade' in disguise.[13]

French antislavery was clearly distinguished by an inability to combine a stable élite leadership with a mass appeal. It is not just that the radicalization of the French Revolution after 1791 destroyed or scattered the élite of the first French abolitionist society long before the National Assembly certified the first emancipation. From its founding in 1788 the relative fragility of the *Amis des Noirs* was apparent.[14] A comparison between the results of the first British petition campaign in 1788 and the French *Cahiers de doléance* of 1789 is illuminating in this respect. In France, calls for acting against Atlantic slavery, in any form whatever, appeared in only a handful of the general cahiers. In Britain requests for action on the slave trade constituted more than half the total number of public petitions submitted to the House of Commons during its 1788 session. The

TABLE 3.1 *Frequencies of calls for action related to slavery in the Third Estate* Cahiers de doléances *of 1789, expressed as a percentage of calls for other actions affecting conditions of personal coercion*

Alternative subjects	Percentage of demands for alternative actions*		
	Colonial slavery†	Slave trade†	
Galleys	113	60	66
Prison conditions	28	15	22
Serfdom	18	10	15
Labour services	11	6	7
Personal liberties	9	5	6
Royal *corvées*	6	3	6
Constraint of the person	2	2	5

* Columns (2) and (3) refer to the frequency of slavery-linked grievances per 100 'alternative' subjects; column (4) refers to the frequency of *cahiers* listing slavery-linked grievances per 100 *cahiers* referring to alternative subjects. This is to control for the possibility that a few *cahiers* might have clustered very large numbers of either slave-linked or alternative grievances.

† In order to allow for maximum interest in the question of slavery, all coded statements on slavery, positive, negative and ambiguous, were counted.

SOURCE These data were provided by the 'Quantitative Studies of the French Revolution', a research project at the University of Pittsburgh directed by Gilbert Shapiro and John Markoff. The overall design of the research is described in Gilbert Shapiro, John Markoff and Sasha Weitman, 'Quantitative Studies of the French Revolution', *History and Theory*, 12, no. 2, (1973) 163–91.

Cahiers were not, of course, strictly analogous to public petitioning. They were a harvest of all the grievances in the realm, not the result of single interest social mobilization. Nevertheless, it is clear that slavery and the slave trade counted for very little compared with other problems concerning the status of persons (see Table 3.1). It is perhaps not surprising that demands for action on slavery should be only 2 per cent as frequent as demands for governmental action against general constraints on personal liberty. But since there were probably more slaves in the French colonies than serfs in Eastern France, it is telling that demands for action on serfdom were more than five times as frequent as those on slavery. Finally, considering the ratio of those sent to the French galleys compared with those imported by African slavers each year, it does appear significant that concern for the condition of African slaves appeared only two-thirds as frequently in the *Cahiers* as those on the slave trade.[15] In France's first general canvass of popular grievances in more than a century,

overseas slavery and the slave trade were among the least conspicuous issues.

The relative weakness of the French abolition movement was most
dramatically revealed when Thomas Clarkson visited Paris in 1789 to
stimulate the *Amis des Noirs* to more vigorous action. The French
abolitionists' proposal for a national petition campaign to pressure
the French government could hardly have found a more enthusiastic
supporter than the peripatetic Clarkson, who was to travel 33 000
miles on horseback during the first British abolitionist campaigns
between 1787 and 1792. But he was dismayed to find that what they
had in mind was a massive *British* petition to the French government.
Clarkson politely pointed out that the French legislature might react
sourly to such a massive outside intrusion.[16] He rightly anticipated
the charge of foreign influence that was to plague French abolitionism into the Second Empire.

There is scattered evidence of a good deal of hostility to colonial
slavery in revolutionary France, but it was expressed only spasmodi-
cally and occasionally. The most famous members of the *Amis des
Noirs* were dead, exiled or silenced when the National Assembly
decreed the first emancipation. At the Revolution's end the first
liberation could not easily be integrated even into a consensual
national ideology. None of those connected with the first French
emancipation achieved an apotheosis in the official French pantheon
comparable to that of Wilberforce or of Clarkson in Britain. Brissot
de Warville and Condorcet died on the guillotine, branded as traitors.
Toussaint L'ouverture, the black liberator of St Domingue, died in a
Napoleonic prison. Sonthonax, the Commissioner and author of the
emancipation decree in St Domingue, died in complete obscurity.
Abbé Gregoire's later life was spent in internal exile, his very
existence a deterrent to the formation of a new abolitionist movement. The anniversary date of the first French emancipation was
never declared a national holiday even under the First Republic.

By the end of the Napoleonic régime abolitionism was identified
with the climactic violence of the radical phase of the French Revolution. Even those within the élite who wished to align France with
democratic liberalism were deterred by the double traumas of the
French and St Domingue Revolutions. No French abolitionist society
was reconstituted during the First Empire or the Restoration and
there was no continuity of personnel between the *Amis des Noirs* of
1789 and the *Société Française pour l'abolition de l'esclavage*, formed
in the wake of British abolition, in 1834.[17]

The divergence between Britain and France increased during the latter's 'second slavery'. France restored its slave system in 1802 and reopened its slave trade for a third time in 1814. Just when the British public was massively reaffirming its position as the world's premier abolitionist society, foreign observers reported that French opinion was indifferent to the restoration of the slave trade and hostile to British petitions demanding the renegotiation of the sanction for France's slave trade in the Anglo-French peace treaty of 1814. The élite pressure group acting on behalf of abolition was no more than one branch of a philanthropic society during the Restoration and a small coterie of notables for most of the July Monarchy.[18] The French Abolition Society of 1834 included little more than 50 members, drawn almost exclusively from the intellectual and political élite of Paris. Many were members of the Chamber of Deputies, representing a Parliamentary caucus drawn from the Left and Centre Left. Their one attempt to hold a public meeting in Paris in 1843, in imitation of London's world antislavery convention two years earlier, was forbidden by the government on grounds of possible violence. No general antislavery meeting took place in France during the entire period of its 'second slavery'.[19]

The two French petition campaigns which achieved some minor success in the 1840s were both the result of activities originating outside the French abolitionist élite. The first, in 1844, was a petition by French workers calling for slave emancipation. The second, in 1847, was organized primarily by a West Indian *homme de couleur* and a provincial French protestant. The Revolution of 1848 interrupted the beginnings of a third petition campaign. Although the French governmental restrictions on public meetings hindered petition campaigns they certainly do not account for the feeble French response to both the British political example and the strategic threat to French slavery posed by British emancipation. By 1840, when France moved toward the brink of armed conflict with Britain, every French politician realized that the British could mobilize both their own freedmen and the French slaves in an easy sweep of their colonies at the outbreak of hostilities.[20]

Emancipation never became an electoral issue within the *pays légal* in France. It did not even become a major campaign adornment for French abolitionist Deputies. I have been unable to find a record of any political campaign before 1848 in which a French candidate mentioned his antislavery position as a reason for his constituents' support. Indeed, because of Anglo-French tension in the early 1840s, some French abolitionists went out of their way to demonstrate their opposition to the Anglo-French treaty providing for mutual rights of search on suspected slave carriers. It was not only fear of nationalist Anglophobia which bothered French abolitionists. One of their most prominent members, Alexis de Tocqueville, became inactive precisely when new adherents, who wished to popularize and radicalize the issue, began to emerge shortly before 1848.[21]

In striking contrast with Britain after 1814, French governments conducted their foreign policy without any abolitionist overtones. To Continentals pressured by British diplomacy, abolitionism was often regarded as an expression of hegemonic power and Machiavellian deception. Britain often called upon the most formidable navy in the world to extend its diplomatic initiatives. Mere capability did not entail abolitionist activity. The French had the second most powerful navy in Europe in the second quarter of the nineteenth century, and they too were legally committed to the prohibition of the Atlantic slave trade. Yet the French record of captures was certainly not remotely proportionate to its relative naval capacity between 1820 and 1860, the critical years in the closing down of the Atlantic trade.[22] (The same can be said of the US which prohibited the trade to its nationals in 1808.)

The decision not to approach Britain's level of enforcement implies that African suppression was not seen as an important means of projecting or utilizing power. France not only lagged in slave-trade enforcement and emancipation; there was a discrepancy in Anglo-French attitudes toward slave-holding and trading within their respective Old World colonies as well. Britain abolished slavery in its South African Cape Colony in 1834 (even at the cost of alienating many Afrikaaner settlers), and in its East Indian possessions in 1842. Meanwhile the French governor-general in Algeria was allowed to advocate openly the continued toleration of slavery. Without sufficient counter-pressure from within the metropolis the French government supported the existing social structure.[23]

Despite intermittent surges, French abolitionism was clearly less embedded in its metropolitan environment than its British counterpart. The structural weakness in French abolitionism therefore produced a remarkable divergence in policy between the two societies in the 50 years after the Great French Revolution. France, the paragon of revolutionary explosions, was also the paradigm of revolutionary abolitions and reactionary retrenchments.

This overview of French abolitionism gives us some idea of where we must look to discover the sources of British abolitionism, its durability, its aggressiveness, and its growth from a small committee in London to a social movement dedicated to extinguishing the institution from the entire globe. British abolitionism differed in one way from its Continental imitators, and in another from the North American variety. Northern US antislavery was analogous to its British counterpart in using techniques of mass agitation. It differed above all in the relative strength of the slave interest and the counter-mobilization which that interest could organize. British antislavery did have to deal with a West Indian parliamentary presence. But aside from the port of Liverpool, antiabolitionism had no geographical base within the metropolis. In the emancipation petitions of 1833 the abolitionists outcanvassed their opponents by more than 250 to one. Within America even Northern opinion alone never approached that ratio before the ratification of the Thirteenth Amendment. The British political structure was amenable enough to abolitionist influence through normal popular channels. From the first petition of 1788 to emancipation English abolitionists generally behaved as though they were an ecumenical movement.[24] Their American counterparts were more frequently enmeshed in sectarianism, having to react to a world which they could not remake short of an apocalypse.

This international survey of abolitionism highlights three important features of its historical context. With their slower economic and political development, Continental societies lacked strong internal pressure to conform to the British pattern. This was true despite the fact that Britain, as with industrialization, provided an additional external stimulus to restrict and phase out other slave systems. Indeed part of the ideological argument against slavery outside Britain derived from both its positive and threatening existential link with the world's leading industrial and naval power. Antislavery was thus joined to the wave of the future, and at least reflexive discussions were stimulated everywhere by the successive stages in British abolitionism. As with industrialization, in the British case, what was generated as an external stimulus in other countries had to be the result of internal forces.

British popular abolition clearly differed from all its Continental neighbours in breadth and duration. It emerged at the end of the 1780s. It was characterized by a series of campaigns for the abolition of the slave trade between 1788 and 1814 and a lower but visible profile of popular mobilization in 1806–7. These were followed by successive campaigns for amelioration in 1823, emancipation in 1830–3 and a final mobilization for the early end of the Negro apprenticeship

TABLE 3.2   *Ratio of British abolition petitions to all public petitions to Parliament 1785–1833*

Period	Year and number of abolition petitions (1)	Total petitions (per year)(2)	Ratio of (1):(2) (percentage)
1785–9	1787–8 (102)	176	58
1811–15	1814 (774)	899	86
1828–33	average 1831 and 1833 (5252)	3520	149

SOURCES Indices to *House of Commons Journals*; *Parliamentary Papers, Sessional Papers*, 1852–53, 83, pp. 104–5, 'Return of Petitions' for various periods 1785–1852.

system in 1838. Thereafter the movement ebbed and fragmented, with much less effective revivals before, during and following the American Civil War. But for 50 years between 1788 and 1838 abolitionism was virtually unsurpassed in terms of its base of support. There were more petitions for abolition in the 1780s, the 1790s, the 1810s, and the 1830s than for any other single issue (see Table 3.2).[25]

What significance should be attached to the emergence of popular antislavery, and how did it affect the political configuration of Great Britain and ultimately of the whole world? Traditionally, British abolitionist mobilization in 1787–8 has been viewed as simply one more input in a series of familiar and equally important benchmarks along the road to liberation. Historians begin with the forerunners in the philosophical and intellectual tradition and continue through a set of events: the Somerset case of 1772; the Quaker petition to Parliament and the Zong affair in 1783; the Quaker-Evangelical alliance of 1787 to form the first London Abolition Society; and, finally, the decision by the younger Pitt and William Wilberforce to bring the issue before Parliament.[26] Let us critically examine these precursors: the Somerset case, the Zong case, the 'Saints', Pitt, and above all what David Brion Davis evocatively calls the Quaker Antislavery International.[27]

As far as the courts were concerned, the Somerset decision, however broadly defined, had not impinged at all on the institution of overseas slavery or permanently shaken planter confidence.[28] Granville Sharp and Somerset's lawyers, for the sake of their client, and Lord Mansfield for the sake of imperial commercial stability, had all emphasized the supremacy of positive law and therefore the legality of overseas slavery. Right up until the Emancipation Act the courts, of course, upheld the validity of the slave status in the colonies, even for those blacks who had resided in Britain and voluntarily returned.

The Zong case in 1783, far from subverting the distinction between Britain and the world beyond, underscored it. The case concerned a slave ship whose captain, fearing a shortage of water, had thrown 133 of his cargo of slaves overboard. The incident came before the courts only because of a dispute between the slave merchants and the insurance company about claims to reimbursement in a situation where the captain had deliberately destroyed the insured goods. Mansfield, presiding over the case, treated the issue as one strictly within the confines of property and commercial law. 'The case,' he ruled, 'was the same as if horses had been thrown overboard.'[29] Second, Sharp's attempts to bring either a private prosecution or to have the Admiralty prosecute for murder got absolutely nowhere. Most importantly, from our point of view, the case, which was over insurance liability not homicide, got no publicity before and very little after the trial. An isolated letter of protest to a London news-paper after the Mansfield decision was its sole immediate public result, though even Mansfield was shocked by the details.[30] There was no move in or out of Parliament even to change the insurance law concerning slaves, in order to counteract the motives for such actions or to regulate the middle passage. The Zong case became the Zong affair only in retrospect, *after* the emergence of popular abolitionism. It serves rather to underline the legal strength of overseas slavery after Somerset.[31]

If one wishes to discover links between the history of black slavery and the expansion of the British welfare agenda, a more forceful intrusion on metropolitan awareness occurred as an unforeseen consequence of the American conflict. At the end of the American War a new wave of blacks, who had entered the British services, made their way to England.[32] As already indicated, all were assumed to be free and none were entitled to parish relief. As destitute beggars in London many became the focus of a scheme in 1786 to establish a free labour colony on the African coast at Sierra Leone. Beyond intensifying the awareness of black poverty in London the impact of the event on the broader public is not clear. On the one hand, for the first time blacks, as a social group, became the discreet object of state intervention in Britain itself. On the other hand, the British government's willingness to transport blacks to Africa has been interpreted as an implicit attempt at the forced repatriation to

Africa of the black poor from Britain.[33] This seems unlikely either as a general motive or operative premise. No more than 500 were ever boarded, the outports were never involved, and more than 95 per cent of the black population was left untouched by the operation.[34]

The black poor could have had a significant if narrow impact on a few of the élite. It may have been the problem of destitute blacks in Britain which first suggested to William Pitt the possibility of breaking through the bloody cycle of the Atlantic slave system by helping to introduce free labour into Africa. Just after the government launched the first colonizing voyage to Sierra Leone in 1786, Pitt suggested that Wilberforce interest himself in the cause of abolition in Parliament.[35] At least one small group in London was now prepared to act aggressively toward the African continent, attempting to change the social structure at the source of slave supply. Beyond this, the impact of the Sierra Leone experiment on the emergence of political abolitionism is very dubious. News of the disaster of the first colonization rendered the scheme useless to the abolitionists by 1788.[36] It was revived on a more massive scale with impressive capital backing only in 1791, long after abolition had become a major political issue.

We should also consider the impact of the Clapham sect, of Wilberforce and above all of Pitt. Abolitionism certainly gained an invaluable Parliamentary advantage when Wilberforce and Pitt decided to explore the possibilities of abolition. Both politicians, however, initially took the royal road to abolition. In 1787 Pitt unsuccessfully tried to negotiate an international agreement with the French monarchy for the mutual abandonment of the slave trade.[37]

The intervention of Pitt and the Parliamentary 'Saints' must be set in comparative perspective. In 1788, Pitt represented little more than himself in the Cabinet. Neither the King nor the majority in the Cabinet would allow him to make the question a ministerial measure. His principal trade adviser in the Privy Council was opposed to abolition from first to last. The limit of Pitt's power in Parliament, even combined with that of Charles Fox, the leader of the opposition, was demonstrated as late as 1791 by the decisive defeat of the first abolition Bill.[38] Pitt rarely found himself with so small a share of a Parliamentary division in the first decade of his ministerial career.

There remain the most important candidates thus far put forward by historians as the launchers of political abolitionism. The Quakers do qualify in a number of ways as the originators of the social movement. They were the first group in Anglo-America to begin to

discourage their membership's participation in Atlantic slavery during the third quarter of the eighteenth century. They provided a
model of disengagement even before the American revolution. The
Quakers were also institutional pioneers in some of the methods
which were subsequently to be used in abolitionist campaigns. They
formed the first network of local agents in England to distribute
antislavery propaganda on a national scale. They were the first to
resort to petitioning Parliament on the slave trade in 1783. They
constituted three-quarters of the original 12-man membership of the
London abolition committee in 1787. Anstey, Davis and others
therefore plausibly identify the Quakers as the major link in the
transition from abolitionist thought to action in the 1780s.[39]

The balanced distribution of Quakers in Anglo-America also placed
them in a position to act as solvents of the 'line' which underlay the
world view of most eighteenth-century Europeans. The Quakers
were truly 'international' in that their centre of demographic and
economic gravity was less clearly dominated by a metropolitan/
colony mentality. By the last third of the eighteenth century antislavery initiatives were moving from West to East as Pennsylvania
Quakers ceased to have a frontier attitude towards the need for black
labour.[40] They were able to co-ordinate their moves against the slave
trade on both sides of the Atlantic.

What were the results of their initiatives between 1772 and 1787?
In 1783 the Quakers presented the first public petition to Parliament
against the slave trade. Lord North, the British Prime Minister,
gently complimented them for their generous feelings and then
dismissed the petition with a cool dose of policy, reiterating that
unfortunately the Euopean maritime powers had to make use of the
African trade. None of the soon to be Parliamentary champions of
abolition alluded to, or took issue with, the policy assumption of
Lord North, either that day or for four years afterward. The Quaker
initiative of 1783 was stillborn. The Bill to regulate the African trade,
which had been the occasion of the petition, passed through Parliament without a division or further discussion.[41]

It was not just the MPs, great and small, who were silent. The
presentation of the petition was duly reported in most of the nation's
newspapers as part of their extensive coverage of Parliamentary
proceedings. It was emphatically not one of those events which
periodically stirred up flurries of editorial postscripts or correspondence demanding action. Neither in Parliament nor with the public
did the Quaker initiative cause a stir, much less light a spark. Only in

retrospect was the petition accorded the honours of a political milestone.

The next stage of Quaker organization is equally revealing. Following the petition the Quakers decided to lobby the political élite. A new edition of Anthony Benezet's *The Case of our Fellow Creatures, the Oppressed Africans*, was distributed to the Royal Family, to members of both Houses of Parliament and to the notables of England including the Justices of the Peace and the clergy. More than 11 000 in all were delivered through a network of 150 provincial correspondents. As with the petition, the distribution produced, in the words of its initiators, 'an approbation of our benevolence . . . but little prospect of success'. The minutes of the Quaker slave trade committee record no positive response whatsoever, either among the national political élite in London, or from the 150 provincial agents who distributed the pamphlet.[42] The slave interest was neither aroused nor alarmed.

A self-limiting tendency is also evident in the Quaker agitational style. Having initiated the first abolitionist petition of 1783 after much internal hesitation, the Quakers were not in the van of the mass petitioning of 1788 and 1792 which had overtones of a political campaign. Quaker self-segregation had worked well in enabling the group to detach itself from the dominant latitudinarian attitude towards overseas slavery during the third quarter of the eighteenth century. It also acted as a constricting element in the universalization of abolition. Sociologically, British abolitionism was to emerge as an ecumenical and not a sectarian mobilization.[43]

If there is clear evidence of the poor response to the first Quaker petition and to their élite propaganda campaign in 1783–4, it is less easy to measure the cumulative result of their initiatives over three years. Davis argues that there can be no question that the dissemination 'had tremendous impact; by 1787 the slave trade had become a lively issue for a considerable segment of the English reading public', preparing it for the flood of pamphlets and reports to come. Anstey emphasizes the Quakers' own far more sombre assessment at the end of 1786. At that point they saw as little prospect of immediate success for their initiative in England as Lenin saw for a revolution in Russia in 1916. As late as the summer of 1787, Quaker efforts were still focused on Parliamentary canvassing.[44] Whether one chooses to emphasize the contemporary assessment or subsequent achievements it remains clear that as long as the Quakers concentrated on addressing only the powerful, they had, after more than three years of quiet lobbying, succeeded in converting two or three MPs to the idea of Parliamentary action. Quaker organization had not succeeded in transforming their efforts into a highly visible movement. Various segments of the later abolitionist leadership were still working in virtual isolation from each other. While writing his prize essay against slavery at Cambridge in 1785 Clarkson knew nothing of the achievements of Granville Sharp and was astonished in 1786 to find that the Quakers had formed an antislave-trade committee three years earlier.[45]

Before 1787 the slave interest was far more impressed by the general indifference than by the Quaker initiatives. The Quaker petition to Parliament was published in *Williamson's Liverpool Advertiser*, as everywhere else in England, without editorial comment and without rebuttal. A Liverpool newspaper publisher could casually approve of the occasional calls for more humane treatment of slaves right up to the beginning of the first abolitionist campaign without fear of offending his readers.[46] Throughout 1786 and early 1787 Wilberforce made his initial enquiries into the slave trade 'amongst the African Merchants themselves – at that time ready enough to give him information freely'.[47] One year later Clarkson would pursue such an investigation in Liverpool at the risk of his life.

There is little real evidence that the slave interest thought itself any more threatened in 1786 than it would have felt six years before when Richard Watson sermonized at Cambridge against the 'traffic in blood' from Africa, while acknowledging that, speaking 'as plainly as we can, we can have no great expectation of being regarded'.[48] It took a great deal of faith to disagree with the anonymous antislavery correspondent who declared, in 1785, that 'to expect any relief from Parliament is to expect an impossibility, till Negroes, by having boroughs for their property . . . shall have a party in the House of Commons'. This was fundamentally the same conclusion to which John Wesley had come when he had considered what was to be done about the slave trade in the 1770s. 'Should we appeal to the English nation in general? This also is striking wide, and is never likely to procure any redress for the sore evil we complain of. As little would it in all probability avail, to apply to the Parliament.' For Wesley the only remedy lay in appeals to individuals engaged in the slave trade or slavery. Only weeks before the great petition campaign opened at the end of 1787 another correspondent catalogued long-simmering antislavery sensibility among the other futile 'manias' of the British. He recalled once knowing a guest who rose from the table in a large company and walked across the floor, stamping and swearing, in a fit of 'insanity', upon hearing a gentleman say a few words in favour of the slave trade. His host, a sensible Scotsman, brought the guest to his senses by a very simple rebuke: 'Hod, hod, man-you conno put the world to rights-come-tak your soup.'[49]

Whether one uses either newspaper coverage or pamphlet publications as indicators of abolitionism's emergence as a public issue, the quantitative and qualitative evidence dramatically supports the view that the expression of public interest was exponential, not incremental, between 1783 and 1788, and that the take-off took place only toward the *end* of 1787.[50] Until then slavery and the slave trade remained at the pre-political level of unsavoury but unassailable. There was no radical revaluation of the commercial benefits of the British slave system either during the conflict with America or in the immediate post-war era. The vast pamphlet literature on the settlement of 1783 and the Parliamentary debates until late 1787 reveal a virtual consensus on the continued value of the Afro-Caribbean to the mother country. As late as 1787 William Pitt himself was still 'a great favorite' with the West India interest.[51] No MP apparently considered abolition to be a serious political option. Yet by mid-1788 Fox, the leader of the Opposition, could claim that if Wilberforce and Pitt had not decided to raise the issue he would have done so himself. And the Prime Minister, against the inclinations of a majority of his own Cabinet, successfully argued that Parliament now had to respond to the surge of national opinion by carefully considering the abolition of the slave trade.[52] In the spring of 1787 neither Wilberforce, who first wished to avoid recourse to mass pressure, nor the London Committee dominated by Quakers, nor the slave interest foresaw either the advent of public petitioning or the quantum leap in salience which that technique gave to the issue of abolition.[53]

There is a final but little-noted means of testing the relative efficacy of the post-war activities of the Quakers and the early clerical abolitionists like Ramsay and Clarkson until 1787. Peter Marshall has shown that in the 1770s and 1780s manifestations of moral concern about the West Indies and India overlapped one another quite closely.[54] However, until 1787, criticism of British behaviour in East India was more strident, persistent and politically explosive. At the end of the war with America a survey of British imperial outrages listed injuries to Africans, Caribs, Corsicans, Turks and Poles, but first and foremost to East Indians. Another survey quantified the comparison, beginning with three million victims of the British African slave trade, five million destroyed or expelled in Bengal, and culminating with 'the fifteen to twenty millions of carcasses' with which the British had 'strewn the plains of Indostan'.[55]

Politically, India was by far the more volatile imperial reform question of the early and mid–1780s, completely overshadowing both Africa and the Caribbean during the years of Quaker pamphleteering. Immediately after peace with America, the reform of India became the focus of stormy debates in very full Houses of Parliament. It was the occasion for the dismissal of a government and became a major issue in one of the most hotly-contested general elections of the eighteenth century. No sooner did the campaign rhetoric subside than the 'rape of India' became the dramatic backdrop for one of the most famous political trials in British history, the impeachment of Warren Hastings.[56] As late as the summer of 1787, well after the formation of the London Abolition Committee, the *Public Advertiser* predicted that India would be the big question of the forthcoming Parliamentary session. And well it might have been if the choice had been left to the dramatic taste of most Members of Parliament. It was certainly more difficult to get 40 members to attend dreary committee hearings on the number of slaves packed into slave vessels than to attract 400 MPs to the opening salvos of the trial of Hastings.[57] By early 1788, however, India and the slave trade were rapidly exchanging places as objects of legislative attention.[58] This humanitarian swing to the West came less from three years of persistent Quaker dissemination than from the new style of political mobilization. It was this mobilization which was the 'great surprise' of 1788 and constituted the abolitionist 'revolution' of public opinion.

4 The Breakthrough 1787–92

Many historians of the late eighteenth century, especially of high politics, have been inclined to treat with scepticism the concept of public opinion as an autonomous causal factor.[1] Popular abolitionism, located on the very cusp of the age of the modern social movements, is difficult to fit into a political frame of reference still so generally oligarchic.[2] Yet it was the mobilization of public opinion which ushered in the consciousness that one was in a new period in the history of slavery; not in the sense of inaugurating an era of uninterrupted victories but in the sense that the terms of public discourse about the institution in Britain were dramatically and forever altered.

The core area of the take-off is of special interest to a historical analysis that seeks to link developments of antislavery, capitalism and public opinion. It was the booming industrializing North and, above all, Manchester, which made mass petitioning the principal political weapon of abolitionism. Manchester converted a London committee which was little more than a low-key lobby, like the Protestant dissenters' delegates working against the Test Acts, or the Quakers' representatives handing out pamphlets to MPs at the doors of Parliament, into the prototype of the modern social reform movement. E. M. Hunt gave us the first detailed account of the abolitionist movement in the North of England.[3] His analysis can be extended to emphasize both the critical new social mass which was forming in the North during the 1780s and its changing relationship to national decision-making. The combination of the two made Manchester ripe for abolitionism when Clarkson passed through the city during his first abolitionist tour in the autumn of 1787.

There was undoubtedly a general intensification of British popular politics in the 25 years following the accession of George III. The links between local and national political ideology became more tightly knit with a coalescence of partisan voting and affiliation.[4]

National political crises from Wilkes to colonial embargoes, to the American War, East India reform and the constitutional confrontation of the early 1780s, occurred frequently enough, and were significant enough at even the local level, to mobilize clear choices for an increasingly politicized electorate in each general election after 1780.[5] Unimpeded newspaper reporting on Parliamentary debates after the 1770s gave readers a clearer sense of national policy as a continuous and changeable process, susceptible to external pressures. A French traveller was astonished at an English sailors' pub brawl over Parliamentary speeches by Pitt and Fox. Just two years before the Great Revolution he could not conceive of such an event happening in Paris.[6]

One of the important developments of the late eighteenth century was the silent revolution in the meaning of 'public opinion' in political discourse. Professor J. Gunn has recently traced the accelerated movement of the term into the everyday language of politics in the 1780s. For a time, at least, many commentators assumed in the years after 1784 that an era of benign and informed public opinion had arrived. There was an explicit recognition that participation in the political process extended vaguely but quite broadly beyond the confines of Parliament and even of the enfranchised electorate. On the other hand, the agitation over the major national controversies during the generation before 1787 was not centred in the industrializing North, and certainly not led by it.[7] In the case of abolitionism the organizational linkage between a rising capitalism and antislavery may be more direct than references to various religious and political forerunners implies. It is as tempting to extrapolate abolitionism from the radical political organizations as from the Quaker International of the 1780s.[8] Yet the abolitionist take-off did not emanate from the established radical network of London or Norwich or the Yorkshire gentry any more than it did from the Quaker network.[9]

Lancashire was not particularly active in political reform either before or immediately after the war with America. On the eve of the American Revolution Manchester's principal public concern with Africa was with the need to bolster national protection of British traders against natives and foreign interlopers.[10] Only in isolated pockets like Warrington Academy was there a hint of sustained antislavery opinion.[11] On the other hand, the early 1780s witnessed an extraordinary burst of capitalist development and interest-based agitation in Lancashire. Immediately after 1783 Britain's imports of raw cotton increased at a faster rate than in any other period of its dramatic history. Meanwhile a government coping with vastly increased indebtedness sought to enhance its revenues by tapping into this explosive development. When the new Pitt administration attempted to tax the fustian manufacturers, Manchester organized a massive repeal petition in the name of tens of thousands of Lancastrians whose livelihood depended upon the cotton industry. The Prime Minister backed down, significantly acknowledging that his decision was made in direct response to the overwhelming popular reaction, although he himself considered their fears to be economically unfounded.[12]

Lancashire manufacturers also played a leading role in the broader petition campaign against a customs union with Ireland. Here Manchester's interests were aligned with other regional industrialists. Thomas Walker, the leader of the fustian campaign, now joined forces with Josiah Wedgwood of the Potteries to bring maximum extra-Parliamentary pressure to bear upon the government. Again Pitt backed down from his initiative when industrial opinion clearly swung against the measure.[13] This is not to imply the formation of anything like a united industrial interest in the 1780s. The General Chamber of Manufactures which was created in the wake of the coalition against free trade with Ireland immediately disintegrated over the next major issue of political economy, Anglo-French trade liberalization. Walker and Wedgwood split over the treaty of 1787. Indeed Lancashire itself was divided and the government carried the treaty with the support of much of Lancashire. These and other issues of the 1780s revealed that Manchester was by no means the fortress of free trade that it was to become more than two generations later. The abolitionist movement was to be led by Manchester's most consistent anti-free trader of the 1780s and the slave trade, like the French treaty, was to divide rather than to unite the Mancunian manufacturing élite.[14]

The linkage between Manchester and abolition must be sought within a slightly different context. Although its merchants and manufacturers had by no means become the cutting edge of international free trade which they were to be two generations later, Manchester was as wedded to the practice of international free enterprise as any city in Britain in 1788. Its interest-oriented battles of the mid-1780s created the organizational expertise which could open the sluices of enthusiasm otherwise confined within the narrow institutional boundaries that existed for such popular expression in those times. Manchester was of necessity more inclined to experiment with such extra-Parliamentary pressure. It lacked both a corporate local government and a representative in Parliament. Thus there was no line between those with qualifications for participation in electoral decision-making and those without it. As a city which had doubled in population between 1774 and 1788 and was to triple by 1800 it was a 'town of strangers', pioneering in the formation of more impersonal organization. It also led in the development of voluntary welfare organizations including one of the earliest and most successful Sunday-school systems in the nation.[15] Nor was the voluntary system confined to philanthropy. Manchester was perfectly poised in the late 1780s to extrapolate the organizational and agitational skills forged in its economic policy battles.[16]

Manchester's mode of petitioning was highly unusual for England in the 1780s. It launched the petition campaign without consulting with the London Committee or the regional Quaker network. As far as can be seen from newspaper accounts it had the most massively subscribed list of local contributors to the first abolition campaign. No other city in England in the immediate pre-abolition period even attempted to gather 10 000 signatures at a time. It also aimed at a mass enrolment of the male inhabitants. In December 1787 the almost 11 000 who signed the Manchester petition formed fully 20 per cent of the total population of the city.[17] Even if, because of migration, the proportion of adult males represented 30 per cent of the city's total population, two-thirds of Manchester's eligible men subscribed to the first petition for the abolition of the slave trade. This conservative estimate is still astonishingly high. National consciousness of the breadth of Manchester's petition reverberated through the subsequent intense discussion.

The new social reform movement moved smoothly along other important channels provided by contemporary economic development. Britain's relatively dense network of provincial newspapers, with their extensive advertisements, fostered a nationalization of the market by innovative entrepreneurs in the second half of the eighteenth century.[18] The abolitionists of Manchester innovatively decided to use their subscription fund to purchase advertisements of their own petition in every major newspaper in England, calling for similar actions. At a stroke they placed Manchester on the national map as the pace-setter in popular abolitionism, and gave their resolutions a ubiquitousness usually reserved only for Parliamentary debates and Royal Proclamations.

This position was critical. Before the winter of 1787–8 it was assumed that the industrializing North was wedded to the slave trade. When Manchester's petition was first advertised in London, the city newspapers still carried squibs forecasting that the Manchester petition would certainly be met with countervailing petitions from Liverpool and the other port cities.[19] Similar notices appeared elsewhere, advertising Liverpool's intentions to produce a petition which contained even more signatures than Manchester's. Liverpool's own petition was held back until the following year, and there is some reason to doubt that the figure was nearly as large as the 13 000 or 15 000 promised in the squibs. (The petitions to the House of Lords, which have been preserved, show that Liverpool was never able to mobilize more than one-sixth that many antiabolition signatures between 1792 and 1807.[20]) A putative mass antiabolition petition from Manchester also never materialized.[21]

Where the slaving capital was really overmatched, however, was in the resounding echo Manchester's petition elicited from all parts of England. Liverpool stood virtually alone in its ability to generate other 'inhabitant' petitions in favour of the slave trade. Even in Bristol a large committee petition was signed against the slave trade. Liverpool was simply overwhelmed by Manchester's hundred-and-one unanswered volleys.[22] As far as can be determined from a survey of the Parliamentary Journals, this total was an unprecedented levy of petitions for the decade between the Peace of Versailles and the second abolitionist wave in 1792. Manchester rather than the Quaker religious network pushed Britain across the psychological threshold into the abolitionist era.[23] Setting aside ideological considerations for the moment, this was the manner in which British capitalist development made its first direct contribution to political abolitionism.

The Manchester petition was also significant in another respect. It undermined the policy/morality dualism in British political culture which underlay the response to the Quaker petition, and indeed to all previous suggestions to alter or limit the Anglo-Atlantic slave system. Unlike the Quakers, who could be both praised and discounted by their long tradition of tender conscience and sectarian isolation, Manchester was a hard-nosed manufacturing town. If its economy was not dominated by the African or colonial trades it certainly had a tangible stake in these trades, perhaps a larger share than any other inland city in Britain. One-quarter of its exploding appetite for raw cotton came from Britain's own colonies and fully 70 per cent came from the African-purchasing colonies of the Americas. (Leading Manchester cotton manufacturers, like the famous Peels, were later able to procure smaller-scale petitions against abolitionist bills from other interested Mancunians for two full decades.[24]) Slave-trade supporters could certainly accuse the Manchester abolitionists of indifference to the interests of their fellow capitalists. They could and did accuse its abolitionist workers of also acting contrary to their own interests. They could not credibly accuse the Manchester signatories of making high moral pronouncements in ignorance of economic principles. If England's most successful boom town of the 1780s could come down so overwhelmingly on the side of abolition, Lord North's worldly-wise response to the Quakers in 1783 no longer appeared axiomatic.[25]

Aside from the general social and religious changes which its residents shared with many others, and which will be discussed later, what was it about Manchester that set it in motion towards petitioning, even before the itinerant Clarkson's arrival, and made it respond to abolitionism so far beyond anyone's expectations?[26] Manchester in 1787 had probably just become the largest inland commercial centre in Britain. As in the case of London and its black poor, there was enough involvement in the African trade to arouse self-scrutiny without also arousing an overwhelming self-interest. Manchester was the commercial and communications hub of an industry whose very day-to-day existence, from procurement of distant raw materials to sales, depended on an international perspective. Each major Parliamentary debate on trade policy since 1784 had occasioned Manchester's active participation. Its élite was therefore market- rather than state- or corporation-oriented. If its principal industrialists were still the opposite of internationalist free traders they had already acquired a deep faith in the rewards of the untrammeled marketplace at home. Still more significantly, many of the Manchester workers agreed with the mercantile élite's faith in the market. The status of trade and industry had a resonance in Manchester which was lacking in areas where tradesmen occupied a more subordinate rung in the hierarchy of honour.[27]

Beyond the marketplace, moreover, its workforce was one of the least parochial in Great Britain. Manchester was a town of the uprooted. No other agglomeration could have been so collectively and effectively moved by Clarkson's focus on the peculiar terrors of the slave trade: loss of kin, hearth and community. To be part of a lonely crowd, of a community of the uprooted, even by choice, was to feel the appeal on behalf of those uprooted by violence, and forever. Manchester had begun its long search for a myth which 'would elevate its citizens above the prosaic level of their daily working life'. The myth ultimately found expression in the ideology of free trade. But half-a-century before that it found its first expression in an ideology of liberty.[28]

Rhetorically Manchester's mass petition did not concern itself with the policy aspects of the slave trade, or with potential economic gain or loss. Manchester, like almost all of its 15 000 sequels during the next 50 years, based demands for action on the offensiveness of such a traffic to humanity, justice and national honour. Policy considerations were left to Parliamentary debate. It is of crucial importance that from the opening salvo until the final abolition of 'apprenticeship' just half a century later, antislavery's direct economic beneficiaries were rarely identifiable. The losers always were.[29]

The combination of political strategies drawn from the everyday economic life of Britons in the 1780s could not have been achieved so casually in the 1680s or even the 1730s, despite the fact that the imperial economy was less dependent on slave production in 1685 or 1735 than in 1785. Some opponents were glumly encouraged by the very commercial techniques used to rivet public attention on slavery. If advertising had made abolitionism fashionable, this year's fad might be succeeded by next, perhaps an attempt to do something about men on the moon. In this spirit one peer denied the need for any response whatever to such a 'five days fit of philanthropy'. There were also early attempts to dismiss abolitionism as an exotic or subversive plot designed to undermine British national greatness.[30]

As Manchester was uniquely poised to take the lead in a petition campaign, it was also able to tap the extensive national acquifer of libertarian ideology and aversion to slavery noted in Chapter 1. In some areas the Quaker network was able to set the process in motion. In others a gathering of the Justices of the Peace at Quarter Sessions was the occasion for launching county petitions. In many places, the Manchester advertisement was sufficient to stir local imitation through debating societies and church meetings.[31] A close reading of the surviving local newspapers demonstrates that Manchester was already part of a broader geographical base of popular petitions during the very first campaign of 1788.

Unfortunately, we have cited numbers of signers from only two cities besides Manchester, but something about the social base may be learned from the way in which petitions were gathered and

TABLE 4.1 *Mobilizations 1769–1824*

Occasion	Date	Target	Percentage of petitions restricted to privileged groups (nobility, corporation, freemen, etc.)
Wilkes Dismissal	1769–70	Crown	89
of Fox/North	1784	Crown	57
Slave trade abolition	1788	Parliament	30
King's recovery*	1789	Crown	72
Slave trade	1792	Parliament	15
Sedition Bills	1795	Parliament	62 (pro)
			16 (con)
Slave trade	1814	Parliament	2
Slave trade	1823	Parliament	3
Slave trade	1824	Parliament	1

* This was not a petition but congratulations to the King.
SOURCES   For applications to the Crown, PRO HO55/1–30.
For applications to Parliament, indices to the *House of Commons Journals* for the appropriate sessions.

presented. Before abolitionism petitions usually designated themselves as emanating from some interest or corporate group (nobility, clergy, freemen, corporation members, and so on), with a qualified public or private right to governmental attention. Less frequently a petition declared that it emanated from the publicly-gathered inhabitants of an area. From even summary self-designations it is clear that those without any kind of special claims to participate in the polity entered into a greater proportion of abolitionist petitions than with any previous question brought before the Parliament of Great Britain.

Table 4.1 shows that of the more than 100 petitions submitted to Parliament in 1788, only 15 per cent were self-designated as emanating from some corporate or special status group: nobility, magistracy, clergy, freemen or 'principal' citizens. The rest entered themselves simply as 'inhabitants' of towns and parishes, or as participants in voluntary associations without political privileges. One may compare the proportion of inhabitant petitions with those of major political campaigns of the previous generation. Between the Wilkes affair in the 1760s and the dismissal of the Fox-North ministry in 1784, each mobilization gathered more than half of its petitions from corporate or enfranchised groups. The division between corporate and unincorporated petitioning refers to the self-designation of the petition area and may actually underrepresent the popularity of some 'popular' corporate petitions in 1788. The petitioners of Norwich, submitting a corporation petition, may have had a social profile as representative of their general adult male population as the citizens of York, who petitioned as inhabitants.[32]

Although Manchester's was the most numerously signed petition in 1788, petitioning elsewhere was also quite often a process of canvassing following a large and formal public meeting. This was designed to present the resulting document as a measure of community consensus where possible. In 1788 provincial reporting of local public meetings was still so abbreviated that the record is generally incomplete. Abolition, because it was virtually unopposed in most areas, became a bridge to freer public reporting on local political and contentious activity.[33]

It has been possible to gather evidence of at least 27 public meetings in 1788, more than a quarter of the recorded petitions. Almost all of the larger towns in England were represented. The total number of signatories was rarely mentioned, but Sheffield weighed in with 2000 signatures and York with 1800. Urban public meetings were usually followed by a wide circulation for signatures. Manchester's petition was left in ten public places, Sheffield's in four and the Northampton petition was left in twelve market towns. Nottingham also sent its petition out to surrounding towns. Shrewsbury had two separate meetings, a general county meeting for the freeholders of Shropshire and an open town meeting for the rest of the population. Exeter and Birmingham had two general meetings. According to the newspaper accounts, Birmingham citizens held their second mass meeting specifically to counter an opposition resolution which might have been subsequently advertised as an inhabitants' petition. The Leeds meeting appealed to 'the rough sons of lowest labour'. Where the petition was not circulated it was usually left, as in Bristol and Oakham, at the meeting place for further adhesions.[34]

We have accounts from enough areas to conclude that Manchester's plea for a broad base was heeded. York's 1800 signatures represented up to 40 per cent of the adult males and may have rivaled Manchester for the maximum proportion of adult male signatories. Falmouth was satisfied with the unanimity of those at the public meeting. Northampton county went for large numbers of adhesions and gathered about 2000 signatures. Most meetings follows Manchester's lead in advertising their own resolutions in both regional and London newspapers. These towns were well aware that Manchester had created a competitive humanitarian market. Along with its 2000 signature harvest, Sheffield announced that it had always been first in humanity.[35]

Abolitionism broke through unevenly in 1788. Popular petitioning was not yet a casual form of collective activity. The average annual number of public petitions sent up to the House of Commons between 1785 and 1789 was still only 176 per session. In 1788 more than half the 200 petitions received by the Commons were those dealing with the slave trade. Not all areas felt equally free about the propriety of inhabitant petitioning. It was easier for communities already politicized by contested electoral struggles to respond to Manchester's call for a speedy mobilization. John Phillips has recently noted that of four Parliamentary boroughs he studied between 1760 and 1800 the two most electorally active (Norwich and Maidstone) were the most petition prone. They petitioned against the slave trade in 1788. By contrast, Northampton and Lewes, relatively unpoliticized, rarely petitioned the Commons. Antislavery itself, however, provided a bridge to mobilization. While the normally unroiled borough of Northampton did not petition against the slave trade as a borough in 1788, its inhabitants did join in the county petition. In the second and more systematically organized appeal of 1792 all four of Phillips's towns petitioned against the slave trade. Even the bashful boroughs did not have to be asked more than once.[36]

There were other inertial constraints on petitioners during the abolitionist take-off of 1788. In some cases the activity itself was thought to be beyond the legitimate role of constituted bodies. The Scottish Presbytery and Oxford University demurred, the latter much to the embarrassment of its representative, Sir William Dolben. One small inland town was uncertain whether its insignificant petition would help or hurt the general cause. Petitioning to Parliament in the 1780s was still more 'private' than public, traditionally tied to the claims of specific injured parties or beneficiaries.[37] The novel appearance of 'disinterested' petitions in a matter of trade involved an aggressive redefinition of propriety. At the beginning of 1788 the abolitionists' most difficult task was to get the public to make the leap from an economic to a humanitarian political frame of reference. The agent for Jamaica was himself completely disconcerted by these outlandish dabblers in the imperial economy who gathered in unprecedented numbers, although 'stating no grievance or injury of any sort, affecting the Petitioners themselves'. Lord Hawkesbury, the very model of the mercantile perspective of the Privy Council and Board of Trade, knew that the proper question in all economic legislation was who was injured and who benefited.[38] From the outset the petitioners were breaking this cardinal rule of capitalist interest petitioning. Their grounds of complaint were therefore as unsettling as their economic base was unfathomable. Moreover, instead of beginning with a motion in Parliament, they were 'blowing up the flame first, and then telling you for what purpose afterwards'.[39]

Quite aside from the unsettling nature of the demands, many potential signers felt diffident about any agitation whatever. In smaller towns the élite might decide that a petition emanating from the 'principal' residents was as good, or better, than an inhabitant petition. The Kendal meeting was described as including all of the 'principal inhabitants' of the town. At Olney it was the freeholders who met to congratulate their MP on his proabolitionist stance. At Stamford only the gentlemen of the county met to consider the petition. In the South-west most of the 'principal inhabitants' of Swansea signed. In Falmouth the 'principal inhabitants' included 'none but tradesmen and creditable inhabitants', which leaves the social boundaries rather indeterminate, although it probably meant householders only. In this area, a rotten borough heaven, there seemed to be more attention to social gradation and a mayor might be more hesitant to sanction a petition meeting.[40]

There were clear geographical limits to the first campaign. Almost a third of the petitions came from the 'new' industrial area north of the Severn, between Worcester in the south-west and Yorkshire in the north-east. Smaller clusters came from the area between Bedford and Norwich, and from the Southern towns in the triangle between Southampton, Plymouth and Bristol. Petitioning spilled over into Scotland but only as far as Edinburgh's élite Chamber of Commerce and some Scottish synods and universities. Perhaps because Manchester limited the scope of its advertisement campaign there was no surge of inhabitant response in Scotland or Wales comparable to those in England. Subsequent campaigns reached out to more distant locations. Except for some county magistrates, the campaign was an urban phenomenon. Petitions were circulated through satellite market towns. The general network of commercial communication was the abolitionist channel of 1788.

Abolitionism was also grafted on to other everyday practices of commercial capitalism. For Josiah Wedgwood, slavery in 1788 was no less promising an object for ceramic commemoration than the Peace

Treaty with France, John Wesley, or Captain Cook.[41] So while the pottery workers of Staffordshire were signing up against the African traffic, their principal employer, an early member of the London Abolition Society, was trafficking in a new line of medallions (with a generous seeding of free samples): the famous jasper figure of the kneeling slave asking, 'Am I not a man and a brother?' What was unusual about the slave medallion was the anonymity of the figure, an everyman of a mass age.

From the printing press came the most famous pictorial representation of all the slave-trade campaigns, Clarkson's schematic plan of a loaded slave ship. It was far cheaper to print and to sell than even Wedgwood's medallion. If we may credit the cartoonist's instincts for background realism, the slave ship soon hung in homes throughout England.[42] The initial outburst of abolitionism therefore stimulated its most striking and enduring popular iconography. Two generations later an aging Birmingham orator movingly recalled how his social conscience had first been awakened when his father unrolled the picture of the slave ship before his gathered family.[43]

The campaign of 1788 not only tested the resilience of petitioning as an instrument of public mobilization; it also began to extend the boundaries of political participation. Even the most widely-signed petitions were confined to adult males. One place or another might exclude illiterates, paupers, non-householders, those who were not members of the local corporation or not regarded as principal citizens. Yet the public agitation also created room for other kinds of intervention; in 1788, abolition suddenly became a ubiquitous topic within the formal debating societies. Some discussions, held over from one session to another by popular demand, were also directed at female audiences. On at least one occasion women were the principal speakers. In these debates many English men and women may have seen black public speakers for the first time, describing their personal experiences in the slave system.[44]

By 1791 another abolitionist technique emerged, again without the instigation of the London committee. It brought women and children directly into the orbit of the campaign. A nationwide boycott of slave-grown sugar was begun. It was as closely related to the new sense of consumer power as Wedgwood's capitalist philanthropy was to his pottery. It made the abolitionist élite uncomfortable because it was launched not merely as a symbolic means of pollution avoidance, but as an instrument of economic power.[45]

There is no way of knowing just how many people participated in the slave-sugar abstention (antisaccharite) movement at its height in 1791–2. Clarkson claimed that 300 000 families were involved. In the light of my rough estimate of petition signers in the second slave-trade campaign of 1792, this is not an unreasonable guess. The newspapers confirmed its national breadth. In England it extended from Cornwall to Carlisle. It also spread to the main urban centres of Scotland and even beyond the petition zone into urban Ireland and Wales. Since abstention was a family-oriented strategy, special appeals were directed towards women, emphasizing their otherwise excluded status from the political arena.[46]

As a weapon of consumer capitalism the sugar boycott achieved some peripheral successes. Dealers advertised 'free sugar' in British towns from Ipswich to Edinburgh and Wales. The sugar interest from Bristol to Liverpool acknowledged that abstention had some affect on sugar prices at the height of the petition campaign of 1792.[47] As a political weapon, however, the free-grown sugar movement could hardly have come at a worse time. The St Domingue Revolution of 1791 had produced a sharp upward surge in prices. Throughout the campaign British sugar refiners were complaining about a devastating shortage rather than a glut. Although British sugar consumption may have dropped by up to a third from its pre-French Revolutionary level during the abolitionist campaign of 1792, it remains unclear how much of this was due to abolitionist abstention and how much to rising Continental demand. During the same period the rate of re-exports of British colonial sugar to Europe almost tripled.[48] What is abundantly clear is that the British tropical planters were feeling no profit squeeze whatever in 1791–2. Moreover, while British consumer mobilization was adding a new weapon to the social reform arsenal, Parisian crowds were blending revolutionary rhetoric with the traditional moral economy of the food riot to force French colonial sugar on to the market.[49] On balance, the consumers of Europe easily cancelled out the abstainers of Britain. Even over the long term it would be impossible to determine how much of lowered British home consumption was produced by high prices and how much by high principles. Sugar prices remained buoyant for almost seven more years. Thus the first decade of the abolitionist era coincided with the best average prices sugar growers had seen for at least a century.[50] There was a later attempt to use abstention during the emancipation phase, but its impact remains equally unclear.

The second petition campaign was co-ordinated from London. Agents were sent through England and Scotland to stimulate sympathetic local organization. They were very scrupulous to avoid activities which might support charges that they orchestrated or even initiated local petitions. Typically, a private meeting was called by sympathizers. The agent passed out an edited volume of Parliamentary evidence on the slave trade. Even if the local organizers immediately suggested a petition they were told first to circulate the evidence and to draw up their own resolutions. There was to be no basis for accusations of mindless conformity.[51]

The localities were only asked to time their public meetings so that the petitions would converge on Parliament just as Wilberforce renewed his abolition motion in 1792. The presenters would be able visually to maximize the impression of the *vox populi* as the sheepskin petitions piled up on the table of the House of Commons. In most respects the pattern of 1788 was repeated, but on a more comprehensive scale. The abolitionists capitalized on their virtual monopoly of popular support. The total number of petitions quintupled from 102 to 519, the largest number ever submitted to the House on a single subject or in a single session.[52] Every English county was now represented, although the most massive support still seemed to emanate from the North.[53] In 1788 petitions from north of the Tweed had represented only corporate Scotland: presbyteries, synods, universities, and a chamber of commerce. In 1792 Scotland arrived in full force: municipalities, parishes, professions and trades.[54] No distinction was permitted between backwaters and large towns or between principal and general inhabitants. Popular petitions were explicitly preferred. Towns were warned against submitting only one signature in the name of the community. Single signatures were simply no help. The more open the petition, the greater was the leverage it would exert in Parliament. In some areas trade and friendly societies were specifically invited to intervene. Efforts were more concentrated on canvassing than producing written publicity. Propaganda could be matched by counter-propaganda; signatures could not.[55]

Antiabolitionist strategies of detraction only reinforced the evidence of popularity. After the vigorous vindication of Manchester's 10 000 workers and tradesmen in 1788, no one attempted a similar assault on the reported 20 000 subscribers to the Manchester petition of 1792. Manchester's 50 sheets might be punned away as 'sheepish names on sheepish skins', but no one challenged their authenticity.

No abolitionist responded to sneers at the Nottingham stocking workers or Cornish miners for signing petitions or abstaining from sugar on behalf of people who worked in far less hazardous situations than themselves. Abolitionists objected only when their enemies took the opposite tack, and attempted to keep the poor away from the 'skins' with rumours that signing entailed a financial pledge. In some communities adhesion was so complete that prominent individuals who did not sign were singled out for special mention. One town reported that only six members of the clergy refused to sign. Another announced that only one refused. Olney's William Cowper, already famous as an abolitionist poet, felt obliged to issue a lengthy public statement explaining why his name did not appear on the Olney petition.

In 1792, the abolitionists were more concerned with accusations of excess than paucity. In Parliament, Liverpool's Colonel Tarleton attempted to discredit a few of the petitions, including the major one from Edinburgh. Tarleton claimed that schoolboys had signed its petition.[56] Tarleton's observation was both correct and misleading. A private report to Clarkson on the Edinburgh subscription by a petition-watcher informed him that the skins had been kept open and in his sight for three days and not sent from house to house. No one under 14 years of age was allowed to sign. When some boys did get at one sheet the watcher had cut their names off, at the expense, he sadly concluded, 'of twenty-six good names with them'.[57]

Tarleton's list of frauds also included Ipswich. Ipswich was also one of the few examples of a local challenge. The rebuttal revealed that the canvasser was familiar with every name on the petition. All in all 715 housekeepers had been signed up and others had offered themselves. The signing was public and in the presence of hundreds of witnesses. The defender of the Ipswich petition challenged the anonymous denouncer to offer a single false name. As in Edinburgh, open and public signing apparently had been chosen in anticipation of exactly the sort of challenges levelled in Parliament. In Northampton a resident challenger reported in triumph that a pauper had, in fact, signed the petition. With equal triumph abolitionists cited this accusation as evidence against any massive misrepresentation of the Northampton signatures. Given the heavy preemptive precautions taken by the abolitionists, it is not surprising that only ten petitions were named as fraudulent in Parliament, and those in the vaguest terms. Of those few for which contemporary discussion is available, all seem to have been scrupulously monitored. The probability of more than insignificant fraud seems extremely low. The year 1792 marked the last gasp in Parliament of challenges to the authenticity of any abolitionist petitions.[58] ₔ

The contemporary discussion of who signed or who might have signed also affords us some idea of the ever-disputed boundaries of eighteenth-century legitimacy. In 1792, as in 1788, we have no clear idea of the number of signatures at the national level. Neither the London abolitionists nor MPs seem to have been particularly interested in the grand total. An outstanding number such as Manchester's signers in 1787 or in 1792 might be widely publicized. Otherwise figures were reported only for local consumption. For 1788 it has only been possible to uncover reports for three Northern towns out of a total of 102 petitions. Manchester's 10 639 is the only one purporting to be exact. Manchester, Sheffield, York and two other petitions accounted for over 15 500 signatures. These five petitions together represented, of course, less than 5 per cent of the total. If they represented even as much as five times their proportionate share of the total *signatures*, over 60 000 signed the 1788 petition. The only contemporary claim I have come across was 100 000. It is worthwhile noting that this easily could be the case if the 15 000 signatures represented by the known 5 per cent of the petitions counted for as little as 15 per cent of the signatures.

For 1792 we are on somewhat firmer ground. From a survey of the provincial press it was possible to ascertain figures for 44 petitions. The numbers given would have to be taken as low estimates for their areas since some figures were reported as interim totals while the petitions were still being signed. The 44 known petitions represent one in twelve (8.5 per cent) of the total of 519. They accounted for 97 800 signatures.[59] If the 44 represented even three times as many signatures as they did petitions (that is, one-quarter of the signatures), 390 000 signed in 1792. This figure does not seem unreasonably high. In 1814, in far more hurried circumstances, the abolitionists claimed 750 000 names on 800 abolitionist petitions.[60]

The 1814 total was the first for which Clarkson advanced even a round figure. In 1788–92 the number of localities representing the geographical breadth of petitioning was more significant to the abolitionists than the total number of signers. Only with the coming of counter-mobilizations on other issues in the mid-1790s did more precise numbers of signers appear salient to the protagonists. In November 1795 Manchesters' two petitions to the House of Commons on Pitt's Sedition Bills carried 11 654 signatures (7 351 loyalists as against 4 303 opponents). A month later Manchester's maximum canvass of petitions to the Lords attracted 30 011 signers (12 185 loyalists as against 17 826 opponents). At the national level the petitions to the House of Commons on the Sedition Bills was tabulated at 161 206 (29 922 loyalists as against 131 284 opponents).[61] Exact totals therefore became important when claims to 'public' opinion were actually contested. Manchester's total number of petitioners in 1795 (to the Lords) easily exceeded the abolitionists' 20 000 in 1792, but the anti-sedition mobilization also appears to have been more localized. The abolitionist national mobilization of 1792 was certainly more than double the combined total of 160 000 on the sedition petitions.

The hostile witnesses of the opposition to abolition in 1788–92 demonstrate why the petitioners of 1792 did not have to tally signatures as carefully as the antagonists of 1795. The abolitionists were satisfied with having conveyed the sense of an overwhelming national consensus. In newspapers, pamphlets and in Parliamentary discussions, the slave interest questioned the policy, the efficacy, the sincerity, the humanity and even the sanity of the abolitionists, but not their popularity. Whether the people should be listened to was one thing. Whether they had spoken was another. Most defenders of the trade began with the defiant assertion that they were bravely taking the unpopular side. Their private assessments were no different from the public ones in this respect. The West Indians were stunned and demoralized. In 1788 John Pinney of Nevis vowed never to invest another pound in his West Indian estates. The agent for Jamaica acknowledged that the colonists had been wrong to believe that they could rely on 'policy' alone.[62]

One problem faced by the slave interest was the growing tendency of Parliamentary leaders during the 1780s to accept petitioning as a mode of integrating public opinion into the legislative process. Abolitionism, as we have indicated, was the most logical nominee for such an innovation, having accumulated the most abundant harvest of petitions to Parliament in the 1780s and early 1790s. The overall pattern of acceptance was not entirely smooth or automatic. In the case of the Gordon riots of 1780, petitioning was a preliminary stage of an episode of shattering collective violence. In its wake there were demands for curbing mass petitions. Large political gatherings for any purpose continued to arouse official anxiety. At the abolitionist petition meeting of 1792 in Edinburgh, which attracted more than 3500 people, the magistrates placed the castle troops, the town guard and two troops of horse on alert despite the solemn order with which the meeting was called.[63] On the other hand, no one was more aware than the Prime Minister that the public petition had proved as valuable to the Government as to the Opposition. In 1784 Pitt made effective use of overwhelming petitioning against the Fox–North coalition in order to strengthen his claim to national support. When Pitt demanded some immediate legislative response to the abolition petitions in 1788 he was simply extending a perspective which had served him well.[64] Again, in April of 1792, Pitt issued the last threat of his Parliamentary career to go to the country if the House of Commons voted to postpone gradual abolition for as much as eight years.

In 1788–92, popular national petitioning was still an imponderable element of political behaviour. The ever-cautious Wilberforce discouraged any public meeting by the London Society and the abolitionist petition campaign of 1788 developed beyond his control. Mass abolitionist petitioning was unleashed again only after Parliament's negative vote of 1791, and thereafter not for 20 more years. The campaign of 1788 provoked references to the anti-Catholic campaign of 1780, when petitioning climaxed in London's worst riot of the century. Finally, as the fear of Jacobinism gathered steam during 1792, abolitionism was yoked to emerging British radicalism and attacked as the Trojan horse of political and religious revolution.[65]

Besides raising thorny questions about the legitimacy and weight of petitions in the political process, mass petitioning opened up volatile questions about who was a legitimate signatory. From the early debates in Parliament it seems clear that criminals and children under 14 were not regarded as legitimate signatories. They were assumed, on all sides, to delegitimize petitions. By and large, working men seem to have been acknowledged as legitimate signatories from the outset. Even when working men alone submitted a petition, they were designated by MPs as 'numerous and respectable'. When a West Indian MP challenged the general right of workers to petition (on another matter) in 1794, his motion was immediately rejected. The right to petition the legislature was designated as one of the distinguishing characteristics between free men and slaves.[66]

Signatures of independent working men were one thing; paupers were another. From the controversy over the Ipswich petition it is clear that paupers were not sought out by the petition sponsors, nor did opposition to signatures of paupers necessarily come from conservatives. Radicals denounced signatures obtained by agents of the government from the dependent poor. It is only in 1814 that one finds evidence of an account of a town's dependent poor signing its petition against the slave trade. It may well be that by then the virtual consensus on abolition of the slave trade ensured that no one would challenge the names on ground of dependency to the powerful in the community.[67] After 1788 communities were never left in doubt that what was wanted was signers unlimited.

Women were the principal group whose status as potential signers changed during the age of abolition, and indeed in response to it. In 1788 there was not even public speculation that women should sign petitions, although they were listed as subscribers of funds and vigorously participated in debates.[68] In 1792 their disbarment from petitioning was cited as an injustice by the radical Methodist propagandists of Manchester. Norwich radicals went as far as suggesting the signing of a separate female petition. The gender line was breached at least once, in England at Belford, and a separate women's petition was reported from Scotland.[69] The fear of delegitimation generally outweighed calls for unlimited female signatures. By 1807 women were prominently canvassing in Yorkshire's famous slave-trade election, but in 1814 a news item still reported that a woman had shed tears of frustration at her inability to subscribe to the abolition petition. By 1830 women were signing separate petitions in considerable numbers, and at the climax in 1833 they presented Parliament with the largest antislavery petition of them all. A huge coil signed by 187 000 'ladies' of England was carried into the House of Commons by four MPs. The unrepresented beyond the line of freedom had come to be represented by the unrepresented beyond the line of gender.[70]

What was the result of the abolitionist breakthrough in 1788–92? It was certainly not the immediate abolition of slavery nor even of the slave trade. The only unequivocal political result was the regulation of that trade on terms which still allowed it to reach its all-time peak in the decade after 1788. The man-trade still had a great deal of Parliamentary support, as abolitionists were bitterly to discover during 20 long years. The most significant immediate result was rather the emergence of a new attitude towards slavery and the slave trade.

The arrival of the abolitionist mentality can be documented at a number of levels. Before 1788 even those who were most hostile to slavery tended to be either fatalistic or apocalyptic about the chances of altering the Atlantic economies. When Adam Smith cautioned his students that unfree labour was likely to characterize most of the earth for a long time to come he was merely projecting on to a world scale the hundreds of years required to complete the evolution of Western European labour from largely bound to largely waged or independent labour.[71] On the eve of popular abolitionism the Abbé Raynal's passionately anti–imperialist history of European expansion reflected a sense of global impotence about patterns of overseas behaviour. He still saw only two possible sources of change: a maroon Spartacus in the colonies or a consensus of crowned heads in Europe. Even this involved the intervention of a *deus ex machina* from outside the previous pattern of historical development: 'Isn't the future splendour of these colonies a dream, and wouldn't the happiness of these regions be a still more amazing phenomenon than their original devastation?'[72] It was precisely in the light of such eighteenth-century projections that their reversal was to appear so extraordinary. Even those who condemned slavery root and branch on religious grounds saw no hope of dramatically altering the system before the age of abolition. On the very eve of popular abolitionism in 1787 John Wesley preached at Manchester on one of his last tours, apparently unaware that his path had crossed that of Thomas Clarkson on his first abolitionist journey. A year later Wesley was enthusiastically including abolitionism in his sermons at Bristol and pledging his support to the new crusade.[73]

No better example can be found of sailing with the new wind than in the writings of Arthur Young. In 1772 the quantifier and geographer of liberty and slavery had classified Britain's African trade as intrinsically 'of very great importance; but, besides these circumstances, the immense article of our American colonies on it, renders it to the highest degree advantageous'. In 1788 the same author, reviewing Samuel Estwick's reprinted economic defence of the slave trade (first published in 1773), now dismissed the very thought of such a defence: 'To offer any remarks on such [a] position, and towards the close of the eighteenth century,' he solemnly intoned, 'would be paying a very poor compliment to the understanding of my readers.'[74] Young was neither the first nor the last who would imply that they had known for an age what they had discovered only yesterday.

Reviewing the cultural artifacts on the slave trade produced by the British Parliament during the eighteenth century it is evident that in the case of the slave trade we are not dealing with the cumulative outcome of a slowly shifting moral/economic boundary. On the evidence one would be hard pressed to produce even faint harbingers in Parliament of the cultural revolution of 1787–92. Before 1787

Britain had built up an intricate network of trade relations with various West African rulers and factors and almost nothing else. The last pre-abolitionist Parliamentary enquiries into the conditions of the African and sugar trades were focused exclusively on overhead costs of fortification and threats of international competition. The governmental political enquiries in 1788–92 operated within an entirely new framework. The old economic and demographic questions were extended and even systematized. But entirely new fields of enquiry were now opened: the exact role of British traders in the total transoceanic trade; the motives for intra-African wars resulting in slaves; the relative sources of slaves produced by breeding, capture, or judicial proceedings; African incentives and disincentives to labour; the variety of African political and religious systems; the ways in which slaves viewed their European carriers; relationships between European buyers and African sellers; the antiquity and origins of the slave trade; the nature of property relations in Africa; the nature of African religion; and conditions on the middle passage and in the West Indies.

Reviewing this new pattern of enquiry David Davis has been particularly struck by its cathartic and action-*avoiding* functions: 'From a psychological perspective, the investigations can be seen as a ritual of expiation that temporarily exorcised the slave trade's worst evils.' The 'calling of witnesses, quite apart from the timing of votes, helped to prolong a public catharsis'.[75] Yet, compared with the half-century before 1788, the cognitive impact of the investigation was far more significant than any putatively affective dalliance. What was psychologically new was the entire investigative format. The questioners treated the slave trade as part of a social system with significant political, religious and communal impacts. What had changed, and permanently so, was a cognitive world-view, whether one deals with it in terms of its psychological or its political dimensions. For the first time the political system raised issues revealing concern with Africa and the West Indies as human communities rather than purely trading units. And the range and nature of the questions, even where they highlighted differences between European and African standards, implied that to accept West African standards regarding the slave trade, even beyond the line, was to allow Europeans to accept standards of behaviour rejected by Europeans among themselves.

In the new political atmosphere, when proslave-trade witnesses cited conviction for 'witchcraft' as one of the sources of enslavement in Africa, they were announcing that they accepted West African juridical standards which the European legal community now contemptuously rejected as barbarous.[76] Every African person convicted of witchcraft was *ipso facto* an innocent victim of criminal superstition. On issue after issue the non-economic standards of two worlds collided suddenly and starkly, dogged by the implicit new question: by which set of standards ought British subjects to conduct business around the world? By 1788 witchcraft was already distant enough from educated European culture to be dismissed with contempt. Stunned by this new wave of expansive Eurocentrism, the African traders tacked futilely towards cultural relativism. The Privy Council and Parliamentary hearings on the slave trade between 1788 and 1792, like public discourse out of doors, represented a paradigmatic leap in the relationship between the British metropolis and the Atlantic slave system.[77]

5 The Impact of Popular Mobilization in Britain and the Caribbean

Once institutionalized in 1788–92, abolitionist petitioning followed the same pattern for the next half-century. There were successive extra-Parliamentary campaigns in 1806–7, 1814, 1823, 1830–1, 1832–3 and 1838. All except that of 1806–7 were characterized by a national petition campaign. The longest period without a general call for petitions was between 1792 and 1814. The polarization of politics after 1792 and the active governmental discouragement of public petitioning after 1795 deterred the uneasy London Committee from activity.[1] Most historians view the whole period between 1793 and 1814 as a dormant period for popular abolitionism. In explaining the victory over the slave trade in 1806–7, they therefore tend to focus almost exclusively on Parliamentary activity.[2] Yet the Parliamentary campaigns of 1806–7 were caried out amidst a simultaneous revival of popular canvassing. As in 1791, the abolitionists again adopted this more active strategy in the wake of an unexpected setback for slave trade abolition in Parliament in 1805. They concluded that in the absence of a clear public message an unpressured Parliament was unreliable. The network of local organizations was revived. The leadership now chose to tread a middle path between the massive popular agitation that had ended in the 'Jacobin panic' of 1792 and the total popular inaction which had resulted in only limited Parliamentary achievements between 1793 and 1805.[3]

The relative dearth of public meetings compared with 1792 or 1814 may have led historians to underestimate the significance of the mobilization of 1806–7. Contemporaries whose capital was on the line took it seriously.[4] The Liverpool slave interest began to protest as early as 1805 that the mobilization of Yorkshire, Lancashire and London was killing the slave trade by working up 'violent propaganda'. The Jamaicans complained that popular pressure was a serious, if not absolute, deterrent to new capital investment. The abolitionists stopped short of a petition campaign, but did call for a selective mobilization. One hastily canvassed petition from Manchester, in May 1806, was designed to counter the smaller antiabolitionist petition sponsored by Robert Peel. The signatures were gathered and dispatched in a matter of hours. The abolitionists boasted that they could have easily doubled the number of names with even one additional day to obtain signatures.[5]

The second stage of the 1806-7 mobilization came during the autumn Parliamentary elections of 1806. For the first time abolitionism became a campaign issue in certain areas. (There had been some pressure for MP pledging during the petitioning of 1792, but not as part of the electoral process.[6]) The third stage of the 1807 campaign was the most overt outburst of public abolitionism since 1792. Although confined to Yorkshire, Wilberforce's bid for re-election was blown up into a nationwide referendum on the decision for abolition, and was one of the most hotly-contested elections in the history of the county. A national fund was created to bring eligible Wilberforce supporters from all over Britain back to vote.[7] Wilberforce's principal opponent, a West Indian, clearly testified to the strength of antislavery sentiment in Yorkshire. He pledged himself not only to support abolition of the slave trade, but to work for emancipation if anyone introduced a motion to rescind it.

The impact of the popular campaigns of 1806-7 may be gauged in three ways. The first was the ever-diminishing share of antiabolition votes in the House of Commons from 1805 to 1807 (from just over half in February 1805 to one-eighth in June 1806, to one-twentieth in February 1807). The second indicator is the sense of shock among West Indian MPs (even among those who supported abolition) at the surge of popular hostility against not just slave traders but slave-holders.[8] The final indicator is the fact that domestic radical reformers drew, even from this selective popular campaign, encouragement for the large-scale renewal of their own reform movement for the first time since the mid-1790s. The abolitionist campaign therefore registered its impact on all parts of the political spectrum.[9]

These details of 1807 are noted in order to emphasize the continuity of public opinion as a structural component of abolition. There is no need to discuss the successive extra-Parliamentary campaigns as instruments once the mould was set in 1792. Mass petition campaigns were repeated in 1814, 1823-4, 1830-1, 1832-3 and 1838, each with a generally expanded geographical scope.

It is difficult to select the criteria by which to measure the relative impact of popular antislavery mobilization on British society. By some of the more obvious ones, however, it was one of the most successful movements of its time. Compared with the major constitutional issues of Parliamentary and religious reform, abolitionism managed to extract more positive legislative responses during its first 40 years as a political movement.[10] In 1788 Pitt was able to squeeze through Parliament the first Bill to regulate the slave trade, despite his minority position in the Cabinet. In 1792 the abolition campaign played a decisive role in reversing the negative 1791 vote in the House of Commons. In 1807, according to the public testimony of a member of the Cabinet, the national consensus on abolition prevented the abolition Bill from being aborted at the last minute on a technicality by the administration which assumed power just before the Bill had received royal assent.

In 1814 many of those ministers who had been most clearly identified as hostile to abolition in 1807 were still at the pinnacle of power.[11] Having successfully led Britain through its greatest war, and at the height of their popularity, the engineers of Napoleon's defeat felt freer to act according to their own inclinations or indifference. The Anglo-French treaty of 1814 sanctioned the reopening of the French slave trade for five years and provided no machinery for forcing closure at the end of that period. The abolitionists responded by canvassing the most numerously signed petition in British history.[12] This eruption of petitions forced Lord Castlereagh to elevate international abolition to the status of an imperial priority. It opened a new stage in the unraveling of the Northern European slave trade, beginning with renunciation of the Dutch trade in 1814 and Napoleon's decree of abolition in 1815.[13] The African slave trade became the only extra-Continental issue to be forced on the attention of the Congress of Vienna. It was legitimized as a target for international suppression. The impact of the 1814 campaign extended beyond the international slave trade. It provided momentum for slave-registry schemes in the West Indies and for the direct intrusion of the metropolis into master-slave relationships within all the British colonies. The mass petition campaigns of 1823, 1833 and 1838 were also quickly followed by successive limitations on the coercive powers of the planters.

To achieve this unique stature among contemporary reform movements, abolitionists were required to demonstrate ever more massive displays of support. In the late 1780s, when only 170 public petitions a year were submitted to the House of Commons, abolition made its mark in 1788 by accounting for more than half the annual average. By the early 1810s when a toal of 900 per year was the norm, the abolition petitions of 1814 almost equalled the annual average for 1811–15. In the contentious period 1828–33, when the level of petitions quintupled over that of 1811–15, the number of antislavery petitions increased *more* than five–fold. In both 1831 and 1833 more petitions for emancipation were sent up to Parliament than the annual average for the period 1828–33. Put another way, petitions demanding slave emancipation increased the total number of petitions to Parliament by more than *50 per cent* for the period 1828–33.[14] Abolitionism was probably also unmatched in its ratio of metropolitan supporters to opponents. In terms of signers the 1833 petition canvass for immediate emancipation was in the order of over 99 per cent pro-immediatist. It is difficult to imagine any other major campaign obtaining antislavery's petition ratio of more than 250:1, including the popular agitation for the Great Reform Act of 1832.

The case of France clearly reveals the stir that even a fraction of British mobilization could make in a much smaller pot. The average number of petitions to the French Chamber of Deputies in each of the six years before French emancipation was about 500. This was a tenth of the number reaching Parliament in the five years before British emancipation. The first mass slave-emancipation petition to the French legislature in 1844 was signed by 7000 Parisian workers.[15] This was probably fewer than one-ninth of those who signed the initial British petition of 1788. Miniscule by British standards, the petition of 1844 nevertheless stimulated the introduction of the first mincing metropolitan French legislation to regulate master-slave relations and conditions of manumission.

The second French abolitionist petition campaign brought 10 700 names to the Chamber of Deputies in 1847. This represented less than one adult French male in a thousand, compared with more than one in five in Britain in 1814 and again in 1833. Yet even the petition of 1847 produced shock waves amongst those habituated to the indifference of the French Chambers towards slavery.[16] The Minister of the Colonies was forced to resign after attempting to dismiss the petition outright. Departmental Councils began to increase their support for abolition.[17] The colonial agents were demoralized and broke ranks. Some opened discussions with the more conservative Parliamentary abolitionists, attempting to negotiate a preemptive emancipation plan of their own devising. The colonial agents correctly saw the petitions as the writing on the wall, and fearfully anticipated a nascent alliance between urban working-class and religious constituencies that forecast larger numbers of signatures to come.[18] On the eve of the February Revolution the abolitionists claimed that 30 000 signatures were being collected for the new session. This was still far fewer than the first British petition 60 years before but France appeared to be possibly on the threshold of a real breakthrough to national mobilization. By the Revolution of 1848 at least radical opinion in Paris had been sufficiently mobilized that the Provisional Government made emancipation its first order of colonial business.

All this came in the wake of a petition campaign which had accumulated no more signatures than Manchester alone, at a time when it contained a less than one-fifth of 1 per cent of France's population of 35 million in 1847. Without the Revolution, which gave Parisian Republicans a brief free hand, such small French petitions did not and could not elicit immediate emancipation.[19] If 7000–10 000 signatures were enough to momentarily break down years of indifference in the French Chambers, British MPs had to be presented with more dramatic pressure to vote for innovations. British antislavery had to compete in an arena where ten times as many petitions were annually received and where, economically, the British slave colonies played a role four times greater in their metropolitan economy than did their French slave counterparts. Demographically, there were at least three times as many slaves in the British colonies as in the French. Fiscally, this meant that the tax burden of compensation, and of repression of the slave trade, was heavier per capita in Britain than in France.[20] Psychologically, British legislators had to assume the incalculable social risks of pioneering emancipation within the American plantation economies.

Probably even more important than the short-term results of each abolitionist mobilization considered separately, was the cumulative impact of successive mobilizations. Popular behaviour did not have to be repeated annually in order to induce contemporaries to believe that there was an underlying continuity to collective attitudes, just as historians can infer popular attitudes in food riots or industrial violence even where such events might be separated by a decade or more. Abolitionist opinion was not a series of discrete explosions but a social movement which expanded in size and articulation for over 50 years: from 100 petitions and perhaps 60 000–75 000 signers in 1788, to 500 petitions and 350 000–400 000 signers in 1792, to 800 petitions and 750 000 signers in 1814, to 5000 petitions and almost $1\frac{1}{2}$ million signers in 1833.

The creation of a climate of opinion was therefore the most important residue of frequently renewed petitions. It became part of the consciousness of all those who played a role in shaping British policy regarding Atlantic slavery. Unlike most earlier eighteenth-century contentious gatherings, the abolitionist 'crowds' were acting directly on the imperial legislature. They were certainly not seeking local rectifications within a traditional moral order, but demanding increasing conformity to an evolving moral order. An abolitionist petitioner was also told that he was part of a cumulative social force both spatially and temporally. 'Though for a time . . . unsuccessful', the Baptist Magazine assured potential petitioners, 'the voice of the people could not be continually lifted up in vain'.[21] The abolitionists therefore not only mobilized, they changed the framework of political discourse. Initial dismissal of abolitionism in 1788 as a 'five days fit of philanthropy', the fad of a season, yielded to the sense that a permanent addition of policy considerations had occurred. From the 1790s British 'chronologies' designated 1788 as the *annus mirabilis* of antislavery.

The new climate of opinion can be gauged in a number of ways. The authors of books on international trade, which as late as the mid-1780s treated the slave trade as a deplorable but integral part of the British imperial economy, began to write about the trade as one facing proximate elimination. This occurred regardless of whether the books appeared in high or low periods of antislavery mobilization after 1792. A compliant sense of duration and ubiquity had been replaced in Britain by that of slavery's uncertain future.

It is more difficult to demonstrate conclusively the watershed of British popular attitudes towards slavery through literary sources. Duncan Rice correctly notes that both the theoretical and sentimental arguments against chattel slavery *per se* were complete by the 1760s.[22] Rice's evidence points to a different sort of 'revolution' in literature after 1788. In Britain the idea that slavery was an evil, but as inevitable as war, disease and famine, had all but disappeared between 1788 and the end of the Napoleonic wars.

The attitudes of all Prime Ministers toward the British slave economy also changed, whether historians judge their attitudes favourable, hostile, manipulative or indifferent toward abolition. In hesitating to open the Crown lands of newly-acquired Trinidad to planters in 1802, the Prime Minister least sympathetic towards abolition between 1788 and 1807 cited public opinion as a deterrent.[23] Ten years after 1792 it was simply no longer possible to pursue the old policy of slave business as usual. Even when the House of Commons failed to follow through on its 1792 resolution for gradual abolition of the slave trade, the West Indian contingent in Parliament considered it necessary to try to defuse metropolitan energies by having Parliament resolve to urge the colonies to improve their own slave conditions. Alterations of the West Indian slave codes and religious reforms were explicitly designed to appease metropolitans. In 1804, after the London Abolitionist Society had lain almost dormant for a decade and at a moment when their strategy was to be quite placating, West Indian propagandists continued to concede the 'popular' side to their opponents.[24] They might disdainfully dismiss the abolitionist opinion as 'mists of fanaticism',' but the West Indian representatives conceived of appeals to public opinion as beyond their own reach and the abolitionist influence on it as generally prevalent.[25] 'It is idle to disguise from ourselves that the various parties who from different motives are hostile to the West India interest, are at least as powerful, and act upon a more extensive system, and with greater means of influencing the public mind, than the Proprietors and Merchants connected with the colonies.'[26] This perception was as palpably evident to moulders of public opinion as it was to the slave interest.

During almost three decades of vigorous hostility to abolitionism, emancipation and blacks, William Cobbett fumed over the popularity of abolitionism. Sometimes it was the jostling for popularity among MPs which infuriated him. At other times it was the 'delusions' of his fellow Britons. But whether he spoke of the manipulating or the manipulated within abolitionism, Cobbett never disputed the fact of its popularity. He was ultimately no more immune to the massiveness of abolitionist petitions than were his fellow journalists. He could never go as far as the radical *Examiner* in 1814, and speak proudly of antislavery as one of the instinctive reflexes of an Englishman. But the sheer numbers of signers could momentarily soften his evaluation of abolitionists as 'the ideot [sic] part of the community', and he could momentarily allow that their hearts if not their heads were in the right place.[27]

The antiabolitionist response followed a fairly set pattern during the entire half-century after 1788. Occasionally, the slave interest could mount a vigorous counter–attack at the beginning of a new escalation in the campaign or in the wake of slave uprisings.[28] But the balance of expressed opinion was usually so heavily against them that merchants and planters preferred to work within the more congenial and conventional network of governmental bureaus and sympathetic ministers.

The impact of abolitionist mobilization on its opponents' tactics seems clear, but can its relative impact on the legislative process be measured? One might ambitiously compare it with the two other major national movements, for Parliamentary reorganization and religious liberalization, in the same period. As G. M. Ditchfield has observed, there is no real surprise in the fact that abolition was the first of the three reform questions to witness a major breakthrough in 1807, and to achieve a second major step towards total victory in 1823. Between 1788 and 1833 abolitionism had the broadest popular base and faced the most divided opposition among the political élite.[29] For 40 years after 1788 abolitionist petitioning at least matched the other two movements in sheer numbers and certainly outperformed them in terms of the balance of opinion.

On the other hand, it is clear that towards the end of the age of popular abolition slave emancipation came only in the wake of Catholic emancipation (1829) and the passage of the Great Reform Act (1832). Catholic emancipation passed despite the fact that a clear majority of petitioners to Parliament signed up against the reform, and political reform came only under the duress of mobilizations which threatened to go far beyond petitioning. In the case of both Catholic emancipation and Parliamentary reform there was something 'extra' behind extra-Parliamentary agitation: very tangible reserve armies of violence.

Should the potential for violence in the case of colonial slavery be allotted the same weight usually assigned to Catholic militants in Ireland in 1829, or political militants in Britain in 1832? Given the parallels one must necessarily consider the credibility of alternative forces at the disposal of petitioners. One major difference between antislavery and the two other movements is indisputable. At no point from beginning to end did abolitionism ever intimate that behind its thousands of petitions lay a threat of metropolitan violence. Broken heads over abolitionism were probably rarer than over any other major social issue in Britain during the 50 years after 1788. Yet abolitionists' enemies did operate under the threat of less co-ordinated but quite serious resistance from the overseas colonial slaves themselves.

Caribbean scholarship, harking back to the pioneering work of C. L. R. James and many others, has recently attempted to integrate slaves and slave resistance more decisively into the process of abolition. Although the assertion that 'slaves actually achieved their own emancipation' is recognized as an overstatement in the British case,[30] there is a developing historiography which ties the pace, the timing and the causal links in British emancipation to autonomous processes of economic and social development within the slave zone. The central theme is the elaboration of an autonomous resistance with its roots in the internal social evolution of slave society itself.[31] It is not enough, however, to take note of slave resistance or make general assertions about its destabilizing role. One must also attempt to weigh its significance, both short- and long-term, in relation to other tangible processes and events.

To date, the integration of slave resistance in the British emancipation process has largely been achieved by assigning mutually supporting, but unweighted, roles to each of three major factors in the process: metropolitan ideological transformation, the French Caribbean slave revolution, and British Caribbean 'creolization'. In the words of Barry Higman, creolized slave societies 'were responsive to changing external conditions, created by the St Domingue revolution and the transformation of metropolitan society, but they also depended for their impact on changes internal to the slave society and its demographic structure'.[32]

In comparative terms it is clear that slave mobilizations and massive resistance was of great significance in determining the pace of, or even the metropolitan decision for, some Caribbean emancipations. The St Domingue revolution of 1791 was, of course, the greatest and most successful example of slave resistance in history. The concept that black slaves were incapable of a sustained uprising, used in an occasional argument for black incapacity as late as 1788, was effectively silenced.[33] Slaves had organized a resistance sufficient to defeat the armed intervention of the three most powerful imperial forces in Europe, the British, the Spanish and, ultimately, a veteran Napoleonic army. The slave revolution initially also created a wave of panic among the planters of the entire Caribbean area.

The St Domingue uprising thus fits quite well into the recent historiographical emphasis on the role of West Indian slaves as makers of their own freedom. In the French metropolis, the first decree of slave emancipation in February 1794 was accelerated by, if not entirely a result of, the position of French slave revolutionaries and British counter-revolutionary forces in the Caribbean in 1793–4. The less famous slave rising in Martinique in 1848 probably also ensured that the new French Constituent Assembly would not move to disavow or postpone Schoelcher's French emancipation decree. Danish emancipation was likewise accelerated by a slave uprising in 1848.

Yet the very dependency of French emancipation on military power in the 1790s and early 1800s showed how easily slavery could be revived by the metropolis if the balance of power changed as in Guadeloupe and St Lucia in 1802. Moreover the role of slave resistance in British domestic politics, while probably more significant than in the US before the Civil War, was clearly never as dramatic as in the French, the Danish or certain Latin American cases.

It is important to distinguish between short- and long-term impacts and the very ambivalent role of St Domingue on British policy.[34] We can safely dispense with the argument that St Domingue forever transformed the psychological or social relationship between masters and slaves in the British colonies. The alluring argument that the St Domingue slaves somehow 'broke the spell of the master class' relies far too much on an unproven assumption of socio-psychological planter hegemony before 1790 and a rapid or steady erosion of planter authority thereafter. For the British case it would be both extraordinarily difficult to demonstrate such a process and to tie it to the Haitian revolution. British colonial slavery was an institution, not an incantation. Whatever the primacy of St Domingue's resistance in precipitating the first French emancipation, this formulation fails to demonstrate just how the revolution in Haiti generated British abolition or any of the subsequent emancipations by other Continental powers.

During the decade of the St Domingue revolution (1791–1801) British slavery was, on balance, the most rapidly expanding system in the world. More 'British' slaves aided British colonial rule and slave expansion than rebelled against it. Twelve slave regiments were raised to complement the regular European military forces.[35] For 20 years after 1803 it was possible to treat the Haitian war of independence as a peculiar event within the context of the Atlantic slave economies. Regarding the British case in particular, David Geggus has recently shown the equivocal long-term relationship between Haiti and the British abolitionist cause. Haiti exemplified both economic failure and demographic success, and serving every purpose it did not unequivocally serve any.[35]

Despite some speculative suppositions about the Parliamentary vote of 1792 there is no evidence that it was decisive in the major Parliamentary decisions of 1792, 1799, 1806–7, 1823, 1833 or 1838. In 1814 it may have played a catalytic role as a target for potential re-enslavement,[36] but this was definitely not about Haiti as a threat-by-example, much less as a threat-by-invasion. By the time Lord Stanley introduced the Emancipation Bill to Parliament in 1833 the Government regarded the St Domingue example as both inconclusive and irrelevant.[37] The question as to whether Haiti could thrive or even survive had become divorced from the debate on British slavery. St Domingue remained the most dramatic instance of a Caribbean slave revolution but it is the long-term pattern of British colonial resistance itself which raises the most interesting questions about the connections between metropolitan and overseas mobilizations against slavery.

The historiography of colonial slavery in the British Caribbean itself now generally distinguishes between an Afro-Maroon and a creolized phase of slave resistance. If scholarship has shown that an exact chronological demarcation between the two is tenuous, one must still emphasize the general isolation of slave resistance from metropolitan concerns or consciousness during the long period prior to the age of British abolition. My general chronological division of slave resistance into two stages is therefore analogous to Genovese's dichotomy between slave resistance before and after about 1790.[38]

Setting aside his parallelisms of New and Old World popular resistance (designated on both sides of the ocean as 'restorationist'), early New World slave resistance was clearly 'old régime' in one major sense. It was intensely localized during the course of the seventeenth and for most of the eighteen centuries. Insulated from one another, even the most substantial slave actions and conspiracies before 1790 usually took the form of withdrawal and flight from the imperial system. Attempts at personal or collective liberation simply had to be based on the premise of a world from which no help or quarter could be expected. The strategies of withdrawal and self-enclosure, which Genovese classifies as reactionary, are indeed 'reactions' to what appeared to be a hostile nexus of power and information about the world beyond. There was no inter-island co-ordination between revolts or marronage in different colonies, or between movements in the slave colonies and those in the Old World. Except in the sense that Old World conflicts sent new waves of criminals, prisoners or uprooted victims of war to the islands from both Africa and Europe, Afro-Creole resistance did not stimulate or intensify either wider abolitionist discussion or European revolutionary discourse in the metropolis before 1788. In other words, the relation between colonial resistance and metropolitan mobilization remained a 'latent' one, filtered through the exportation of individuals across the Atlantic, or occasional Caribbean conflicts.

There are two obvious indications that New World slave resistance operated fairly independently of European events. First, the high proportion of African-led and African-inspired revolts in the slave colonies meant that participants were those slaves least integrated into the colonial-metropolitan communications network. Even colony-wide plots (whether African or Afro-Creole in composition and whatever the social outcome) were quite realistically framed either in terms of an interior maroon colony or at most of a maroon island.[39] One could hardly have aspired to create more than an enclave in an unforgiving world. Moreover, even at the plantation level, the slaves were fragmented along both African and European ethno-cultural lines and by their positions within the plantation hierarchies of status and power.

From an imperial and world perspective the most critical historical developments in the liberation process were stages of abolitionism in the metropolises rather than the colonial process of creolization. Up to 1790 the threat of collective resistance actually seems to have declined as the slave population was creolized. Breaking down Michael Craton's chronology of black resistance between 1638 and 1837,[40] one can demonstrate that the second half of the seventeenth century was far more productive of slave revolts in the British islands than the first half of the eighteenth. Between 1649 and 1700 a slave revolt occurred almost every five years. Between 1700 and 1750 a slave revolt occurred only once every 25 years. In the older sugar colonies, except Jamaica, there was a decrease in slave resistance as these slave colonies reached their plateaus of economic development and creolization.[41] The same trend is evident if we compare the second half of the seventeenth and the first 90 years of the eighteenth century. If we exclude colonies intensively developed only *after* 1763,[42] 'old colony' slave resistance occurred only once every 15 years. Significantly Jamaica ran behind, although not against, the overall trend. Between 1650 and 1700 Jamaica had more than one major incident every decade and none were abortive. Jamaica's resistance rate fell slightly to only one every 12 years from 1700 until 1790. But almost all old colony revolts after 1700 were in Jamaica, the one 'old' frontier colony. This seems to be further corroboration that creolization coincided with a diminution of collective resistance. After 1760 the newly-developing colonies seem to have repeated the first stage of the older ones. In the 30 years after 1763 the new colonies (including Belize) had a recorded incident of active resistance once every three years. Excluding Belize, which was not a plantation society, the rate was about once every four years. This roughly parallels the five-year intervals for the old colonies in 1650–1700.

Another interesting set of data reinforces the hypothesis of diminishing recourse to collective violence for the pre-abolitionist era. Craton's chronology includes plots as well as outbreaks of slave resistance. One can therefore measure increasing or decreasing security of the planters by comparing both the combined rates of plots and completed resistance, and the ratios of unsuccessful plots to completed acts of resistance during the seventeenth and eighteenth centuries. The first approach shows that the 'combined' resistance rate (plots plus acts) decreased as the colonies moved from the seventeenth to the eighteenth century, just as in the case of acts alone. The 'combined' rate for the 'old' colonies in the second half of the seventeenth century was about one incident every $3\frac{1}{2}$ years. In the same colonies between 1700 and 1788 there was one incident every $5\frac{1}{2}$ years. Turning to the ratio of plots to outbreaks, we find that the completed action rate was only one-third as great in 1700–87 as in 1649–99 and the total resistance rate was only 38 per cent as great.

In other words slave plots had relatively less chance of reaching fruition with progressive creolization. From the Seven Years' War until the beginning of the age of abolition (1788), overt slave resistance in the old colonies had but one chance in three of achieving the name of action. Thus, while the eighteenth-century rate of resistance in these colonies fell to half that of the previous century, the rate of *aborted* plots rose from four out of ten before 1700 to almost two out of three. So just when the rate of resistance was declining the odds against even momentarily successful collective outbreaks were rising. Finally, Craton's chronology shows that, Jamaica aside, not one instance of resistance came to fruition between 1700 and 1790 in all of the older islands combined, and there were only five plots. Indeed, during the last half-century before 1790, only a single plot appears in the record.

While recognizing that Craton's chronology may be incomplete, it probably reflects relative trends over time with sufficient accuracy. One may conclude that the largely creolized slave islands were either too socially fragmented or too well integrated into the older Caribbean plantations for potential rebels to have had much hope of success in large-scale flight or revolt. Until the Seven Years' War, and the acquisition of new colonies, grandees on both sides of the Atlantic seem to have felt equally secure as lords of creation. There were brief threats from 'highlanders' in both Scotland and Jamaica during the second quarter of the eighteenth century, but many were co-opted as agents of the empire.[43]

Without any sign of metropolitan intervention, violent resistance and flight must have seemed less and less viable to slaves in the pre-abolitionist era. On the one hand the mechanism of the slave trade offered slaves differential opportunities for individual mobility, and on the other, slaves confronted a solid phalanx of masters backed by an imperial régime with apparently unlimited reinforcements. Creoles, of course, understood the odds even better than the Africans.

When a new upsurge of British slave resistance began after 1760, it was almost exclusively confined to the newly-conquered islands and rapidly developing Jamaica. In the dozen years after 1763, the outburst of slave resistance which greeted new British developers was matched only during the pioneering period (1673–86) of the previous century. There were nine attempts at resistance in each period. This burst of slave resistance occurred quite independently of the relative quiescence in the older British islands. Moreover, a decisive new division appeared between different Creole cultures. Creole slaves of the conquered French planters, free coloureds and the free Black Caribs became major new sources of resistance.

Before the age of abolitionism, then, popular resistance in the British Caribbean tended to occur in areas which were either in the early stages of development or newly integrated into the British empire. In the old islands, both the rate of resistance and the rate of conspiracy remained very low for the entire period between the end of the seventeenth century and the end of the Napoleonic wars. Moreover, almost all of the resistance which we have been discussing thus far involved resistance to enslavement more than resistance to slavery. Some slaves undoubtedly had elements of 'restorationism' in view, and desired to create autonomous social units dominated by African culture. Some may have planned to set up independent commercialized states, keeping some or all of the plantation system, including slavery. Others quite clearly accommodated to the plantation environment, accepting autonomous status within the general system and English as their own language.[44]

As far as one can see, neither pre-abolitionist British opinion nor general British policy towards the slave islands had any measurable impact on the timing of slave resistance. (The Black Caribs, whose plight was the subject of a brief Parliamentary discussion in the early 1770s, were not slaves.) Extraordinarily brutal uprisings or repressions might result in occasional journalistic notice or in an isolated letter of protest to a British newspaper. Significantly, West Indian writing was relatively free of accusations of metropolitan incitement to slave resistance before the late 1780s. There was no network of support to encourage potential resisters in the colonies.

In terms of interoceanic popular mobilizations, how does the age of abolitionism compare with the period which preceded it? Comparing the first nine decades of the eighteenth century with the four decades which followed, one notes that the incidence rate of resistance rose by over 60 per cent in the period 1790–1832. If one excludes aborted plots, outbreaks of resistance more than doubled between the first period and the second. The planters' rate of 'uncovering' plots dropped from 40 per cent for the whole pre-abolitionist period to only half that for the period between 1788 and emancipation. Even more significantly, the magnitude of successful collective resistance dramatically increased. For the first time there were slave revolts involving many thousands of slaves in Grenada (1795), Barbados (1816), Demerara (1823) and Jamaica (1831). The parallelism with metropolitan mobilization was, however, not complete. There appears to have been an important difference between slave resistance during the period of revolution in Europe and of a 'slave-trade' focus in British abolitionism (1788–1814), and the final period of direct British intervention into the colonial slave system (1815–32). In the first period (1788–1814) the rate of revolt remained much higher in the newer and frontier colonies than in the older ones. In this respect the pre-abolitionist pattern continued in the islands. In the post–Napoleonic period, however, the older, most Anglo-Creolized, colonies experienced a higher than average rate of resistance than for British Caribbean slavery as a whole. The rate of actual outbreaks rose to more than triple that for the pre-abolitionist period. Even more remarkably, the planters' ability to abort slave conspiracies plummeted. During the first half of the eighteenth century the planters had got wind of nine out of ten plots in time to take preventive action. Even during the revolutionary period, one out of three potential outbreaks had been stopped at the planning stage. From 1815 onwards only one out of the 14 slave actions was completely forestalled. The fact that slave resistance shifted from those areas *least* integrated into the empire before 1814 to those *most* integrated thereafter, leads one to distinguish between slave mobilizations before and after 1815.

There has been some attempt to ascribe post-revolutionary slave resistance to the latent impact of the abolition of the British slave trade in 1807. According to this reasoning the cessation of imports generated slave discontent through its alteration of the labour system. Planters, confronted with a diminishing supply of labour, were forced to reduce incentives for social mobility, to squeeze their slave-labour force and to shift slaves from cotton and coffee into sugar, the most onerous crop.[45] However, balanced against this argument it should be noted that after 1815 the resurgence of slave resistance occurred in the old sugar colonies and Jamaica where the shift to sugar was least dramatic, and in the marginal colonies which, whether old or new, were not sugar colonies. After 1814 slave resistance was less evident in the newer colonies where the shift to sugar was greatest. Moreover, the one crop in which there may have been a *reduction* in slave hours of labour was in sugar production during the crop season.[46]

A less equivocal and more direct correlation can be made between slave resistance and the changing political focus of metropolitan abolitionism after 1814. In this sense the age of British abolitionism did not arrive in the West Indies until *after* the age of the French Revolution. British metropolitan abolitionism was directed until 1814 mainly at the Atlantic slave trade. The outburst of slave resistance in the British Islands in the mid-1790s was in response rather to the opportunities occasioned by revolutionary warfare in the Caribbean, when the British abolitionist movement was in suspension. Moreover, slave resistance was more formidable in those islands, and among those groups, least integrated into the British plantation system: the Francophone free blacks and slaves in the ceded islands of Dominica, Grenada and St Lucia; among the black Caribs in St Vincent; and among the Maroons of Jamaica. The French revolutionaries sent their agents primarily to the French-speaking blacks in the British colonies. British plantation slaves were less readily mobilized by these groups and in some cases the slaves mobilized against them.[47] This was also the basis for the British planters' belief that 'outsiders' were more prone to take up hostilities against them. Finally, the uprisings of 1794–6 came in response to French military and not to British political mobilization. The high level of resistance in the British Caribbean of the 1790s was linked to French initiatives.

In the 1790s the locus of Caribbean resistance was still similar to what it had been in 1763–90. The great change was in the enormous increase in opportunities from beyond the line. Jamaica, the least creolized of the 'old' colonies and the most turbulent one before 1790, seems to have occupied an intermediate position in slave resistance from 1791 to 1815. The reaction of Jamaican slaves to the rising in St Domingue in 1791 caused a preemptive planter mobilization. In 1795 some of Jamaica's maroons rose in a serious revolt at the moment of maximum French Revolutionary success. On the other hand, the mutiny and unrest in Jamaica in 1808 may have been the first significant resurgence of 'old' island slaves to the major metropolitan triumph in 1807 over the most vociferous planter opposition to abolition among the colonies of the empire.[48]

This temporal pattern also reveals the negative impact of British slave resistance on imperial abolitionism before 1806–7. Grenada and St Vincent in 1795–6 clearly presented the British with the most serious threat to the social system of one of their West Indian colonies since the settlement of Barbados 150 years earlier. In terms of loss of both property and duration of the conflict Grenada was the most serious uprising in the history of British slavery, including Jamaica's Baptist War 35 years later. Yet the event literally disappeared from metropolitan abolitionist consciousness. Without public discussion the British quickly restored the *status quo* as soon as they reconquered Grenada and St Vincent in 1796, just as the French restored slavery as soon as they recovered Guadeloupe in 1802. Almost alone, Granville Sharp protested the re-enslavement of free blacks in the conquered French islands. Apparently no one challenged Britain's right to restore the old legal and political order in the reoccupied British islands.[49] Many British planters were pleased with their slaves' unwillingness to abandon their plantations despite French appeals or threats.

Within the British metropolis one can detect even less evidence of any long–run impact of the Grenadian than of the Haitian revolution. This is strikingly demonstrated by Lord Howick's motion introducing the Aboliton Bill in the House of Commons in February 1807. Howick noted that the British islands had never been so free of slave revolts as in the previous 20 years.[50] Remarkably, no one challenged him, not even the more informed West Indian MPs. Apparently they, like Howick, believed, as they argued, that their Creole slaves were 'loyal'.[51] In imperial consciousness the uprisings of the mid-1790s were French invasions, abetted by free foreign blacks. Whatever the reasons, Howick's remarkable and unchallenged account of slave resistance calls for careful notice by historians of British abolitionism. The Black Caribs deported from St Vincent and the maroons deported from Jamaica were dispatched out of mind as well as sight, and the crushed black Republic of Grenada sank like a stone from metropolitan memory.

From this historical perspective the reversal of post-Waterloo slave mobilization is all the more remarkable. The planters were less prescient about their fellow Britons than about their slaves. After 1815 the slave-owners found themselves between two enemies. Once that happened creolization simply worked in exactly the opposite way from 1700–1800. Only then did the line between metropolis and colony disintegrate at both the level of slave consciousness and behaviour. In the metropolis, Parliamentary abolitionists began their first direct interference between masters and slaves by moving for the introduction of slave registration. In 1823 the first mass campaign for the gradual abolition of colonial slavery led to further intrusions into the masters' control. The final stage of the metropolitan crusade came with the shift to demands for immediate emancipation in the two mass campaigns of 1830–1 and 1832–3.

Unlike the campaigns for abolition of the slave trade in 1788, 1791–2, 1806–7 and 1814, each of these last three major initiatives (slave registration, amelioration and emancipation) was followed within months by three of the most massive and co-ordinated slave uprisings in the history of British slavery: Barbados in 1816, Demerara in 1823, and Jamaica in 1831. Unlike the outbreaks in Grenada and St Vincent in 1795, these risings were not sparked by any military intervention, nor could they be described as the initiatives of free coloured subcultures.

The upheaval in Barbados signaled the most remarkable reversal of perspectives in the history of British slave resistance. In 1816 Barbados was the most creolized of the British colonies, a densely settled and well-cultivated island. It had experienced no major risings or plots for over a century and had remained quiet during the entire French Revolutionary period and the British struggle with Napoleon. Barbados was not a part-African Haiti, a part-French Grenada or a part-Carib St Vincent. Barbados was 'little England' in the Caribbean. The Barbadian resistance stemmed from a highly acculturated segment of British slave society.

The Demerara rising also challenges, it seems to me, a demographic variant of what can be called the 'natural history' of British slave resistance. Viewing slave mobilization from a British Caribbean angle one might take the position that 'creole resistance' was a biocultural phenomenon, based on a gradually evolving creole population and culture.[52] Viewed in comparative perspective, however, the most significant change in the structure of slave resistance appears to have been far more dependent on political than biocultural development. The Demerara revolt of 1823, occurring in the newest of Britain's possessions, came from within a segment of the slave population already culturally mobilized by the British missionaries.

Only in these terms can one account for the fact that Africans in Demerara achieved in little more than a decade what creolized Barbados did only after more than a century. The decisive variable was the stage of *metropolitan* abolitionism, not demographic creolization. At the very least creolization was more dependent on political communication than birthplace. There is no more reason why Africans could not become as easily 'seasoned' to the organizational forms and discourse of missionaries, colonial governors and new modes of slave solidarity in ten years as to the novel regimen of the plantations in three. A biocultural creolization theory is therefore rendered more problematic by the fact that massive slave resistance appeared so suddenly, giving a 'three bears' model of late British slave revolts: first in the oldest, Barbados, then in the youngest, Demerara, and finally just midway, in Jamaica.

The timing of the Demerara, Jamaica and Barbados events with metropolitan development is striking compared with their otherwise divergent Afro-Creole ratios, sex ratios, or man-land ratios.[53] The catalyst was the stage of metropolitan abolitionism, not the level of colonial demographic creolization. The three revolts were also ideologically linked to British abolitionism to a degree that almost no previous rising was. The very possibility of support from beyond the line played a more conspicuous role than before in the leaders' appeals to adherents. Whether the assumptions about such support were unrealistic is less significant than the impression that large friendly forces from the metropolis might finally intervene on behalf of the slaves. This is reinforced not only by the terms used to gather adherents but by those used to confront masters and public authorities. When the slaves of Demerara met the command to disperse with a counter-demand for their 'rights', they assumed terms of discourse readily understood in the metropolis. And the language of messianic Christianity in the last two revolts demonstrated how rapidly the slaves, whether African or Caribbean-born, could instrumentally adopt the language of nineteenth-century Britons.

The penultimate metropolitan petition campaign before emancipation in 1830–1 was the one which obtained the most meagre reward from Parliament because of the Reform Bill crisis. By contrast, it had the most direct impact on the West Indies. In demanding immediate and total emancipation, the petitioners sparked a dramatic planter counter-mobilization in Jamaica. It was replete with public meetings, protest petitions, demands for armed resistance and threats of secession to the US. It also stirred the organization of the most massive uprising among Jamaican slaves in the history of slavery. The 'Baptist War' spread over an area of 600 square miles. As early as April 1831 a loose network of conspiracies gradually formed among élite slaves on almost 100 estates. It is significant that the rebellion came despite improvements in conditions for slaves.[54] The movement was led by slaves most in touch with British culture and metropolitan events just as the petition campaign of 1830–1 in Britain came to a head. The slaves' movement bore an indisputable relationship to its transatlantic counterpart. It was organized at religious meetings, and was planned to take the form of a mass strike, coupled with demands for wages in exchange for work and liberty under British law.

Sam Sharpe informed other prospective resisters that freedom had already been granted by Britain. As Mary Turner notes, this carefully planned uprising was neither a Maroon communal flight to the forested hinterlands nor an apocalyptic spasm of despair.[55] Although the plot was partly uncovered shortly before the outbreak of hostilities, its unprecedented extent assured some initial success. As a military venture it failed. Large-scale but military tactics were as much beyond the experience of the slaves as they would have been beyond those of most petitioners across the ocean.

The Baptist War has often been identified as principal catalyst in the swift passage of emancipation.[56] However, the first reaction of Parliament was rather the formation of a Committee in the upper House intended to undermine abolitionist claims. As late as the opening of the new reformed Parliament the next year, the Baptist War and its residue of desperate planters was instead cited by a minister as a reason for postponing legislative action.[57] Emancipation was not mentioned in the King's opening speech. It took yet one more massive metropolitan campaign to bring the issue to a head late in the spring of 1833.

As an instrument of pressure the slaves did not function as effectively as their metropolitan counterparts among Catholic and political reformers in 1829 and 1832. The issue was not courage. Even slaves demanding much less than freedom risked far more than any metropolitan reformer between 1829 and 1832. The slaves were quite literally laying their lives on the line, while most metropolitan abolitionists contributed a small portion of their time, money or energies. It was the political position of the metropolitan abolitionists which gave them the decisive advantage over the most heroic of Caribbean rebels.

The cases of St Vincent and Grenada seemed to show that, without metropolitan mobilization, British governmental reaction to slave uprisings would have been no different from those of the other European imperial powers before and afterwards. Troops were first dispatched to crush the uprising. Then the plantation system was restored in every detail. British Grenada and St Vincent in 1796 foreshadowed French Guadeloupe and St Lucia in 1802. Located at a periphery, even the Haitians, with the longest, the most extensive, the bloodiest and the most decisive slave liberation in the history of the world could liberate only themselves. The huge human and material costs of the West Indian campaigns of the 1790s no more deterred Britain from subsequently reconquering every enemy island (except Haiti) in the following decade than the American Revolutionary War deterred the British from extending their Indian empire or founding both their African and Australian empires within a decade after 1783. Once the cost in white mortality had been diminished by the formation of the African slave regiments it was no more difficult to have black soldiers pouncing on Caribbean islands than to have Irish soldiers policing the Emerald Isle or Sepoys expanding the British Raj in India.

By contrast one cannot overemphasize one implication of the Baptist War for the metropolis, regardless of its immediate failure. It demonstrated that the slaves of Jamaica had become so well attuned to metropolitan mobilization that abolitionist campaigns would henceforth reverberate through the islands whatever the immediate disposition of petitions by Parliament. The reciprocal mobilizations in the colonies and in the metropolis finally converged in the political imagination like two armies, one massive, pacific and meticulously quantifiable, the other furtive, violent and immeasurable.

By 1832 the rhythm of resistance between Britain and the Caribbean islands had become predictable enough that the idea of separating the mobilizations of slaves and citizens seemed futile. What had begun in 1788 as a purely metropolitan campaign to help remote Africans had become a transatlantic exchange between fellow British subjects and Christians.[58] In this respect at least, the once potent geocultural line between freedom and slavery had ceased to exist.

6 God's Work: Antislavery and Religious Mobilization

Having explored the magnitude and impact of political mobilization for abolition one must turn towards its social sources. The religious dimension of British abolition has always claimed and usually received pride of place in such discussions, from Thomas Clarkson in 1808 to Roger Anstey and David Brion Davis. The abolitionist leaders were known to contemporaries and to posterity as the 'Saints'. Nothing in the abolitionist historiographical tradition infuriated the iconoclastic Eric Williams so much as Reginald Coupland's imaginary interview with Wilberforce. To the historian's question on the significance of the abolition of British slavery, Wilberforce was made to reply: 'It was God's work. It signifies the triumph of His will over human selfishness. It teaches that no obstacle of interest or prejudice is irremovable by faith and prayer.'[1]

Just as economically-oriented historians have been drawn to reflect upon the general correlation between British abolitionism and the industrial revolution, so religiously-oriented historians take as their point of departure the chronological correlation between the British abolitionist take-off and the rise of evangelicalism. Some historians, including Roger Anstey, have identified antislavery as derivative of emergent Protestant nonconformity in theology, ideology, rhetoric and organization. Thus behind the specific problem of British abolition lies the wider question of the relation of organized Christianity to the demise of slavery.[2]

Within this wider framework linking Christianity and abolition presents at least as many anomalies as does the correlation between industrialization and abolition. It is difficult to overlook the coexistence of Christianity with ancient and medieval Mediterranean slavery, with Eastern Christian slavery and with Atlantic slavery. Christianity made its peace with the institution as readily as Judaism or Islam. Europeans transported both African slaves and Christian institutions to the New World.[3]

What was true of Christianity in general for more than a millennium and a half was true of British Christianity in the slave colonies for a century and a half after the settlement of Barbados. In the British, as in every other New World system, Christian institutions, liturgy and theology were established alongside the institution of slavery. The Established Church of England and the various dissenting groups made adjustments to the new colonial system within and beyond the plantation areas. The Anglican Church functioned much like other Old Régime churches in the sugar, coffee, cotton, rice and tobacco areas. Its clergy made no attempt to mobilize the slave population as a whole for conversion nor were they pressed to do so by their metropolitan superiors. Anglicanism enjoyed its dominant position in the plantation colonies, endowed with glebe lands, housed in parish churches, and staffed with a university-educated clergy.[4] If they were characterized by a general lack of evangelical zeal even among their white parishioners, this was no more than was expected of them in eighteenth-century Britain itself.[5]

A clergy so dependent on the paternal support of the English squirearchy at home could scarcely have been shocked by the fact that Caribbean plantation owners determined the religious setting of their estates. They were already nurtured within an oligarchic social system before they ever set foot in the islands. The Anglican clergy certainly contributed to the maintenance of communal solidarity in the islands through its recurrent rites, even if opportunities for marriage and baptismal ceremonies were relatively fewer, and the occasions for funerals were greater, than in England. For their part, before the age of abolitionism, the slave-owners put no pressure on London for colonial Bishops. On both sides of the Atlantic the agents of the church, almost without exception, fitted themselves into a decentralized religious system in which landowners set the boundaries of devotional practice.

The clergy emulated the social and economic behaviour of their secular co-religionists as individual and corporate owners of slaves, as sexual exploiters, and as defenders of the legitimacy, if not the glory, of the slave system to the very end. The Anglican Society for the Propagation of the Gospel (SPG) ran its own plantation endowment on Barbados along the same lines as other well-run plantations. David Davis rightly concludes that without the pressure of metropolitan abolitionism it is impossible to say whether the SPG would have been shaken from its acceptance of slavery and its integration with the master class.[6]

The Established Church beyond the line differed very little from its counterparts in other rapidly developing Catholic plantation colonies. Like its English equivalent, French Christianity in the islands was the religion of the planters and their fellow Europeans. Its clergy refrained from any basic criticism of the institution of slavery as it did of any other aspect of plantation life. As with the Anglican church, the French slave system belonged to Caesar.[7] Religious sanctification was equally available for slavery overseas whether the colonial power was predominantly Catholic, Anglican, Lutheran or Reformed.

Where the British slave system differed most from its Catholic, although not from its Protestant, counterparts was in the multiplicity of its colonial denominations. Both the relative political autonomy of the British colonies and the greater degree of British religious toleration allowed for more experimentation and diversity within the colonies of religious relationships between masters and slaves. Although no colony and no denomination moved to abolish the slave trade or slavery until the last third of the eighteenth century there appears to have been more leeway in the Anglo-American than in the Continental empires for the smattering of sectarian pre-abolitionists who emerged from time to time in the century before 1788.

In such a latitudinarian setting there could also be no metropolitan pretence that the slave trade was being conducted in order to incorporate heathen Africans into the one true Protestant faith. On the other hand, within such a pluralistic context the Quakers of Britain and the Northern Continental Colonies were able to effect their own collecting withdrawal from the Atlantic slave trade and slave ownership even before the age of abolition.[8] Others were free to underwrite the conversion of their slaves on the sugar islands. English proprietor-patrons established Moravian missions for some slaves in Jamaica in 1754, as did converts to Methodism in the islands later in the eighteenth century. Within limits, the principle of *cuius regio, eus religio* applied to every individual overseas plantation.

However, one must also note the significance of the major religious difference between the metropolis and the islands even before the age of abolition. Whatever the other parallels between squire and planter, West Indian Christianity did not act as an agent of communal reinforcement. If one out of ten English parishes were unattended to by ministers of the Establishment, nine out of ten souls in the islands were not served at all by its clergy.[9] The religious rituals and rites of passage which, in England, were designed to bind local society together from top to bottom in dependent solidarity, bound only the

Europeans together and separated them from the mass of the population over which they ruled. Most planters, like the slave traders, never pretended that the massive conversion of slaves was either the norm of the islands or their particular aim.[10] The plantation system was held together not by a paternal religious system but by a tacit acceptance of the slaves' cultural autonomy in religion and social customs as long as it did not threaten the economic system. As the English Establishment had made its tacit peace with the 'half-pagan popular culture' of the metropolis, with its fairs, its sports, its drink and its hedonism, so the planters made an even greater accommodation with their wholly pagan slaves. With relatively little opposition the Afro-Caribbeans developed their own spiritual hierarchy, myths, festivals, musical and dance forms. They created a cultural world of their own as distinctive as their autonomous marketing system beyond the plantation.[11]

However, the same cultural autonomy which mitigated the masters' control also acted to insulate the slaves against new cultural offers from beyond the line. Before abolitionism, most planters clearly found this balance of social control and autonomy much more palatable than mass conversion to Christianity. In addition to the punishments of whips, chains, branding and mutilation, they could capitalize on the inherently divisive ethnic disparities produced by the African slave trade and on the differential opportunities for individual mobility accorded to colour, concubinage and craftsmanship. It seems clear that left to themselves the sugar planters found the presumed risks of conversion far greater than the benefits. The traditional Established Church therefore had little difficulty in effecting a *modus vivendi* between Chistianity and New World planters. It endured not only until the end of the eighteenth century, but in many respects until the actual passage of emancipation.[12]

What, then, was the impact of the new evangelical crusade which coincided with the age of abolition and which has led historians like Anstey and Edith Hurwitz to conclude that abolitionism was essentially a product of religious revival? In terms of temporal priorities, the pressure for religious change clearly came from the metropolitan side. The great social shift which was slowly undermining the position of the Established Church in England before 1790 had no parallel in the contemporary Caribbean. In the islands there was no wave of enclosures, no erosion of the remnants of a traditional agrarian economy, no surge of popular evangelical religion from below, and no general demand for a cultural awakening from above.

The most dynamic centre of Protestant expansion in the age of abolition is as easily identified as the most dynamic centre of antislavery. The peak period of mass abolitionism in Britain coincided almost precisely with the foundation of a world-wide Anglo-American missionary network abroad. Between 1790 and 1820 British missionary enterprise overwhelmingly dominated Protestant Christianity. Of the missions founded outside Anglo-America between 1792 and 1820 three-quarters were British, and all but one of the remainder were American. America's own great surge of overseas enterprise caught up with Britain's in the generation after 1820, while its own abolitionist movement entered a new intensive phase.[13]

Just when Britain began its most dramatic era of geographical expansion the Catholic overseas empires were moving in precisely the opposite direction. For more than two generations after the American Revolutionary War, European Catholic enterprise was virtually paralysed. The Catholic monarchist attacks on the Society of Jesus, culminating in its dissolution, entailed the recall or displacement of hundreds of colonial missionaries. This erosion accelerated when the French Revolution caused the Catholic Church to concentrate on rebuilding its shaken European core.[14]

During the first half of the nineteenth century, there was little to tempt either the Papacy or its European hierarchies into an attack on slavery. Little of the church's depleted economic and human resources were directed towards overseas conversion. For the entire age of British popular abolitionism the Catholic Church was geo-politically and socially in a defensive posture. Only on the eve of the Revolutions of 1848 were there signs of a modest missionary revival in France as well as an emerging affiliation between popular Catholicism and abolitionism. In 1847 the most activist lay Catholic newspaper in France, *L'Univers*, looked forward to a popular campaign for emancipation in 1848. Abbé Dupanloup, one of the clerical leaders of liberal Catholicism, promised to gather 20 000 signatures for the cause. The Archbishop of Paris, after a decade of silence towards the abolitionist movement, gave evidence that he too would support public clerical action.[15] The spark was snuffed out in the wake of the events of 1848 in France and Italy.

Beyond France the Church of the early nineteenth century was dependent upon political and social régimes which still relied heavily upon various forms of bound labour, serfdom in Central Europe, and slavery in the colonies of Spain and Portugal. The general affiliation of the Catholic episcopacy with the *status quo* was similar to that of its

Establishment Protestant counterparts. Latin American revolutions which moved to abolish slavery did not rely on the clergy for a Catholic mobilization of antislavery opinion. The pattern of transatlantic migration and social conflict before 1840 did not enhance the growth of popular Catholic overseas abolitionism in the Americas. In the US the oldest Southern Catholics of Maryland and Louisiana, aligned with their sectional economic interest. Only after 1840 did the expansion of immigrant working classes in some Southern cities begin to create even potential seedbeds for Catholic working-class antagonism to planter slave capitalism. In the North ethno-class conflict kept the large mass of Irish immigrants at arm's length from Protestant evangelical abolitionism.[16]

Significantly the largest single mass mobilization of Catholics against slavery originated in the British Isles at the very end of the era of British popular abolitionism. In 1841–2 an antislavery address signed by 60 000–70 000 people in Ireland was directed to the Irish in the US. It was headed by a coalition of Catholic and Protestant abolitionists, including Daniel O'Connel and Father Theobald Matthews. Like the English Protestant intrusion into America a few years earlier, it received a hostile reception among the articulate majority of its intended recipients.[17]

Anstey's derivation of abolitionism from evangelical nonconformity seems to be strengthened by this geo-religious survey of the locus of both missionary and abolitionist enterprise at the turn of the nineteenth century. He claims that the very dynamic of the evangelical world-view nurtured sensitivity to the claims of liberty and to the call of benevolent measures. 'Once the law of love is invoked as the supreme criterion, slavery stands condemned.' There 'was a necessary externalisation of the polar opposites of [the Evangelicals'] own religious experience' which gave a drive to antislavery zeal that few mere humanitarians could generate. To counter the plausible objection that many American evangelicals felt they were not called to campaign for abolition Anstey explained British evangelicals 'just were not put to the same test as were American Methodists'.[18]

Closer scrutiny considerably modifies Anstey's general thesis and alerts us both to the limiting and generating factors in the relationship between the new evangelicalism and abolition. In the first place, the mobilization of the eighteenth century began more than a generation before the rise of popular abolitionism. Initially it showed no general concern for slavery as a system. It was not only possible for evangelicals to sanction slavery in warm climates but, as in the famous case of

George Whitefield, to favour establishment of the institution in Georgia, where trustees had originally prohibited it.[19] All the world might be open for preaching, but in eighteenth-century fashion slave-owners could be considered quite useful for bringing their slaves to salvation. A slave-holder founded Methodism in the British West Indies. In the pre-abolitionist period, even the new nonconformity was as capable of adapting to slavery as its denominational predecessors.[20]

As of 1770 the conscience of the revival had not been clearly sensitized to slavery as an overriding moral issue. John Wesley's own great awakening to the evil of slavery seems to have come in response to the sharpening of public discussion over the Somerset case in 1772 and through the writings of the Quaker Anthony Benezet.[21] In a widely publicized essay of 1774, Wesley declared that liberty came not just when one breathed English air but with the breath of life itself.[22] From the mid-1770s there was an increasingly clear recognition of slavery as an internal moral problem for the Methodist faithful. The 'second generation' of evangelicals also gave notice in America of the emergence, if not the dominance, of a new attitude towards slaves as members of the community of the faithful, and towards slave–owners as embodiments of excessive wealth and arbitrary power.[23]

Since Methodism was the most centralized of all the new revivalist sects, the fate of Wesley's abolitionist impulse may provide us with the best proxy indicator for the general relationship between the Anglo-evangelical religious and antislavery mobilizations. As noted before, he originally had scant hope of effecting any good by an appeal to the popular will on such an issue. Wesley and Clarkson were working the same fertile grounds in Manchester in 1787, Wesley on one of his last great circuits for Methodism, Clarkson on his first in support of abolition.[24] As soon as Manchester demonstrated the full potential of mass political abolitionism Wesley threw his personal influence behind the movement. Although they were never more than a substantial minority of the British abolitionists, the Methodists may also afford us the best means of understanding the social context of mass abolitionism. In our international context their network developed almost simultaneously in Britain and the Americas. In the metropolitan context, as we shall see, they offer us the most complete evidence linking membership and mass abolitionist participation of any social grouping in Britain during the age of abolition.

Let us begin with the international comparison. In the free-labour zones of Britain and the Northern US, Methodists moved toward more abolitionist positions in the 1780s.[25] In Britain they became identified as abolitionists *par excellence* through each phase of their movement. In the American upper South, Methodism also seemed to veer towards antislavery in the first flush of evangelical mobilization. Only after a sharp internal struggle did Southern evangelicalism surrender the nascent abolitionism it originally shared with the free-labour zones and develop a strong evangelical rationalization for slavery in the South.[26] Both the first impulse and the sequence are important.

To explain the divergent paths taken by Methodists in Britain and in the American South, David Davis draws a distinction between the populist and expansionist nonconformity of the South and the more deferential nonconformity of Britain. His emphasis on the primacy of conversion within all the new dissenting groups is convincing but his distinction between Southern and English Methodism seems unwarranted. The real difference was not between a populistic Southern and a deferential English Methodism but in the social characteristics of the areas proselytized by Methodism.[27] In the South, as in Britain, the missionary effort evolved out of a rejection of the paternalist culture of the gentry. Both areas had large free white populations accessible to conversion. The decisive difference was the South's large black slave population. Methodists at first attempted to transfer the whole ethos of the British variant, including antislavery, to the American mainland. In the South this produced a short-term challenge, but a long-term accommodation. The fact that the pool of potential evangelical converts contained large numbers of slaves and slave-holders meant that the primacy of conversion was consciously deflected away from the issue of slavery.

Moreover it was not, as some historians hold, that the South alone among the plantation societies was tested by dissent, and resolved the moral challenge by assimilating it. Evangelicals in the British West Indies followed the same path to accommodation. The difference was that their stage of accommodation was not preceded by a period of challenge and the accommodation itself was undermined from without.

Where West Indian nonconformity did follow a different trajectory from that of the South toward slavery was in the inversion of stages between 1780 and 1840. In the islands it was accommodation first and abolitionism afterwards. Missionaries began by adjusting their doctrine to slavery and reached their high point of adaptation in the early 1820s. Only after 1823 did nonconformist religious mobilization begin to take on overtones of abolitionism.[28] What explains this inversion of the Southern stages? The normal target population for nonconformists, the free poor, constituted only a tiny fraction of the Caribbean population. Penetration of the world of the plantation slaves was entirely dependent, in the first instance, on the masters. Nonconformity had to be far more deferential in the West Indies than in England or America. In Virginia, the English missionary Thomas Coke ran into a storm of threats when attempting to enforce Wesley's prohibition on Methodist slave-holding. In the islands he never even made the attempt.[29] In the Chesapeake slavery seemed to have a chance to be in God's realm in 1790; in the Caribbean it was clearly in Caesar's. At the *extremes* (Britain and the West Indies) preachers immediately knew exactly how far they could go regarding antislavery. In the American South what transpired was a very quick lesson about the inverse relationship between maximum conversion and abolitionism. Given the situation, what is most interesting is not that the outcome was proslavery, but that so many evangelicals initially assumed that conversion implied the necessity to do something about slavery.

Regarding abolition, the most important difference between the American Southern and West Indian developments involved the *changing* relationship of each area to its non-slave metropolis. Before the age of abolitionism, nonconformity was, like conformity, in the hands of proprietors. The Moravians had demonstrated, at least for the time being, that converted Negroes were not more dangerous slaves.[30] Most planters, however, seem to have assumed that they were well enough off with Christianity at the top and Afro-Creole religion at the bottom. If some planters wished to ease their tender consciences, *chacun à son dieu*. Only a handful of planters availed themselves of the opportunity. A new period began with the initiatives of Thomas Coke and the founding of a few Baptist and Methodist missions. This was a period punctuated by sporadic planter crackdowns on missionaries in response to outside events like the St Domingue revolution of 1791, the Caribbean revolutionary war of 1795–6, the Napoleonic restoration of French slavery in 1802, and the abolition of the British slave trade in 1807. A split developed between tolerant and intransigent planters. When the intransigents attempted to rid themselves entirely of their troublesome preachers, they were simply overruled by the imperial government.[31]

The phase of accomodation lasted beyond Waterloo to the first metropolitan emancipation drive in 1823. As long as the abolitionist movement was quiescent the 'moderate' planters actually won the battle to co-opt nonconformity into a Southern mould. The second phase of disaccommodation came in the decade before emancipation. It was characterized by a dynamic expansion of the missions backed by the metropolitan government, growing planter mobilization against the missionaries and increasing identification of the missionaries with religious freedom for the slaves. At this stage the slaves began to test both their masters and the religious system, forcing increased missionary intervention.[32] This final period of internecine conflict was climaxed by the great slave uprising in Jamaica in 1831.

In the very early years of the revival, the unmobilized planters had tolerated, if they did not encourage, various experiments on Moravian and Methodist plantations. As in Britain there was no fundamental change in attitude before the abolitionist take-off. As late as the 1780s even black Baptists from America were allowed to establish themselves as preachers to black converts, to preach before open-air meetings and to build chapels, as long as they did not attempt to convert slaves without their master's approval.[33] Not every contemporary Southern American community was so amenable. Coke's first service in the West Indies to an integrated audience was interrupted by gentlemen 'inflamed by liquor' but this was no more than standard operating fare for Methodist preachers in England. Coke was genuinely impressed by the courtesy shown him by most whites. Above all, the authorities did not interfere. Coke's reception was far more civil than it had been in Virginia where he faced angry mobs and threats of flogging or lynching. One of the essential differences, of course, was that Coke never mentioned an antislavery requirement as the *sine qua non* for Methodist membership in the islands.[34]

For their part, the subsequent Caribbean missionary movements carefully attempted to separate themselves from their abolitionist counterparts within the metropolis. They drew a rigorous line between missionaries and abolitionists, even between Wilberforce the abolitionist and Wilberforce the evangelical patron. Nonconformist preachers were told by their metropolitan dispatchers to render unto Caesar, to refrain from all political discussion, and to preach and practise obedience to legitimate authority. They were enjoined to be meek before authority, whether civil or Anglican, and not to associate on intimate terms with free coloured people. They were urged to accept their dependent status in order to be licensed by the magistracy, and to set an example to their communicants, softening arrogance by obedience and humility.[35]

Missionaries in the field often went even further along the road to creolization than expected to at home. They adopted standards of living customary for whites. They employed numbers of servants or hired slaves on a 'colonial' scale. They did not accept free blacks or coloureds as fellow ministers. In the crisis of the mid-1820s some took the ultimate ideological step of identifying emancipation as injurious to the slaves, unjust to the proprietors, ruinous to the colonies, and destructive of Christianity. Caribbean missionaries showed the same capacity to defend their peculiar institution as did their counterparts in the American South.[36]

For all this, nonconformity proved to be *more* dangerous and subversive than its counterpart on the American mainland. This was obviously not because conversion was itself inherently subversive of slavery or on account of the symbolism of liberation embedded in evangelical ideology. Christianity did provide slaves with a new sense of individual worth, an alternative hierarchy of status and new opportunities for leadership, but it also divided slaves. It competed with the status hierarchy of the plantation which had its own material and social rewards. It required converts to withdraw from Afro-Creole amenities in the same way that English converts were required to withdraw from the hedonistic culture of their compatriots.

Still, British mobilization for overseas religious activity after 1790 decisively affected the rate of slave conversion in the short run and the pace of emancipation in the longer run. The new missionary movement in Britain produced a decisive shift in the relationship between the metropolis and the colonies. The 'latent' event in the British colonies in the years after 1780, and especially after 1800, was the entrance of a pluralistic missionary enterprise, sanctioned by the metropolitan government and focused primarily on the black population.[37] Faced with the subversion of their African trade by the abolitionists and prevented by the imperial government from retaliating against the missionaries for the actions of their metropolitan patrons, many planters attempted to make the most of the line drawn by Coke between the abolitionist evangelicals in Britain and neutral missionaries in the colonies. As long as the primary focus of metropolitan abolitionism was on the African slave trade this appeared to be a workable compromise. By the time the metropolitan evangelicals began to attack slavery itself in the 1820s the transformation had occurred. It was one of the principal elements in eroding the line between metropolis and colony. In the years between the 1780s and the 1820s the heathen African became a fellow Christian. It was precisely such a change which helped to override the perception of racial and cultural differences.

On balance, as Mary Turner concludes, nonconformity was ultimately more subversive of slavery than the prior creole religious traditions. This was not primarily because it allowed slaves more autonomy within the slave system.[38] The slaves already had evolved both religious and economic institutions for serving such functions on and off the plantation. At best the competitive market of the missionary entrepreneurs became an additional resource of Afro-Creole sects beyond white control. Nonconformity was more subversive because of its association with evolving antislavery. Despite the officially neutral attitude of the missionaries, planters were aware that the missionaries and slaves alike belonged to the same metropolitan groups as the abolitionists and that the missionaries were bound to reflect the diminishing range of metropolitan tolerance for slavery. As deferentially as they might act toward the planters, missionaries were hired, fired and supported for life by their transatlantic superiors. Like the planters in Britain they were 'absentees', ultimately drawing economic, psychological and social sustenance from an overseas community.

In any crisis of authority they would be reminded, with penalty, that 'you are not sent to the West Indies to lose your Christian and English feeling on the subject of Slavery, nor to acquire the prejudices of caste and colour; nor to surrender in conversation, or by any act, any principle of Christian truth and justice to obtain favour from any man'.[39] As the situation changed dramatically after the political mobilization of 1823–4, a missionary who wished to stay at his station discovered not only what Christian truth was but just which way it was heading. Regardless of how a missionary might resolve the psychological tensions between serving his West Indian flock, the secular authorities in the colonies and his patrons in Britain, as the metropolis radicalized so did the missionary community.

The West Indians were therefore neither stupid nor irrational in seeing the dissenting missionaries as refractions if not reflections of their metropolitan masters, and not as harmless evangelicals breathing St Paul's accommodating advice to the slaves. In1790 there was still some identity of interest between Anglican and nonconformist potential conversion in the colonies. All missions made clear their official respect for the legal status of slavery as distinguished from abolitionist activity in the metropolis. There were sufficiently large numbers of slaves that each home organization could theoretically hope for an abundant harvest. All denominations made their initial peace with the West Indians by placating the planter magistracy.

By the 1820s nonconformists had functioning organizations among the slaves, serving tens of thousands of converts. The Anglican clergy, perhaps because of their identification with the planter class, had played no significant role in converting the slaves. On the contrary, some of its clergy took an active and hostile role against the nonconformist missionaries.[40] Still, as long as nonconformist metropolitans did not turn their fire directly on the slave system, there had emerged an interim 'Southern' solution to the problem of conversion and slavery. However, as metropolitan nonconformity was approaching a new militant stage of agitation at home, its social interests abroad diverged more than ever from those of even metropolitan evangelical Anglicans. In institutional terms metropolitan mobilization after 1823 not only fostered slave resistance and planter repression but created missionary 'martyrs' in Demerara and Jamaica. The relationship of missionaries to metropolitans meant that such missionary persecutions triggered secondary mobilizations of British nonconformists.[41] It is to that mobilization which we must finally turn to identify the religious connection which in the end destroyed British slavery.

There is a close parallel between the pattern of British overseas mission formation and British religious evolution between the 1780s and the 1830s. At the moment of take-off in 1788–92 the abolitionist support and initiative came from sources much wider than those of organized nonconformity, whether old or new. The attitude of John Wesley in the 1770s, and of occasional sermonizers on the slave trade in the early 1780s, showed how uncertain early religious figures remained about the potential for public support until the eve of the first campaign. After four years of minimal results the Quakers in 1787 joined their own stymied effort to a broader movement in order to incorporate as much as possible of the British religious and secular spectrum.

In its religious aspect the early mobilizations exhibit two important features. In appeal, the movement was designed to be a coalition of the whole range of philosophical and religious discourse. Potential ideological differences were muted.[42] The slave trade was attacked by the unitarian Joseph Priestley, the deist Tom Paine, evangelicals and high Anglican bishops alike. In this setting the dissenters as a whole were aware of their minority position in the movement and the nation. They displayed no aspirations to leadership. This ecumenical characteristic profited from the unusual fluidity of religious and doctrinal ideas in Britain during the 1780s. It was a moment of muted denominational strife.[43] Tension between dissent and the Establishment was at a particularly low ebb. For dissenters it appeared that there might even be a chance of quietly repealing the Test and Corporation Acts without arousing any major alarm among the Anglican clergy or laity. Like the broad-based Sunday-school movement, abolition was seen by dissenters as a way of combining forces with members of the more powerful Established Church which would lower mutual distrust.

The nondenominational element was underlined by the community-centred organization of early abolitionism.[44] Petition meetings were not requisitioned on behalf of specific denominations nor held in chapels, but were called as general meetings in town halls or other public places. There was clearly no antagonism between popular radical and popular religious abolitionism in 1788–92. James Walvin has already noted the close interaction of radicals and abolitionists in the early 1790s. Thomas Hardy extended his hospitality to Equiano, who reciprocated by putting Hardy in touch with contacts garnered from his abolitionist campaigns.[45] At the conservative end of the socio–religious spectrum the Anglican presence was quite conspicuous. Almost a quarter of the petitions of 1788 and one-sixth of those of 1792 were sponsored by clergy of the Established Church. The Scottish clergy were even more prominent in the first mass levy of petitions north of the Tweed in 1792. The broad range of abolitionist support out-of-doors seems to have been echoed in Parliament, where the unsaintly Charles Fox joined forces with Wilberforce over the issue of abolition.

Even when religious mobilization in defence of Establishment privileges began to rise again in 1789, abolitionism was resistant to the divisive trend and retained something of its original privileged and cross-denominational position. Grayson Ditchfield has demonstrated that abolition was politically much more broadly based in Parliament in the 1790s (or, one might add, in 1807) than support for the relief of religious disabilities. Thus in the earlier abolitionist campaigns nonconformity clearly played a supporting and not a dominant role.

If there was a notable difference between early Anglican and nonconformist participation it lay in the fact that the nonconformists seemed to participate with almost total unanimity. The Baptists gave official public support from the outset. The Methodists, breaking with their strictures on participation in politics, ensured maximum enthusiasm for the petition campaigns of 1792. The Nottingham Methodists circularized their connection in other areas of England just as the city of Manchester had done in 1788.[46] In contrast, there were indications even in 1788–92 of ambivalence or hostility from the Establishment. Sometimes corporate Anglican hesitation was expressed in a refusal to petition Parliament on grounds of impropriety, as when Oxford refused to petition in 1788, or when the Archdeacon of Leicester attempted to prevent his clergy from petitioning in 1792. More often individual Anglican clergymen simply refused to sign petitions. I have no idea of the numbers or proportion, but when clerical abstainers were mentioned they were referred to as High Tories.[47]

The opponents of abolitionism were by and large ineffective in designating nonconformity and religious radicalism as the early mainstays of abolitionism, and in trying to brand it as a Quaker plot, as a Methodist plot, or, in more inflamed moments, as a revival of the Fifth Monarchy men. This was simply part of the counter-abolitionist strategy to drive any available wedge between the heterogeneous elements in abolitionism.[48] Opponents did state correctly that abolitionism appeared to be more unifying and ecumenical for the new nonconformity than for Anglicans. Nevertheless, up until the end of the Napoleonic Wars, the prominence of the Anglican evangelicals in abolitionist campaigns and positions of Parliamentary leadership overrode observed but untallied defections among the Anglican clergy.

In the generation before 1815, the slave trade phase of abolition, popular support for abolition seems to have been well reflected in Parliamentary debates and votes. The dissenting and reforming interests, those who supported both religious liberalism and Parliamentary reform, were solidly behind abolitionism.[49] The latter movement simply had a wider base, including some who opposed the other metropolitan reform movements.

By the time the metropolis focused on slavery itself in the 1820s, there was still a strong evangelical Anglican component which supported abolition, but the rift between nonconformity and Anglicanism was becoming progressively deeper and more bitter. As the balance of affiliation in Britain shifted rapidly in favour of nonconformity, Anglicanism sank to its lowest point. Relative to total population the proportion of Anglican communicants reached its absolute nadir at the beginning of the 1830s, just as abolitionism reached its climax.[50] In the meantime, Methodists had been officially thrust out of the Church, openly adding their burgeoning numbers to the ranks of nonconformity. By the late 1820s nonconformists felt strong enough to make a frontal attack on the exclusive position of the Anglicans. One after another the legal underpinnings of the Established Church were dismantled. The repeal of the Test and Corporation Acts (1828), the Roman Catholic Relief Act (1829) and the passage of the Reform Act (1832) signaled the end of the old legal bulwarks.[51]

This had important consequences for the way in which both the Anglicans and nonconformists viewed the climactic antislavery campaigns of 1830–3. While the evangelical wing of the Established Church still supported abolitionism and urged full participation in the petitioning, Anglicans increasingly felt that the movement had been taken out of the hands of their leaders and replaced by a nonconformist/radical coalition.[52] The final campaign for emancipation ended in a flurry of bitter recriminations over the absorption of abolitionism by radicals. The Anglican residue felt bitter nostalgia for the days when Wilberforce and James Stephen had led the movement and abolitionism had been uncontaminated by 'the dubious Rights of Man'. As we shall see, the realities of early abolitionism were already fading into the hazy mythology of a golden age.[53] By 1832, when the fate of Anglicanism in the colonies was tied almost exclusively to a slave-owning class on the brink of slave emancipation, it was linked in the metropolis to an unreformed Establishment on the brink of political emasculation.

Domestic and overseas developments combined to induce High Tories to be more outspoken in defence of the planters than before Waterloo. When the *Preston Pilot* discovered, in 1832, that members of the Anti-slavery Society were openly distributing anti-tithe literature, they encouraged the embattled West Indians with the thought that their best chance of avoiding emancipation lay in the growing fusion of abolitionism with attacks on the Established Church.[54] The intervention of abolitionist Anglicans had probably been decisive in legitimizing and depoliticizing abolitionism during its fragile early days. Some 40 years later their heirs felt that the movement had become exactly what many conservatives had called it as early as 1792, a stalking horse for constitutional dismemberment. The results of the nonconformist 'take-over' in England by 1830–3 are clearly visible in Table 6.1. By the 1820s the proportion of abolitionist petitions sponsored by Establishment clergy had dropped to 3–6 per

TABLE 6.1   *Percentage of English denominational antislavery petitions 1788–1831**

	Anglican	Dissenter
1788	13	2
1792	9	1
1814†	N.A.	3
1823	6	1
1824	3	1
1826	5	6
1830–1	3	70
1833	N.A.	56

* includes all petitions by clergymen alone and by clergymen and inhabitants but not from inhabitants of a parish alone.
† From 1814 Methodists are included within Dissent.

SOURCE House of Commons *Journals*, indices.

cent. Correspondingly, dissenters had explicitly sponsored no more than 2 per cent of the first two abolitionist petitions. By 1830–3 they accounted for over half the total number of petitions. If abolitionism never actually became a nonconformist preserve, emancipation in the 1830s marked a new stage in the political emergence of organized nonconformity. Its missionary commitment in the colonies was now reinforced by an ideology of religious liberation in a way that the interests of the Established Church were not.[55]

Since the fate of colonial Anglicanism was linked almost exclusively to the planter class it was not merely a general conservatism which made the evangelical Anglican *Record* come out loudly in favour of compensation against the voice of nonconformity during the debates over emancipation. The *Record* had always publicized arguments supporting biblical hostility to slavery. Now, at the last minute, and to the shock of some of its own readers, the *Record* went out of its way to defend the biblical sanction of slavery on behalf of equity to the planters. Metropolitan and colonial developments thus reinforced each other in accounting both for the denominational intensification of antislavery and its increasingly confessional lines of division.[56]

The fact that nonconformity represented a significant and growing proportion of the social base of abolitionism on both sides of the Atlantic affords us the best empirical opening into the connection between British economic development, popular mobilization and religion. To take full advantage of it, however, I must take a slightly different tack from historiographical tradition. Most studies of abolition, both sympathetic and critical, have equated abolitionism with its leadership. The Quaker leaders, the Saints and their Parliamentary allies, the nonconformist theologians, constitute the socio-religious representatives of antislavery. When historians move outwards from this core it is usually to pick up one more élite: political economists, Methodist leaders, Parliamentary notables, or prominent capitalists.[57] The social base of abolitionism, when not dealt with in terms of these élite categories is most often simply characterized as a movement of the nonconformist middle class. The ideological basis of abolitionism, when not defined in terms of the religious ideas of the above groups, is most often characterized as an expression or hegemonic offshoot of nonconformist capitalism.[58]

In attempting to relate abolitionism to the rapid industrial transformation of Britain, one of the few ways to analyze its social base is from its religious affiliations. In all but a handful of cases we lack the petition lists that would enable us to make the nominal linkages which have proved so fruitful in the study of popular political and social behaviour. We do, however, have an opportunity to work from some aggregate religious figures. In the case of the Wesleyan Methodists there was an extraordinarily complete signing-up of the membership for the great emancipation petition of 1833.[59] If one combines the estimates of A. D. Gilbert on Methodist membership and the signature count of the Parliamentary Select Committee on Petitions, well over nine Wesleyans out of ten seem to have responded to the canvass. This information can be combined with evidence of the social composition of the Methodists during the age of abolition.

In the Methodists we also have a denomination with an outstanding record of long-term antislavery commitment. Methodists were canvassed for abolition on a nationwide basis as early as 1791–2.[60] They were singled out by early opponents as a source of popular abolition. In the famous Yorkshire election of 1807, the Methodist ministers supported Wilberforce when competing religious and economic issues pulled other nonconformists away from him. When Methodists were not ready to move, as during the post-Napoleonic years of social conflict, Wilberforce suspended renewed agitation. In the final stage, as we have noted, Wesleyan Methodists achieved a confessionally identifiable adherence to petitions matched by no other group.[61]

Abolitionism also reached its peak at the moment when Methodism's growth rate was reaching its peak. Indeed five out of the six abolitionist mass petitions occurred when Methodism, and nonconformity in general, were in periods of high growth.[62] In relation to other denominations the Methodist sign-up for emancipation represented about half of the nonconformists who signed up *confessionally* in 1833. Therefore, using the Methodists, we can obtain a breakdown by occupation for a group which represented more than half of the nonconformity who signed up by congregation and almost one-fifth of the total signatories to the 1833 petition. The relative proportions of the Wesleyan occupational breakdown are quite close to those of nonconformity as a whole. My assumption will be that all the new nonconformity of the abolitionist period should be treated as socially analogous, with relatively minor variations in occupational distribution.[63]

If we take the Methodists as our proxy for abolitionist support, we find that relative to the whole society abolitionism was greatly underrepresented in the ranks of the aristocracy and the farmers, somewhat underrepresented among merchants, manufacturers and labourers, slightly underrepresented among tradesmen, and heavily overrepresented among artisans, colliers, and miners (Table 6.2). Taken together the largest Methodist occupational groups, artisans, colliers, miners and labourers, constituted almost three-quarters of the Methodist share of the petitioners. If the Methodist sample is roughly indicative of the abolitionist social base the core of the English abolitionist movement would seem to have been supported by its artisanry. Unfortunately, even rough as this is, we have no comparable way of estimating the occupational participation for earlier campaigns so that we might establish some occupation trends between petitions. However, because of their sheer numbers, the Manchester petitions of 1787 and 1792 had to have a preponderance of artisanal working men. Since the other public meetings of 1788 and 1792 were located primarily in market towns and searching for maximum adherents there, it is also probable that overrepresentation of urban artisans also prevailed in 1792.[64] Moreover the strenuous appeal made by the Methodists in 1792 for a total sign-up in Manchester, Nottingham and elsewhere strongly suggests that the heavily artisan adherence of 1833 was at least as evident among its membership in 1792.

The Methodist sample may indeed give us an overly 'artisanized'

TABLE 6.2 *Occupational structure of nonconformity with high participation in anti-slavery petitions (sample 1830–7)*

Occupation	English society (%)	Wesleyans (%)	Baptists and Congregationalists (%)
Aristocracy	1.4	0	0
Merchants/ Manufacturers	2.2	1.7	5.4
Tradesmen	6.2	5.8	8.2
Farmers	14.0	5.5	7.1
Artisans	23.5	62.7	63.0
Labourers	17.0	9.5	3.9
Miners, etc.	2.5	7.6	2.1
Others	33.2	7.2	10.3

SOURCE A. D. Gilbert, *Religion and Society in Industrial England: Church, Chapel, and Social Change 1740–1914* (1976), pp. 63, 67.

portrait of the abolitionist social base, especially outside the ranks of nonconformity. Nevertheless one may conclude, even at this point in the social analysis of British abolitionism, that the known data squares poorly with the attribution of abolitionism as a nonconformist middle-class movement. In other words, it is precisely within nonconformity that the middle-class label seems inappropriate. At the very least, historians will have seriously to modify characterizations which are so socially constricted. The likelihood is that British abolitionism was more cross-class than most accounts of abolition, whether sympathetic or critical, have usually implied.

What may one say of the relationship of the nonconformist revival to abolitionism? First, the abolitionist take-off occurred when nonconformity still represented a distinctly minority element and well before it became clearly distinguished from the general evangelical revival at the end of the eighteenth century. If nonconformists were as numerous as Anglican communicants by the time of emancipation they were not yet one-third as large by the beginning of the nineteenth century. In this ecumenical venture of the late eighteenth century even the boundaries between religion and irreligion had not clearly hardened.[65] Thomas Paine had started out apprenticed to a Methodist preacher and was reported to have conducted a Methodist service.

Given its putative social profile it would appear that abolitionism was indirectly linked to the rapid changes that were produced by the early stages of the British industrial revolution but not in the way usually portrayed. Evangelicalism did not create mass abolitionism; rather, abolitionism proliferated in the same social and ideological context which was favourable to the growth of nonconformity. It took root within a range of groups with certain similarities. Abolitionism burst into the public arena just as its artisanal social base was rapidly expanding in the various mining and manufacturing regions, especially in Lancashire, the West Riding of Yorkshire, the Midlands, southern Scotland and Cornwall. In the early 1790s radicals universally supported the abolition of the slave trade. The Scottish campaign of 1792 did especially well in obtaining petitions from specific skilled trades. Antislavery flourished in nonagricultural milieus, but one must bear in mind that until the 1830s the dominant pattern of industrial settlement was largely determined by the expansion characteristics of early capitalistic outwork.[66]

Abolitionism, in other words, was less a response to the nascent factory system or the enclosure movement than to the concomitant artisanal expansion of the industrial revolution during the half-century after 1780. Outwork and artisanal industry, not the factory, provided the 'articulation' of the capitalist mode of production.[67] It flourished in urban towns and small industrial and mining villages. In this transitional era, as Alan Gilbert has argued from a religious, and John Rule and others from a working-class, perspective, involvement in a trade in manufacturing, mining or commerce represented the broadest route of emancipation from the paternalistic dependency system of the eighteenth century. What John Rule concludes about Methodism and labour therefore seems equally applicable to abolitionism and labour. Whatever the anti-radical views of the Clapham Saints, the movement was one of the symptoms of the weakening hold of paternalism over artisans and miners in the initial period of the industrial revolution.[68] The phenomenon was not just a characteristic of expanding Methodism in the North. Baptist preachers of the generation of 1790 were similarly struck by the fact that Cornishmen, being miners or fishermen, 'were more in a state of independence', more open to itinerant preachers and less subject to paternal control than labourers in agricultural areas.[69] These same Cornish miners were willing to participate in the boycott movement against West Indian sugar during the abolitionist campaign of 1791–2.

The social independency and aspirations of the artisans, rather than their despondency over the new economic order (what E. P. Thompson called the chiliasm of despair) have been emphasized for reasons which will be more evident in the next chapter. At any given moment sectors of the industrial capitalist economy were viewed by workers as relatively free from paternalistic authority. In terms of both work and workplace the artisans remained on the traditional side of the Thompsonian divide between pre- and post-industrial work discipline, and probably obstinately so.[70] Some indeed became factory owners themselves while remaining ardent abolitionists. Others, like Richard Oastler's father, refused to become factory owners for the very reasons that they had become abolitionists.[71] In any event, as we shall see, working men were able to discern these similarities and differences quite clearly.

Artisans could also realistically subscribe to a work discipline quite unlike that demanded by the factory system. They might trade off traditional leisure patterns for social mobility, or at least respectability, in the pre-Victorian sense.[72] Here I think we may relate the life experience which tied together the artisan's distaste for factory labour and his willingness to subscribe to antislavery. Abolitionists were not being distracted from what went on within the factory walls by the image of the plantation or the slave ship.[73] The unrelenting *externality* of both slave and factory discipline would have struck a deep chord of enmity in the artisanry. The institution of slavery affronted their moral economy at its source, depriving its field workers of supplementary gain from any extension of their labour. Thus antislavery appeals made special sense both to those who were succeeding through their own reinvestment of time and resources and to those who aspired to do so. As we shall see, they would have seemed especially true in the booming 1780s. Conversion to the new evangelicalism fortified this moral economy by communal fellowship. It would be misleading to impose a sharp line between artisan workers and small capitalists at this early stage of industrialization. The ranks of nonconformity thrived in an expanding economy of independency where the artisan might still feel closer to the petty capitalist than to the unskilled labourer.[74]

International comparisons seem to confirm the heavily artisanal sources of popular antislavery, even in the absence of Anglo-American nonconformity. The French case presents a striking example. Since there was so little room for mass petitioning in France in the decades before 1848 we have only a few hints about abolitionism's potential social base. We do know that the first mass petition in favour of French abolition was organized among the skilled artisans of Paris in 1844. The petitions were gathered at the workplace, and in most cases were sent to the Chamber of Deputies workshop by workshop. The workers of Lyons joined in, designating themselves as 'Proletarians'.[75] The working-class petitioners explicitly rejected the ideological analogy between themselves and plantation slaves, whether preferred by the spokesmen of slave-owners or by socialists.[76] At that point no major French élite or bourgeois initiatives at mass mobilization had ever been undertaken on behalf of emancipation. A generation later French middle-class organizers of a drive on behalf of American freedmen were still astounded to find that their single greatest tally of contributors turned out to be 10 000 workers of Mulhouse, supported by workers in Paris and Lyons.[77]

On the other side of the Atlantic, John Jentz has also discovered that New York artisans were subscribing to antislavery petitions both before and after the mass intrusion of evangelicalism in the early 1830s. He notes that English immigrant artisans were most likely to be among the signers.[78] In another study of the social base of Northern antislavery petitions to Congress from 1836 to 1839, Edward Magdol discovered the prominence of skilled artisans in samples from four cities in Massachusetts and western New York state. He incidentally notes that 63 per cent of the Methodist petitioners were skilled artisans. This is precisely the same percentage of artisans Alan Gilbert finds among the English Methodists between 1800 and 1837.[79] Immigrant artisans were also a source of rising anxiety for political leaders in the American South in the years before secession. As in New York, many immigrants apparently transferred attitudes towards slavery formed in metropolitan abolitionist zones.[80] Jentz's studies lead him to conclude that historians of American antislavery must look beyond the boundaries of the evangelical revival 'for the values and ideas which led a broadly diverse constituency to support the cause'.[81]

While further research may alter the proportions, on the basis of the evidence at hand it appears that abolitionism struck an especially responsive chord among the artisanry during the early industrial revolution. This finding may also lead historians to take another look at the putative relationship between British abolitionism and its 'free labour ideology'. Howard Temperley, David Davis and David Eltis, among other recent historians, have emphasized the fact that abolitionists invested heavily in Adam Smith's affirmation of the superiority of free labour in his *Wealth of Nations*. Smith claimed that slave labour was both more expensive and less inventive than free labour, a claim which was incidentally, commonplace long before 1776.[82]

Temperley and Eltis assume that this was essentially a bourgeois conception during the succeeding age of abolition.[83] The essential formulation is accurate but its class specificity strikes me as at once too broad and too narrow. Smith's economic universal was of course irrelevant to almost every capitalist planter beyond the line. It was also less than obvious to many metropolitan political economists and some abolitionists even during the age of abolition.[84] It might have seemed true to British factory owners, and bitterly true to factory workers, but at the end of the eighteenth century it must have seemed both true and completely relevant to workers in those expanding industries in which they retained some control over either their working conditions or their skills. It is probably not accidental that Smith used comparative production among miners to illustrate the superiority of free labour in his *Wealth of Nations*.[85] It is certainly no accident that he did not choose to compare the sugar plantation and his famous pin factory for comparative analysis.[86]

A connection between the economic experience of industrial artisans, their nonconformist religious outlook, and their support of abolitionism has been hypothesized. If this reasoning is sound we may now be in a position to restate the social linkage between free labour and the new religious ideologies of the late eighteenth century. Howard Temperley has emphasized the nice fit between Adam Smith's famous judgment on slave labour and the abolitionist credo. The pluralistic economic, religious and imperial context of late eighteenth-century Britain was especially conducive to fusing autonomous workers and non-slave-owning capitalists and intellectuals into a liberation movement with global dimensions. Only where an independent artisanry was located in a free labour society, however, did the rejection of 'dependency' entail a full antislavery commitment.[87]

Ironically the most overrepresented social category yet discovered in abolitionism was the most overrepresented category in the conflict with metropolitan state authority during the early stages of the industrial revolution. Thus the problem of relating abolitionists to the class struggle must command our attention.

7 Class Conflict, Hegemony and the Costs of Antislavery

For the abolitionists, freedom was the avowed central issue in the debate over slavery. For the planters and their allies, the central concern was labour, as it had been during the whole history of the British Caribbean. It has also increasingly been so defined by historians as the central problem of the empire, and of the abolitionists as well. It is therefore important to consider both the costs of abolition and the fate of labour during the age of British abolition.

The abolitionist leadership and the historians who followed them felt little need explicitly to locate their conflict within or to align themselves directly with any of the enormous domestic issues which emerged in Britain during the 50 dramatic years between 1788 and the end of colonial apprenticeship. They simply considered their victory as part of a more universal extension of civil and social rights throughout the globe. The critical tradition, precisely because it defined the major locus of historical development in terms of social conflict and deception, has been much more apt to treat the entire process in terms of contending domestic social forces. Yet despite what ought to have been its inclination towards closer social analysis, the critical tradition has remained content to treat abolitionism as the instrument of a loosely defined ruling class or the outcome of an evangelical–capitalist ideological hegemony. Indeed, the sympathetic school's concentration on the Saints as heroes helped the critical school to portray antislavery as the preserve of a group of evangelicals, operating in the interests of nascent capitalists.[1]

This perspective was reinforced by post-emancipation apprenticeship and indentured servitude as substitutes for slave labour in the colonies. In these terms abolitionism has been portrayed as a hegemonic hoax beyond the line. It has also been treated as a hegemonic displacement of social tensions in the metropolis. In both these interpretations of emancipation there is embedded an implicit or explicit model of compensated change. Both emphasize the 'deceptive aspects' of the social transformation. The colonial society exchanged one form of servitude for another. The metropolitan society failed, at least for a time, to see the new forms of degradation being fastened upon it.[2]

In broad comparative terms this perspective has the added advantage of conflating modern emancipation with pre-eighteenth-century transformations of slavery. Declines of prior major historical forms of slavery have been linked to compensatory increases of bondage among the surrounding labouring populations. Moses Finley plausibly argues that ancient slavery declined in conjunction with the gradual emergence of an increasingly coerced and bound rural peasantry. Richard Hellie notes a similar process at work in early modern Eastern Europe and Russia, where domestic chattel slavery declined or was abolished in tandem with the rise of rural serfdom. In both cases some new form of coerced labour was an adequate or even advantageous substitute of personal bondage for the preceding form of chattel slavery.[3]

Does a similar compensatory labour-substitution pattern emerge in the Americas? In most cases, abolition of the African slave trade and American emancipations were carried out over the opposition of the majority of the slave traders and owners and by an external force located in the free-labour area. The only major exception was the St Domingue revolution. The first French emancipation was initiated by slaves and some free allies against the determined opposition of the planters, and ultimately against the armed might of Europe's most powerful colonial states. The Haitian exception, however, strengthens at least one part of the rule. From the perspective of colonial proprietors it was the most unsatisfactory outcome of all, and no other planter class in modern history lobbied for so long to undo the revolution. From the perspective of the post-revolutionary black élite, beginning with Toussaint L'Ouverture, successive efforts to impose a coercive labour system on the Haitian peasantry were an indication of the limits of free labour in reconstituting an adequate substitute for the old plantation labour force.

The abolition of the British slave trade conforms even more poorly to the Roman/Russian paradigm. In terms of compensatory labour, the post–abolition recruitment system was hopelessly in arrears of the declining plantation labour population. For more than three decades after 1807, the British planters were faced with a diminishing, less mobile and more expensive workforce. The British colonial system, which accounted for more than half of North Atlantic sugar in 1808, languished helplessly as its share of world production dropped throughout the first half of the nineteenth century (see Table 1.2). Emancipation sharpened the crisis. It took several decades for a large-scale substitute plantation labour system to be established. During the first four decades of the nineteenth century 'imperial Britain exhibited little interest in protecting the productive and exploitative interests of the West India planters'.[4] The belated West Indian turn toward indentured servants from the East was undertaken primarily because of the relative failure of the emancipation experiment as a system of staple production.

The net gainers by this process were the expanding and slave-importing zones of Latin America. On the eve of British abolition Britain's biggest new frontier colonies were importing more slaves than booming Cuba.[5] Following the opening of the indentured labour market to Britain's ex-slave colonies, more than three-quarters of the new labour flow to the world's tropical areas went to the British frontier colonies which had hitherto been restricted from importing slaves.[6] By the 1860s the British sugar colonies had recovered their overall pre-emancipation level of production but never again did they approach their early nineteenth-century share of world production. In terms of the Roman/Russian precedent the system was neither offered to the planters in exchange for slave-trade abolition nor adopted by the imperial government in time to prevent large sections of the planter class from succumbing to the economic pressures generated by emancipation itself.

To address the distribution of costs and benefits of British abolition fully one would have to deal with short- and longer-run impacts on a truly global scale. The peoples of Africa, Europe, Asia and the Americas would all enter into the equation.[7] Seeking to confine the question to manageable proportions we will look at the impact of British abolitionism on the metropolitan masses who agitated for the general principle, if by no means the actual consequences, of the abolition of the African slave trade and emancipation.

One must begin by emphasizing that a damage-control perspective was certainly operative in British abolition. The slave merchants and planters by no means paid the full price of antislavery. On the contrary the popular demands for abolition and emancipation were converted by Parliament into a heavy burden for British metropolitan subjects and West Indian labourers.[8] Metropolitans paid a heavier price than the inhabitants of all other European nations to destroy the system voluntarily. The financial burdens of abolition were many times greater for the British than for mainland taxpayers. The British compensation of £20 million to the slave-owners was equal to 40 per cent of British revenue in 1833.[9] The radical working-class press noted that the compensation clause cost the taxpayer almost three times the annual outlay for the English poor.[10] The much more leisurely Dutch emancipation, after 30 years more of slave labour, was only half as burdensome in terms of metropolitan annual revenues. Compared to the French, the British were also tampering with a sector of their economy which was more than twice as valuable to them as France's slave colonies to their metropolis at the time of their respective emancipations (see Figure 7.1).[11]

Beside the once-and-for-all cost of compensation, the policy of British pressure on other powers after 1808 and the naval patrols on the African coast entailed another loss. For long periods when other states still connived at slave trading, the British squadron attempted to reduce the flow of slaves into the non-British Americas. The British were probably responsible for intercepting ten times as many slaves *en route* as the Americans and the French combined. These expenses added another 50 per cent to the abolition bill. According to David Eltis the resources which the British expended on suppressing the traffic after abolition were probably almost equal to the total profits accrued from the trade before abolition.[12] The British consumer also paid an added price in reduced consumption as the cost of sustaining the West Indian sugar economy for more than a decade after the emancipation of the slaves.

The most interesting vision of compensatory abolition is an indirect version of the traditional perspective. In this paradigm, the hegemonic class interest is identified not as that of colonial but of metropolitan capitalism. David Davis carefully elaborates this theme in the second volume of his projected trilogy on Western slavery. No direct analogy is drawn between the fate of Euro-American labour and the earlier Roman and Russian peasantries. There was no legislative trend in Britain between 1780 and 1840 towards diminishing labour mobility, or increasing the labourer's legal liability to penal servitude or personal dependency. On the contrary, in Britain, as in Western Europe generally, the remnants of personal bondage clearly diminished during the age of British abolitionism.

However, the very success of abolitionism as a colonial reform is reinterpreted by Davis as an example of capitalist hegemony. It

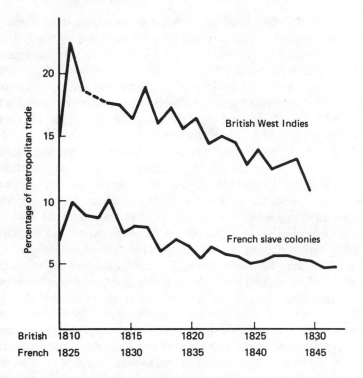

FIGURE 7.1 *Trade of the slave colonies of Britain* and France in the generation before their respective emancipations, as a percentage of the total trade (including re-exports) of each*

* This does not include the British trade with colonies using slave labour in the Eastern hemisphere. The value of the trade of the Cape Colony and Ceylon might theoretically be added to the British figure.

SOURCES For the British system: B. R. Mitchell and P. Deane, *Abstract of British Historical Statistics* (Cambridge, 1962), pp. 309–11; *Parliamentary Papers* 1831–2, vol. 20; for the French system: *Statistique de la France*, Imprimerie royale, 1835–47 (tables of colonial commerce).

putatively operated not to open the way to a freer or more egalitarian society, but to diminish sensitivity towards increasing metropolitan class domination and exploitation. Can one test the thesis that antislavery, at least before 1833, 're-inforced or legitimized' hegemony?[13]

To begin with, was there a hegemonic convergence of the imperial 'ruling class', or even of its metropolitan components, over slavery which one could identify as an exercise in social control? What we know of the pattern of hierarchical opposition points in precisely the opposite direction. If one can formulate any empirical generalization about the British élite's relation to abolitionism from 1788 to 1833 it is that the higher the social level the deeper was the opposition to abolition. For almost 20 years the monarch opposed abolition. One prince, later also a king, was identified with the West Indies from the time of his royal visit to the islands in 1787.[14]

Only one rung lower, the great landowners represented in the House of Lords were always less inclined to vote for abolitionist measures than the Commons. In 1788 the Lords almost defeated the first minimal slave-trade regulation. For years after 1792 they delayed action on the Commons' resolution. In 1794 they shunted aside the Commons' foreign slave-trade bill; in 1799 they defeated the Commons' bill to restrict the coastal area of the African slave trade. As late as 1833, they held out for higher compensation for the slave-owners. In every session where both Lords and Commons voted on a major abolitionist measure the proportion of peers against abolition was higher than the opposition in the Commons. Similarly, if one compares the abolition/opposition petition ratios to the voting ratios in the lower House the ruling class as represented in the Commons was more hesitant to proceed than the mobilized country at large.

As for the entrepreneurial capitalists themselves, it is not clear from the existing evidence whether they disproportionately supported or opposed abolitionism. Merchants, manufacturers and tradesmen represented about the same proportion of nonconformity as they did of the whole society during the age of abolition.[15] At a more microcivic if atypical level, Manchester's two extant petitions to the House of Lords in 1806 show that entrepreneurs were divided over the slave trade with a majority of traceable entrepreneurial signers in favour of abolition.[16] There is a dearth of even impressionistic evidence that capitalists were, like some High Tories, notable abstainers from abolitionist petitions. Given the ratio of abolitionist to antiabolitionist adhesions, it is as difficult to accept the proposition that entrepreneurs as a class, 'for the most part detested abolitionists', as to see any basis for the assumption that a hegemonic coalition of British capitalists and rulers underlay the abolitionist process in the generations after 1788.[17]

If abolitionism was not the initiative of a limited ruling class, was it a response to an otherwise sharpening general crisis of authority, a mode of channeling discontents generated from below that threatened the hierarchical order?[18] Here the timing of the abolitionist breakthrough would seem to indicate that it did not emerge in order to preempt a mounting crisis in the British political or industrial order. It became a national movement at what must have been one of the most benign conjunctures in British history between the end of the Seven Years' War and the Crystal Palace Exposition almost a century later.

From most perspectives the late 1780s were a halcyon moment. By 1787 the rapid recovery of the economy from the effects of the American war struck contemporaries as nothing short of miraculous.[19] Overseas trade was flourishing on every horizon including the Atlantic slave system.[20] From Russia to the East Indies trade was expanding. At the turn of 1787–8 the newspapers were happily announcing record flows of goods through customs.[21] Across the Atlantic Britain was clearly holding on to the lion's share of the foreign trade of her old colonies. In agriculture, from Cornwall to Aberdeen, the harvest of 1787 was the best in the memory of man.[22] In the industrial sector the press was exulting over Britain's lead in technology, entrepreneurs and skilled artisans. Bank stocks were rising steadily.[23] A Royal Family visit to the mammoth new Whitbread brewery in the summer of 1787 was reported nationwide as testimony to Britain's benign attitude towards industrial innovation. The British cotton industry was expanding at a rate never equalled before or after and in Northern England real wages were rising.[24]

Diplomatically, Britain's international ascendancy had rebounded almost as completely as her trade. Looking westwards, the newspapers in 1787 carried condescending stories about the tribulations of the new transatlantic republic, divided internally and humililated by North African corsairs on the high seas. It was difficult for British correspondents to resist drawing attention to the routine enslavement of independent Americans, while the head of an Algerian sea captain was on display in Algiers because he had dared to seize a British vessel. British newspapers brimmed with equal satisfaction over the condition of their erstwhile rival France, just four years after the Peace of 1783. The French had become booming trading partners of the British while their government foundered on the brink of bankruptcy and receded as a credible military threat. The Dutch were deeply embroiled in civil conflict at home and economically distressed in the West Indies.[25]

Within Britain confrontation was at an ebb. Popular rioting, that barometer of social discontent, hovered at a low point. The Home Office papers for the late 1780s reveal only sporadic outbreaks of violence. There were none which even faintly resembled London's Gordon Riots of 1780 or the politically linked agitation which was to frighten the authorities only a few years later.[26] After years of deep worry, the national deficit had been brought under control by the younger Pitt. The post-war struggle between Pitt and Fox had subsided in both victory for Pitt and a clear subsidence of partisan politics.[27] The Royal Addresses of 1787 and 1788 passed through Parliament without a division. As already indicated, religious conflict was muted while popular religious mobilization was flowing through the explicitly undenominational channel of the Sunday-school movement. Even Ireland was affording British ministers a moment of tranquillity amidst all its late eighteenth-century turbulence. The newspapers of 1787–8 were awash with national euphoria.[28]

Without trying it mechanically to the business cycle, abolitionism may be classified at its origin as a 'fair-weather' movement, taking advantage of sustained prosperity and a socially harmonious landscape to achieve its relatively swift addition to the agenda of the unreformed Parliament. Until close to emancipation, it remained a movement for good seasons, thriving in relative prosperity and waning in periods or areas of deep economic and social crisis.

One might pursue further difficulties entailed in the capitalist-hegemonic paradigm. Elsewhere I have analysed it with special reference to the climactic period just before emancipation.[29] Here I would like to suggest an alternative framework. Seeds of conflict were, as always, latent in this burgeoning of economic activity. If 1788–91 was not a period of industrial crisis, the political situation clearly provided the basis for group pride and self-assertion, for a wide variety of political radicalisms, for nonconformist moves towards equality and for abolitionist extensions of libertarian values to domestic demands.[30] In the midst of Britain's great interwar boom and the French Revolution, abolitionism became entwined with more general assertions of human rights and with the diffuse movements to make England a more equal society.

Even for Thomas Clarkson, abolitionism did not function as a channeling instrument of the ruling class in resisting egalitarian demands. As he made his rounds through England in 1791 he freely expressed his belief in the identity of the aims of abolitionism and the French Revolution.[31] In the early 1790s abolitionism stimulated innumerable ideological challenges to the image of British society as a perfected instrument of human organization.

The mobilization of 1792 made it abundantly clear that even the generally apolitical Methodist flock was drawing sustenance from the stimulus of general reformist agitation and from the French Revolution across the Channel. Its most widely-publicized call for abolition signatures was written by Salford Methodist Samuel Bradburn. Riding the wave of artisan radicalism in the North, Bradburn took as his motto, *vox populi*. From his pulpit he demanded *unbounded liberty* founded upon the *Rights of Man*. His call to action was not at all illustrative of a sense of disillusionment and powerlessness in the dissenting public. On the contrary it exemplified, if anything, an overoptimistic assessment of the power of mass petitioning and the sugar boycott in the spring time of 1792.

Bradburn's appeal to the Methodists to join with their neighbours on behalf of the abolition campaign brimmed with italicized social compact metaphors and democratic radicalism. He referred not to suppliant Africans but to 'our *fellow-subjects*, the negroes'. Abolition was not charity at a distance but a preemptive strike against the aristocracy at home. 'The same usurping power' which made slaves of blacks 'might try to enslave you and your posterity'. The line was dissolved. The British empire was one *'large society'* and the flock had to use every legal means including petitioning and abstention from sugar. Against counsels of caution Bradburn called in the French Revolution: 'If *moderate men* had been attended to in France, that infernal mansion the Bastille had still remained.'[32]

Neither Bradburn nor his flock were Bastille stormers in 1792. They bent before the governmental reaction which began to consolidate within weeks of the abolitionist victory in the Commons in April 1792. But the evidence was already abundant that abolitionism was not a theatrical or ceremonial catharsis being played out by Parliamentary or evangelical hegemons for the distraction of the masses.

From the very outset, abolition was a double-edged sword confronting the authorities of the metropolis. On the one hand its petitions affirmed the metropolitan experience, British civil liberty, and the Constitution, Christianity, European mores and customs, and more occasionally, the market economy and free labour. There is no reason to doubt that on this general level the subscribers 'endorsed' their society. On the other hand abolitionism demonstrably heightened the sense of national shortcomings, and the possibility of actively changing those defects. It articulated ideals which were as fundamental to Paine's *Rights of Man* as Bradburn's address on the slave trade.

The relationship of abolitionism to politico-economic cycles in

Britain seems to sustain the hypothesis that mass abolitionism was activated in periods of relative prosperity and declined or was even suspended at moments of deepest economic or political crisis. The second abolitionist wave of 1791–2 was terminated by the counter–mobilization against radical reform and France.[33] The more limited abolitionist mobilization of 1806 again occurred early in a new cycle of radicalism which lasted until after the passage of the abolition of the slave trade in 1807. The fourth abolitionist mobilizaion in 1814 came in the brief interlude of British prosperity between the crumbling of the Continental system and the onset of the post-war cycle of depression, mass discontent and governmental repression.[34] There was as little appeal to popular abolitionism in the years from the Hampden clubs to Peterloo as there had been in the anti-Jacobin crusade of the later 1790s. For four decades after 1788 mass abolitionism was not quite the stalking horse of revolution envisioned by conservatives. It was, however, the crocus of reform movements. Its periodicity therefore indicates that abolitionism was a harbinger or catalyst of other popular mobilizations, rather than a deflector of social conflict.

With the final two campaigns of 1830–1 and 1832–3 there was a shift in the relationship between abolitionist mobilization and the social reform cycle. While abolitionism appeared to be stronger than ever in its climactic moments of maximum mobilization, it was bidding for support within increasingly polarized as well as politicized constituencies. Emancipation in 1833, unlike abolition of the slave trade in 1806–7, came only *after* a restructuring of the distribution of metropolitan religious and political privilege. In the political arena, repeal of the Test and Corporation Acts, Catholic Emancipation and Parliamentary reform all preceded slave emancipation. The abolitionist petition campaign of 1830–1 was itself displaced by the political reform crisis of 1831.[35] The mass petitions of 1830–1 and 1832–3 did not occur during the worst points in British economic cycles, but it would be difficult to describe them as coinciding with moments of confident prosperity such as 1787–8, 1791–92, or 1814.

On the contrary, the campaign of 1830–1 triggered a fundamental ideological challenge to abolitionism's social justice credentials in its very core. The mass factory movement of Yorkshire arose directly out of a sharp division over factory reform among abolitionists. The final petition campaign and, even more clearly, the passage of the Act of 1833 intensified this ideological challenge. Abolitionism retained its cross-class and cross-denominational constituency through emancipation, but under increasing cross-pressures from competing social mobilizations.[36] In other words the heightened multi-class mobilization of antislavery proceeded coincidentally with an intensified class mobilization.

One may illustrate this point by considering the relationship between political reform, slave emancipation, and factory child labour at the end of the age of abolition. The struggle for Parliamentary reform between 1830 and 1832 had mobilized large numbers of the working class and left many with an even sharper sense of exclusion from the political process. At the same time, as the class lines sharpened after 1830, the factory operatives found allies among strong abolitionists willing to transfer the ideology of antislavery from the abolitionist to the factory movement.[37] If old radical campaigners who attempted to force working-class grievances into abolitionist rallies were ruled out of order, abolitionist spokesmen in Yorkshire were attracted, for the first time, into a popular movement against factory child labour. The interweaving of the rhetoric of the two campaigns has been detailed elsewhere.[38] The important point is that antislavery was being used as the ideological point of departure for a sustained demand of factory workers in the old abolitionist heartland.

The burgeoning working-class press and leadership of the early 1830s was also more divided in its approach to antislavery than the older radical press.[39] Before the end of the Napoleonic wars William Cobbett stood virtually alone in his denunciation of the 'negrophile' hypocrisy of British abolitionism. By 1830 London working-class radicals, distant from both the deep abolitionist traditions of the industrial North and the social realignment of the Factory Movement, tended to treat abolitionism in the old Cobbett style, as a diversion from the real miseries of white slaves at home in favour of remote and even comfortable colonial slaves abroad.[40]

In the North, however, antislavery did not lose its popular base. William Cobbet himself had to cross over into abolitionism as the campaign for emancipation entered its final phase. Cobbett, who for 30 polemical years had opposed every abolitionist initiative,[41] finally pledged himself to immediate emancipation when he ran for Manchester's new seat in Parliament in 1832. He did so only in explicit deference to his working- and middle-class constituents, refusing to withdraw from his assessment of the comparative comfort of black slaves and British workers. He still only wished to God that 'all working people were as well fed, as lightly worked and . . . as civilly treated as the negro slaves. But it is the general wish of the people in these great towns of the north that the slaves should be totally emancipated; and I am for no half emancipation.' Cobbett concluded his pledge with a touch of a Freudian slip: 'if any one will bring forward a motion for the total and complete abolition of the slaves at once, I would be for that measure'.[42]

Cobbett repeated his pledge to Manchester even after he knew that he was already likely to win an alternative seat at Oldham.[43] At Oldham itself he won with the important backing of the antislavery society. An occupational breakdown of the Oldham vote confirms the global evidence of differential class support for both radicalism and antislavery. If emancipation was a triumph of capitalist hegemony the Oldham cotton capitalists had no share in it; either that or in Oldham the role of industrial capitalism in emancipation proved to be among the best examples yet unearthed of a truly invisible hand. Only one out of seven cotton manufacturers voted exclusively for either antislavery candidate. Whether it was because the Oldham antislavery candidates were too radical or too abolitionist the cotton manufacturers gave their votes to neither of the contenders supported by the antislavery society. On the opposite side were the shoemakers, weavers and retail traders, who cast between 95 and 100 per cent of their votes for the radical/antislavery candidates. The cotton spinners seem to have occupied an intermediate position. They voted slightly *higher* than average for the non-abolitionist candidates. Either they were less radical, or less antislavery (or more deferential to the manufacturers), than Oldham's weavers and shoemakers. If the Oldham figures are too localized to be considered representative of support for antislavery, they further indicate persistence in the social base of abolitionism. And while retailers were also below average in voting for the candidates opposed by the abolitionists, they were still three times as likely to vote for them as were the weavers. Like the Methodist figures, the pattern at Oldham indicates that the Northern artisanal constituency of abolitionism remained extremely loyal.[44]

The West Riding of Yorkshire's indigenous radical working-class newspaper shows the same pattern despite the sharpening social divisions in the region. The *Voice of the West Riding* gave full coverage to the mass factory movement of 1833 featuring hatbands and banners proclaiming 'No white slavery'. It provided its readers with a delightful description of an antislavery delegate returning from London in June 1833 to be boycotted by his chapel and Sunday-school scholars over his hostility to working-class demands. Yet the *Voice of the West Riding* simultaneously aligned itself with the drive to destroy the 'monster' 3000 miles off. It proudly recounted the history of Yorkshire's popular antislavery mobilization, and drew attention to the more than one million signatures against slavery in 1833. It predicted that legislative inaction 'even on this point alone' would lead to the newly-reformed House being swept out of office. Of all questions, this one entailed 'the greatest results to humanity'.[45]

The electoral, petition and ideological evidence all indicate that the worker component of abolitionism held fast in its old industrial heartland. But it was clearly operating under a new set of pressures. One bit of evidence of both the new social context and its impact on abolitionism may be found in the open effort by the antislavery movement to adjust its propaganda to growing working-class interest in factory reform. The most widely distributed antislavery tract of the final campaign of 1833 was Henry Whitely's *Three Months in Jamaica, in 1832*. No less than 200 000 copies were distributed in two weeks. Extensive excerpts were published in newspapers and read aloud at public meetings. Whitely was a colleague of Richard Oastler, veteran abolitionist and the 'Clarkson' of the Factory Movement in Yorkshire and Lancashire. Whitely's credentials as a Methodist member of the Central Committee of the Factory Movement in Leeds and his personal ties to Oastler were both prominently included in his publication. Thomas Buxton led off a great antislavery rally at Exeter Hall by referring to Whitely's endorsement by the Factory Movement leadership. Most significantly, *Three Months in Jamaica* ended with a joint plea for slave emancipation and factory reform.[46]

For the antislavery movement this represented a striking change of policy. For 50 years abolitionist leaders had carefully preserved their autonomy from political parties and other social movements. As the most consensual cross-class and cross-denominational movement in England, and as the most successful from the late 1780s to the mid-1820s, this strategy made good political sense. By 1832, however, the terms of the 'movement' trade were clearly shifting. Some incorporation and recognition of the planter-factory analogy was becoming necessary to avert a major loss of abolition's social base. It was becoming as difficult for the movement to tack between the polarized currents of class as of religious and political conflict.

How is one to measure the impact of the contemporary denunciations of abolitionism as a class-based political displacement (now reconceptualized by historians as a psychological displacement of reforming energies)? At the level of popular mobilization neither the calls for rejection of the movement by most of the radical working-class press of London nor the more sympathetic perspective of Robert Owen in *The Crisis* appear to have played an important role in the national campaigns of 1832–3. Only two antislavery meetings were interrupted in the name of working-class demands: one was repudiated by the workers in whose name the intervention was made, and the other was overborne by a meeting of the Political Union whose member had initiated the disruption.[47]

There was, of course, a more subtle tactic available to antiabolitionists than outright repudiation. In towns with large working-class populations those hostile to the 'diversionary' influence of emancipation petitions were free to move amendments at popular antislavery meetings, demanding equal action on behalf of wage slaves or of factory children. A Tory newspaper in Leicester claimed that such a possibility had foreclosed a public petition meeting in that town. The technique of fusion was actually employed by the 844 petitioners of Bowling, Yorkshire, during the campaign of 1833. Bowling's petition affirmed that no one had a right to hold another in bondage because of a black skin, 'nor to constrain him to labour without a just and equitable remuneration, whether he be white or black'. But if the petitioners were ashamed to think that 'the hated name of Slave should ever be heard', they were still more ashamed to

> know that in these manufacturing districts where they live, a system of Infant Slavery prevails . . . and Your Petitioners believe that the conduct of many persons in the manufacturing districts who have professed a mortal hatred to black Slavery, but have winked at, and in some cases enriched themselves by white Slavery, has been very disastrous to the interests of the anti-Slavery cause in these parts, and to the cause of Christianity too, especially when such persons have made high-sounding professions of religion.[48]

The Bowling Petitioners therefore prayed that 'charity may begin at home' and that the first Reform Parliament should distinguish itself by passing both an effective 'Ten Hours Bill and the eternal abolition of British Colonial Slavery'. That the Bowling antislavery petition coincided with the first great wave of petitions to restrict child labour in factories was clear evidence of a new note of class impatience,[49] but the fact that Bowling's 'linked' petition had no recorded imitators among the more than 5000 antislavery petitions presented in the same year indicates this novel formulation of anti-abolitionism was exceptional.

The stress of the factory movement was only one source of pressure. The final emancipation formula worked out by the government was a greater tax on abolitionist unity than the factory movement. Instead of 'immediate' emancipation, the country was confronted with a six-year intermediary stage and huge liquidation costs. The petitioners had not been led to expect either. If the abolitionist élite was most disturbed by the length of apprenticeship, the radical press was clearly more outraged by the size of the bill. Denunciations of the antislavery 'humbug', which had been muted during the height of the mass petition campaign, were now intensified by the 'swindle' of 'English tax-ridden slaves'. Cobbett, true to his pledge, had supported emancipation solely on the grounds of the wishes of his Oldham supporters, maintaining all the while that the slaves were better fed than his constituents. With the introduction of compensation he could return to his more comfortable role of abolition baiting: 'When the 187,000 females were signing their pretty names, they little thought that they were petitioning to have the bread taken from the mouths of their children!'[50]

There was clearly a crisis of confidence, even in antislavery's Northern heartland. Since compensation alone assured passage of the Bill through the House of Lords, the Parliamentary abolitionists made no attempt to launch community-wide protests against the monetary terms of the Act. The *Voice of the West Riding* now taunted that an anticompensation petition meeting was held at a 'hole-and-corner' Wesleyan chapel for fear of unleashing the full backlash of public indignation against the terms assented to by the Parliamentary abolitionists.[51] A special canvass was necessary among the Methodist poor to keep them from deserting the abolitionist ranks. In Oldham 6000 inhabitants, petitioning for the ballot just as the Emancipation Bill moved through Parliament, were incensed enough to tag a denunciation of West Indian compensation on to their petition.[52]

Popular anger against compensation to planters sometimes spilled over into anger against blacks. London workers, who had fed for 30 years on Cobbett's images of blacks lolling in luxury, did not always draw a sharp line between the lazy white planter and the lazy black slave who worked 'only 55 hours and had everything provided for his comfort (hear, hear . . .)' while 'the mechanic of England procured a bare subsistence by 84 hours hard work'. Such words did not go unchallenged, but they lingered ominously.[53] Lacking a means of measuring the relative influence of radical working-class editors it has been assumed only that they represented a substantial proportion of politicized workers in the early 1830s. At the very minimum one can conclude that class tensions were far more salient in the final pre-emancipation campaign than they had ever been before.

To say that abolitionism reflected class tensions in Britain during the early 1830s is not to say that it succumbed to them. Those with a metropolitan socialist perspective could be quite sympathetic to antislavery. Thus did a reader of Owen's *The Crisis* report the introduction of the Emancipation Bill:

> Well then, Sir, I was in the House of Commons last night, and a glorious scence it was, for all around me seemed to take a most lively interest in the proceedings; placed as I was in the gallery of the Commons, I could obtain a side way view of all the faces there crowded together; one could easily distinguish the friends from the foes of emancipation by their very looks; *Quakers, dissenting preachers, West Indian merchants, grocers*, and *grocers' clerks*, and a few chopsticks (as Cobbett would call them) composed chiefly the heterogeneous mass. The moving nostrils, the parched lips, and snarling expression of some, indicated enough the dread and apprehension of the monied man, whose cash has been as it were squeezed out of the negro's flesh; the thought was painful, but I was amply repaid by the contrast presented by many happy countenances, who seemed actually to breathe a new life, in the fond hope that what was falling from the secretary's [Stanley's] lips would that very night realize their so-long delayed wishes. Had a painter been there, how well he might have portrayed to the life faces beaming with that natural and lively expression, so seldom to be met with, of humanity, benevolence, rectitude of conscience, and disinterested gratitude to providence, for having at last brought on the day when slavery was doomed to be for ever annihilated![54]

Popular antislavery survived a withering drumfire even from radical working-class spokesmen until the end of apprenticeship. At the great Birmingham Chartist rally of 1838, launching the first national petition, the resolution's mover was the working man, Henry Sansum. Sansum began his speech by adverting, amidst cheers, that he had attended Birmingham town hall to 'celebrate the emancipation of the blacks in Jamaica' and now he was joining 'to work out the emancipation of the whites at home'. Two weeks later a correspondent from Birmingham also sought out the same common ground for women. This correspondent ignored Cobbett's taunt that 187 000 ladies of England had petitioned for black freedom in exchange for their children's food. Calling for a petition of 50 000 in favour of universal suffrage, she evoked not the cost of female abolitionism but its potency. The agency of women had 'redeemed the slavery of the negroes . . . and it shall now secure the most glorious and perfect of victories'.[55]

Abolitionism, far from deflecting attention away from metropolitan grievances, delivered a message of long-term popular power. This was not merely a case of what Brian Harrison has called the spur of 'reciprocal rebuke', with one reform constituency storming into action against the misplaced efforts of another.[56] Whatever room or necessity there was at the top of the abolitionist heap for telescopic vision, those who spoke at Birmingham to launch the great Chartist crusade considered it not only reasonable but natural for someone to march from a slave emancipation rally one day to a universal suffrage rally the next. Despite Cobbett's decades of denunciation of abolition as a humbug, despite years of infuriating comparisons of the hours of British workers and Caribbean blacks, despite cries of fraud against the staggering cost of compensation and the postponed liberation of apprenticeship, the pages of the *Northern Star* eloquently reiterated the ability of its audience to distinguish between means and ends.

In this connection we should also consider another complementary linkage between abolition and domestic repression. Davis ascribes the passage of the Poor Law Amendment Act of 1834 to the same political triumph of the middle class that ensured slave emancipation the year before: it was hardly coincidental 'that in 1834 the newly-reformed British Parliament not only transformed West Indian slaves into "apprentices" but enacted a New Poor Law which required British paupers to be incarcerated in workhouses where the regimentation, surveillance, and separation of families would surpass the "social control" of the most notorious West Indian plantations.'[57]

Here one most closely approximates the classic compensatory model of institutional transformation. The linkage is, of course, ideological and indirect. English paupers were not shipped to the West Indies nor offered a choice between the workhouse and colonial apprenticeship. Yet there is no doubt that the New Poor Law was intended to degrade able-bodied paupers with respect to their past treatment in the parish. Before referring emancipation and Poor Law incarceration to a common social milieu, however, one must also consider the narrow limits of such an identification.

The age of popular abolitionism as a whole far more clearly coincides with the late eighteenth-century *expansion* of outdoor relief between 1795 and 1834 (the 'Speenhamland era') than the constriction of relief from the mid-1830s.[58] One might more readily conclude that abolitionism coincided with the apex of outdoor relief under the old Poor Law system. Moreover the Speenhamland system derived from a compounding of local initiatives like the abolitionist petitions of 1788. Although Speenhamland was not a Parliamentary Act, it was openly debated and extensively 'nationalized' at the local level during the 1790s. The New Poor Law was implemented in a distinctively unpopular way. It was investigated and reworked behind closed doors. The Act of 1834 was as close to a closet revolution as any major piece of legislation of the reform era between 1828 and 1835.[59]

Finally, the abolitionist heartland was not the area for which the Poor Law of 1834 was framed. Unlike the geographical overlap and organizational analogue of the factory and antislavery movements, the Poor Law reform was designed for and addressed to agricultural problems. For sound political reasons, the industrial North was the last area into which the new system was introduced, to the accompaniment of massive opposition.

Where emancipation and the New Poor Law had a common ground was not in the apparent parallelism of sugar mill and workhouse, with institutional incarceration, surveillance and legal constraint. The intention of supporters of each reform was to have labour allocated as much as possible through a free market.[60] The two groups, however, were not as congruent as this convergence of market values seems to imply. The underlying aim of the Poor Law in 1834 was not to deter labour but to uproot the able-bodied and to steer them into the labour market. Apprenticeship, on the other hand, was merely a sop to the West Indians against free-labour principles. It was designed temporarily to *halt* the flight of able-bodied labour from the plantation labour market. Even in Parliament on this issue of constraint it was among the abolitionists that both forms of coercion caused more than average opposition.[61] No one has ventured to suggest that enthusiasm for the new workhouse system was greater among the abolitionist poor than among the Parliamentary élite.

From the available evidence it is certainly clear that abolitionists were less supportive of 'incarceration' in both cases. Even if the same 'free labour' ideology legitimized slave emancipation and the degradation of the English pauper other values were obviously also at issue. Finally one must come back to the point that emancipation rather than apprenticeship was the desired popular abolitionist outcome. Otherwise it is impossible to account for the simple fact that the bulk of abolitionists who denounced apprenticeship before emancipation were infuriated by its passage and worked for its repeal almost as soon as it was in place.[62]

Beyond the relationship of the antislavery constituency to other reforms and beneath the cyclical ebb-and-flow of popular support for abolition it may be possible to detect a sea change in British antislavery over time. In part this reflected a basic structural change in the British economy. In its popular base abolitionism rested upon the nexus of the early industrial revolution.[63] By the climax of abolitionism in 1830–3 the transition to the factory was rapidly diluting the earlier artisanal dominance of labour. The demoralization as well as the decline of the handloom weavers from the 1820s was the most dramatic example of the change. Second, the rapid expansion of nonconformity, which had counteracted its tendency to 'rise' with its constituency out of the working class, was also coming to an end in the early 1830s. Both these trends were reflected in denominational schisms which accentuated social differentiation after 1833. The tendency of abolitionism to become increasingly denominational in the campaigns after 1830 therefore coincided with the inclination of the predominantly abolitionist denominations to become increasingly middle class.[64] The domestic expansionism, which had counteracted bourgeoisification, was now converted mainly to the overseas missionary enterprise. The great phase of nonconformist growth in the ex-slave colonies, immediately following emancipation, may be seen as a transference of the earlier stage of religious growth within the metropolis.

With the ending of colonial apprenticeship the age of popular abolition drew to a close. The 'hungry forties' in Britain offered sharp new contrasts. Colonial blacks were experiencing the once-and-for-all advantages of emancipation: reduction of labour for children and women on the plantations, the opportunities for more flexible combinations of wages and nonstaple farming and the generally higher price for labour at the critical periods in the annual cycle.[65] All this took place against the counterpoint of one of the severest metropolitan depressions in 20 years, including sharply rising prices for protected West Indian produce. From 1840–5 British per capita consumption of sugar hit its nineteenth-century low.[66] Despite some genuine distress caused by the sugar shortage, most radical working-class newspapers seem to have been inclined to regard the sugar-duty debate between supporters of free (high-priced) and slave (low-priced) sugar as a relatively minor problem. However, pro-labour MPs now felt freer to reiterate West Indian claims about the superior social condition of their black workers, and working-class editors felt free to publicize such comparisons.[67]

It is not yet clear whether such speeches in Parliament and the enthusiastic missionary reports of rising standards of black leisure, living or autonomy deepened the influence of long-standing claims that blacks in the British colonies lived 'more comfortably' than the British labourer and worked shorter hours than British women and children. William Knibb, the most famous abolitionist missionary in the West Indies, now openly declared that the freedmen were materially better off than British workers, and the government shared his views.[68] With slavery gone the undergrowth of racism may also have had more room to flourish. Carlyle's vitriolic 'Occasional Discourse on the Nigger Question' (1849) was symptomatic of an increasing public receptivity to racial explanations of the causes of reduced West Indian production.[69] On the other hand, we must be wary of attributing resentment over West Indian 'comfort' to a generalized popular racism. We know that American ex-slaves crossing the Atlantic to agitate against Southern slavery were still cordially received by British workers.[70]

What is beyond doubt is that the antislavery movement, which had been able to hold on to its mass base for 50 years after 1788, saw its agitational power wane after the end of Negro apprenticeship. In 1840 the first world anti-slavery convention met in London and as late as the Spring of 1841 a government Bill to diminish the protection of 'free' sugar was defeated, followed shortly by the fall of the government itself.[71] However, sugar protection could not survive the abolition of the Corn Laws. If colonial blacks had been integrated into the imperial free-*labour* zone in 1838 how could one object to their integration into the free-*trade* zone in 1846? Part of the enfranchised middle class split bitterly against the abolitionists. By the end of the 1840s antislavery was the preserve of a more staid nonconformity.[72]

How then does popular abolitionism relate to the development of class in Britain? Abolitionism was born in the flush of early industrialization. It waned with the hardening of class and denominational lines at the end of the decentralized, small-town phase of industrialization. Arising well before the triumph of the mass urban factory, abolitionism was a democratic revolution in a Tocquevillian rather than a classical Marxian sense. Without attacking the proprietary society it set limits to the claims of property in the name of greater equality of social relations and the values of independency. Its popularity depended on a degree of fluidity and a vagueness of class lines between the artisanal workers and the small tradesmen, and an identification of the aristocracy and monopoly capitalists as the privileged enemy. If one takes seriously E. P. Thompson's admonition that conflict creates classes rather than classes creating conflict, it was also a class struggle, if not in the Victorian sense.[73]

Did abolitionism, in responding to capitalist industrialization, remove the focus from evils at home to evils abroad? One might address this question in terms of intellectual history. David Davis relies predominantly on the conservative perspective of a Wilberforce or a James Stephen; Betty Fladeland on the more radical Granville Sharp and Joseph Sturge.[74] Cowper or Blake, Paine or Paley will offer different 'abolitionist' world-views. Using this exemplary approach it is impossible to establish whether British abolitionism after 1786 tended to idealize the hierarchical social order, as Davis maintains, or to generate greater sensitivity and activity against the inequities of industrializing England, as Fladeland concludes. For Davis, radical abolitionists were atypical before 1833. For Anstey, on the other hand, even Wilberforce exhibited the potential for 'a more modern syndrome', and Fladeland easily invokes a list of certified radicals who worked for abolition, and of abolitionists who worked for domestic political social reform.[75]

A more mundane kind of evidence is more revealing of the impact of abolitionist agitation on popular political discourse. Do newspapers, petitions and pamphlets indicate that abolitionism distracted or silenced popular awareness of exploitation and inequality in Britain? I previously attempted to answer this question in the negative for the industrializing North of England during the decade before emancipation.[76] Such an approach can be extended to demonstrate that, except during times when all political expression was curtailed by police power, abolitionism generated powerful radical resonance. The mobilizations of abolitionism inspired other movements for political and social reform. Its victories were never interpreted, except by the most conservative abolitionists, as sacred moments of redemption which were dispensations against further reform.[77]

In the early 1790s one line of reform literature abounded with domestic analogues to the slave trade and slavery. Conscription and flogging in the military, the agricultural poor, debtors, domestic servants, parish apprentices, abused schoolchildren, wives, tenants, animals, the Celtic poor of Scotland and Ireland, the forced emigration of Highlanders, the unrepresentative House of Commons, were all linked to slavery by reformers in public celebrations, pamphlets, speeches, newspapers and subversive handbills. Abolition was intensively drawn into the popular discourse by affirmations about the unity of popular liberties. What was true in the 1790s was equally true in the early 1800s, when popular reformism began to re-emerge. After the victory of abolition in 1807 distressed Englishmen felt free to invoke Parliament's magnanimity toward Africa as evidence that it could also come to the aid of Lancastrians. The instigator of the Spa Fields Riots in 1816 stirred his audience to action with the admonition that they could not allow themselves to be treated like enslaved Africans.[78]

Even at sacred moments of ritualized nationalism, a large abolitionist burr could be placed in the seat of complacency. The most famous instance of this was the popular reaction to the Peace of Paris in 1814. Lord Castlereagh returned from France flushed with the greatest victory in British history. He was then deluged by the greatest wave of petitions in British history against the opening he had granted to the renewal of the slave trade.[79] Victory celebrations throughout Britain were laced with symbolic evocations of African desolation. Castlereagh and Wellington spent the next months attempting to modify the clause of the treaty which had sanctioned the French slave trade. The African slave trade became the only extra-European problem to generate an international declaration at the Congress of Vienna.[80] Five years later, while many journalists were commemorating the triumphs of the 50-year reign of George III, the radical *Black Dwarf* observed that the abolition of 1807, one of the glories of the reign, owed nothing whatever to the deceased king.[81]

Radicals were equally adept at separating men from measures. In the reform press Wilberforce was attacked as a hypocrite for his domestic political positions by frustrated reformers.[82] The *Black Dwarf* insisted, however, that Wilberforce's political record on domestic issues would not keep it from supporting abolitionism, just as it would welcome any West Indian planter's support in advocating Irish reform.[83] One could assemble massive evidence of such distinctions throughout the whole course of British political dialogue.

Whatever else it may have done, abolitionism did not deter radical reformers from domestic social concerns.

Antislavery did not even distract the abolitionists. One must be extremely wary of attributing to emotionally charged symbolic moments any sustained power to displace functional political analysis. Abolitionists were certainly not hypnotized by the revitalizing rituals of victory into ignoring unfinished business. David Davis's extensive discussion of the sanctification of emancipation in August 1834 asserts that although they eventually concluded that 'apprenticeship was as oppressive as slavery' the abolitionists were 'at first dazzled by the radiant reports' from the West Indies.[84] Thomas Fowell Buxton may have been dazzled but others were demonstrably not. In November of 1834 *The Abolitionist* referred to apprenticeship as a 'humbug', designed to defraud the slaves of their freedom.[85] Given that it must have taken at least a month for the first reports on Caribbean emancipation to reach Britain, the honeymoon was at best brief, despite the size and solemnity of the celebration. The representatives of abolitionism outside parliament had disavowed all connection with Apprenticeship from the very outset as a governmental *fait accompli*, avowedly imposed at the insistence of the slave-owners.[86] Among abolitionists, the duration of satisfaction with Apprenticeship may well have been directly proportionate to their original sense of outrage at its imposition and to their general preference for voluntary institutions over those fashioned for administrative social control.

Can one move beyond the illustration of the continuity of radical extensions of antislavery to a more convincing demonstration of a *structural* ideological relationship between abolitionism and a continuous critique of British society? It seems so. From 1788 on, the abolitionist attack on the slave interest elicited a vigorous counter-attack. This counter-attack by one prominent element of British society against another ensured a campaign designating evils at home in defence of evils abroad. The counter-abolitionist propaganda touched on every sore in the British Isles. The most cursory review of the relation of abolitionism to antiabolitionism reveals the former's limits as a mechanism of displacement. The slave interest invoked dreadful examples of the insecurity of English labour, the awful poverty of the Irish, the pathos of the short-lived chimney sweeps, the dangers of the miners, the sale of pauper children, the abuse of apprentices, the · pangs of hunger, the flogging of soldiers, the impressment of seamen, the mortality of Manchester, the uprooted of Scotland, the black beggars and the white debtors of London. The slave interest matched the wrongs of Africa with the wrongs of Britannia. Had they wished to have every social sore catalogued in the newspapers and pamphlets of Britain, the abolitionist leaders could hardly have done better. If they did not learn that lesson the first time they surely must have had some inkling of the pattern by the second or the third.[87]

Each abolitionist assault entailed an inevitable counter-attack. This dialectic relationship was characteristic of the entire abolitionist era. The strategy was not only predictable but increasingly effective as plantation-slave working hours were reduced and protection for slaves increased under metropolitan pressure. Since the standards and values of the metropolis were the usually explicit baseline for transatlantic comparisons, any expansion of abolitionist demands called forth a corresponding escalation of disparaging comparisons with the metropolis. At the climax of emancipation in 1832–3 abolitionist lecturers were pursued by West Indian agents who probed deeply into very specific comparisons between the new industrial order and the old plantations. Both sets of specialists provided workers with food for thought of their own.[88]

The effectiveness of the early West Indian critique was initially diminished by the abolitionist focus on the slave trade. The quantum of routinized violence, death, dislocation and disposal was impossible to match anywhere in contemporary Britain.[89] When the target shifted to settled slave communities, however, the range of disparity was comparatively narrower; but an equally important change was occurring in Britain itself. As we have indicated, at the final stage of popular antislavery abolitionism had increasingly to accommodate demands for domestic reform. These demands were couched as critiques of British society drawn from abolitionism itself. It was therefore not the case that liberation of the slaves was being won at the cost of debasing the metropolitan subject, whether worker, woman or child. Rather the effort to liberate the slave escalated the claims of metropolitan movements. As the West Indian labourer increasingly approached the civil and social condition of his British working-class counterpart, comparisons became more pointed. As abolitionists closed the legal and social gap between metropolitans and colonials the question of material well-being was brought out into ever sharper relief. With the more articulated class consciousness of the early 1830s the intrinsic abolitionist arguments achieved an unprecedented salience and poignancy.

Workers who flocked to hear abolitionist lectures might be aroused by depictions of 'the infamous, inhuman and debasing traffic in human flesh', yet the detailed accounts of the high prices paid by slaves for privileges short of freedom made them reflect on their own condition. On a British worker's wages how could anyone have accumulated the sums saved by West Indian slaves for their manumission? The increasing restrictions on the hours of plantation labour became a rallying point for the short-time and child-labour movements. When the government proposed the Emancipation Bill in 1833 a Leeds newspaper appended an editorial paragraph headlined 'TEN HOURS A DAY'. If that was justice for an adult Negro, why was it not for British children?[90]

The above argument, however, only repeats at a more general ideological level the example-by-example argument which Fladeland and Davis make on the level of individually selected abolitionists. In order to escape from the inherent limitations of such an ideational approach let us review the same question in comparative societal terms. Can one correlate the presence, timing and strength of abolitionism with that of concern with other social problems and with the level of social movement activity in general? Did abolitionism, as one of the first modern social movements, act as a depressant to further social awareness or action? At this point what follows is no more than a presumptive overview of the issue.

In these most general terms the evidence seems to weigh heavily against the hypothesis of abolition as a 'hegemonic depressive' for social control. Looking at Western Europe from 1788 to 1838 one could hardly contend that association for the expansion of civil, political and social rights occurred where antislavery was conspicuously absent. No one, for example, concludes that the French slave emancipation of 1794 diluted or diverted attention from domestic agitation. At the one moment in French history (1847–8) when it appeared as though abolitionism might become rooted in a mass movement it was swept aside in the Revolution of 1848.[91] It could therefore hardly have served a general hegemonic function of displacing a challenge to the metropolitan political or social order. Moreover, since abolitionism was never widely embraced by Continental ruling élites or capitalist proprietary classes, however defined, it could not have served even the more limited class function of guilt aversion, diverting attention from metropolitan inequalities. On the contrary, European mainland antislavery lacked the fundamental prerequisite of any hegemonic displacement function. Without diversion there could be no displacement.

Furthermore, a positive correlation appears in regard to action for social change. In Britain itself, when abolitionists were quiescent, political reformers were being silenced. The parallel rates of abolitionist and total petitions to Parliament are a conspicuous indicator of such synchronization. The movements for the rights of women, of children, of animals, of religious minorities and of workers were conspicuously pioneered in Britain during its age of abolition. Workers gained more opportunity to communicate, demonstrate and even participate in regional and national politics than elsewhere during the first four decades of the century. In France the national movements for women's rights, for limiting child labour, for the legitimation of trade unions, for an organization of workers, and against cruelty to animals appeared later than in their British counterparts. Except during the French Revolution, more workers had the Parliamentary franchise in England than in any Continental metropolis in the age of popular abolition.

The positive correlation appears to hold true regionally as well as nationally. The first mass abolitionist petitions in France came from two of its most highly class-conscious urban centers, Paris and Lyons. Within Britain it was easier to launch a child labour movement in the Northern heartland of abolitionism than elsewhere, as it was easier to organize massive resistance to the New Poor Law and to initiate the mass Chartist movement for universal suffrage. One can pursue the same comparison regionally as between the American North and South. Labour was better organized, political participation was broader, social reform movements were more abundant, and education was more widely diffused where abolitionism was present than where it was absent.[92]

Before one can attribute any social displacement function to abolitionism it would therefore be necessary, either comparatively or counter-factually, to devise some convincing method of testing such a hypothesis. At the very least it is not heuristically very useful to relate abolitionism to industrialization by a few arbitrarily chosen coincidences: the abolition of the slave trade in 1806–7 with the Parliamentary refusal to establish a minimum wage for weavers, or slave emancipation in 1833 with the passage of the New Poor Law Amendment of 1834. This approach never broaches the question of why the British Parliament never sensed the advantage of 'diverting' attention from more obvious domestic British coercion Bills in 1796 by passing slave-trade abolition, or why Napoleon complemented the Eighteenth Brumaire in France by restoring slavery in the French colonies. In fact the whole tradition of abolitionist historiography, which emphasizes élite needs for levers of 'compensatory' popularity, implicitly recognizes that 'public' or 'national' opinion was a structural force to be reckoned with in Britain.[93]

Even in rough outline certain features of the ecology of abolitionism seem obvious. British abolitionism was not a capitalist weed, drawing nutrients from other forms of social consciousness and political action. It was a very hardy perennial of late Georgian political life, flourishing in a climate favourable to other forms of libertarian social contention and political organization.

8 Antislavery and Capitalism

In accounting for the destruction of British slavery it is necessary to emphasize how closely it was embedded in its social and economic world even when it chose to shift or change one element of that world. Without the context of a rising industrial order there would have been no social leverage available to destroy one of the original components of the old order. Yet linking the rise of antislavery to the evolution of capitalism alone leaves us far short of explaining the dynamic of abolitionism. I have taken issue with accounts whose point of departure is a capitalist political domination of antislavery, its socially controlling methods, its ideological hegemony, or its artful transference of one form of social domination into another. I have attempted to change the frame of reference by emphasizing abolitionism's broad social base and the heuristic utility of viewing its history as a power struggle rather than a display of hegemonic symbol manipulation.

However, this hardly does full justice to the historical significance rather than historical conditions of abolitionism. That significance goes beyond one opportunity opened up for democratic agitation by early capitalist industrialization and constricted by its further development. At the beginning the last chapter I mentioned that the expansion of freedom was the central problem to the abolitionists (including the slaves), whereas continuity of labour was the central problem to the planters. Historiographically, it would almost appear as though the planters triumphed in at least one respect. Much of the recent discussion has been grounded in the assumption that continuity of labour was the central concern of both abolitionists and their enemies, indeed of all salient groups, except, perhaps, the slaves.

In discussing the abolitionists, it is assumed that theirs was primarily an ideology of free labour, not of freedom, and that they as well as the planters were obsessed by the problem of staple production and labour discipline.[1] It would not be difficult to demonstrate that many abolitionists, both conservative and radical, were far less certain of the validity of the free-trade or free-labour ideologies in colonial than in metropolitan areas. There is also abundant evidence that abolitionists explicitly rejected the proposition that abolition of the slave trade or emancipation should be contingent upon the maintenance of levels of British or plantation staple exports.[2]

The recent emphasis on the problem of labour for planters and for industrial capitalists in the Atlantic economies has drawn historiography away from the latent anthropological and political roots of hostility to Afro-American slavery. One must recall just how many taboos of British society were violated by the system. The first was the market itself. Thomas Clarkson's first book was significantly an *Essay on the Slavery and Commerce of the Human Species*. His focus was on the corruption of the free market, in metropolitan terms, not the mere existence of forced labour in the colonies.[3] Clarkson, in fact, acknowledged that forced labour, as a criminal punishment, was well within the *ius gentium* of all Europe. Penal labour was not outlawed by British emancipation, the Thirteenth Amendment to the American Constitution or the socialist revolutions of the twentieth century. One must not, however, tease from the *limits* of Clarkson's attack on coercion some presumed preference for 'bureaucratic' over 'feudal' and personal dependence.[4] Bureaucratic authority over labour in Britain was comparatively weak, and weakening, during the period between 1780 and 1840.

It was not the old feudal or paternalistic relationship but the primacy of internal authority within the impersonal constraints of the market which was the decisive frame of reference for Clarkson. Eighteenth-century England had evolved a labour market on a scale unprecedented in history. Abolitionism's propaganda centrepiece in 1792 precisely followed the structure of Clarkson's argument. It focused on the perversion of the metropolitan distinction between human beings as buyers and sellers, and the complete marketability of everything else, including labour power in the Afro-West Indian market. The 'stain' was all the deeper because British capitalists were the largest single polluters of the moral order of the market.[5]

The second violated institution was community itself. The slave trade eradicated villages and devastated regions. Human networks were destroyed. People were uprooted from their lands and sent among strangers as strangers even to one another. Where could the tale of the violently uprooted have had more resonance than in the industrializing North, above all in Manchester, that town of strangers?[6] Third, the institution of the nuclear family, was literally destroyed among the enslaved and never, in the eyes of contemporary Britons, restored in the West Indies. The corruption of this primary human organization remained one of the most enduring indictments against the slave system.[7] Its pollution of sexual and family relationships among both masters and slaves was regarded as an unequivocal evil.

Finally, slavery negated all political institutions which tended to allow the expression of popular grievances and to secure the less from the more powerful. This was what Bradburn meant in assuring his fellow Methodists that the signing of the public petition was a preemptive strike for freedom and equality at home. The same 'usurping' aristocratic power might otherwise try to enslave the signers. Clarkson also emphasized that petition-signing was a demonstration of freedom and power on behalf of those who lacked both.[8]

It was therefore not just the forms of labour control which were at issue. The disparity between metropolitan and colonial norms made the wrongs of Africa seem more nearly the negation of all rights than any other abuse in the empire. The extremity of slavery helped to sharpen the meaning of human rights in a way which a less multiform deviation could not have done.[9] It is possible, as I have indicated, to argue that in referring to the British market, family, community and political institutions, abolitionists diminished attention to domestic inequalities or coercions. It is possible, but very problematic, for British abolitionism flourished in an environment with a thick undergrowth of multiple movements. Its historical role as a pioneer among social movement remains clear. Its role as a hegemonic ideology is, at best, equivocal and based on a narrow range of élite evidence.

One institution of millennial durability was mastered by a collective effort on both sides of the Atlantic. On a planetary scale abolition entailed a global change over more than a century. The decisive groups were neither masters nor slaves. Many were even outsiders by economic status or gender to their own electoral system. In the political process most members of the Parliamentary élite were reacting to, not initiating, change. Viewed over the long run Mill and Tocqueville were more realistic than naive in attributing British emancipation to the power of public opinion, just as Marx was more realistic than naive in ultimately attributing American emancipation to 'ordinary people' rather than to a single hero.[10]

The serial description of successive legislative 'handlings' of opinion will show us only the trees, not the forest. Those who persist in trying abolition to various combinations of commercial interest, hegemonic classes, or successive stages of false consciousness and middle–class sensibility have limited historical understanding rather than compelling a more comprehensive social assay of British abolition. When both the Whiggish-liberal and Marxist versions of progressive historiography were depleted by the brutalities and the bureaucracies of the twentieth century what was eroded was not just our hopes, but our imaginations. Between us and the story of slave emancipations now lie the institutions where coerced labour and racism were carried beyond social death to mass annihilation, since refueled by everyday reports of mass murder, degradation, and indifference to human suffering.

In the closing years of the twentieth century we also remain in the wake of 50 years of anti- and post-colonial scholarship concerning the era of European expansion. In this retrospect antislavery was a legitimizer of imperialism before and after the fact. Viewed across these twentieth-century lesions, British abolition is not merely 'too good to be true',[11] but too true to be good.

The recent historiography of slavery has also evolved within a more general discourse, which tends to devalue not only the abolition of slavery but also the broader 'age of improvement' in which it was historically embedded. There has been a vigorous and stimulating reinterpretation of modern history focusing on the role of economic power and professional élites in constraining the masses. This perspective conceives of modern social change primarily as the invention of new institutions and agents of social control which maintain or perfect domination. Historiographical interpretation veers away from the traditional view of abolition as a movement of liberation and links it with nineteenth-century examples of mass confinement in prisons, workhouses, poorhouses, madhouses and schoolhouses.[12]

A final observation on international context is in order. Three hundred years ago Britain was what she is again, a medium-sized island off the coast of Eurasia. Between then and now she became the centre of a world economy. And just midway upon this imperial passage the people of the empire, free Britons and colonial slaves, secured the destruction of slavery and hastened its demise throughout the world. Those who were part of Britain's Atlantic economy but free of direct economic dependency were the most effective agents in that process. This was not because they were better human beings than their Continental or American counterparts, or braver than the slaves. They happened to be located in the best political position. They, above all, could call a halt to the imperial slave system at the meridian of its expansion.[13] To do this in an age before mass suffrage, the abolitionists had to establish themselves as a structure of opinion, with a weight so unequivocal and so persistent that emancipation came to seem natural, inevitable and irreversible long before its denouement. Before the emergence of such a sea change the duration of slavery had seemed indefinite. Afterwards, its demise seemed only a matter of time. It literally had no future.

Antislavery is most worth studying not because it created a whole new post-exploitative world – no revolution has ever done that – but because it created a new way of viewing and ordering the world. It ultimately excluded one communally sanctioned institution which had uprooted, constrained and abbreviated millions of lives. The great novelty of this process lay in the fact that for the first time in history the non-slave masses, including working men and women, played a direct and decisive role in bringing chattel slavery to an end. In comparative terms this not only set Britain apart from ancient Rome, medieval Western Europe, Renaissance Italy and early modern Russia but, in scale and duration, from nineteenth-century Eurasia as well.

To summarize that story, I deliberately paraphrased the opening passage of Dante's *Divine Comedy*. Attempting to draw attention to the ordinary roots of an extraordinary journey, I have tried to add to the rich interpretative legacy which historians from Clarkson to Anstey and from Williams to Davis have already given us. Antislavery was ultimately a political extension of the daily patterns of everyday life and imagination. Roger Anstey knew that the political and religious aspirations of a people cannot be separated from their economic relations, but he also knew that the economic policies of a people are an extension of their idea of human relations.

Notes and References

1 THE FOUNDATIONS OF SLAVERY AND ANTISLAVERY

1. Roger Anstey, *The Atlantic Slave Trade and British Abolition, 1760–1810* (London, 1975); David Brion Davis, 'An appreciation of Roger Anstey', in Christine Bolt and Seymour Drescher (eds), *Anti-Slavery, Religion, and Reform: Essays in Memory of Roger Anstey* (Folkestone, Kent/Hamden, Conn., 1980), 10–15; Thomas Clarkson, *History of the Rise, Progress and Accomplishment of the Abolition of the African Slave-trade by the British Parliament* (London, 1808); Reginald Coupland, *The British Anti-slavery Movement* (London, 1933). For recent general surveys of antislavery historiography, see R. Anstey, 'The historical debate on the abolition of the British slave trade', in Roger Anstey and P. E. H. Hair, *Liverpool, the African Slave Trade, and Abolition* (Liverpool 1976), 157–66; S. Drescher, 'The Historical Context of British Abolition', in David Richardson (ed.), *Abolition and its Aftermath in the West Indies, I, The Historical Context, 1790–1870* (London, 1985), Chapter 1.
2. E. Williams, *Capitalism and Slavery* (Chapel Hill, 1944; reprinted 1964); C. L. R. James, *The Black Jacobins: Toussaint L'Ouverture and the San Domingo Revolution* (London, 1938); and Franz Hochstetter, *Die wirtschaftlichen und politischen Motive für die Abschaffung des britischen Sklavenhandels im Jahre 1806–07* (Leipzig, 1905).
3. Anstey, *Atlantic Slave Trade*, xx.
4. S. Drescher, *Econocide: British Slavery in the Era of Abolition* (Pittsburgh, 1977); S. H. H. Carrington, 'Econocide – Myth or Reality – The Question of West Indian Decline, 1783–1806', and S. Drescher, 'Econocide, Capitalism and Slavery: A Commentary', *Boletin de Estudios Latinoamericanos y del Caribe*, 36 (June, 1984), 13–67; S. Drescher, 'Paradigms tossed: The Decline Thesis of British Slavery since the Mid-Seventies', in Barbara Solow and Stanley Engerman (eds), *Caribbean Slavery and British Capitalism* (forthcoming).
5. David Brion Davis, *The Problem of Slavery in the Age of Revolution, 1770–1823* (Ithaca, New York, 1975) (hereafter, *Slavery in . . . Revolution*); D. B. Davis, *Slavery and Human Progress* (New York, 1984); Stanley Engerman and David Eltis, 'Economic aspects of the abolition debate', in Bolt and Drescher, (eds), *Anti-Slavery*, 272–93; David Eltis, 'Economic Growth and Coercion: The Ending of the Atlantic Slave Trade' (Mss), 2 vols, esp. 1, Sec. 2 (forthcoming, and kindly sent by the

author). Howard Temperley, 'Capitalism, Slavery and Ideology', *Past and Present*, 75 (May 1977), 94–118; H. Temperley, 'Anti-slavery as cultural imperialism', in Bolt and Drescher (eds), *Anti-Slavery*, 335–50; H. Temperley, 'The Ideology of Antislavery', in D. Eltis and J. Walvin (eds), *The Abolition of the Atlantic Slave Trade: Origins and Effects in Europe, Africa, and the Americas* (Madison, 1981), 21–35; James Walvin, 'The Public Campaign in England against Slavery, 1787–1834', in Eltis and Walvin, *The Abolition*, 63–79; S. Drescher, 'Capitalism and the Decline of Slavery: The British Case in Comparative Perspective', in Vera Rubin and Arthur Tuden (eds), *Comparative Perspectives on Slavery in New World Plantation Societies: Annals of the New York Academy of Sciences*, 292 (1977), 132–142; Thomas Haskell, 'Capitalism and the Origins of Humanitarian Sensibility: Some Analytical Considerations', in *The American Historical Review*, 90, 2 and 3 (April and June 1985), 339–61, and 547–66.

6. On the post-emancipation era, see H. Temperley, *British Antislavery 1833–1870* (London, 1972).

7. See, *inter alia*, Drescher, 'The Historical Context of British Abolition', Part II; Henry A. Gemery and Jan S. Hogendorn (eds), *The Uncommon Market: Essays in the Economic History of the Atlantic Slave Trade* (New York, 1979). On the switch to African slave labour see D. W. Galenson's survey of the literature in *White Servitude in Colonial America: An Economic Analysis* (New York, 1981), 141–68; R. P. Thomas and R. N. Bean, 'The Fishers of Men: The Profits of the Slave Trade', *Journal of Economic History*, 34 (1974), 885–914; H. Gemery and J. Hogendorn, 'The Atlantic Slave Trade: A Tentative Model', *Journal of African History*, 15 (1974), 225. H. Gemery and J. Hogendorn, 'Elasticity of Slave Labor Supply and the Development of Slave Economics in the British Caribbean: The Seventeenth Century Experience', in Rubin and Tuden, eds. *Comparative Perspectives*, 72–84; H. McD. Beckles, 'The Economic Origins of Black Slavery in the British West Indies, 1640–1680: A Tentative Analysis of the Barbados Model', *Journal of Caribbean History*, 16 (1982), 36–56.

8. Eltis, *Economic Growth and Coercion*, ch. 6 (original sequence).

9. See British Library (hereafter BL) Add. Mss 43,845, Sturge Papers, ff. 12–15, John Bright to Joseph Sturge, Rochdale, 1843. Bright deplored all anti-slave trade policy since the outlawing of the slave trade as 'useless' and a 'delusion'. Enquiries into the 'moral condition of every people', in a trading country like Britain, 'seems to me most irrational'. Cobden was less sweeping but condemned the use of force of any kind in furthering action against the slave trade. For Richard Cobden, one needed to help England first. The rest should have 'the crumbs only that fall from the table. But you are giving the entire feast to the Natives of Africa and the people here are in a fair way of starving'. BL Add. Mss 50,131, Sturge Papers, Cobden to Sturge, 15 May 1839.

10. Drescher, Capitalism and the Decline of Slavery' 132–42; S. L. Engerman, 'Slavery and Emancipation in Comparative Perspective: a look at some recent debates' (forthcoming).

11. See, *inter alia*, Paul E. Lovejoy, *Transformations in Slavery: A History*

of Slavery in Africa (Cambridge, 1983); Suzanne Meirs and Igor Kopy-toff, *Slavery in Africa: Historical and Anthropological Perspectives* (Madison, (1977); Eltis and Walvin (eds), *The Abolition* (Part II).

12. Patrick Manning, 'Contours of Slavery and Social Change in Africa', *American Historical Review*, 88, 4 (October 1983), 835–57; Davis Eltis, 'Free and Coerced Transatlantic Migrations: Some Comparisons', ibid., 88, 2 (April 1983), 251–80, Table I. On African, Cuban and Brazilian prices, see Eltis, 'Economic Growth and Coercion', Appendix 6, Figure 1.

13. See Philip D. Curtin, *The Image of Africa: British Ideas and Action, 1780–1850* (Madison, 1964), Chapters 4 and 5. I compared editions of William Guthrie's *A New Geographical, Historical and Commercial Dictionary* (London, 1771, 1779, 1787, 1790, 1795, 1806, 1808, 1819 and 1843). The coverage of Sierra Leone expanded dramatically in the 1795 edition but contracted again by the 1819 edition. Gustavus Vassa (Olaudah Equiano) wrote an early rejoinder to Lord Sydney's use of Sierra Leone as an argument in favour of the African slave trade (*Public Advertiser*, 28 June 1788). In 1791 Clarkson was predicting an African trade through Sierra Leone with 50 000 000 consumers within five years. Salop Record Office, Plymly Diaries, 20 October 1791. Sierra Leone's difficulties soon became a sore point for abolitionists. *The Philanthropist*, a vigorously abolitionist periodical, wrote of Sierra Leone in 1816 that 'Africa had not been energized, and habituated to husbandry' (VI, 297). See also Chapter 6, note 84, below.

14. See the 'prefaces' to the African section of Guthrie's geographies from 1771 to 1819. Guthrie's book was declared to be the most widely read geography of the 1780s. (John Lettsom, *Some Account of the late John Fothergill, M.D.*, (London, 1783), xcii.) My own analysis of space devoted to Africa in British popular geographies between 1680 and 1830 shows very little variation around a low percentage of the total. In France, the African sections of geographical works from the sixteenth to the eighteenth centuries was also limited to between 6 and 8 per cent, and there was no upward trend whatever during the eighteenth century. William B. Cohen, *The French Encounter with Africans: White Response to Blacks 1530–1880* (Bloomington, 1980), 7, 262, 292, perceives a fundamental perceptual continuity about Africa in France. Peter J. Marshall and Gwynn Williams also note the lack of any fundamental change in attitudes towards indigenous Africans before 1800: *The Great Map of Mankind: Perceptions of New Worlds in the Age of Enlightenment* (Cambridge, Mass., 1982), 251.

15. Anthony J. Barker, *The African Link: British Attitudes to the Negro in the Era of the Atlantic Slave Trade, 1550–1807* (London, 1978), Chapter 10.

16. See William Thompson, *An Inquiry into the Principle of the Distribution of Wealth Most Conducive to Human Happiness* (London, 1824, reprinted New York, 1963), 336.

17. On the Atlantic migration, see Eltis, 'Free and Coerced Transatlantic Migrations', 251–6, and 'Economic Growth and Coercion'. Davis, *Slavery and Human Progress*, Chapter 5; and Robert William Fogel, *Without Consent or Contract: The Rise and Fall of American Slavery*, Chapter 1 (kindly sent by the author and forthcoming).

18. Drescher, *Econocide*, 83–4; Ralph Davis, *The Industrial Revolution and British Overseas Trade* (Leicester, 1979), 112–21. As late as 1835, 88 per cent of British raw cotton came from slave-labour areas of the Americas. I estimate the 'slave' share of British cotton by considering all imports of Eurasian and African origin as free. Some of this cotton, designated as from Northern Europe or Africa, might well have derived from slave labour.

19. Drescher, *Econocide*, 78. The *Liverpool Courier*, 22 August 1832, estimated that three-quarters of Britain's coffee, fifteen-sixteenths of its cotton, twenty-two twenty-thirds of its sugar, and thirty-four thirty-fifths of its tobacco were still produced by slaves.

20. Drescher, 'Econocide, Capitalism and Slavery', 56–7, Tables 4 and 5.

21. S. Engerman, 'Contract Labor, Sugar, and Technology in the Nineteenth Century', *Journal of Economic History*, 43, 3 (September 1983), 635–59. Estimate derived from p. 642, Table I, on intercontinental flows of contract labour, 1838–1922.

22. J. R. Ward, 'The Profitability and Viability of British West Indian Plantation Slavery, 1807–1834', unpublished paper given at the University of London, February 1979.

23. William H. McNeill, 'Slavery as a Moral Ambiguity', a review of *Slavery and Human Progress*, in *The Washington Post National Weekly Edition*, 5 November 1984, 34; E. A. Wrigley and R. S. Schofield, *The Population History of England: A Reconstruction* (Cambridge, 1982), 218–21, Table 7.1 and Figure 7.5. Nor can one shift from objective data to a 'subjective' Malthusianism in attempting to explain the great abolitionist watershed of 1760–90. Moreover, see Bernard Bailyn, 'The Challenge of Modern Historiography', *American Historical Review*, 87, 1 (February 1982), 1–24. In the 1770s Scottish and Irish absentee landlords in high office in London were shaping imperial policy based on the fear that their domains would be *depopulated* 'by the extension of settlement in America, threatening their own economic stability' (ibid., 15).

24. In the 1780s capitalists in the Austrian Netherlands attempted to retain their foothold in the slave trade created by the Anglo-French conflict over American Independence. There was also a flow of capital from the same region into the French slave system (Belgian National Archives, Brussels, Archives du Comité du Commerce, 180, no. 2150–3, report concerning the influence of the Peace of 1783 on the commerce of Ostend with the French slave islands and the African coast). The Ostend merchants wanted the Emperor to acquire Tobago, Curacao, or some foothold in Guiana, to be used as a slave entrepôt. See also the reports of Cte Charles de Proli, of Antwerp; the widow of Vanschoor and son, of Brussels; Heries, a merchant of Ostend; Sr Du Roissi's report on the possibilities of entering the West Indian trade; and the report of the 'Comité du 6 fevrier 1783', on permission to ship slaves to the French Windward Islands until August 1786.

Other European merchants were also interested in entering the Atlantic slave system. In 1786, a Tuscan company planned to trade with America and the West Indies from Leghorn, Italy. (*General Advertiser* 17 March 1786). At the end of the same year the King of Sweden chartered a new company of merchants trading to the West Indies via the island of St Bartholomew (*Morning Chronicle*, 2 January 1787) while a new company of Dutch merchants was formed at The Hague for trading with new areas of Africa (*London Chronicle*, 24–7 February 1787). Hanover became a growing centre for the exportation of clothes and lumber to the slave islands (see a letter dated Ostend, 2 July 1787, published in the *London Chronicle*, 11–13 July 1787, and *General Advertiser*, 15 July 1787). The Spanish showed renewed interest in entering the slave trade and the French trade considerably expanded. On the latter see Robert Louis Stein, *The French Slave Trade in the Eighteenth Century* (Madison, 1979), 13–42. Not since the late seventeenth century did there seem to be so many interested newcomers.

The British were also optimistic about enlarged opportunities in the slave system on the eve of the age of abolitionism (Drescher, *Econocide*, Chapters 3, 4). A new enterprise for enlarging the African slave trade was advertised (*Morning Chronicle*, 27 February 1786) the same day that the *Public Advertiser* reminded its readers that almost three million acres remained to be developed on Jamaica. About 48 per cent of the patented lands were still uncultivated in 1790 (*Diary* of 16 February 1790). The late eighteenth century also witnessed a rise in slaving in South–east Asia. It was related to the rising consumption of tea in Europe. See James Francis Warren, *The Sulu Zone 1768–1898* (Singapore, 1981).

25. This point is made by K. G. Davies, *The North Atlantic World in the Seventeenth Century* (Minneapolis, 1974), Chapter 2; Ralph Davis, *The Rise of the Atlantic Economies* (London, 1973), Chapter 8. For the continuity of old and New World slavery, see Charles Verlinden, *The Beginnings of Modern Colonization: Eleven Essays with an Introduction*, transl. Yvone Freccero (Ithaca, New York, 1970), 80–97; Sidney M. Greenfield, 'Plantations, Sugar Cane and Slavery', in Michael Craton (ed.), *Roots and Branches: Current Directions in Slave Studies* (Toronto, 1979), 85–119, and most recently, David Brion Davis, *Slavery and Human Progress* Chapter 4.

26. Elizabeth Fox–Genovese and Eugene D. Genovese, *Fruits of Merchant Capital: Slavery and Bourgeois Property in the Rise and Expansion of Capitalism* (New York, 1983), 12–13. Eugene Genovese exaggerates the parallelism in the evolution of 'seigneurial' Europe and slave–holding America in *The World the Slaveholders Made: Two Essays in Interpretation* (New York, 1969), Pt. I. It is the autonomy of American slaveries, despite the variety of European social systems to which they were attached, which is their striking structural feature. (See Davies, *North Atlantic World*, 109). The shift towards the flexibility of merchant capital in their more recent *Fruits of Merchant Capital* is more attuned to this feature. Their emphasis on the correlation of New World slavery with *pre*-bourgeois European social systems, however, leaves the British case as an outstanding paradox. Why did an already 'bourgeois' English society construct a new colonial slave-labour system *after* 1660 which was larger by 1760 than those of any seigneurial European power?

27. One aspect of this argument has been outlined in S. Drescher, 'Capitalism and abolition: values and forces in Britain, 1783–1814', in Anstey and Hair, *Liverpool, The African Slave Trade*, 167–95. For a discussion

of the moral 'tremors' created by New World slavery, see also David Davis, *The Problem of Slavery in Western Culture* (Ithaca, 1966), Chapter 4. On slavery in South–east Asia, see Anthony Reid (ed.), *Slavery, Bondage and Dependency in Southeast Asia* (St Lucia, Queensland, 1983), 18.

28. Shelby T. McCloy, *The Negro in France* (Lexington, Kentucky, 1961), Chapters 2 and 3. Slavery was certainly legally recognized in sixteenth-century Antwerp. By the beginning of the eighteenth century, however, 'the Slaves which the *Spaniards* bring with them into *Flanders* are Free upon their arrival, as has been adjudged by the Grand Council of State at Mechlin'. (Anthony Hill, *Afer Baptizatus: or, the Negro Turn'd Christian* (London, 1702), 44.) This was the result of 'particular Customs and Provincial Councils'. Every country has to be 'left to the Liberty of its Constitution'. (ibid., 45).

29. Davis, *Slavery and Human Progress*, Chapter 4; Sidney Mintz, *Sweetness and Power* (New York, 1985); Greenfield, 'Plantations, Sugar Cane and Slavery', 85–119; Stuart B. Schwartz 'Indian Labor and New World Plantations: European Demands and Indian Responses in Northeastern Brazil', *American Historical Review*, 83, 1 (February 1978), 43–79; Colin A. Palmer, *Slaves of the White God: Blacks in Mexico, 1570–1650* (Cambridge, Mass., 1976); Richard S. Dunn, *Sugar and Slaves: The Rise of the Planter Class in the English West Indies 1624–1713* (Chapel Hill, 1972); Richard N. Bean and Robert P. Thomas, 'The Adoption of Slave Labor in British America', in Gemery and Hogendorn (eds), *The Uncommon Market*, 381–94. On the flow of black slaves of the New World, see Philip Curtin, *The Atlantic Slave Trade: A Census* (Madison, 1969); and Paul E. Lovejoy's summary of the recent literature, 'The Volume of the Atlantic Slave Trade: a Synthesis', *Journal of African History*, 23, 4 (1982), 473–501. On the use of white bound labour see David W. Galenson, *White Servitude in Colonial America: An Economic Analysis* (Cambridge, 1981); Hilary M. Beckles, 'White Labour in Black Slave Plantation Society and Economy: A Case Study of Indentured Labour in Seventeenth-Century Barbados', PhD dissertation, University of Hull, 1980.

30. Charles Verlinden, *L'esclavage dans l'Europe médiévale*, vol. 1, (Brugge, 1955), I, 814–19; A. C. DE C. M. Saunders, *A Social History of Black Slaves and Freedmen in Portugal 1441–1555* (Cambridge, 1982), Chapter 2. The Spaniards restricted the importation of slaves from North Africa, the Levant and Spain into America for reasons of social control. Joseph de Veitia, *The Spanish Rule of Trade to the West Indies* (London, 1702), 154–5. The Portuguese legislation of 1773, which provided for the emancipation of slaves imported into the metropolis, was an attempt to bring Portugal into alignment with the 'modern states' of Europe *c.* 1770. It belatedly affirmed the Northern European distinction between metropolitan and colonial labour systems. Jose Calvet de Magalhaes, *Historia do Pensamento Economico em Portugal: De Idade-media ao mercantilismo* (Coimbra, 1967), 376–85.

31. See Howell's *State Trials*, 33 vols (London, 1814), 20, no. 548, The Case of James Somersett, 59 and note. In the 1660s the States-General ordered their admirals to sell all captured Mediterranean pirates into

slavery. Cornelius van Bynkershoek, *Quaestionum Juris Publici Libri Duo*, 2 vols, transl. of the 1737 edition by Tenney Frank (Oxford, 1930), 2, 28. In his first work on slavery D. B. Davis referred to, but did not develop, a dichotomy between a Europe 'increasingly devoted to liberty and a mercantilist system based on Negro labor in America' (*Problem of Slavery*, 108). Moreover, his most recent work even more emphatically favours the *continuity* rather than the dissimilarity between early modern Europe and America. Davis draws his dividing line in the history of slavery'

> not so much between Old World and New as between the standards and expections of two eras . . . It is easy to miss the simple fact that Europeans behaved in the Caribbean much as they had behaved in the Mediterranean and the Canary Islands. To the Caribbean and South America, they simply transferred customary patterns of piracy, banditry, plunder, cruelty and ruthless reprisals, along with slavery (*Slavery and Human Progress*, 69–70.)

This sets aside a crucial *discontinuity* in the early modern period between North–western Europe on the one hand, and the circum-Mediterranean world on the other. Slavery and the slave trade simply did not follow the expansion of trade routes to Northern Europe in the fifteenth century. Davis notes that Madeira was an entrepôt where merchants of North–western Europe mingled freely with slave traders (ibid., 63). Yet there is no evidence that slaves moved northwards to England along this route during the late fifteenth century, at a time when England was still recovering from its earlier demographic losses.

The Scottish reduction of their colliers and salters to virtual slavery during the seventeenth century forms an interesting contrast to the general trend in England, the Netherlands and France and shows similarities to the process of second enserfment in Eastern Europe. See 'Slavery in Modern Scotland', *Edinburgh Review* 387(1899), 119–148. Enslavement, however, was exceptional to the norm and Adam Smith considered that a Negro servant, coming to Scotland, was a freeman while there. *Lectures on Jurisprudence*, R. L. Meek *et al.* (eds) (Oxford, 1978), 456, report dated 1766.

32. Dunn, *Sugar and Slaves*, 3–83, and Noel Deerr, *The History of Sugar*, 2 vols (London, 1949–50).

33. Marcel Trudel, *L'Esclavage au Canada Francais: Histoire et conditions de l'esclavage* (Quebec, 1960), 52; McCloy, *The Negro in France*, 44–5. Except for the recruitment of Africans for the galleys, black slaves were initially not allowed in France on grounds that they were freed by French soil. The principle was breached in 1716 when slave–owners coming from the islands with blacks were allowed to retain them. In 1738 this allowance was restricted to three years for training slaves to a trade. No slave was allowed to marry in France. In 1777 special port depots were set aside for black slaves of colonists residing temporarily in France. (McCloy, *The Negro in France*, 47; Cohen, *French Encounter*, 12). Cohen concludes that the comparative lack of similar legislation in

England seems to reveal a less profound level of racial hostility than was the case in France (ibid). The extent to which one should credit the presence or absence of 'slave' legislation in England to racial hostility is debatable. It may simply have been easier for colonials to obtain such legislative action in an absolute monarchy.

34. Charles Leslie, *A New History of Jamaica . . . In Thirteen letters*, etc. (London, 1740), first letter. The shock of slave markets can be traced all through the eighteenth and nineteenth centuries. See, for example, *Lloyd's Evening Post*, 1–3 June 1767, 523; George Pinchard, *Notes on the West Indies*, 3 vols (London, 1806), 2, 216; *Votes and Proceedings of the House of Commons*, (1830–1831), petitions from Canterbury, Swindon, Accrington, Langarren, Oxford and Christchurch, etc. In the famous Somerset case, Counsel Mansfield conjured up the possibility of 'slaves being sold in Britain in open market', (*The Craftsman, or Say's Weekly Journal* no. 720, 16 May 1772). There is one record of 11 blacks being offered for sale in Liverpool, in September 1766. This would seem to indicate that in England's chief slaving port, that exceptional event took place without any local public outcry. Blacks were almost always sold singly or in pairs in Bristol or London. See Peter Fryer, *Staying Power: The History of Black People in Great Britain* (London and Sydney, 1984), 58–64. For the radical Thomas Spence, the great divide between classical antiquity and contemporary Britain was also that in the earlier period great numbers 'were bought and sold like cattle'. *The Important Trial of Thomas Spence on May 27, 1801* (2nd ed., London, 1807), preface, 30. The shame of such sales was embedded in English children's literature even before the second half of the eighteenth century. See John Newbery, *Circle of the Sciences*, 7 vols 1748, 6, 250. In Ireland, the first and most shocking image of colonial slaves was of 'wretches' whom 'fate had doomed to be sold in the common market, like so many herd of black cattle', *Dublin Evening Post*, 17 January 1788. The critical factor in all such reactions was the presumed variance of such practices from everyday metropolitan norms. Generations before the abolitionist propaganda campaigns of the late eighteenth century the wholesale marketing practices of the slave trade were apparently a yardstick of shocking behaviour. When English orphan parish apprentices were brought northwards to Lancashire in large numbers to feed the expanding cotton trade in the early 1770s, the check weavers reflexively compared their plight to that of blacks in the Americas. (A. P. Wadsworth and J. de L. Mann, *The Cotton Trade and Industrial Lancashire 1600–1780* (Manchester 1931, reprinted 1965), 407.) The slave merchants of Liverpool never developed a branch of their African trade to Lancashire in response to the labour shortages of that booming region.

35. James Walvin, *Black and White: The Negro and English Society, 1555–1945* (London, 1973), 8.

36. For the complaints of cavaliers against being sold, and whipped 'at pleasure' in Barbados, see *Diary of Thomas Burton*, esq. John Towhill Ruth (ed), 4 vols (London, 1828), 4, 254–68. Apparently news of the enslavement created a public uproar, ibid., 261. The distaste for the buying and selling 'of our own species as our wealth and possessions' was

reflected in Thomas Tryon's *Friendly Advice to the Gentlemen-Planters of the East and West Indies* (1684), 82.

One superficial analogue to slave trading which did not unduly bother most contemporaries was wife selling. On 27 November 1787 the *York Courant* indignantly denounced the implements of the 'Negro trade' displayed at Liverpool. In the following issue (4 December) the same newspaper amusedly described a wife sale in a local market. The great difference was, of course, the voluntary nature of the exchange: the wife 'was happy to think that she was going to have another Husband, for she well knew who would be the Purchaser. When they came to the Place, Goward [the husband] embraced his wife, and wished her well, upon which she returned the compliment'.

37. Richard Bagwell, *Ireland under the Stuarts and During the Interregnum*, 3 vols (London, 1909–1916, reprinted 1963), 2, 345, and Patrick J. Corish, 'The Cromwellian Conquest, 1649–53' in *A New History of Ireland* (Oxford, 1978), 362–3.

38. Dunn, *Sugar and Slaves*, 335 ff. See also Ira Berlin, 'Time, Space and the Evolution of Afro-American Society on British Mainland North America', *American Historical Review*, 85, 1 (February, 1980), 44–78. On conformity to plantation pressures and the drift away from traditional English political values, see Gary A. Puckrein, *Little England: Plantation Society and Anglo–Barbadian Politics, 1627–1700* (New York, 1984), 85–6. Early in his campaign for blacks in England Granville Sharp emphasized that plantation laws and customs 'must certainly be esteemed as different and *distant* from our own, as the *climate itself*'. See G. Sharp, *A Representation of the . . . Dangerous Tendency of Tolerating Slavery* (London, 1769), 134. Morgan Godwyn drew the same distinction in *Trade preferr'd before Religion and Christ made to give place to Mammon, first preached at Westminster-Abbey, and afterwards in divers Churches* (London, 1685). The slave trade in Java was resigned to those 'remote parts where men may perhaps supposed to act as they please, without control' (p. 3).

39. The one sixteenth-century attempt to restore slavery as a form of labour discipline could not be enforced. See C. S. L. Davies, 'Slavery and Protector Somerset: The Vagrancy Act of 1547', *Economic History Review*, 1–3 (1966), 533–49, esp. 545 ff. In *The Commonwealth of England* (London, 1601), 139, Thomas Smith wrote of scruples against bondage and bondmen: 'This persuasion . . . of Christians, not to make nor keep his brother in Christ servile, bond, and underling for ever unto him, as a beast rather than as a man, [is] . . . engendered through Realmes (not neere to Turkes and Barbarians)'. Note the geographical distinction even within the zone of old world Christianity, described in note 34, above. Early advocates for Britain as a zone of freedom were fully aware of 'local exceptions' in the Scottish mines. See Sharp's *A Representation of the . . . Dangerous Tendency*, 159–60, and his correspondence with Henry Douglas, 15, 21 December 1772, (in York Minster Library, Granville Sharp Letterbook).

40. On liberty as characteristically 'English' throughout the eighteenth century, see, *inter alia*, Herman Moll, *A New System of Geography* (London, 1701), 364; *Geography Epitomised* (Philadelphia and London,

1786), 17; Newbery, *Circle of the Sciences* (London, 1748), 4, 186; *Thesaurus Geographicus* (London, 1695), 6; T. Smollett, *Present State of all Nations* (London, 1768), 2, 164; and Jonathan Carver, *The New Universal Traveller* (London, 1779), 499. The claim was a commonplace in newspapers, letters, poems and sermons. Britons were attuned to casual comparisons like these in a sermon preached at the High Church in Hull in January 1779: 'The wretched, the crouching Slavery of France, of Spain, of Prussia, Germany, Turkey and Morocco, of which an Englishmen cannot speak but with indignation and horror', etc. The 'equal liberty of England' was lodged in each Englishman's breast, and obedience was due first to God, then country, then the law, and finally the King. *The Duty and Character of a National Soldier* (London, 1779), 30, 34. The absence of liberty was the distinguishing characteristic of other societies and continents: 'Nor is mention to be found in the whole annals of Asia, of a people that ever formed a resolution of asserting their rights to liberty' (Carver, *The New Universal Traveller*, introduction to 'Asia'). Slavery was *not* colour-coded in the British pre-abolitionist world. For a scathing description of Caucasian slave trading among Christian Georgians, see W. F. Martyn, *Geographical Magazine*, 1, 70. Even children 'were exposed like beasts to the highest bidder to gratify avarice'. Caucasian women, like African, could be described as 'libidinous', ibid., 73). See also J. Carver, *The Beauties of Nature and Art Displayed in a Tour Throughout the World*, 13 vols (London, 1763–4), 9, 140; and Carver, *New Universal Traveller* 23, 100. Slavery also became ascribed to certain peoples. Polish peasants were almost invariably presented as 'slaves'. See Patrick Gordon, *Geography Anatomized* (London, 1693), 130, ibid. (20th edn, 1754), 134; John Mair, *A Brief Survey of the Terraqueous Globe* (Edinburgh, 1762), 111; ibid. (edn of 1789), 138; *Geography for Youth* (London, 1790), 82; *Geography Epitomised*, 23; *Geography Made Easy for Children* (London, 1793), 83; D. Fenning and J. Collyer (revised by Frederick Hervey), *A New System of Geography*, 2 vols (London, 1785), 2, 57–8; Evan Lloyd, *A Plain System of Geography* (Edinburgh, 1797), 87; Newbery, *Circle of the Sciences*, IV, 142; For the beginning of the century, in addition to Patrick Gordon, see Moll, *A New System of Geography*, 364; Robert Morden, *Geography Rectified* (London, 1688), 71; ibid. (1700), 83; *Thesaurus Geographicus*, 349. For mid-century, see Bowen, *A Complete System of Geography*, 2 vols (London, 1747), 1, 979. Carver, *The Beauties of Nature and Art* 9, 57. 'Abject slavery' was equally characteristic of the Russians *The Manchester Mercury*, 18 February 1772 and *The Public Advertiser*, 4 May 1787. One could skip lightly from white to brown to black slavery in a few couplets of *Geography Epitomised*:

Poland: 'The Jews at two millions are rated and more
              Her Nobles are tyrants – their Slaves are the poor'.

Tartary: 'Her absolute Despots by Slaves are rever'd
              Whose voice like the voice of the Lion is feared.'

Guinea: 'For war crimes, alas! have the Men here we find
Been doomed to be *Slaves* for the rest of mankind!'

41. [Arthur Young] *Political Essays Concerning the Present State of the British Empire* (London, 1772), 20–1. Adam Smith, *Lectures on Jurisprondence*, R. L. Meek *et al.* (eds) (Oxford, 1978), 186–7. The same ratio was accepted in the newspapers at the onset of political abolitionism. See also William Knox, *Three Tracts Respecting Conversion* (London, 1767, 1780), 19–20. In the famous Somerset case, counsel for the master opened his argument with the observation that slavery was widely accepted in three-quarters of the world and sanctioned even in Europe.

42. The early distinction seems clear in Charles Molloy, *De Jure Maritimo et Navali; or, a Treatise of Affairs Maritime and of Commerce*, 3rd edn enlarged (London, 1682), 335–6: 'Though *Slavery* and *Bondage* are now become discontinued in most parts of Christendom, and to that degree, that for the person of a man be he *More* or other *Indian*, a Trover is not maintainable by the laws of *England*; yet there may be a servitude which may amount to a labour or suffering *equal* to that of Captives', etc. To this was appended an explanatory note: 'The English Merchants and others at the *Canaries* do here support this unnatural Custom. So likewise at Virginia and other Plantations.' Note the geographical delineation and the adjective implying its 'unnatural' status. The sea was clearly in Molloy's mind when he spoke of 'our floating and circumstantiated [human] laws' in contrast to the uniformity of laws of natural phenomena (ibid., 428). Alongside an account of the revolt of African slaves in Jamaica, newspaper readers would find an item on 200 European slaves redeemed from North Africa (see *The Public Advertiser*, 25 June 1760). For a report on the enslavement and sale of a Liverpudlian on the Barbary Coast, see the *Gazetteer*, 14 April 1772. On the eve of political abolitionism there were regular accounts of prices demanded for European slaves in North Africa and of the public sale of hundreds of Europeans at a place as near as Belgrade. *London Chronicle* 27–9 July, 29 July–1 August, 1786; *Morning Chronicle*, 1 August 1786). Algerian pirates were cruising as far afield as the West Indies for Americans (*Morning Herald*, 9 August 1786; *Morning Chronicle*, 15 August 1786; *Public Advertiser*, 24 June 1786) and seizing the subjects of the Pope and of the princes of Europe in the Mediterranean (*Morning Herald*, 1 June 1787). Algerian raiders, captured by an English-led force at Madiera, were likewise routinely sold as slaves on that island in 1787 (*Morning Chronicle*, 4 May 1787). A British captain might still be taken into an African town and flogged (Journal of the Commissioners for Trade and Plantations from January 1776–May 1782 (London, 1938), 133). As late as 1830 Russian ships were plying the Caucasian slave trade to Constantinople (*Sheffield Iris*, 19 October 1830).

43. Halley's *Atlas Maritimus and Commercialis* (London, 1728), was a handsomely bound volume with a list of 500 subscribers. Among the sponsors were Sir Robert Walpole, William Pitt, James Oglethorpe, 50

peers and dozens of honorables and esquires, with merchants, booksellers and watchmakers filling out the rank and file. Its tone was generally calm and judicious but the description of Africa began with '"tis the worst peopled of any part of the World great or small'. It ended with the famous line: 'They barter baubles for the Souls of Men' (237). Bartering was the major stress point from the beginning. In 1685 Morgan Godwyn wrote:

'And here, to omit all enquiry into the *Equity* and Right of the first purchase, where *Parents* do sell their *Children, Husbands* their *Wives, Brothers* their *Sisters* . . . I shall not stand to enquire how agreeable to Christianity . . . nor how suitable the pretence of *Trade* and *Commerce* is to that *undergoing* of the *Cross* and of self-*denial*.' See Godwyn, *Trade Preferr'd*, 17, 19. There was a frequent recognition that the slave trade was an 'uncommon' market: 'This trade seems inhuman to those who do not know that these poor people are idolators or Mohammedans', etc. See Jacques Savary, *Le parfait Negociant ou instruction générale pour ce qui regarde le Commerce de toute sorte de Marchandises* (Geneva, 1676), Part 2, Chapter 54, 254–6. See also note 65 below.

44. See Adam Smith, *The Theory of Moral Sentiments* (Oxford, 1976), 206; Josiah Child, *A New Discourse of Trade* (London, 1698), 183; J. Oldmixon, *The British Empire in America* (London, 1708); Patrick Browne, *The Civil and Natural History of Jamaica* (London, 1756), 23; *Public Advertiser*, 12 September 1786. In 1680 Morgan Godwyn referred to the planters as 'degenerated English' in possessions formed, 'as it were, in the dark', freed of scruples and prompted by an avarice equalled only by Holland 'whose religion is also governed by their trade'. Godwyn *The Negro's and Indians Advocate* (London, 1780), 2–3. West Indians refusing to baptize slaves in England were a 'leprosy', 'crossing the seas to Europe' (Godwyn, *Trade Preferr'd*, 3). 'And tho such Practices may seem strange to People in England, yet the same Persons going thither are suddenly changed, so that they make nothing of it.' (Godwyn, *The Negro's*, 13.) Samuel Johnson was especially scathing towards those living beyond the line. After the death of a Jamaican acquaintance he was reported as observing that the man 'would not suffer much by the change, for he was gone to a place where he would find very little difference between either the *climate* or the *inhabitants*' (*Public Advertiser*, 12 September 1786).

45. Roy Porter, *English Society in the Eighteenth Century* (London, 1982), 101, citing Josiah Tucker. See also *Some Observations which may contribute to afford a just idea of the Nature, Importance and Settlement of Our New West–Indian Colonies* (London, 1764), Sec. II, 10–13, describing the English poor as dreading 'adventure' into the West Indies. 'These islands are not the promised land of milk and honey.'

46. Always high on the list of Parliamentary corrupters stood the 'Creoles, who being bred the tyrants of their slavish blacks, may endeavor to reduce the whites to the same condition by an aristocracy' (*Gazetteer*, 2 November 1767.)

47. Alderman Beckford of London, a West Indian grandee, was called 'Alderman sugar-cane' and lampooned in political ballads:

> For B . . . . f . . . d he was chosen May'r,
> A Wight of high Renown,
> To see a slave he could not bear,
> Unless it were his own. (*Public Advertiser*, 18 November 1769)

For a more extended poetic contrast between English liberty, civilization, and beauty with Caribbean heat, avarice and slavery, see *A Poetical Epistle, from the Island of Jamaica* (Kingston, Jamaica, 1776).

48. The French *Encyclopédie* was similarly bifurcated. Alongside unyieldingly antislavery articles on the 'slave trade' and 'slavery', its article on 'Africa' stated: 'It remains for us to speak of another trade which is conducted only in Africa, about which men have not yet blushed . . . We render no judgement here concerning this kind of traffic.' (*Encyclopédie Raisonée*, Geneva edn, 1776–9, I, 598.) The article on 'Nègres (commerce)', vol. 5, xxii, referred to the trade as 'odious', but offered a full apologia, on economic and environmental grounds, two pages later. The last relevant article, 'Zone torride', concluded: 'The very sun seems to tyrannize this world of slaves.'

49. William Playfair, *The Commercial and Political Atlas* (London, 1786), section on Africa, and 31, 65–8, 92. John Hamilton Moore's *New and Complete Collection of Voyages and Travels*, 2 vols (London, 1780), 2, 729–30, described the slave trade as 'a triumph of avarice over the laws of humanity'. The British West Indies were 'almost necessary for the existence of our commerce'. For Carver, *The New Universal Traveller*, 143, the African slave trade was also the 'disgrace of humanity', but Georgia's attempt to exclude slavery was an 'error' corrected by overseas experience (ibid., 607). Malachy Postlethwayt's *Universal Dictionary*. (London, 1774), art. *Africa*, speculated on the possibility of substituting civilization for slavery but finally reflected, 'We must, however, at present take the state of the trade as it stands.' As it stood, it was as good as any in Postlethwayt's *Dictionary*. See also his *National and Private Advantages of the African Trade Considered*, 2nd edn (London, 1772), 4–5.

50. Barker, *The African Link*, 61–4, 162–6, 198.

51. For Godwyn, the African slave market itself was proof of the humanity and intelligence of Africans: 'How should they otherwise be capable of *Trades* and no less Manly employments?' (*The Negro's*, 13). See also Lewis Roberts, *The Merchant's Map of Commerce* (London, 1677), 77. A Century Later, William Frederick Martyn's *The Geographical Magazine*, 2 vols (London, 1785), 664, described the growing African use of credit systems in the slave trade. The inhabitants of Whydah were compared to the Chinese in industry, ingenuity and desire for wealth. Given their illiteracy, they showed a genius for figures beyond that of Europeans. Negroland's Sherbros were generous, friendly, assiduous, and neat (*ibid.*, 659, 680). On the basis of their market behaviour many groups of Africans were accorded admiring recognition. On trading as evidence of African intellectual capacity, see also Richard Morgan Kain, 'Primitivism, The Theory of Equality, and the Idea of Progress in English Anti-Slavery Literature, 1772–1808', PhD dissertation,

University of Chicago, 1934, 31. Liverpudlians were equally ready to testify in this respect. See PRO BT 6/9, Privy Council Hearings on the Slave Trade, f. 266, Examination of James Penny, Liverpool delegate, 6 March 1788; *Leeds Mercury*, 30 October 1830.

52. See Philip D. Curtin, *Economic Change in Pre-colonial Africa: Senegambia in the Era of the Slave Trade* 2 vols (Madison, 1975), 1, Chapter 3.

53. The most sustained argument on racial inferiority appeared in the *Morning Chronicle* by 'Civis' and his opponents. See issues of 5, 23, 27 June, 1, 4 July, 19 August, 19 September 1788. On the biblical arguments, see Davis, *Slavery . . . in Revolution*, Chapter 11.

54. Ibid., 461.

55. Barker, *The African Link*, 157–8. But see Fryer, *Staying Power, passim*, for a differing view.

56. Elizabeth Donnan, *Documents Illustrative of the History of the Slave Trade to America*, 4 vols (Washington, 1930–5), I, 88. (my emphasis).

57. House of Lords Record Office, 6 May 1806, petition of merchants, ship owners and manufacturers of Liverpool in the slave trade, cited in Drescher, *Econocide*, 137–8. For direct linkages of the African trade with the free trade ideology see, *inter alia*, [William Wood] *A Survey of Trade, in Four Parts* (London, 1718), 180–1, 191, 260; John Carey, *An Essay on the State of England in relation to its Trade* (Bristol, 1695), 71, and *The West India Merchant* (London, 1778), 98. See also a copy of Earl Westmoreland's speech against the abolition of the foreign slave trade in May 1806: 'The only positive effect . . . [will be] the prevention, not of the supply of those colonies with Negroes, but of a number of British subjects from employing their capital in a particular way . . . Experience has shown that legislative attempts to circumscribe capital, are generally fruitless. Capital is not of a nature to be hedged in.' (PRO T 70/1585, Westmoreland's speech, 8.)

A Scottish poem of 1697 summed up the early marriage of free trade, free labour and free slave trading as well as any:

> Trade needs no fertile acres for support,
> Wherever Freedom lives it makes its Court,
> And only craves a safe and open Port.

> Free Trade will give, and teach us how to use,
> Instruct us what to take and what refuse,

> To that [new land] the weary labourer may go,
> and gain an easie Wealth in doing so,
> Small use of tiresome labour will be there,
> That Clyme richly rewards a little Care,
> There every Man may choose a pleasant Seat,
> Which *poor Men* will make rich and *rich Men* Great.

Black Slaves like bussie Bees will plant them Canes,
Have juice more sweet than Honey in their Veins.

By Manufactures here the Poor will live,
So they that go and they that stay will thrive
(From a *Poem upon the Undertaking of the Royal Company of
Scotland Trading to Africa and the Indies*, Edinburgh, 1697).

58. Anstey, *Atlantic Slave Trade*, Chapter 9; Davis, *Slavery in . . . Revolution*, Chapter 5.
59. Ibid., 233–54. For the most closely reasoned analysis of this hypothesis
see Thomas L. Haskell, 'Capitalism and the Origins', 339–61. Haskell
argues for a 'threshold' effect of capitalism on 'exceptionally scrupulous
individuals' in 'the particular circumstances' of late eighteenth-century
Anglo-America. However, since the market was rewarding capitalist-
cum-slavery causal perceptions in the tropics throughout the century
before 1790 and the half-century thereafter, it remains unclear to what
extent the argument from the market to antislavery explains the less
exceptional political and social support of abolition. For a description of
Liverpool's three-year revolving credit and discounting system, see
James Wallace, *A General and Descriptive History of . . . the Town of
Liverpool . . . together with . . . its extensive African Trade* (Liverpool,
1794), 232–3. For ordinary people the market presumably cut both ways
in the particular circumstances of late eighteenth–century Anglo-
America. In Jonas Hanway's circle, 'many merchants' held the slave in
contempt (*Distribution, Justice and Mercy*, London, 1781, 133). On the
other hand John Newton had no scruples about beginning his slave
trading career: *Letters* (Edinburgh, 1781), 74, 95.
60. R. Anstey, 'The Volume and Profitability of the British Slave Trade,
1761–1807', in *Race and Slavery in the Western Hemisphere: Quantitative
Studies*, Stanley Engerman and Eugene D. Genovese (eds), (Princeton,
1974), 3–31; R. Anstey, 'The Profitability of the Slave Trade in the
1840's', in Rubin and Tuden, *Comparative Perspectives*, 84–93; and
essays by W. E. Minchinton, David Richardson and Barry Drake in
Anstey and Hair, *Liverpool, The African Slave Trade*.
61. For Dalby Thomas, the only liberty in question for the West Indies was
the traders' and planters' 'full liberty to buy Blacks at the best market
they can', saving the Navigation Act restrictions. *An Historical Account
of the Rise and Growth of the West India Colonies* (London, 1690), 39,
51. On the suggested extension of slave plantations to Africa see [Daniel
Defoe], *A Plan of English Commerce* (London, 1728), 328–37. Planners
for the expansion of trade with Africa saw no difficulty in linking it with
an increase in the slave trade. [M. Postlethwayt] *The African Trade, The
Great Pillar and Support of the Plantation Trade in General* (London,
1745), 40–1.
62. Howard Temperley, 'Capitalism, Slavery and Ideology', 98. The British
were aware that a wage labour market, like that in England, did not

exist in the ancient Mediterranean world. (See *The Morning Chronicle*, 11 June 1788, letter of 'Pliny' against the abolitionists.) Nor was the relative inefficiency of coerced labour a 'discovery' of the end of the eighteenth century. See Chapter 6, note 84.

63. Drescher, 'Capitalism and the Decline of Slavery', 141.

64. Olaudah Equiano, *The Interesting Narrative of the Life of Olaudah Equiano, or Gustavus Vasa, written by himself*, 2 vols (London, 1789); even its victims were not knowledgeable about all aspects of Africa or the slave trade. Vassa maintained that credit was not to be found in Africa. (See the letter of "Gustavus Vassa" in the *Public Advertiser*, 31 March 1788.) Vassa offered this in the belief that cash and barter would be more attractive to British manufacturers in the African trade.

65. Clarkson, *History*, I, 293. As early as the 1660s Richard Baxter unequivocally condemned the slave trade. To

> go as pirates and catch up poor Negros, or people of another land, that never forfeited life or liberty, and to make them slaves and sell them, is one of the worst kinds of theft in the world, and such persons are to be taken as the common enemies of mankind; and they that buy them and use them as beasts for their mere commodity, and betray or destroy, or neglect their souls, are fitter to be called incarnate Devils, than Christians. (*Chapters from a Christian Directory, or a Summ of Practical Theology and Cases of Conscience*, J. Tawney (ed.) (London, 1925), reprint of an edition of 1673)

Baxter's words cut so clearly at the root of plantation slavery that his passage was quoted verbatim in abolitionist propaganda more than a century later. Yet even Baxter, whose position approached a total rejection of the ideological foundation of the capitalist slave trade, followed seventeenth-century form in bowing to the accomplished fact of slavery. A century later *The Present State of the West Indies, including all Possessions* (London, 1778), 11, similarly concluded: 'This [slave] trade, to the disgrace of the age, has so deeply taken root, it is become as necessary to the present state of affairs, and our wants have justified it in a manner so absolute, that it is now almost a ridiculous common-place to cry out against the barbarity and cruelty of it.' In 1780 Edmund Burke considered introducing a measure to mitigate and gradually abolish the slave trade. He abondoned the idea because of his sense of the strength of the slave interest. Robin Furneaux, *William Wilberforce* (London, 1974), 71.

66. David Davis and Robert Fogel have both recently asserted the existence of a general belief, before 1750, that slavery furthered 'progress'. (Davis, *Slavery and Human Progress*, xvi, 5; Fogel, 'Without Consent', Chapter 7.) The belief is inferred from the fact that major civilizations from antiquity to the overseas empires of the eighteenth century tolerated or promoted slavery. One might perhaps draw a historical distinction between modern conceptions of *human* progress on the one hand and pre-enlightenment pragmatic assumptions about requisites of wealth or power for an empire or a religion on the other. Even in the

narrower sense of material progress, British prosperity was never dependent upon British slavery or the slave trade. It 'would have been easier to eliminate British slavery in 1685 than in 1785' (Drescher, *Econocide*, 183). No 'vital national interest', it is true, was endangered by abolition (Davis, *Slavery and Human Progress*, 335, note 121). But some historical paradoxes remain. 'No single trade was crucial to the nations prosperity'. R. P. Thomas and D. N. McClosky, 'Overseas trade and empire 1700–1860', in Roderick Floud and Donald McClosky, *The Economic History of Britain since 1700*, 2 vols (Cambridge, 1981), 1, 87–102, esp. 100. This still brings us no closer to accounting for Britain's beginning the destruction process at the end of the eighteenth rather than the end of the seventeenth century. Nor does it prompt one to ask why Britain completed the process before other states whose systems were far less vital to metropolitan prosperity and even less costly to dismantle.

67. The slave trade offered little ammunition for the ideologists of trade against the aristocratic-warrior ethic. Albert Hirschman, *The Passions and the Interests: Political Arguments for Capitalism before its Triumph* (Princeton, 1977), does not deal with this potentially intriguing example of eighteenth-century capitalism. This is probably because most exponents did not treat the African branch within their general observations on the nature of trade. Even for its most vigorous proponents, like Defoe and Postlethwayt, the slave trade was justified as a means to an approved end and not, as with commerce in general, as a self-evidently good activity. Or it required, as with Savary, a set of rationalizing arguments *sui generis*. Even in its heyday, it was an 'uncommon market'.

When the major political attack on the slave trade got under way, British slavery continued to be located within the orbit of commerce and capitalism, not of agrarian seigneurialism, or 'feudalism': if

> self–interest be the leading motive, as well as the ultimate end of all commercial systems, yet an appearance at least of reciprocal advantage, if not always the reality, is proposed by the contracting parties. In this point, however, as in most others, the Slave Trade has this demerit, by presenting no one benefit to the natives of Africa, in return for all the voilence and miseries it occasions ('Africanus' to the *General Evening Post*, 25–7 October 1787)

See also letters III and IV of 'Africanus' to the *Norwich Mercury* (15, 25, August 1787). Writers rarely evoked 'feudal' rather than 'mercantile' images even of slave–owners. The West Indians were portrayed as entrepreneurs by friends and as speculators and 'slave-driving capitalists' by foes. See William Wilberforce, *A Letter on the Abolition of the Slave Trade* (London, 1807), 41, 177, 191, 288, and *Bell's Weekly Messenger*, 4 January 1808, clipping in Friends House Library, Box H.

68. Nicholas Rogers, 'London politics from Walpole to Pitt: patriotism and independency in an era of commercial imperialism, 1738–63', PhD thesis, University of Toronto, 1974, 508–9, quoted by Robert W. Malcolmson, *Life and Labour in England 1700–1780* (Hutchinson, 1981), 132, and Peter Fryer, *Staying Power*, 206.

69. On the *ius gentium*, see Hargrave's speech, Howell's *State Trials*, 20, no. 25. Locke is often cited in evidence of a modern philosophical defence of slavery as late as the end of the seventeenth century. Locke's characterization of enslavement as private war perpetuated is set alongside his provision for slavery in the Constitution of Carolina and his participation in the African trade. Locke also clearly accepted both the fact and the legitimacy of English West Indian slavery. What is not clear is how such facts could be integrated into his political theory. Englishmen had no way of knowing whether their purchased Africans had, by their *own fault*, forfeited life by 'some Act that deserves Death' (*Two Treatises of Government*, Peter Laslett (ed.), Cambridge, 1970, 2, Sec. 23). Planter authority was neither contractual nor patriarchal. It was proprietary, as with their horses (ibid., 1, Sec. 130). The tension between slavery as a condition of war continued and as a condition of sale concluded was never addressed. At the Somerset trial Locke was cited only by Somerset's counsel, in favour of liberty.

70. There was one important divergence between British and other imperial systems which roused metropolitan attention to slavery as a problem during the third quarter of the eighteenth century. Antislavery protest among early European colonists in seventeenth-century Pennsylvania and eighteenth-century Georgia were localized. By the third quarter of the eighteenth century, however, New England and Pennsylvania had developed into Euro-American settler societies using little slave labour and operating under libertarian political and legal institutions. By 1772 Arthur Young casually included the 2 500 000 whites of Anglo-America among the world's 33 000 000 'free' people. No other part of the non-European world was drawn into the orbit of freedom. From these same colonies came the first successful transatlantic efforts to prohibit the slave trade and to condemn Britain for American slavery during their mobilization for national liberation.

2 BORDER SKIRMISH: NEITHER WAGES NOR THE WHIP

1. See F. O. Shyllon, *Black Slaves in Britain* (London, 1974), Chapter 1; F. O. Shyllon *Black People in Britain, 1555–1833* (Oxford, 1977), Chapter 1; J. Walvin, *Black and White: The Negro and English Society, 1555–1945* (London, 1973), Chapters 7, 8, esp. 135–141; Betty Fladeland, *Abolitionists and Working-Class Problems in the Age of Industrialization* (London, 1984), 179 note 1; D. B. Davis, *Slavery in . . . Revolution* (Ithaca, New York, 1984), 498. Advertisements offering or asking for blacks or Indians were publicized in London coffee houses throughout the eighteenth century before 1770. See Bryant Lillywhite, *London Coffee Houses: A Reference Book* (London, 1963), 89, 211, 282, 385, 465, 693, 695. The dates ranged from 1660 to 1769. For the most extensive survey of the variety of sales in eighteenth-century English ports see Peter Fryer, *Staying Power: The History of Black People in Britain* (London and Sydney, 1984), 58–64.

2. *Calendar of State Papers, Colonial America and West Indies, 1677–1680*, 102; *Butts* v. *Penny* (1677), in H. T. Catterall (ed.), *Judicial Cases Concerning American Slavery and the Negro*, 5 vols (Washington, 1926–36), 1, 9.
3. Walvin, *Black and White*, Chapter 3.
4. Orlando Patterson, *Slavery and Social Death* (Cambridge, Mass., 1982), 22–3; also Moses Finley, *Ancient Slavery and Modern Ideology*, Chapter 3.
5. In 1669 E. Chamberlayne's *Angliae Notitia* (London), 462, claimed that there were no slaves in England, domestic or foreign, but that the latter were not thereby free from service. This text remained unchanged through mid-eighteenth century editions of *Magnae Britanniae Notitia*.
6. Bernard Bailyn, 'The Challenge of Modern Historiography', *American Historical Review*, 87, 1 (February 1982), 10–11.
7. *Smith* v. *Gould*, in Catterall, *Judicial Cases*, 1, 11–12. Contrary to other established forms of authority, like villeinange and wardship, 'the law took no notice of a Negro'. This was the opinion of Judge Powell in *Smith* v. *Brown* and Cooper (1706), and was reaffirmed by Chief Justice John Holt (1706): 'the common law takes no notice of negroes being different from the other men'. See Carol P. Bauer, 'Law, Slavery and Sommerset's Case', PhD dissertation, New York University, 1976, 11–16. Charles Molloy, *De Jure Maritimo* (London, 1676), Book III, 338, denied the validity of any contract where the provision of service extended to heirs.
8. See *The British Merchant: A Collection of Papers Relating to the Trade and Commerce of Great Britain and Ireland*, 2nd edn, 3 vols (London, 1743), 1, 73–5; Samuel Foster, *A Digest of all the Laws relating to Customs, to Trade and Navigation* (London, 1727), esp. 119, 240.
9. See *Jus Imperij et Servitutis or, the Law Concerning Masters, Apprentices, Bayliffs, Receivers, Stewards* (London, 1707); [C.S.] *Legal Provisions for the Poor* (London, 1710); M. Dutton, *The Law of Masters and Servants in Ireland* (Dublin, 1723); [George Meriton], *A Guide for Constables, Churchwardens, and Overseers of the Poor*, etc. (London, 1682).
10. Justice Mansfield estimated the number of slaves in England at 14 000 or 15 000 valued at £50 each for a total of £700 000 sterling (Howell's, *State Trials*, 33 vols (London, 1814), 20, 79. *The Gentleman's Magazine*, 34 (1767), 493, set the number of slaves at 20 000 in London alone. Fletcher Norton, a London lawyer, offered the same London figure (P. Hoare, *Memoirs of Granville Sharp* (London, 1820) Appendix II, vi). Edward Long's initial estimate was 3000 for England but he raised the number to 15 000 in a postscript: E. Long, *Candid Reflections Upon the Judgement . . . in Westminster-Hall on what is Commonly Called the Negro-Cause, by a Planter* (London, 1772), 51, 75–76. A correspondent of Liverpool's *General Advertiser*, 26 June 1772, set the total at 1400. Finally 15 000 became the most used figure. Sharp privately adopted 20 000 as the national total. Paul Edwards and James Walvin accept Sharp's higher figure as an informed guess of a sympathetic contemporary: *Black Personalities in the Era of the Slave Trade* (Baton Rouge, 1983), 18–19. Howard Temperley, F. O. Shyllon, and Peter Fryer favour a lower-end figure of 10 000. At the beginning of the abolition debate

Jamaica's House of Assembly offered a figure for the outward flow of slaves from Jamaica until 1787. It set the total (including both escapees and departures with masters) at 13 000. Assuming that there were no escapees, that all slaves who accompanied their masters went to Britain, and that the flow of blacks to Britain from Jamaica was proportionate to the island's share of the total West Indian slave population, the Caribbean flow to Britain for the period 1670 to 1770 was *c.* 28 000. What was then the⁻ *maximum* number of potential slaves in Britain 1770? With plausible mortality tables there were around 9000 in England in 1770. The assertion, in 1772, that property rights to *14 000* persons in Britain were at risk seems to have involved the notion that *all* blacks were to be counted as chattels.

11. As early as 1710 some runaway blacks were identified as apprentices (*London Courant*, 2–3 January 1710). There is another danger in identifying early notices for runaways who were identified as 'black' as slaves. Seventeenth– and early eighteenth-century references to a man as 'black' often implied their colour or dark complexion. See *The Post-Man*, no. 1608, 2–4 May 1706; *London Gazette*, 27–30 January, 12–16 March, 10–13 August 1695.

12. Stephen J. Braidwood, 'Initiatives and Organisation of the Black Poor', *Slavery and Abolition*, 3, 3 (December 1982), 212–13. I surveyed the *Daily Advertiser* employment advertisements for three-month intervals in the years 1772, 1773, 1775 and 1783.

13. See the studies of Shyllon, Walvin, and Fryer.

14. American colonies routinely taxed slaves both as imports and as slaves. Robert A. Becker, *Revolution, Reform and the Politics of American Taxation 1763–1783* (Baton Rouge, 1980), 44 ff.

15. In 1788 there were still rural inhabitants of Southern England who had never seen a black person (*Salisbury and Winchester Journal*, 27 January 1788).

16. A Bristol merchant left his 'negro boy' to a Mrs Mary Becher. It is unclear from the published account whether the legacy was deemed a capital asset or a form of a guardianship. See John Latimer, *The Annals of Bristol in the Eighteenth Century* (n. p. 1893), 15. Otherwise the evidence of English blacks bequeathed as property is quite slim. At least one English master took his Negro 'to be in the nature and quality of my goods and chattels' (Walvin, *Black and White*, 42). Slave colliers in Scotland, on the other hand, were regularly valued as chattel assets: Baron F. Duckham, *A History of the Scottish Coal Industry*, 2 vols (Newton Abbot, 1970), 1, 245. Compared with runaway advertisements in England those in America show a much greater institutional articulation. See Lathan A. Windley (ed.), *Runaway Slave Advertisements*, 4 vols (Westport, Conn./London, England, 1983), 2, 352.

17. On Packwood's advertisements, see N. McKendrick, *The Birth of a Consumer Society* (Bloomington, 1982), 155–6.

18. See *St. James's Chronicle* 30 August–1 September, 4–6, 6–8 September, 4–6 October 1764; 8–10 January 1765 on the 'swarming' Scots; *The London Chronicle* 28 September–1 October 1765 on the Irish; and ibid., 19–22 October 1765, on Negro and East India servants; the *Gazetteer*, 21

April 1767, and *Lloyds Evening Post* 4–6 January 1769 on the French. When Somerset was before Mansfield in 1771–2, it was the Jews who were being singled out for public hostility. One newspaper correspondent remarked that they 'now swarm in divers parts of the country'. Others called for deprivation of due process, registration, special taxation and collective liability. (See *The Westminster Journal and London Political Miscellany*, 14 and 28 December 1771; 29 February 1772; *The Gazetteer and New Daily Advertiser* 7, 20, 25 and 28 December 1771; *The Public Advertiser*, 24 December 1771; *Baldwin's London Weekly Journal*, 3 October 1772. Disliked foreigners risked being taken for even more disliked foreigners. A French teacher was attacked as a Jew and only saved from lynching by a soldier (*Westminster Journal*, 14 December 1771). While Somerset was legally resisting his deportation in the Courts, Sir John Fielding was also quite legally deporting Jews (*Westminster Journal*, 28 December–4 January 1772). There were other parallels between blacks and Jews. The 'middle passage' of Continental Jews to England was sufficiently brutal to elicit a protest in *Lloyds Evening Post*, 24–7 January 1769. Calls for the expulsion of black people from England were rare but not entirely absent before the Somerset case. The decision itself stimulated a call for expulsion. See Fryer, *Staying Power*, 155–6.

A decade later, *London Unmask'd or the New Town Spy* (1783), 45, 117, took notice of the 'scum and filth of the world' swallowed by London: Jews, Italians, Frenchmen, Germans, Scots and Irishmen. It made no mention of blacks. Despite many instances of mistreatment, blacks were not the prime targets of *collective* violence during the eighteenth century: 'And who are all those whom the mob treat uncivil?/ Why Dutchmen, and Scotchmen and Jews and the Devil' (lines from a poem: 'Conversation between two heads upon Temple Bar', published in the *Gazetteer*, 27 March 1769).

19. Walvin, *Black and White*, 111–12. Bauer also maintains that the majority of the people believed that slavery was a valid institution in Britain. (Bauer, 'Law, Slavery', 45). However, the lawyers who advised Equiano when he was still a slave clearly disagreed with that conclusion. Major legal compendia, published both before and after Yorke-Talbot, also disagreed. Thomas Wood's *New Institute of Imperial or Civil Law* (London, 1704), 31, stated unequivocally that slaves might claim their freedom as soon as they entered England. None of his *Institutes of the Laws of England*, whether published before or after the Yorke-Talbot opinion stated or inferred that trover would lie for a slave (compare the edition of 1720 with the 10th edition of 1772). T. Cunningham's law dictionary, published the year before Sharp's first major tract, declared: 'Trover lies not for a Negro; for men may be owners, and therefore not the subject of property'. (cited in Bauer, 'Law, Slavery', 63–4). Mansfield himself was cautious about the possible inaccuracy of this 1729 opinion. Howell's *State Trials* (London, 1814), 20, 70.

20. *Gentleman's Magazine*, 33 (1763), 45.

21. For Hardwicke's habitual reliance on commercial customs as explained to him by merchants, see Bauer, 'Law, Slavery', 22.

22. Walvin, *Black and White*, 109.
23. Bauer, 'Law, Slavery', 7, 18.
24. *An Abridgement of the Laws of England in Force and Use in Her Majesty's Plantations* (London, 1704), 7, made it clear that baptism in the colonies did not confer freedom. On the tradition of runaways seeking baptism as a form of patronage, see also T. Clarkson, *History of The Rise, Progress and Accomplishment of The Abolition of The African Slave Trade* (London, 1808), 1, 64. One version of an early legal decision (*Butts* v. *Penny*, 1677), following the precedent of Calvin's case (1607) in which infidels as 'perpetual enemies' might be enslaved, stated that Negroes might be held 'until they become Christians; and thereby they are enfranchised'. (See Bauer, 'Law, Slavery', 5–6; also the arguments in *Chamberline* v. *Harvey* ibid., 12.) The uncertainty continued throughout the century before abolitionism. Already in 1680 Godwyn wrote of many Creoles who brought blacks to England, and fashionably baptized them. Then, taking them back to the islands, they untwisted 'as it were that Web, they seemed to weave in *England*'. (M. Godwyn, *The Negro's and Indians Advocate* (London, 1680), 37, 103. *Lloyds Evening Post*, of 3–5 November 1760, 433, published the following account:

> Last week a Negro girl about nine years old, having eloped from her mistress on account of ill usage, was brought to a Church in Westminster by two housekeepers, to be baptised. But the mistress of the girl, getting intelligence of it, while the Minister was reading the churching service, seized upon her in the face of the congregation, and violently forced her out of the Church, regardless of her cries and tears; telling the people about her that she was her slave, and would use her as she pleased. We should be glad to be informed, first, whether, it is in the power of a master or mistress of a Negro slave to prevent her being baptized after her arrival in England? Secondly, whether in this free country such a Negro still continues a slave after baptism? Lastly, whether upon complaint of ill usage, it is not in the power of a Justice of the Peace to discharge such a Negro from her slavery?

No reply was forthcoming, but one may note that in this world of private enforcement it would be far more difficult for a child or a woman to escape from control than an adult male.

Peter Fryer maintains that masters baptized blacks only when it was clear that baptism did *not* mean freedom (*Staying Power*, 74). He does not consider that freedom may sometimes have accompanied baptism as part of a mutually desired social change. In other words the link between incorporation into the Christian community and recognition of personal liberty may have been as implicit for those who allowed baptism as for those who prohibited it. One correspondent to the *Gazetteer* (14 February 1772) believed that baptism by leave of the master was a public declaration of freedom by 'admitted custom', but that baptism without consent had no effect on the situation. On the widespread denial of baptism by masters see the letter of 'Z.Y.P.' in the *Gazetteer*, 22 February 1772. Another writer maintained that public opinion held that

baptism conferred freedom. *London Evening Post*, 23–5 June 1772. Baptism was used as a rite of passage into *enslavement* for native-born Scottish colliers. 'Slavery in Modern Scotland', 121.
25. Sir John Fielding described the rapid social process. The West Indians brought their trained servants

> to *England* as cheap Servants, having no Right to Wages; they no sooner arrive here than they put themselves on a Footing with other Servants, become intoxicated with Liberty, grow refractory and either by Persuasion of others, or from their own inclinations, begin to expect Wages according to their own opinion of their Merits; and as there are already a great number of black Men and Women who have made themselves so troublesome and dangerous to the Families who brought them over as to get themselves discharged, these enter into Societies, and make it their business to corrupt and dissatisfy the mind of every fresh black Servant that comes to England, first by getting them christened or married, which they inform them makes them free (tho' it has been adjudged by our most able Lawyers, that neither of these circumstances alter the Master's Property in a Slave). However it so far answers their purpose, that *it gets the Mob on their side* and makes it not only difficult but dangerous to the Proprietors of these Slaves to recover the Possession of them, when once they are spirited away; and indeed, it is the less Evil of the two, to let them go about their business (From Sir John Fielding, *Extracts from . . . the Penal Laws . . . of this Metropolis* (London, 1768), 144, my italics)

The market, the mob, the general lack of regulations for domestics (ibid., 141), and the leeway afforded by London to autonomous black social organization show why it was ultimately the masters who hoped that the higher courts might give them some institutional leverage to hold onto their *disappearing* property rights. The London Justices had given the masters little relief: 'Magistrates are frequently applied to, to cause such Negroes as run away to be apprehended; this is a mistake, for Justices have nothing to do with Blacks but when they offend against the Law, by the commission of Fraud, Felony or Breach of the Peace' (ibid., 145). (Peter Fryer logically concludes from this passage that the poor had helped to make London a centre of black resistance by the 1760s: *Staying Power*, 72.)

The case of Jonathan Strong, in 1767, reinforces Fielding's observation. The Lord Mayor, Sir Robert Kite, discharged Strong because 'the lad . . . was not guilty of any offense, and was therefore at liberty to go away'. Granville Sharp also threatened Strong's claimant with assault if he took any private action and agreed with Fielding on the role of magistrates. He identified all but one London Justice of the Peace as non-enforcers of slavery. G. Sharp, *A Representation of the Dangerous Tendency of Tolerating Slavery* (London, 1769), 7. For corroboration from a hostile witness see note 34, below. In France blacks could apparently be thrown into prison on the whim of their masters. (S. McCoy, *The Negro in France* (Lexington Ky., 1961), 45.)

26. On casual notices of intermarriage see *London Chronicle*, 9–11 September 1766, and *Chester Chronicle*, 2 December 1791. In 1827 the *Edinburgh Review* noted that unlike the West Indies, 'in England white women not unfrequently marry black men' ('Papers Relating to Captured Negroes' in ibid., 45 (March, 1827), 394). At the time of the Parliamentary slave–trade debates of 1792, 'Gustavus Vassa (Equiano Olaudah), the African, well known in England as the champion and advocate for procuring a suppression of the Slave Trade, was married at Soham, in Cambridgeshire to Miss [Susan] Cullen daughter of Mr. [James] Cullen of Ely, in the same County, in the presence of a vast number of people assembled on the occasion.' (*General Evening Post*, 19–21 April 1792). This item appeared without implying any sense of norm-breaking on the part of the couple, or hostility on the part of the audience. For a fuller discussion of Equiano's life, see Paul Edward's introduction to *The Life of Olaudah Equiano or Gustavus Vasa the African* (London, 1969). Equiano had earlier advocated, without creating any public furor, the institutionalization of racial intermarriage. (letter to *The Public Advertiser*, 28 January 1788, a reply to J. T.'s 'Cursory Remarks'). See also Herbert Marshall and Mildred Stock, *Ira Aldridge: The Negro Tragedian* (London, 1958) 119. On the rights of blacks in Britain before Somerset see John Fothergill to Sharp (1769), B. C. Corner and C. C. Booth (eds), *Chain of Friendship: Selected Letters of Dr. John Fothergill of London, 1735–1780* (Cambridge, Mass. 1971), 33.

27. *Cobbett's Political Register*, 5 (1804), 438–9; ibid., 7 (1805), 366–72; for a reader's objection to Cobbett's racial hostility, see ibid., 6 (1804), 178. Blacks were apparently so well integrated into British popular culture that they participated in wife sales. Cobbett reported a wife 'sold for 6d to a Mulatto, the long drummer, belonging to the barracks. Do we denounce this trade?' Ibid., 7 (1805), 446. Visiting American blacks spoke of a great difference of attitudes in Britain: *Black Abolitionist Papers*, 1, 73–74, Charles Lenon Remond to Charles B. Ray, 30, June 1840.

28. In the year 1728, just prior to the West Indian request for the Yorke –Talbot opinion, at least three out of seven London notices for runaway blacks either indicated that indentured servants were being sought or were couched as *requests* to return with promises of kindly treatment, unaccompanied by threats (see *Daily Journal*, 17, 22 January, 3 February, 10 April, 7, 21, 26 August 1728). Slave–owners brought the question before sympathetic officers of the Crown after dinner in order to avoid having to bring the question before the public courts (Clarkson, *History*, 1, 64). Significantly, the whip was not the punishment of choice in England. 'There is no known slaveholding society where the whip was not considered an indispensable instrument.' Patterson, *Slavery and Social Death*, 4. On private whipping, see Catterall, *Judicial Cases*, 1, 9. Dunning, the lawyer who defended Somerset's master, acknowledged that slaves brought to England could only be disciplined like other servants (Howell's *State Trials*, 20, 72 ff.

29. Olaudah Equiano, *Interesting Narrative of the life of Olaudah Equiano*,

1, 176–9. Relevant passages are also reprinted in Paul Edwards and James Walvin (eds), *Black Personalities in the Era of the Slave Trade* (Baton Rouge, 1983), 130–3. Equiano's belief about his freedom was widely shared. See letter of 'Anglicanus' in the *London Chronicle*, 29 September–2 October 1764. Generally, slaves who had left wives and children behind in the colonies found it more difficult to refuse to return. (See Long, *Candid Reflections*, 49.) Granville Sharp recognized this private world of sales, detentions, imprisonments and transportation. (*The Injustice*, 28–9, 87–8.)

30. On the growing difficulty of compelling either return to the islands or to service in England, see the case of John Hylas and his wife (1768), in Granville Sharp's Letterbook, York Minster Library, 18. The tenuous legal status of the Yorke-Talbot opinion was widely publicized during the Somerset hearings. (See the letter from 'Negro' in *The Craftsman*, 6 June 1772, regarding Lord Hardwicke's opinion: 'the law pays no respect to persons, much less to *obiter* sayings;' see also *General Evening Post*, 6–9 June 1772). Adam Smith's *Lectures on Jurisprudence*, 466, indicate that the power of repatriation was crucial for slaveowners in Scotland too. A Negro servant was otherwise 'entitled to the privileges of a freeman while he is here.'

31. As is usual with rightless people, it was sometimes better to be a 'slave' than a free criminal in England. A black servant robbing his master might be transported to the West Indies for a crime for which free subjects were hanged (see *Public Advertiser*, 24 February 1772).

32. William Blizard, *Desultory Reflections on Police* (London, 1785), 46.

33. Some blacks did of course qualify for relief, as witnessed by a notice for a black who had absconded from the workhouse of St. Martin's-in-the-Fields with its provisions (*Daily Advertiser*, 3 December 1772).

34.   Whereas a black Servant, . . . Henry King, has within these few days absconded from his Master, and has written him a very insolent letter, declaring it to be his intention not to return with him to the West Indies, . . . [he] is still the property of his foresaid Master, who is undoubtedly entitled to his Services, and will most certainly prosecute any person that shall attempt to harbour or employ him. (Advertisement in the *Public Advertiser*, 7 October 1771.)

Another notice, offering an extraordinary 25 Guineas for the return of a young black added a postscript which sheds light on the balance of forces in this struggle: 'As the said NEGRO knows his master's affection for him, if he will immediately return he will be forgiven; if freedom be what he wishes for he shall have it, with reasonable wages. If he neglects this present forgiving disposition of his master, he may be assured that more effectual measures will soon be taken'. (*Gazetteer*, 10 March 1769.) By 1769 some advertisements did not even bother threatening for harbouring runaways. They merely offered a reward for getting the runaway on outward bound vessels (*Public Advertiser*, 16 March 1769). Edward Long summed up the odds against the master in his *Candid Reflections*, Sec. V, 46:

the owners of Negroes . . . have frequently endeavoured to send them back, and have as often been defeated, by the quirks of Negro solicitors, and the extra-judicial opinions of some lawyers. The truth is, the Legislature . . . have not expressed any means by which he may continue to exercise that claim. A Negro running away from his master here is not by statute declared liable to imprisonment for any such offence. Advantaging themselves of this silence, they have always, by the advice of their solicitor, applied for a *Habeas Corpus*, and have been thereupon set at liberty of course, the judges not interesting themselves [as with Villeins] . . . to *recommit*, when the cause . . . appeared to be *a refusal to serve their masters*.'

Long and Sir John Fielding agreed on both the social process and the outcome of black flight even *before* Somerset.

35. Reginald Coupland, *The British Anti-Slavery Movement* (London, 1933), 55.
36. For recent reaffirmations of this view see, *inter alia*, John Pollock, *Wilberforce* (New York, 1977), 52; and William Reilley, *William Pitt the Younger* (New York, 1979), 251.
37. Mansfield first inclined to see the question as of 'general and extreme concern'. (Hoare, *Memoirs*, 71.) He then narrowed the question in the penultimate hearing. (*The Craftsman*, no. 722, 30 May 1772).
38. Walvin, *Black and White*, 120; Shyllon, *Black Slaves*, 116; Hoare, *Memoirs*, 60.
39. Mansfield's general objective was 'to make the law more serviceable to the commercial community' and 'to incorporate large areas of commercial practice into law'. See P. S. Atiyah, *The Rise and Fall of Freedom of Contract* (Oxford, 1979), 122–3.
40. Shyllon, *Black Slaves*, 108. Liverpool was probably not as densely populated with black servants as was London. The Somerset case was reported there without eliciting editorial statements or correspondence in favour of the masters. (See *Liverpool's General Advertiser* 22 May–3 July 1772).
41. G. Sharp, *The Just Limitation of Slavery in the Laws of God, compared with the unbounded Claims of the African Traders and British Slaveholders* (London, 1776), appendix 8. Antiabolitionists were equally certain that Mansfield had made it clear that the only choice the courts had was either to *remand* Somerset or to discharge him. See Samuel Estwick's *Considerations on the Negro Cause* (London, 1773), ix, xi. All versions agree on the *unconditional* discharge of Somerset.
42. Bauer, 'Law, Slavery', 147; Davis, *Slavery in . . . Revolution*, 500–1. Only a few days before the Somerset decision *The Gazetteer* of 5 June 1772 contained a notice for a runaway black cook by a Captain Gunn of the Heart of Oak, offering a guinea for the cook's return. There were nuances of 'partial' interpretations. *The Manchester Mercury* of 23 June 1772, understood Mansfield's decision to mean that no master could sell a slave in Britain but that the former could sue anyone who hired his black in service.
43. See, above all, Walvin, *Black and White*, 128–9; Shyllon, *Black Slaves*, Chapter 10; Shyllon, *Black People*, 26–7; Fryer, *Staying Power*, 125–6;

Edwards and Walvin, *Black Personalities*, 24; R. J. Hind, 'We have no Colonies', 10, and note 44.

44. Shyllon, *Black Slaves*, Chapter 11; Davis, *Slavery in . . . Revolution*, 500–1. A recent social history of eighteenth century England concludes that 'despite the much trumpeted Somerset ruling of 1772, even the rights to own Negro slaves in England remained stubbornly secure through the whole of the [eighteenth] century'. Roy Porter, *English Society in the Eighteenth Century* (London, 1982) 153. Fryer, *Staying Power*, 132, more correctly observes that slavery 'had in practice almost entirely disappeared' from Britain several decades before the end of colonial slavery in 1834.

45. Shyllon, *Black Slaves*, 167–8; Charles Stuart, *A Memoir of Granville Sharp* (New York, 1836 reprinted Westport, Conn., 1970), 32. Even Edward Long was under the impression that Mansfield had decided not only that a master could not transport his servant out of the kingdom, but also could not reclaim his 'fugitive slave'. See Long, *Candid Observations*, 56. According to Long's account (ibid., 46–8), this actually meant little more than a ratification of the *de facto* situation. Samuel Estwick also understood that by Mansfield's decision the laws did not allow Somerset to be either sold or remanded, and hence he was discharged (*Considerations*, xi). Mansfield made quite clear to Stuart's counsel that this particular master/servant situation was irrelevant to 'every idea of a contract between parties' (*The Craftsman*, 16 May 1772). Mansfield reiterated this point in his summary. The West Indians were equally clear that there was no contract between master and man, no indenture, and no written or oral agreement: See Estwick, *Considerations*, 68.

46. Catterall, *Judicial Cases*, 1, 20, 22. In 1762 a similar case of enfranchisement in France had resulted in the award of back wages. See McCloy, *The Negro in France*, 45.

47. Walvin, *Black and White*, 135.

48. Mansfield's reasoning was consistent. Slavery could only apply to a black as a result of positive law. Nothing in the statutes located them in a parish if they had or were serving without a contract. See *The Daily Universal Register*, 29 April 1785, on the microfilm of *The Times* for 1785.

49. M. Godwyn, *A Supplement to the Negro's and Indians Advocate* (London, 1681), 6–9.

50. Hoare, *Memoirs*, 58, 60.

51. Mansfield also twice advised the West Indians to seek Parliamentary redress or to resolve the question out of court (Howell, *State Trials*, 20, 70, 79–80). Denunciations of Mansfield for delaying, and for urging the planters to seek Parliamentary intervention, became pointed after six months of continuances: 'Mean spirited, pitiable old Man! How much you've dodged that Holt would have gloried in . . . Good God! Is this the language of an English Judge? *Fiat Justicia, ruat Coelum* – Dastardly Braggard!' (*Public Advertiser*, 13 June 1772, 'Emilius' to Lord Mansfield.) On the abuse of Mansfield for avoiding a decision, see also C. Stuart to James Murray, 15 June 1772, cited in Bauer, 'Law, Slavery', 124; *Gazetteer*, 20 June 1772; and the *Public Ledger*, 17 July 1772.

52. Immediately after 1772, Mansfield's decision was interpreted broadly even in the courts. In *Cay* v. *Crichton* (1773), the court refused to enforce a will transferring a black, even though the benefactor had died in 1769, before the Mansfield judgment. Both sides accepted the premise that there were no slaves in England. In terms of claims to *property* even the *ex post facto* exemption applied by Mansfield to wages was not followed. In an Admiralty Court case in 1776, the judge, again ruling in favour of the black, drew a clear distinction between the commercial world and British law: 'The practice of buying and selling slaves was certainly very common in England before the case of Somersett . . . but however it might have been the law of the "Royal Exchange," I hope it never was the law of England.' (Bauer, 'Law, Slavery', 157.)

'Mandingo', writing in the *Morning Chronicle* on 1 September 1772, correctly located the crucial point of the decision, 'that all relations between man and man must arise from municipal law, or from a contract agreeable thereto.' Since no law covered any part of Somerset's service, which did not arise from municipal law, he was not bound to any form of uncontracted service. Soon after the Somerset decision a London play had an Irish widow informing her two white footmen that the laws had lately made her third servant, a black man, their equal. (*The Gazetteer*, 26 October 1772.) A long series of abolitionist letters and sermons began and ended with the premise, never contradicted, that every slave landing in Britain was free. See, for example, *Norwich Mercury*, 7 August and 27 November 1787, and Robert Robinson, *A Sermon* (n.p. 1788), 19. On the equally 'broad' libertarian interpretation of the Somerset decision in Ireland, see the *Dublin Evening Post*, 17 January 1788: 'Tis not more than 17 years since the blacks, or slaves from Africa, were liberated in Great Britain.'

53. Some historians, like Mansfield's successors, take the Chief Justice to task for his failure to confine the issue from the outset of the hearings to the narrow decision at which he ultimately arrived. They fail to note that Mansfield himself initially thought that the broader question was involved, to the extent of warning the court that he might have to consult all the judges because of the subject was of 'so general and extreme concern'. During the trial he urged alternative solutions precisely because he saw the question as a broader one. Mansfield himself seems to have been unsure at first how the claims of rights in the Somerset case might be divided.

54. Davis, *Slavery in . . . Revolution*, 500. Had Mansfield allowed back-wages to black servants it is difficult to know just how the average cost would have been calculated. Presumably, the oft-cited '£50' of property at risk was derived from an overseas average price, which included the cost of maintaining a domestic slave over a lifetime. However, a back-wages claim might conceivably have been assessed by using the average annual wages offered to London footmen. A footman's annual wage in London, in 1785, was estimated at £14, plus livery. (See Dr Trusler, *The London Adviser and Guide, Useful also to Foreigners* (London, 1786), 49.) In 1762 a French Court of Admiralty awarded a freed black back wages of 100 livres a year from the day of his arrival in France. (McCloy, *The Negro in France*, 45.)

It was again clear from the case of *King* v. *Thames Ditton* in 1785, that black servants without indentures were no longer under any constraint to serve. The servant in question had simply abandoned her master's wife five or six months after the death of her master. Mansfield would not allow that such service had been a 'hiring'. She could therefore neither claim wages nor claim a parish under the rules for settlement. Catterall, *Judicial Cases*, 1, 20. Other justices also refused to grant back wages unless (or until) the two parties had entered into a contract or promise of wages. There was no implicit original contract. Ibid., 2–23, *Alfred* v. *Marquis of Fitz James* (1799).

55. Catterall, *Judicial Cases*, 1, 23, *Williams* v. *Brown* (1802).
56. Walvin, *Black and White*, 136.
57. Catterall, *Judicial Cases*, 1, 21n. *The Craftsman, or Say's Weekly Journal*, no. 720, 16 May 1772, noted that a French galley slave, on reaching Britain, was never returned, nor were any British black runaways who reached France. Barry Bird's *The Laws respecting Masters and Servants; Articled Clerks, Apprentices etc . . . Up to the Present Term* (London, 1795), made no mention of the Somerset decision's impact on the status of black servants or their wages. However, for all servants held on indentures, 'a master cannot assign over his apprentice as he may another chattel, but it must be with his own consent, for the person of a man is not legally assignable'. (Ibid., 35.) Indentured blacks therefore had a right of refusal. As *indentured* servants they were now covered not just by the common law of *habeas corpus* statutes, but the more precise laws of masters and servants.
58. Shyllon, *Black Slaves,* 167–170; Bauer, 'Law, Slavery', 89.
59. Walvin, *Black and White*, 138.
60. Shyllon, *Black Slaves*, 230. There is further evidence from the period immediately after Somerset. The 'Black Society' of London was forced to continue its search in the public press for a black servant maid who had been claimed as a chattel before the Somerset decision. See letters of Mungo to Mr Richard Swords in the *Public Ledger*, 23 October 1772. Moreover, a few months *after* the Somerset decision a notice appeared in the newspapers warning persons against harbouring a 'black woman belonging to Mrs Grant'. A second explicitly claimed 'a Negro Man called Cato' as *property* and offered 5 guineas to 'whoever will bring him in'. Another advertised for a black boy who had already run away a dozen times (*Daily Advertiser*, 4, 9 September, 10 October, 13 November 1772). Such notices had apparently dissappeared in London by the late 1770s. It therefore seems unlikely, as Peter Fryer infers, that those referred to as 'out of place' in 1778 meant blacks living 'under cover' after escaping from servitude (*Staying Power*, 70). See also note 62 below.
61. The Bristol Quakers got a warrant by which they kept the girl 'in defiance of all the human flesh merchants'. *Horace Walpole's Correspondence*, 1, 350. After 1772, slaves illegally boarded on ships for the colonies were certainly no longer regarded as secure property. In 1773, prospective buyers refused to purchase a slave who claimed that he had been taken to the islands against his will (Bauer, 'Law, Slavery', 157). The 1779 advertisement of a Liverpool slave sale was not only the last

but, without any doubt, the most publicized auction of a black person in British history. The notice, for the auction of a 14-year-old boy, was brought to Granville Sharp's attention only in 1782 and remained unpublicized. In 1788 it was brought to the attention of all Britain. (See, for example, *Edinburgh Evening Courant*, 2 February 1788). At that point it was exclusively the *abolitionists* who were citing it. If it were still commonplace why did they have to go back into Sharp's six-year-old file for a nine-year-old item? In 1788 one could obviously no longer compile parallel catalogues of slave sales in London and American cities, as Granville Sharp had done 20 years before. The *Public Advertiser* of 14 February 1788 could disdainfully point to an American slave advertisement offering a black for sale '*with or without her female child*, near four years old'. Public slave sales in Britain had simply disappeared by the beginning of the age of abolition. In London, perhaps one of the last public advertisements appeared just before Mansfield's decision offering to purchase a 'little Negro girl from six to fourteen years old'. (*Gazetteer* of 15 June 1772.) I have discovered no offers to purchase blacks in London after 1772.

On further evidence of African Institution intervention for young blacks, see also Fryer, *Staying Power*, 228, and 547–8, notes 1–3. It is even possible to argue that there has been a deterioration of foreign servants' status *since* the age of abolition. Coerced labour has reappeared within the confines of wealthy households in Britain. (See the article by Peter Kingston in *The Sunday Times*, 10 February 1985.) Wageless domestics who now enter Britain as part of a diplomatic retinue are immune from police action and are unprotected by employment statutes. Once again, the law takes no notice of Afro-Asian servants. Once again, there are no statistics on their numbers, and once again they simply go underground when they can make contact with members of their ethnic group or a friendly lawyer.

62. Shyllon, *Black Slaves*, Chapter 9, contains the most detailed discussion to date on the relationship between public opinion and the Somerset case at the time of the decision. We focus attention on the impact of subsequent public opinion.

63. On the self-perception of black people as free in Britain, see the collective letter to Granville Sharp in Shyllon, *Black People*, appendix 2, 267. On a West Indian acknowledgement of the finality of Mansfield's decision see G. Turnbull, *An Apology for Negro Slavery* (London, 1786), 15–16. An antiabolitionist letter published in *St James's Chronicle* 9–12 February 1788, purported to record an interview with 'an African Black slave now living at Bath' named John Williams. To the question of whether he would prefer to live as a slave in the West Indies or a day labourer in Britain, Williams replied: 'A Slave in the West Indies is infinitely superior to the Day Labourer's condition here. My foolish Countrymen think when they get here they are Freemen. They are so, but such of them as have a good Master are fools for taking it.' Whether Williams's interview was real or fictional, he certainly imagined that the choice was the servant's. The testimony was repeated in a letter from 'M. M.' ibid., 25–7 March 1788. A letter from 'Veritas' the same day asked

how many hundreds have come with masters, 'knew they were on *free ground* and returned?'

64. Ellen Gibson Wilson, *The Loyal Blacks* (New York, 1976); Mary Beth Norton, *The British Americans: The Loyalist Exiles in England 1774–1789* (Constable, 1974).

65. See PRO AO 12/99 (Loyalist claims), f. 82, 3 September 1783; f. 353, 1 September 1783; f. 155, 30 November 1783; f. 265, 21 May 1783.

66. To the last, Mansfield spoke out against consulting 'popular declamation' or the new philosophy on the slave-trade question: *The Diary*, 13 April 1793.

67. From a series of newspaper clippings in Daniel Lysons (comp.), *Collectanea: Or, a Collection of Advertisements and Paragraphs from the Newspapers relating to Various Subjects*, 5 vols, n.d., British Library Pressmark 1889, e. 5., fols 100–4. The manager turned the free-soil rhetoric on his accusers: 'This woman was my servant at the Cape, and not my slave, much less can she be so in England, where all breathe the air of freedom. She is brought of her own free will.' Letter of Hendrick Caesar to the *Morning Herald*, 13 October 1810. Radical newspapers also closely followed the 'Hottentot Venus' affair (see *The Examiner*, 21 October–4 November 1810).

68. Roscoe wrote that full freedom was guaranteed after an affidavit was obtained that the black had been a slave in Brazil. Liverpool Public Library, Roscoe Papers 920 ROS (2447), 9 July 1809. A watchdog legal service was set up in Liverpool to oversee enforcement: ibid., ROS (1776, 2493, 2495), correspondence with Zachary Macaulay.

69. Fryer, *Staying Power*, 132, 203–7, does assign an ideological supporting role to the popular libertarian heritage. An ideological constant which spans the entire eighteenth century, however, can not really go very far in explaining why black slavery rose *and* fell against this popular backdrop. Rebelliousness in defence of custom could only operate sporadically and locally against specific intrusions of imported slavery, like the Portuguese crowd of 1444. (See E. P. Thompson, 'Eighteenth-century English society: class struggle without class', *Social History*, 3 (1978), 154, 158, 165.)

70. Shyllon, *Black People*, 27–8, cites the case of Mary Prince to prove that chattel slavery continued in Britain until 1834. Brought to England from Antigua by her owners in 1828, she suffered abuse and was threatened with expulsion from the house. The case however seems to demonstrate the opposite of Shyllon's contention. Mary Prince was threatened with discharge, not compulsory retention or transportation. She knew she was free in England but lacked choices and therefore feared to leave. She did leave as soon as she found employment through the intervention of the Secretary of the Anti-Slavery Society. She was not only free to leave her mistress but had a network unavailable to other immigrants to England. For examples of similar rescues of children, see note 62, above.

71. *Leeds Intelligencer*, 24 January 1833. For similar liberations at Cork and Belfast see ibid., 25 November 1830; *Sheffield Iris*, 24 August 1830; also *The Record*, 28 March 1833.

72. James Mansfield, counsel for Somerset, was still defensive in his use of

the geographical metaphor during the proceedings: 'Where is the mighty magic of the air of the West Indies, [that] by transplanting them for a while *there*, . . . they should become our absolute property *here*?' For a popular example of the more aggressive redirection of the free-air metaphor from England towards the West Indies, see the *Morning Chronicle*, 31 January 1788.

73. Bauer, 'Law, Slavery', 162. Contrast this with the letter from '*A Guinea Merchant*' to the *Public Advertiser*, 24 February 1772: 'Our first connection with them commands a property. . . . We send our Ships to Africa with cargoes of immense value, to purchase these Negroes. . . . And if we have a power to buy and sell them in the Plantations, how can that Right be diminished by a Voyage of six or seven weeks?'

74. Lysons, *Collectanea*, ff. 100–4.

75. The West Indians united on the need to secure a judicial decision: Liverpool's *General Advertiser*, 15 June 1772. Even before Somerset a slave–owners' spokesman acknowledged that there was some diminution of power over black servants in England. He emphasized that masters did not have power over life or limb or that 'we can harness them like an Ox or a Horse' as in the West Indies (*The Public Advertiser*, 24 February 1772, letter 'To the Twelve Judges' from 'A Guinea Merchant'). The merchant merely insisted, with Blackstone, that the 'Servant' [sic] was bound to some undefined service (ibid., 25 April 1772). See also letter of 'Caius' to the *Gazetteer*, 20 February 1772. The attorneys arguing against Somerset implied no more than that he was a servant serving for life (Howell, *State Trials*, 20, 76). As the *Manchester Mercury* reported on 2 June 1772, for the West Indians, 'suspense would be productive of almost all the consequences Lord Mansfield seems to dread from Judgement in Favour of the Negro'. See also *The Craftsman*, 27 May 1772; and the *General Evening Post*, 26–8 May 1772. See also note 45 above.

76. Leon F. Litwack, *North of Slavery: The Negro in the Free States, 1790–1860* (Chicago, 1961).

77. The chief concern of Somerset's lawyers was to 'draw the line' between colonies and metropolis for the sake of their client: Hoare, *Memoirs*, 76.

3 THE DISTINCTIVENESS OF BRITISH ABOLITIONIST MOBILIZATION

1. The German Antislavery Society made an ephemeral appearance shortly before the Revolutions of 1848: See *Aufruf zu Bildung eines Deutschen Nationalvereins fur Abschaffung der Sklaverei* (Heidelberg, 15 March 1848), printed single-sheet among the Gregoire and Carnot papers, Chateau de Presles, France. Thomas Haskell treats abolitionism as part of 'an unprecedented wave of humanitarian reform sentiment [which] swept through the societies of Western Europe, England and North America' in the hundred years following 1750: 'Capitalism and the Origins of the Humanitarian Sensibility', in *The American Historical Review*, 90, 2 (April and June 1985), 339). Comparatively speaking,

abolitionism was more like a ripple than a wave in most of Western Europe in the century before 1850. The difference between the Anglo-American and Continental variants may, in fact, serve as a useful point of departure for delineating the relationship between capitalist Euro-America and slavery in that century. Haskell's account attempts to move straight from the evolution of the market to abolitionist sensibility without taking account of the mediating role of political development and class conflict in the process.

2. Philip S. Foner, 'Alexander von Humboldt on Slavery in America', *Science and Society*, 47, 3 (Fall, 1983), 330–42, esp. 340–1.

3. The various French abolitionist societies between 1788 and 1848 ranged from less than 70 members for the 'notable' *Société Française pour l'abolition de l'esclavage* of the July Monarchy, to almost 150 for the *Société des Amis des Noirs* of the first French Revolution, and slightly over 200 for the popular *Club des Amis des Noirs* of 1848 (Archives Nationales, hereafter AN, C 942, Enquête sur les événements de mai et juin 1848) dr. 4. On the general exclusivity of organized French abolitionism see also Daniel P. Resnick, 'The *Société des Amis des Noirs* and the Abolition of Slavery', *French Historical Studies*, 7, 4 (Fall, 1972), 558–69; Seymour Drescher, *Dilemmas of Democracy: Tocqueville and Modernization* (Pittsburgh, 1968), Chapter 6.

4. After 15 years of activity, the less élite Dutch Anti-Slavery Society counted 450 members. An abolitionist petition to the King from Amsterdam was signed by only 355 persons (RHASSP G/104, Report of Wolbers, 4 May 1855). According to the *Anti-Slavery Reporter* (1841), 256–7, the first and only abolitionist public meeting in the Netherlands took place in the *English* Church in Utrecht. Nothing like the antislavery meetings in the towns of Anglo-America took place in the French metropolis prior to 1848. The Spanish Antislavery Society, which developed quite late (1866), counted about 700 members. For British efforts to spread abolitionism to Latin–America, see D. Eltis, 'Economic Growth and the Coercion: The Ending of the Atlantic Slave Trade' (Mss), 2 vols (forthcoming), Chapter 7.

5. Svend E. Green-Pedersen, 'Slave Demography in the Danish West Indies and the Abolition of the Danish Slave Trade', in David Eltis and James Walvin (eds), *The Abolition of the Atlantic Slave Trade* (Madison, 1981), 231–57, esp. 232–3. See also Green-Pedersen, 'The Scope and Structure of the Danish Negro Slave Trade', *Scandinavian Economic History Review*, 19:2 (1971), 149–97. Very early in the abolition campaign, Richard How wrote from England to I. J. de Jager in Bergen that he was writing to his influential Danish friends, calling for an international concurrence in abolition. He also suggested contacting Portuguese and German Jews and Irish Catholics (Bedfordshire County Record Office, HJW 87/411, How Family Papers, letter of 9 August 1788, and 1 January 1790).

6. S. Drescher, *Econocide: British Slavery in the Era of Abolition* (Pittsburgh, 1977), 256 n.

7. See E. D. Genovese, *The World the Slaveholders Made: Two Essays in Interpretation* (New York, 1969), 38–9; Waldeman Westergaard, *The Danish West Indies under Company Rule (1671–1754)* (New York, 1917).

8. The Danish decision for gradual abolition was hailed in Britain as a noble extension of Denmark's emancipation of its own peasantry. See *Morning Chronicle*, 26 March 1792.) This coincidence is also suggested in S. Engerman's introduction to Eltis and Walvin, *The Abolition*, 5.

9. P. C. Emmer, 'Anti-Slavery and the Dutch: Abolition without reform', in C. Bolt and S. Drescher (eds), *Antislavery, Religion and Reform: Essays in Memory of Roger Anstey* (Folkestone, Kent/Hamden, Conn., 1980), 80–98.

10. See the general argument in E. Fox-Genovese and E. D. Genovese, *Fruits of Merchant Capital: Slavery and Bourgeois Property in the Rise and Expansion of Capitalism* (New York, 1983), Chapter 2, esp. 41–3.

11. For Brazil, see Leslie Bethell, *The Abolition of the Brazilian Slave Trade: Britain, Brazil and the Slave Trade Question 1807–1869*, (Cambridge, 1970); for Portuguese West Africa, see George E. Brooks, 'A Nhara of the Guinea – Bissau Region: Mae Aurelia Correia', in Claire C. Robertson and Martin A. Klein (eds), *Women and Slavery in Africa* (Madison, 1983), 295–339, esp. 308–10; for Cuba, see David R. Murray, *Odious Commerce: Britain, Spain and the Abolition of the Cuban Slave Trade* (Cambridge, 1980). The nature of the polity was equally important in the Americas. In oligarchically dominated areas of Latin America where slavery remained economically rewarding, nineteenth-century régimes postponed or even reversed the abolition process until well after the age of British abolition.

12. See S. Drescher, 'Two Variants of Anti-Slavery: Religious Organization and Social Mobilization in Britain and France, 1780–1870', in Bolt and Drescher, *Anti-Slavery*, 43–63; see also note 5 above. On the politics of the first French emancipation, see Gabriel Debien, *Les Colons de Saint-Domingue et la Révolution: Essai sur le club Massiac* (Paris, 1953); Yvan Debbasch, *Couleur et liberté* (Paris, 1967); Valerie Quinney, 'The Committee on Colonies of the French Constituent Assembly, 1789–1791', PhD dissertation, University of Wisconsin, 1967; Ruth F. Necheles, *The Abbé Gregoire 1788–1831: The Odyssey of an Egalitarian* (Westport, Conn., 1971); D. P. Resnick, 'Political Economy and French Anti-Slavery: The Case of J-B Say', *Proceedings of the 3rd Annual Meeting of the Western Society for French History* (1976), 179–86. On French antislavery activity after 1814 see also Serge Daget, 'France, Suppression of the Illegal Trade, and England, 1817–1850', in Eltis and Walvin (eds), *Abolition*, 193–217; and L. C. Jennings, 'The French Press and Great Britain's campaign against the Slave Trade', *Revue Française d'Histoire d'Outre-Mer*, 67, nos 246–7 (1980), 5–24.

There is evidence of popular sympathy in Paris for blacks during the radical phase of the French Revolution. The *Diary* of 4 June 1793, reported that 'a band of Blacks of both sexes, amidst the sound of martial music, and escorted by a great mob of Parisians, came into [the National Assembly] to return thanks to the Legislators, for having raised them to the rank of men'. At the same moment, however, French slavers were still cruising off the coast of Africa (ibid., 26 June, 23 July, 8, 16 August 1793.) A few days after the National Assembly decreed the abolition of French slavery in February 1794, a deputation from the 48 sections of Paris congratulated the Convention on its decree.

13. P. Curtin, *The Atlantic Slave Trade: A Census*, (Madison, 1969), 250. Many French abolitionists also viewed the decree of 1794 as the ratification of a *fait accompli* forced on the French by the slaves of St Domingue (*Le Semeur*, 16 May 1838, 153. *Le Semeur* noted that Napoleon reinstituted the slave trade on the same day as the promulgation of the Peace Treaty of Amiens in 1802, and speculated that he would have rescinded his 1815 abolition decree if he had won at Waterloo.

14. Those who favoured a more popular French movement condemned the French abolitionist society for confining the question 'within a certain aristocratic circle instead of carrying the debate before the whole people'. See *Le Semeur*, 23 September 1846, 297. Just one week before the French Revolution of 1848 *Le Semeur*, lamented,

> Hasn't the reader more than once observed that in the reformist banquets, where everything is discussed, our poor slaves haven't obtained the least space? The lot of the working classes in our country has elicited generous advocacy, and we are as happy about that as anyone. But the incomparably more abject condition of the blacks in our Antilles has been left in the shadows. Someone informed us that an honorable Deputy would speak in favour of the abolition of slavery at the Lille banquet but we recall how this banquet was so torn apart by political disputes that the slaves lost the chance for the one mention that was to have been made of their miserable fate. . . . When it moves beyond the Chamber to address the masses the Opposition is an echo, and when it ignores the cause of the slaves, it is because France itself is but feebly stirred. (Ibid., 16 February 1848.)

(On Schoelcher's defence of the executive decree by the Provisional Government, see AN Colonies, K1 and K2, *procès verbeaux* of the commission to prepare the regulations for the indemnity of former proprietors of slaves, 1848.)

Ten years after emancipation Louis Veuillot's *L'Univers*, having abandoned its pre-1848 abolitionism, dismissed British Parliamentary complaints about the French policy of shipping purchased Africans to the French colonies. British protests were dismissed as 'comedies of philanthropism' (24 September 1858). Newspapers like the *Journal des Débats* and the *Siècle* which questioned the imperial policy were branded as 'Jewish newspapers', brought by 'the house of Jacob' (ibid., 18 and 22 October 1858). See also *Anti-Slavery Reporter*, 1 January, 11 November, 1 December 1858). In Africa, David Livingston took armed action against this 'third' French slave trade. See BL Add. Mss 43, 845, ff63–4, Livingston to Sturge, 11 December 1858.

15. Albert Soboul, *La France à la veille de la Révolution*, 2 vols (Paris, 1966), 1, 59, estimates about one million serfs in France in 1789. According to J. Q. C. Mackrell, *The Attack on 'Feudalism' in Eighteenth–Century France* (London, 1973), 109, there were no more than 140 000 French serfs, although contemporaries often used figures up to ten times that number. At the outbreak of the Revolution there were about 675 000 slaves in the French colonies (Drescher, *Econocide*, 34, Table 10). The number of French galley slaves was 5400. See Gordon

Wright, *Between the Guillotine and Liberty: Two Centuries of the Crime Problem in France* (New York, 1983), 6.

16. See T. Clarkson, *History of the Rise, Progress and Accomplishment of the Abolition of the African Slave-trade* (London, 1808), 1, 125–126; also Claviere's letter to Necker, June, 1789 reprinted in the *Diary*, 28 August 1789.
17. See Drescher, *Dilemmas of Democracy*, 153–64.
18. *Ibid.*, Chapter 6; André-Jean Tudesq, *Les Grands Notables en France (1840–9): Etude historique d'une psychologie sociale*, 2 vols (Paris, 1964), 1, 834–8.
19. On French opinion in 1814, see Drescher, *Econocide*, 254, note 30; S. Daget, 'A Model of the French Abolitionist Movement and its variations', in Bolt and Drescher, *Anti-Slavery*, 64–79. In 1840 the difference between Britain and France in the political salience of abolitionism was still as great as it had been half-a-century before. Isambert, a French delegate at the first world antislavery meeting in London, remarked that his country would scarcely believe that 12 days were spent in London discussing slavery. (*Le Siècle*, 30 June 1840, Bibliothèque Nationale, Nouvelles Acquisitions (hereafter, BN NA), 23769, Isambert Papers. During the July Monarchy the French press was favourable in principle to British slave-trade repression although indifferent in terms of actual coverage. This indifference was briefly ended by an outburst of hostility against Britain following the Anglo-French war scare of 1840 (Jennings, 'The French Press and Great Britain's campaign', 5–24. On the cancellation of the public meeting see BN NA 23769, Isambert Papers, Letter of the Minister of the Interior to the Duc de Broglie, president of the French abolitionist society. See also *Le Semeur* (9, 16 March 1842, 72, 88), for details. The minister feared a violent counter-demonstration against the British antislavery representatives. The meetings of the French abolitionist society followed the rhythm (and the long interims) of the French Chamber of Deputies (*Le Semeur*, 3 January 1838, 7).
20. See S. Drescher, *Tocqueville and Beaumont on Social Reform* (New York, 1968), 142–3. On the strategic necessity for emancipation see also the [Broglie] report, *Commission instituée . . . 26 mai 1840, pour l'examen des questions relatives à l'esclavage* (Paris 1843), 49–52; *L'Atelier, Organe des intérets moraux et materiels des Ouvriers*, 4, 8 (May, 1844), 119; and *Le Siècle*, 21 January 1839. C. A. Bissette claimed that the French abolitionist society would not even print a sufficient number of petitions for the 1847 campaign. See RHASSP, C 13/119 Bissette to Scoble, 19 January 1847. The petition of 1846–7 seems to have been launched by G. de Felice, of Toulouse, and Bissette, an *homme de couleur* in Paris. For the model French petition of 1847 see BN Lk⁹751, dated 30 August 1847. Its covering letter specifically pointed to mass petitioning: 'the entire English people, workers, peasants, nobles, bourgeois, men, and women insisted on the deliverance of the blacks'. As signs of popular abolitionism emerged in 1846–7 'notables' like Tocqueville drew back from abolitionist activity. He felt that he could not budge the colonists, and he did not want to ally himself with men who wanted to resolve the question 'at any price and whose ideas could

lead to ruin and disorder'. (See BN NA 3629, Schoelcher papers, Correspondence of the delegates of Guadeloupe, 29 April 1847.)
21. On electoral proclamations, see the "Le⁵⁴" series in the BN. Bissette unsuccessfully attempted to make slavery an issue in Rennes, the electoral district of Martinique's agent Thomas Jollivet (Le⁵⁴ 1894, 23 July 1846). Even before the Anglo-French war scare of 1840, Isambert's political manifesto of 28 February 1838 made no mention of slavery in appeals to his electorate at Chartres (BN NA 23769, Isambert papers). Only when appealing to the Parisian working class after the Revolution of 1848 did Isambert's election propaganda mention his abolitionist activity as evidence of his sympathy for *workers*. ('Aux electeurs de la Seine', ibid., 23,770.) Nor did any major Parliamentary figure identify emancipation as an urgent reform to his constituents in the elections of 1839. (See *Chambre des Deputés. Elections 1839–1841*, BN no. Le⁵⁴1072 to 1397.) French abolitionists felt obliged to affirm that slave emancipation was not an 'English' idea but one with purely French antecedants going back to Philippe Auguste. (*L'Abolitioniste Francaise*, 1 (1844) 104.) On the electoral strength of antiabolitionism in the French ports see *Anti-Slavery Reporter* (1842), 58. As late as the spring of 1848 many capitalists and Chambers of Commerce petitioned for a delay of emancipation by the Provisional Government. See AN, Section Outre-Mer Généralités, 153 (1275), communications from Montpellier, Lyons, L'Orient, La Rochelle, Rochefort, Toulon, Saint-Mâlo, Nantes, Dieppe, St Brieux, Dunkerque, Morlaix, and Paris.
22. See Daget, 'France, Suppression of the Illegal Trade', 193–217.
23. The French government tended to dissociate itself from policy conflicts over slavery. Even a nominally abolitionist French Foreign Minister like François Guizot viewed France's interest in an independent Texas entirely in terms of the balance of power, European monarchical principles and the commercial possibilities in expanding cotton production. Slavery was not even mentioned. (Archives des Affaires Etrangères, Etats-Unis, Correspondance Politique, vol. 100, Guizot to Pageot, 10 February, 28 May, 12 August 1844.) There was no French analogue to the heated Anglo-American exchange over Britain's opposition to the expansion of slavery. Marshall Bugeaud, the French Governor-General of Algeria, could resist demands for slave emancipation in Algeria on practical grounds and could dismiss *rêveurs* in the metropolis far more easily than a British Indian proconsul. Without a large abolitionist movement it was also easier for the French colonial party to buy the sympathy or silence of Parisian newspapers. See the accounts of the delegates of Martinique, BN NA 3629, and 3631, Schoelcher papers. During the 1840s more than a dozen newspapers were given colonial financial support by the Colonial Councils.
24. D. B. Davis, *Slavery and Human Progress* (New York, 1984), 142–53, 259; H. Temperley, *British Anti-Slavery 1883–1870* (London, 1972), xiii–xiv.
25. As a problem in intellectual history, one may probably approach the development of abolitionist élite culture within the context of an emerging 'progressivist' ideology at the end of the eighteenth century.

However, in order to analyse the popular role comparatively, historians must begin with the opposite premise. Public opinion clearly did not everywhere give an overwhelming and positive reception to antislavery. After 50 years of praising the voice of the people as the voice of God, British abolitionists in the 1830s were stunned by the rejection of abolitionism in America and denounced American public opinion as a *'demon of oppression'* (Davis, *Slavery and Human Progress*, 141).

26. The most detailed account to date is in R. Anstey, *The Atlantic Slave Trade and British Abolition, 1760–1810* (London, 1975), Parts II–IV.

27. See D. B. Davis, *Slavery in . . . Revolution* (Ithaca, New York, 1984), 5. The Somerset affair seems to have aroused planters only momentarily. Contrast the serene preface of *An Essay upon Plantership* (London, 1765), v, citing Virgil, with the 5th edition of that work published in the aftermath of the Somerset case (1773). An aggressive new preface now declared that the slaves were happier in the islands than in Africa, and 'at least as happy as the Labourers of Britain'. The preface was 'necessary at this time, to put an end to the many publications upon the Freedom of the Negroes'. For the 1785 edition however, the situation again seemed stable and the Preface of 1773 was dropped.

28. F. O. Shyllon, *Black Slaves in Britain* (London, 1974), Chapter 12.

29. Ibid., 193–9.

30. The reaction to the Zong case was significant precisely for its lack of immediate resonance. The case was heard on 6 March 1783, but the only news relating to slavery on the following day was an item on the West India Committee's request for a reduction of sugar duties (*Morning Chronicle*, 7 March 1783). An exceptional letter on the case appeared on 18 March (ibid.). The next newspaper comment on Mansfield was the following item on 26 May 1783: 'It is wonderful to see with what ease Lord Mansfield gets through the business of his Court'. He was so 'pleasant and punctual' that 'it makes everyone happy who has any matter to transact before him' (ibid.). The *Morning Chronicle's* coverage of the Quaker petition to Parliament in June 1783 contained no reference whatever to the Zong case. *Gentleman's Magazine* did not mention the Zong case in its monthly 'remarkable trials' sections in the spring of 1783. Elsewhere it mentioned Sharp's effort to press criminal charges. See Shyllon, *Black People*, 228. It was Sharp's extraordinary step, not the facts of the case which were deemed newsworthy. I have been unable to discover any British newspaper which mentioned the Zong in connection with the Quaker petition. Four years later, when a provincial abolitionist began to illustrate how insurance nullified the interest that a slave trader had in preserving the lives of all his cargo (self-interest was really only the *'price of insurance'*), the Zong case was still not cited. See Letter VIII of 'Africanus', dated 'Norwich, October 8', in the *Norwich Mercury*, 13 October 1787.

31. Two years after the Zong trial newspapers still echoed the traditional dichotomy between moral aversion and *de facto* acceptance. On 8 January 1785, *The Daily Universal Register* called the Negro trade shocking to humanity, cruel, wicked and diabolical, but on 1 July it reported, without comment a jury decision awarding insurance for all

slaves in a mutiny who had died of wounds, bruises and salt water. The jury refused payment only for those who leaped into the sea. As Mansfield again calmly explained, the suicide of a slave from despair was not like his being thrown overboard by the captain to save the rest of the crew and cargo. Slave insurance emerged as separate legal 'problem' only in 1788, after the passage of the Dolben Act. See Samuel Marshall, *A Treatise on the Law of Insurance*, 2 vols (Boston, 1805), 77, 132–5, 385–6, 419, 616.

32. See C. Fyfe, *A History of Sierra Leone* (Oxford, 1962); M. B. Norton, 'The fate of some Black Loyalists of the American Revolution', *Journal of Negro History*, 58 (1973), 402–26; J. Walvin, *Black and White: The Negro and English Society, 1555–1945* (London, 1973), Chapter 9; Ellen G. Wilson, *The Loyal Blacks* (New York, 1976); F. O. Shyllon, *Black People in Britain, 1555–1833* (Oxford, 1977), Chapter 10; and S. Braidwood, 'Initiatives and Organization of the Black Poor', *Slavery and Abolition*, 3, 3 (December 1982), 219–24.

33. Shyllon, *Black People*, 134 ff; Walvin, *Black and White*, Chapter 9; P. Edwards and J. Walvin, *Black Personalities in the Era of the Slave Trade* (Baton Rouge, 1983), 24, 47.

34. Rather than maximizing the exodus of blacks from London, special precautions were taken to prevent the emigration of any person 'against the Rights of Parents or Masters'. (PRO TS/632/1513, meeting of 14 June 1786.) For the protective certificates granted to each settler, see ibid., 2430, 9 October 1786. Shyllon interprets this procedure as a provision for 'owners of runaway blacks' to 'recover their chattels' (*Black People*, 134). It is unclear on what grounds historians interpret the term 'masters' to mean owners of chattels. Ottabah Cugoano's extensive criticisms of the management of the enterprise contained no charge of slave-catching. (See Cugoano, *Thoughts and Sentiments on the Evil of Slavery* (London, 1787), 139–42; also quoted at length in Shyllon, *Black People*, 138–9.) Generalized racism may have played a greater role in *preventing* blacks from going to Sierra Leone a few years later than in forcibly repatriating them in 1786–7. London's *General Evening Post* of 9–11 February 1792, reported that the proprietors of the Sierra Leone Company generally declined 'giving a passage to any black person from hence, in consequence of their having observed that the habits of those blacks who had been living in London, were far from being regular and industrious'. Philip Curtin thinks that the principal sponsors of the project of 1785–7 were dominated by humanitarian motives (*Image of Africa*, Chapter 4). Despite his criticisms of its execution, Cugoano took the same position: *Thoughts and Sentiments*, 138. The subscription list for relief of the black poor included future abolitionists like the Thorntons, Sir Rowland Hill, William Wilberforce, Granville Sharp, the Duke of Montagu, Samuel Hoare, Thomas Walker, Thomas Erskine and William Pitt. But it also included some future antiabolitionists like Lord Romney. See *Public Advertiser*, 27 January, 17 February, *Morning Chronicle*, 3, 13 February 1786. In some ways Sharp's plan for a multi-racial colony clearly foreshadows agricultural utopian projects of the nineteenth century. But it accommodated

to both English and African pre-abolitionist realities, providing for slaves bought from African neighbours to work off the costs of their purchase in five years of public indentured servitude. G. Sharp, *Short Sketch of Temporary Regulations . . . for the Intended Settlement . . . near Sierra Leone* (London, 1786), 1–11, 22–32.

35. Anstey, *Atlantic Slave Trade*, 251.
36. *General Evening Post*, 3 January 1788.
37. Anstey, *Atlantic Slave Trade*, 323–4.
38. Ibid., 300–3, also citing Wilberforce's view. For Clarkson's similar acknowledgement of Pitt's political weakness, see Salop County Record Office, Katherine Plymly Diaries, vol. 1, 1791, entry dated 20 October 1791; also Liverpool Record office, 920 ROS (1444), Roscoe Papers, R. Enfield to Roscoe, 24 October 1789.
39. Davis, *Slavery in . . . Revolution*, Chapter 5; Anstey, *Atlantic Slave Trade*, Chapter 9.
40. Gary B. Nash, 'Slaves and Slaveowners in Colonial Philadephia', *William and Mary Quarterly*, 30 (1973), 226–52.
41. Cobbett's *Parliamentary History*, 23 (1782–3), 1026. The discussion in the newspapers was dominated by the economic consequences of the peace on Africa and the West Indies.
42. Anstey, *Atlantic Slave Trade*, 230. On the lack of response from the Parliamentary or provincial élites, see Friends House Library, London, Box F, Minutes of Meeting for Sufferings, Committee on the Slave Trade, 1783–1792, esp. minutes of 5 May 1784.
43. Davis, *Slavery in . . . Revolution*, 223. These were isolated responses. The Society for Constitutional Information did respond to the Quaker petition, and published statements of support in 1783 and 1784 (PRO TS 11, 961/3507). In September 1786 the Quaker literature was readvertised after the *London Chronicle* gave prominent notice to Clarkson's essay on slavery, (31 August–7 September); see also *Public Advertiser*, 4 September 1786.
44. Ibid., 224; Anstey, *Atlantic Slave Trade*, 230; *Leeds Mercury* 3 July 1787.
45. Clarkson, *History*, 1, 215.
46. *Williamson's Liverpool Advertiser*, 26 June 1783; D. Clare, 'The Growth and Importance of the Newspaper Press in Manchester, Liverpool, Sheffield, and Leeds between 1780 and 1800', MA thesis, University of Manchester, 1960, 117.
47. Anstey, *Atlantic Slave Trade*, 251, citing R. I. and S. Wilberforce, *The Life of William Wilberforce*, 5 vols (London, 1838), 1, 149. 'It needs not be told that the abolition of the slave trade first applied for by Quakers were treated as the chimeras of a wild imagination, which no man thought deserving of a serious discussion.' *The Case of the Sugar-Colonies* (London, 1792), 19. Early in 1789 a pro-slavery correspondent to the *British Journal* (19 April 1789) claimed that the complete failure of legislators to respond to the Quaker petition had quite reasonably left the slave interest unprepared for the onslaught of 1788. See also Clarkson, *History*, 1, 296.

48. Richard Watson, DD, *A Sermon Preached before the University of Cambridge* on 4 February 1780 (Cambridge, 1780), 6, 9. In 1783 even sympathizers with American abolitionists openly assumed that slavery might wither away in North America, but would continue in the West Indies as long as the pecuniary interests of Europe flowed in that direction. The only hope was some alternative investment in Africa itself. (John Lettsom, *Some Account of the Late John Fothergill, M.D.* (London, 1783), lxvi. The Sermon of John Warren, Bishop of Bangor, delivered to the Society for the Propagation of the Gospel in February 1787, also referred to the slave trade as 'infamous' but contained no suggestion for considering its alteration.

49. *Public Advertiser*, 21 January 1785; *The Times*, 28 August 1787; *Morning Chronicle*, 23 November 1787. The quote from John Wesley is from his *Works*, 11, 75, quoted in Wellman J. Warner, *The Wesleyan Movement and the Industrial Revolution* (New York, 1930), 91. Once the popular campaign got underway late in 1787 Wesley immediately signed on.

50. Both the pamphlet literature and newspaper attention indicate that the abolitionist explosion occurred precisely at the end of 1787. Just before the American War of Independence about three antislavery tracts were published each year. Output rose to an annual average of under six in 1783–7, and then soared to over 46 per year in 1788–92. (Calculated from the Catalogue at the Anti-Slavery Society Library by Joyce Bert, 1958, plus Lowell Ragatz's *Guide for the Study of British Caribbean History, 1763–1834* (Washington, DC, 1932), and P. C. Lipscomb's bibliography in 'William Pitt and the Abolition of the Slave Trade', PhD thesis, University of Texas, 1960.) The new version of *The Times Index*, for 1785–9, illustrates the same pattern in the newspapers. From January 1785 to September 1787 there are 19 items entered under 'slave trade' or about 18 items every two months. Items relating only to the *abolition* of the slave trade appeared *once* every *ten* months between January 1785 and September 1787. From September 1787 to December 1788, abolition-related items appeared at a rate of 90 every ten months. All told, in the 2 ¾ years before October 1787, only four of fifteen items in *The Times* on the slave trade were related to abolition. The others were simply traditional trade reports. In the 15 months beginning October 1787, 136 out of 140 items were related to abolition. During the first trimester of 1788, before the subject was mentioned in Parliament, more than half of the items consisted of announcements of the various abolitionist petitions. The 'slave trade' items in *The Times* of London 1787–9 were reported as shown in the table below (items include correspondence, reports, petitions, etc.).

51. See the Duke University Library, Stephen Fuller Letterbooks, 1, Fuller to the Jamaica Assembly, 28 February 1787. Fuller was Jamaica's agent in England. See also *Morning Chronicle*, 2 January, 19 March, 25 September 1787; *London Chronicle*, 11–13 January, 20–2 February, 8–10 March 1787; and *Parliamentary History*, 28 February 1787. In 1777, the last 'pre–abolitionist' Parliamentary report on the *General State of*

Date	Reports on 'normal' slaving activities	Reports on moral or political activity against slavery	Total reports	'Abolitionist' reports as percentage of total reports
Jan. 1785–Sept. 1787	15	4	19	21
Oct. 1787–Dec. 1788	4	136	140	97
Jan.–Dec. 1789	6	74	80	92.5

SOURCE   New index of *The Times* (1786–9).

the Trade to Africa had no more to say about the morality of the slave trade than had the *Valuation of the Company's Forts, Castles and Factories, in Africa* in 1713.

52. *Parliamentary History*, 27 (1788–9), 396–7, 495–6.
53. Anstey, *Atlantic Slave Trade*, 264–6. In the spring of 1787 the Jamaica merchants' and planters' chief concern was the smuggling of foreign sugar and coffee into British Caribbean freeports. See Duke University Library, Fuller letterbooks, 1, 117, 1 May 1787.
54. Peter Marshall, 'The Moral Swing to the East: British Humanitarianism, India and the West Indies' (kindly sent in manuscript by the author). Marshall notes that there was a divergence in concern over these two previously related subjects around 1790. I would contend that the 'swing' of humanitarian concern was rather to the West and that it occurred in 1788. Regarding the retrospective perception of the slave trade as a particularly bad one for sailors, and therefore an inherently vulnerable target for reform, one must note that for contemporaries in the summer of 1787, *East* India captains were the particular target of lawyers 'trepanning sailors to prosecute their commanders and officers for supposed pretences of ill-uses' (*Felix Farley's Bristol Journal*, 25 August 1787).
55. See Parker, *Evidence of our Transactions in the East Indies, with an Enquiry into the General Conduct* (London, 1783), vi–ix; and *The Political Progress of Britain* (London, 1792), 3; 'Humanitas' to *Gore's General Advertiser* (Liverpool), 21 February 1788.
56. See John Ehrman, *The Younger Pitt: The Years of Acclaim* (New York, 1969), 443–51; P. Marshall, *The Impeachment of Warren Hastings* (Oxford, 1965), 188.
57. *Public Advertiser*, 11 July 1787; *Morning Chronicle*, 13 June 1788 (letter of 'Observator').
58. Marshall, *The Impeachment*, 188; L. G. Mitchell, 'Charles James Fox and the Distintegration of the Whig Party, 1782–1794,' D Phil, Oxford University, 1969, 148–160. Prosecutions for the illegal selling of East

Indians began immediately after the first British mobilization against the *African* slave trade. See *Horace Walpole's Correspondence*, 2, 485.

4 THE BREAKTHROUGH 1787–92

1. See, for example, A. D. Harvey, *Britain in the Early Nineteenth Century* (New York, 1978), 44–7. As with all political terms which imply the community as a whole, or its entire public space, the definition of 'public opinion' was always a matter of ideological conflict. Yet although political antagonists usually deny their opponents such an a priori advantage, antislavery opinion was never denied 'popularity'.

2. Charles Tilly, 'Britain creates the Social Movement', in James E. Cronin and Jonathan Schneer (eds), *Social Conflict and the Political Order in Modern Britain* (New Brunswick, 1982), 21–51.

3. E. M. Hunt, 'The North of England Agitation for the Abolition of the Slave Trade 1780–1800', MA thesis, University of Manchester, 1959.

4. See John A. Phillips, *Electoral Behavior in Unreformed England, Plumpers, Splitters and Straights* (Princeton, New Jersey 1982), 15–19; also John Brewer, *Party Ideology and Popular Politics at the Accession of George III* (Cambridge, 1976), 41–56.

5. Phillips, *Electoral Behavior*, 12–19. Before the abolition campaign in 1788 the largest single set of petitions sent to Parliament seems to have been on the subject of hawkers and peddlers, between 1729 and 1731.

6. *Voyage Philosophique d'Angleterre* (London, 1786), 1, 176–83. Englishmen were often proud that the butcher, the grocer, the leather-seller, the apothecary and the fishmonger discussed the politics of Prussia, Canada and Africa every morning, and related the price of veal to the British policy towards Germany or Portugal. (See *Lloyds Evening Post*, 19 May 1762, 481; *Morning Chronicle*, 11 June 1788.) For further links between communications, commercialism and the broadening of civility, see John Brewer, 'Commercialization and Politics', in N. McKendrick *The Birth of a Consumer Society: The Commercialization of Eighteenth-Century England* (Bloomington, 1982), 197–262.

7. J. A. W. Gunn, *Beyond Liberty and Property: The Process of Self-Recognition in Eighteenth Century Political Thought* (Kingston and Montreal, 1983, Chapter 8, 'Public Spirit to Public Opinion', esp. 281 ff., and 312. See also *London Unmask'd, or the New Town Spy* (London, 1783), 54, 60. The 'Guide to the House of Lords Papers and Petitions' (typescript Record Office Memo no. 20, 26), dates the modern system of public petitioning from 1779.

8. The principal engine of Parliamentary reform during the 1780s, the Society for Constitutional Information, adopted an abolitionist position in the wake of the first Quaker initiative. See, *inter alia*, J. Walvin, 'The Impact of Slavery on British Radical Politics: 1787–1838' in V. Rubin and A. Tuden (eds), *Comparative Perspectives on Slavery in New World Plantation Societies: Annals of the New York Academy of Sciences*, 292 (1977), 343–55.

9. See George Rudé, *Wilkes and Liberty* (Oxford, 1962). In the Wilkes affair the initiative came from London: 'Till of late we were all very happy here in Yorkshire . . . when all of a sudden down comes a troop of your London patriots and Bill of Rights Men.' (*Public Advertiser*, 14 November 1769.) The Wilkes petitions were usually freeholders' petitions. For self-conscious concern over the social level of petitioners in the Wilkes affair, see *Public Advertiser*, 2, 4 November 1769.

10. *Manchester Mercury*, 5 November 1771. On the eve of the American Revolution Granville Sharp began to use American petitions from Virginia and Pennsylvania and abolitionist incidents in New York and Boston to agitate privately against the British slave trade. (See Gloucester Record Office, Hardwicke Court Muniments, Sharp papers, Box 28-F, letter of 7 January 1774.) The Pennsylvania petition against the slave trade in 1773 was signed by about 200 persons 'of most weight' in Philadelphia. Huntington Library, BR Box 12 (21).

11. See G. M. Ditchfield, 'Manchester College and Anti-Slavery' (Mss kindly sent by the author).

12. Blanchard Jerrold (ed.), *The Original*, 2 vols (London, 1874), 1, 3. Lancashire petitioners claimed 80 000 signers. See Stockdale's *Parliamentary Debates*, 5th ser. (London, 1785), 2, 208–9. Pitt was impressed and moved for immediate attention to their claims. D. A. Farnie notes that cotton from the mid-1780s began to differentiate its fiscal role from that of the woollen industry; *The English Cotton Industry and the World Market 1815–1896* (Oxford, 1979), 38.

13. On the Irish Resolutions, see John Ehrman, *The Younger Pitt*, 330–6. On the political significance of petitioning see Josiah Wedgwood to Thomas Walker, 23 May 1785, in Jerrold, *The Original*, 1, 93. On national recognition of Manchester petitioning see the *Public Advertiser*, 20 June 1785. Another London paper reported that a Manchester petition signed by 18 'houses' represented 42 000 workers (*Morning Herald*, 7 April 1785).

14. See S. Drescher, *Econocide: British Slavery in the Era of Abolition* (Pittsburgh, 1977), 58–60.

15. On Manchester's development see John Bohstedt, *Riots and Community Politics in England* (Cambridge, Mass., 1983). For a parallel use of the newspaper as the foundation of a mass movement in the provinces, see Thomas Walter Laqueur, *Religion and Respectability: Sunday Schools and Working Class Culture* (New Haven, Conn., 1976), 23.

16. Thomas Cooper appealed particularly to Manchester's new reputation as a leader of popular expression: *Supplement to Mr. Cooper's Letters on the Slave Trade* (Manchester, 1787), 28.

17. See J. Walvin, 'The Rise of British Popular Sentiment for Abolition, 1787–1832', in C. Bolt and S. Drescher (eds), *Anti-Slavery, Religion, and Reform* (Folkestone, Kent/Hamden, Conn., 1980), 149–162; S. Drescher, 'Public Opinion and the Destruction of British Colonial Slavery', in J. Walvin (ed.), *Slavery and British Society*, (London, 1982) 1–22. Manchester decided to petition Parliament despite the fact that the London Committee felt that 'the time was not yet ripe', and that there was as yet no likelihood of success because of 'the great "interests" involved in the trade', *Manchester Mercury*, 11, 17 December 1787, and

letters of Thomas Cooper, cited in Lillie Robinson, 'Thomas Walker and Manchester Politics', BA thesis, University of Manchester, 1931, 14.

18. McKendrick, *Birth of the Consumer Society*, 91, 267–70 and *passim*.

19. Before the petitions of 1788 it was anticipated that the towns of the North would line up in favour of the slave trade. See letter from 'Real Humanity', *Public Advertiser*, 26 July 1787. After Manchester surprised them, London newspapers still expected it to be countered by Liverpool, Bristol, Lancaster and Poole. (*World*, 30 January 1788.) Immediately after the first wave of Northern petitions it was the turn of abolitionists to point out that some of the 'very towns which furnish commodities for the trade' had turned against it. Letter from 'Penn', *Morning Chronicle*, 11 February 1788.

20. *The Morning Chronicle*, 24 June 1788 reported 15 000; The *Morning Post*, on 13 March 1788, 14 000. An unsubmitted petition, intended for the House of Lords in 1796, is the largest Liverpool canvass I have been able to locate. It was drawn up as a 'Merchant, Trader and Inhabitant' document, but contained only 2320 names; Liverpool Public Library Mss, 900 MD 2 (1796). When one of Liverpool's MPs claimed that he was deputed to support the slave trade by the Corporation of Liverpool and *'ten thousand of its inhabitants'* he was challenged even in the Liverpool press. 'The honorable general', wrote a correspondent, 'has never received so respectable a sanction.' (*Liverpool Chronicle and Commercial Advertiser*, 27 February 1805, letter of 'Argus.') There is no doubt, however, that the trade had some popular support in Bristol and, above all, in Liverpool. In 1792 when the Commons voted for gradual abolition, the journeymen carpenters of Liverpool discussed pulling down some abolitionist houses if the trade were abolished. (PRO HO 42/20 (1792), fs 59–62, Henry Blundell, Mayor of Liverpool, to Henry Dundas, 14 April 1792.) See also S. Drescher, 'The Slaving Capital of the World: Liverpool and National Opinion in the Age of Abolition', Mss presented at the Nantes Colloquium on the Slave Trade (1985).

21. An antiabolitionist letter to the *Morning Chronicle* claimed that '4,580 gentlemen, of equal consequence to Mr. T. Walker' signed a counter–petition, one gentleman employing 3000 manufacturers. ('R.O.' to T. Walker, esq., *Morning Chronicle*, 11 April 1788.) A reply in ibid., 9 May denied the existence of any such counter-petition of Manchester inhabitants, signed by 4580 gentlemen. There had been no public requisition for a meeting. If anything it must be a private petition of those interested in the African slave trade. The writer challenged R.O. to list the names, and boasted that if he could not offer ten equally respectable names for each of R.O.'s he would acknowledge 'at least the shadow of truth for his side'. 'R.O.' never took up the challenge. Such scrutinies of Manchester opinion received national publicity (see *Morning Chronicle*, 24 March 1788). The Manchester petition was also quickly dispatched to Jamaica by its agent in England. Duke University Library, Stephen Fuller Letterbook, 1, 16 January 1788.

22. *House of Commons Journals*, 1788. The *Bristol Gazette and Public Advertiser*, 24 January 1788, described the port's abolitionism as a broadly-based movement.

23. There is evidence that even the Quakers on the abolitionist committee were overtaken by events. In the summer of 1787, on the eve of mobilization, John Barton informed William Roscoe that he was afraid of Clarkson's zeal and his lack of caution. (Liverpool Record Office 920 ROS, John Barton to Roscoe, 17 August 1787.) Public opinion helped to strengthen those on the London Committee who favoured immediate rather than gradual abolition. (Ibid., Barton to Roscoe, 6 March 1788.) As late as January 1788 the Quakers had not yet committed themselves to join the national petitioning. Abolitionism was probably the first social movement to use the provincial press systematically on a national scale. A special agent was hired to ensure the republication of the Manchester resolutions. (See Donald Clare, 'The Growth and Import- ance of the Newspaper Press in Manchester, Liverpool, Sheffield, and Leeds between 1780 and 1800', MA Thesis, University of Manchester, 1960, 36.) Manchester also made contact with the Edinburgh Chamber of Commerce which petitioned Parliament as a corporation. (*Gazetteer*, 12 February 1788.)

24. Drescher, *Econocide*, 86, 137–8, 178.

25. When a Liverpool writer attacked Manchester for supporting abolition against its own 'cotton interest' a Manchester correspondent replied, 'Why be alarmed for manufacturers and mechanics when they have no fears?' (*Manchester Mercury*, 11 March 1788.) A year later, against a similar West Indian line of criticism, the following account appeared:

> I shall at once appeal to the conduct of the Manufacturers themselves, . . . they may be supposed to know their own interest as well as the Planters and Slave Merchants know theirs. . . . [The] inhabitants of Birmingham and Manchester respectively assembled . . . and with a unanimity which ought to be remembered to their honour, formed committees for the abolition of the slave trade. . . . At Birmingham a base attempt was lately made to defeat the benevolent purpose of their society by procuring a counter-petition. . . . In consequence of an advertisement on the preceeding day, the inhabit- ants assembled on the 19th of last month [May 1789] in such numbers that the public office could not contain them and they were obliged to adjourn to the hotel. A chairman having been elected, the constables were required to give up the names of those who had called the town together, when it was found to have been the influence of *eight*!! manufacturers chiefly interested in *the trade*. This paltry number of persons were, if possible, sufficiently disgraced and mortified by the Resolutions of the Meeting, to support their [the abolitionists'] for- mer petition, and to thank Mr. Wilberforce for the able manner in which he had introduced the business of the Slave Trade into Parliament.

Charles Fox wrote to Thomas Walker, early in January 1788, that he was 'the more happy that the town of Manchester sees the matter in this light, because the cotton manufacturers were one of the classes of men who were expected to think less liberally than they ought upon this subject. . . . I think it will be difficult even for Liverpool, Bristol, etc. to appear openly in support of so invidious a cause.' (Jerrold, *The Original*, 106–107, 11 January 1788.) In 1792 the petitioners of South Shields, including many shipowners and mariners, pointedly rejected the slave trade as a nursery of seamen. (*Newcastle Courant*, 24 March 1792.) A similar petition came from the fishing trade of Dartmouth. (*Diary*, 27 March 1792.) When Nottingham took the lead on 22 December 1791, and launched the 1792 campaign, some petitioners 'reserved opinion' on the resolution that the slave trade was not necessary for the well-being of the West Indies. But no one actually moved the contrary proposition. (*The Derby Mercury*, 3 January 1792.)

26. The *Manchester Mercury* of 7 October 1787 announced that an effort would be made in Manchester to petition Parliament on the slave trade. The first sermon in favour of the petition was given by Rev. Thomas Seddon, weeks before Clarkson preached. (See *Manchester Mercury*, 9, 30 October 1787.)

27. Farnie, *English Cotton*, 61, speaks of Manchester's freedom from tradition, its dynamic young immigrant population, its 'unrestrained and hyperintelligent individualism which contrasted sharply with the corporate tradition of Liverpool'. Its artisans also lacked the support of ancient craft traditions (ibid., 64).

28. Ibid., 66.

29. On the broadly humanitarian emphasis in the name of manufacturing and commercial realists, see Manchester's national advertisement of 29 December 1787 (e.g. *Public Advertiser*, 10 January; *The London Chronicle*, 12–15 January; *The London Gazette*, 15 January 1788). Symptomatic of the difficulty of classifying abolitionists during the early years were the frustrated epithets of their opponents. The West Indians felt that they were figthing 'mists' and 'phantoms', not interests. See Duke University Library, Fuller Letterbooks, 1, 152, letter of 30 January 1787; S. Drescher, 'Capitalism and abolition: values and forces in Britain, 1783–1814,' in R. Anstey and P. E. H. Hair (eds), *Liverpool, the African Slave Trade, and Abolition* (Liverpool, 1976), 195, note 49.

30. Drescher, *Econocide*, 183.

31. 'Is the imaginary cruelty of the *West India Planters* to be the theme of every *drinking club* and *psalm singing meeting*? . . . the cruelties . . . are become as familiar to *children* as the story of *Blue Beard* or *Jack the Giant Killer*.' (Jesse Foot, *A Defence of the Planters in the West Indies* (London, 1792), 72, 75.) Antiabolitionists characterized abolitionism as a general 'delusion' prevailing 'amongst all distinctions of people'. See 'Agricola', to the *Public Advertiser*, 10 March 1788.

32. Phillips, *Electoral Behavior*, Chapter 5.

33. McKendrick, *Consumer Society*, 217.

34. The Northampton County petition was lodged in different towns 'for the Signatures of all those who wish to suppress this abominable traffic': *Northampton Mercury*, 19 January 1788. The petition was explicitly not confined to freeholders (ibid., 26 January 1788). Following the Northern example, the newspaper insisted that numbers were required to overcome avarice (ibid., 2 February 1788). Similarly, the Rutland county petition was left for the signature of those who wished to subscribe.

(*Lincoln, Rutland, and Stamford Mercury*, 22 February 1788. The Salisbury and Nottingham petitions were also open to inhabitants. *Salisbury and Winchester Journal*, 10 March 1788; *Nottingham Journal*, 15 March 1788.

35. On 16 February 1788 the *Sheffield Register* announced 2000 adhesions to Sheffield's petition. York claimed 1800 (*York Chronicle*, 18 January 1788). Not only Manchester, Sheffield and York, but Leeds, Birmingham, Norwich, Coventry, Bristol, Exeter, Middlesex, Leicester, Shrewsbury, Kendal, Mansfield, Blackburn, Rotherham, Hull, Nottingham, Colchester, Ipswich, Reading, Newbury, Halifax, Warwick, Bradford, Swansea and Falmouth were advertised as having held general meetings. County petitions which were widely circulated or signed included Northamptonshire, Staffordshire, and Northumberland. Rudé estimates the number of Wilkesite petitioners at about 55 000: *Wilkes and Liberty*, 134.

36. Phillips, *Electoral Behavior*, 124.

37. Initially, the *World* characterized the Manchester petition as a 'private' rather than a 'public view'.

38. Stephen Fuller, the agent for Jamaica, wrote despairingly that although the petitioners had no particular grievance or injury to complain of, their protests flowed in from all parts of the country. He openly recognized that 'the sentiments of a vast majority of the people of Great Britain' were hostile to the slave interest. See Fuller, Letterbook, 1, 20 February 1788, and *Diary*, 5 October 1790 (report of June 1790).

39. Fuller Letterbook, 1, 20 February 1788.

40. Phillips, *Electoral Behavior*, 57–60.

41. McKendrick, *Consumer Society*, 122. The manufacturers of earthenware in Staffordshire and the cutlers of Sheffield signed their respective petitions in 1788.

42. See Caricatures listed in M.D. George, *Catalogue of Political and Personal Satires*, 11 vols (London, 1978), no. 8074, by Gillray, 'AntiSaccharites, or John Bull and his family leaving off the use of sugar' (27 March 1792); no 8081, 'The Gradual Abolition' (15 April 1792). Cartoons related to abolition appeared in 1788, 1792, 1795, 1796, 1804, 1807, etc. For an early mention of the slave ship print, see the *Morning Post*, 3 April 1788.

43. S. Drescher, 'Cart Whip and Bill Roller: Antislavery and reform symbolism in industrializing Britain', *Journal of Social History*, 15, 1 (1982) 14.

44. The *Morning Herald* of 25 February 1788 carried an advertisement by the Westminster Forum for a debate on the question:

> Can any political or commercial advantage justify a free people in continuing the slave trade? . . . A Native of Africa, many years a Slave in the West Indies, will attend this evening and communicate . . . a number of very remarkable circumstances respecting the treatment of Negro Slaves, and particularly of his being forcibly taken from his family and friends on the coast of Africa, and sold as a slave.

For a similar account of black speakers at Coachmakers Hall the following year, see *Diary*, 13 May 1789.

Even while abolition was being voted down in Parliament in 1791 it won decisive approval in a London debate. The subject was so popular that a decision was held over for at least three sessions. The vote was only three short of unanimity in favour of abolition, and 'a Native African particularly distinguished himself in vindicating the Rights of his much injured countrymen'. *Diary*, 27 May 1791. The presence of Africans at slave trade debates was incorporated into advertisements. A debate was held over for two more sessions in order to allow Africans 'to plead the cause of their fellow-countrymen', one 'which involved the rights of rational beings, the principles of humanity, and the honor of civilized nations'. *Diary*, 23 November and 1 December 1791, and 15 February 1792. By the third session the debate was even more vividly entitled, 'Criminality of Consuming Rum, Sugar, etc.' See also the *Public Advertiser*, 19 April 1792. Equiano's abolitionist activities as far afield as Edinburgh were reported in the press (*Gazetteer*, 30 May 1792).

Just after the first advertisement heralding African participation in the slave trade debates, *The Morning Herald* of 27 February 1788 reported that a lady astonished and enraptured her audience by the dignity, energy and information she displayed at the School of Eloquence on the subject of the slave trade. At Rice's Room in London, there was a 'ladies only' discussion of the proposition: 'Ought not those ladies whose husbands are Peers and Members of Parliament, to exert their influence over them to obtain an abolition of the Slave Trade.' The slave trade was also debated by 'ladies only' at 'La Belle Assemblee', in London. (*Morning Chronicle*, 7 April 1788.) For later conservatives the practice was insidious: 'It was one of the earliest of their [debating societies] tricks to attract females to their indecent discussions', with subjects 'in which the "ladies" were said to be deeply interested': *A Warning to the Frequenters of Debating Clubs, being a short history of the Rise and Progress of those Clubs* (London, 1810), 3.

45. The consumer was 'the master-spring that gives motion to the whole Machine of Cruelties', and abstention could unbend the spring of planter action. (*The Duty of Abstaining from the Use of West India Produce. A Speech delivered at Coach-Maker's Hall, London January 12, 1792*, 7.) All could join: 'Plebian, Peasant, Artist, this is a cause which you may engage secure of conquest; because far more glorious than that of sacking towns, or subduing kingdoms, is that of "bidding the oppressed go free" . . . ye have only to refuse the commodity which is the price of blood, of the blood of brethren . . . unite and conquer'. (*Leicester Journal*, 13 January 1792. See also T. Clarkson, *History of the Rise, Progress and Accomplishment of the Abolition of the African Slave-trade* (London, 1808), 2, 350.) On female initiatives, see the *Newcastle Courant*, 7 January 1792. The first known Welsh advertisement for free sugar was published in 1797. Specific reports on female-initiated abstentions and canvassing were published in Newcastle, Norwich, and Chester.

46. The advertisement for a London debate on the duty of 'ABSTINENCE from Sugar, Rum, etc.', observed that 'since it had been resolved upon by women as well as men', the debate would be 'an appeal to the justice and humanity of both sexes' at Coachmakers Hall. (*Diary*, 5 January and reports of 12 and 18 January 1792). The question was decided 'by an almost unanimous vote of almost six hundred persons in favour of our African brethren'. (Ibid., 18 January.) Popular interpretations of the question at issue were often broader than their Parliamentary counterparts. The question debated was whether to abolish *slavery* and not just the slave trade, and 'the iron mask of the Somerset case' was brought forward. (*Diary*, 12 January 1792.) On London abstention, see also *General Evening Post*, 26–8 January 1792; and *Morning Chronicle*, 23 March 1792. At the 'Society for Free Debate' in Birmingham, sugar consumption was also voted down by 'a very great majority'. (*Sheffield Advertiser*, 30 December 1791.) Apparently two itinerant Quakers made an actual enumeration of the sugar abstainers in Cornwall. (*Star*, 23 March 1792; *Diary*, 28 March 1792.) In Lincoln, 'a party of economical and public spirited ladies' led the campaign for abstention. The inhabitants of Biggleswade did a house-to-house canvass for pledges (*Chester Chronicle*, 2 December 1791. See also *Newcastle Courant*, 7 January 1792). Children in dissenting schools were not allowed to use sugar so that they would never feel deprived of it: Duke University Library, Fuller Letterbook, 2, 7 December 1791. On details concerning the spread of abstention see, *inter alia*, *Shrewsbury Chronicle*, 30 March 1792; *Newcastle Courant*, 7 January, 7 April, 30 June 1792; *Northampton Mercury*, 24 December 1791, 7 January 1792; *Lincoln, Rutland and Stamford Mercury*, 2 December 1791; 30 March 1792; *Edinburgh Evening Courant*, 4, 23 February 1792; *Gloucester Journal*, 6 February 1792; *Norfolk Chronicle*, 9 November, 3 December 1791; *Leicester Journal*, 6 January 1792; *Chester Chronicle*, 18 November, 2 December 1791; *Manchester Herald*, 14 April 1792; *Sheffield Register*, 11 November 1791. Sugar abstention was mentioned in London, Cornwall, Birmingham, Sheffield, Ipswich, Newcastle, North Yorkshire, County Durham, Northamptonshire, Leicester, Norwich, Boston, Manchester, Stamford, Edinburgh, Cork, Limerick, Leslie, Glasgow, Chester, Biggleswade, Derby, Belfast and Dublin. 'Free' sugar advertisements appeared, *inter alia*, in London, Manchester, Ipswich, Newcastle, Northampton, Norwich, Sheffield, Edinburgh, Chester and Birmingham. The West India merchants were sufficiently alarmed by the anitsaccharite movement to form a committee 'for the sole purpose of counteracting the above practices'. Duke University Library, Fuller Letterbook, 2, 7 January 1792.

47. Before the abstention campaign a Liverpool newspaper had sarcastically advised abolitionist souls to refrain from sugar instead of agitating. Four years later another Liverpool paper was upset at the abolitionists for having adopted just that technique. Compare *Gore's General Advertiser*, 31 January 1788, with *Williamson's General Advertiser and Marine Intelligencer*, 3 April 1792. British abolitionists did not envisage a boycott of all slave-related products. They were unwilling to extend the

antisaccharite movement to cotton, which 'might take away the bread of a million of our fellow subjects, the innocent poor of this country'. Salop Record Office, Plymly Diaries, 5, entry of 27 February 1792.

48. Calculated from *A Report from the Committee of Warehouses of the United East India Company Relative to the Price of Sugar* (London, 1792), 23.

49. When news of the St Domingue uprising reached Britain late in 1791 with reports of over 200 sugar plantations destroyed, prices rose and British sugar surged into the Continental market. See the *Shrewsbury Chronicle*, 4 November and 25 November 1791. On the Paris sugar riots, see George Rudé, *The Crowd in the French Revolution* (Oxford, 1959), 95–8; *Morning Chronicle*, 30, 31 January, *Public Advertiser*, 16, 24 February 1792. In London, the most detailed reports on the riots, including excerpts from the National Assembly reports, appeared in the *Diary*, 22, 30 and 31 January 1792. There was also a small French radical current in favour of abstention. After the sugar riots 'several sections of Paris and several societies in the Provinces, . . . abjured the use of these luxuries [coffee and sugar]. The Club of Jacobins . . . took an oath to the same effect.' (Report dated Paris, 2 February 1792, in the *Diary*, 7 February 1792.)

50. Noel Deerr, *A History of Sugar*, 2 vols (London, 1949–50), 530.

51. See Friends House Library, London, Temp Mss, box 10/14, William Dickson, 'Diary of a Visit to Scotland, 5th January – 19th March 1792, on behalf of the Committee for the Abolition of the Slave Trade'.

52. *House of Commons Journals* (indices).

53. William Smith, in the Slave Trade debate of 26 April 1792, noted that 'while the concurrence is undoubtedly general in the southern part of this island, it is yet nothing to that perfect unanimity which prevails on that subject among our brethren in the North'. (*Diary*, 4 May 1792).

54. For the organization of the Scottish campaign of 1792, Dickson took special precautions to avoid all charges of having dicated the decision or the contents of petitions. When boys attempted to sign a petition (Dundee entry, 2 March) the event was scrupulously recorded. Dickson 'visited all the trades in their different corporations, who are with us to a man'. (Salop Record Office, Plymly diaries, 5, 27 February 1792.) In Scotland, and closest precedent to the petitioning of 1792 was the outpouring against Lord North's Catholic Relief Bill from May 1778 to July 1779. That declaration had also been signed by labourers and journeymen of all trades. (See Dickson's Diary, 25 February 1792.) Paisley's abolition petition contained 21 trade societies, including tailors, shoemakers, weavers, smiths, masons, bakers, gardeners, etc. (*The Star*, 29 February 1792.) See *The Edinburgh Evening Courant*, 20, 25 February 1792, 3, 10 March 1792 for the adhesions of skinners, furriers, bonnet makers, dyers, shoemakers, websters, farmers, friendly societies, tradesmen and journeymen.

55. The absence of mass counter-petitioning was one of the abolitionists' most unequivocal advantages. (Friends House Library, Temp Mss 10/14, Dickson Diary, 13 January 1792.) The abolitionist *Abstract of the Evidence . . . on the . . . Slave Trade* (London, 1792), 20–1, their major

propaganda document, took a broad view of the public; 'even those who have not the vote, are nevertheless comprehended in our idea of the public mind'. Clarkson appealed for mass petitions only: see his letter to the Major of Lincoln dated 2 February 1792 (*Lincoln, Rutland and Stamford Mercury*, 15 February 1792). In 1792 the number of abolitionist petitions was so unprecedented that they 'almost obstructed the proceedings of the House [of Commons] by their perpetual introduction'. *Diary*, 12 April 1792.

56. Abolitionists actually welcomed Tarleton's tactics on the petitions of 1792. He claimed that some were signed by 'school masters, schoolboys, with the addition of other names, some real, some fictitious'. What did this prove, replied Sir Richard Hill, but that 'individuals of all sorts, conditions and ages, young and old, master and scholar, high and low, rich and poor, the risen and the rising generation had unanimously set every nerve on stretch. . . . Besides, it is not improbable that some of these lads had just been smarting under the operation of a severe flogging from some too rigorous master.' Who else could so appropriately 'sympathize with the poor African?' Moreover, Tarleton had singled out less than *two* per cent of the documents. (*Letter of Sir Richard Hill to Reverend J. Plymly, Chairman of the Abolitionist Society of Salop, a portion of his undelivered speech in the Commons* (1792).) See also Thornton's defence of 'the peasant, the mechanic and the school boy' as equal in judgment to any member of the House on such a matter (*Diary*, 4 May 1792). One of Tarleton's targets, the Edinburgh petitioners, had deleted the schoolboys' signatures before it went to Parliament. Some opponents of abolition admitted that the petitions in their own localities were valid reflections of local opinion (see Drake's speech in the *Diary*, 26 April 1792). On calls for mass signatures, see Samuel Bradburn, *An Address to the People called Methodists* (Manchester, 1792), 12–15. Notices had to be circulated at Ipswich assuring the poor that signing would cost them nothing (*Diary*, 30 March 1792). The *Chester Chronicle*, 30 March 1792, took note of a 'Reverend Gentleman' in Manchester who refused to sign its abolition petition. On the Manchester figures for 1792 see the *Chester Chronicle*, 9 March 1792. For hostile acknowledgments of working-class petitioners in Leicester and Nottingham, see *The Star*, 7 March 1792. The author of *Farther Reasons of a Country Gentleman for Voting against Mr. Wilberforce's Motion* (London, 1792), 1–2, denounced the abolitionists for 'soliciting the ignorant and illiterate of every village'. *An Appeal to the Candour and Justice of the People of England in Behalf of the West India Merchants and Planters* (London, 1792), 69, condemned the signing up of 'the sick, the indigent, the traveller', the use of students to canvass, and 'the indiscriminate signing of all' in towns like Bolton.

57. Salop County Record office, Plymly Diaries, 9, 16 April 1792; and William Dickson's 'Diary', Friends House Library, entry of 25 February 1792. As late as 1833 14 years remained the general minimal age for petitioning. See *Report of the Select Committee on Public Petitions*, 694 (no. 645), Glasgow antislavery petition, with 31 172 names. Some petitions had a minimum age of 16. (*Wheeler's Manchester Chronicle*, 23 July 1814.)

58. On the Ipswich correspondence, see *The Ipswich Journal*, 17, 31 March 1792. In a parish near Northampton with a population of 2000, 308 signed in 1792. Women, paupers and illiterate labourers were not permitted to sign. Less than a dozen 'eligibles' refused to subscribe. Presumably, the entire literate adult male population of the parish was about 300, or 15 per cent of the parish population. See *Northampton Mercury*, 24, 30 March 1792. One correspondent, attacking the petition, claimed that a pauper *had* signed. The charge was welcomed as a general confirmation of authenticity (ibid., 7, 14 April 1792). Of Northampton's 1079 signatures for abolition 750 were housekeepers: *Northampton Mercury*, 31 March 1792. The Norwich petition committee appealed to all inhabitants. (*Norfolk Chronicle*, 11 February 1792).

   Signatures were not reserved for the 'grave, respectable, and informed part of the community' (Speech of Tarleton, MP for Liverpool, quoted in *An Appeal to the Candour*, 74. One antiabolitionist was outraged that the City of London's commercial majority in favour of the slave trade should be placed on an equal footing with the

   > *englightened miners* of Cornwall, who, it seems, bring up the rear of the Petitioners. But surely, when the first City in the World, after a full and free discussion of any branch of Traffic, gives its decided opinion that it should be preserved, it affords a strong presumption that it cannot be abandoned without the grossest robbery of a great part of our fellow subjects.

   A few days later a London Common Hall carried abolition by a 10 to 1 majority, over the opposition of the Lord Mayor (*Diary*, 28 March, 3 April 1792). The chief complaint about the Ipswich petition was that those who signed were not remarkable for their respectability: 'An apprentice to a Carpenter signed and next day signed for three of his master's journeymen.' (ibid., 30 March 1792.) In Parliament, Tarleton described petitions as seldom coming from town halls but moving 'from Ale House to Ale House' (ibid., 9 April 1792). Another MP complained that MPs had voted against their better judgment because of popular pressure. For Colonel Phipps the petitions were 'contemptible' because they were gathered from 'school boys, farmers, mechanics, and others no way interested in the commerce of the kingdom'. (*Diary*, 24, 26 April 1792).

59. The petitions of Edinburgh, Glasgow, Sheffield and Manchester together contained 'not less than 43,000 names'. (*Diary*, 27 March 1792.) To reach a total of 350 000, the remaining 500 or more petitions needed to average only 600 names each.

60. In 1814 the Freemason's Hall petition in London was signed by nearly 30 000 people in five hours. Huntington Library, Thomas Clarkson Papers, CN42, Clarkson to Catherine Clarkson, 28–9 June 1814.

61. On petition counting for the two Sedition Bills of 1795, see BL Add. Mss 27,808, Francis Place Papers, f. 52.

62. The reaction to public opinion by the slave interest was not always an uncompromising reaffirmation of their rights. The representatives of Barbados expressed more anguish than defiance:

> We consider the system oppressive to master and slave, as tending of both to destroy the moral character, and to perjurate families. The proudest and the most prosperous among us would wish time to go back, to replace our ancestors in their original conditions in Europe, and to give to chance the power of determining our present situations in Great Britain, rather than to take our proper stations in the colonies where many are slaves. (*Diary*, 23 August 1792)

63. See Dickson's Diary, 6 March 1792, entry on Edinburgh. On the evocation of the Gordon Riots, see *Morning Chronicle*, 7 March 1788. There was an occasional threat of violence at peak moments of abolitionist mobilization. *The Manchester Herald* of 19 May 1792 reported that a party of dragoons was marched from York to Scarborough because of anger against Colonel Phipps, its representative, for voting against abolition.

64. Phillips, *Electoral Behavior*, 34. At the first petition meeting of the 1792 campaign, Nottingham resolved that it was proper to instruct its representatives (*The Derby Mercury*, 3 January 1792).

65. An item in the *General Evening Post* at the beginning of the first petition campaign (22–4 January 1788) warned that 'the cry of *No Slavery!* may be as popular in 1788 as *No Popery* was in 1780, or *Wilkes and Liberty* in the time of the *North Briton*'. In some areas launching a petition involved a clear defiance of local authority. The advertisement for the petition of Hertford announced that it had been signed by the 'great majority of inhabitants' (*General Evening Post*, 18–21 February 1792). An item in the *Diary*, 30 March 1792 (supplement) stressed the special role of the slave trade in illustrating 'the virtue of the people triumphing over aristocratic influence. . . . The Mayer [sic] of Hertford refused to lend the inhabitants the Hall to assemble in for agreeing on a Petition to Parliament for the abolition of the horrible traffick. The people, however, met at an inn, and accomplished the point in view.' At Malton, in Yorkshire, 'a letter was read from the great proprietor of the town to the people convened there for the purpose of Petitioning, dissuading his tenants from such a measure. This interference they received with indignation and 600 persons soon afterwards signed their names.' In the County of Monmouth, the Sheriff refused to call a meeting, and other impediments were made use of, but the people would not be disappointed. They met at the town of Usk and completed their wishes. . . .' At Woburn, 12 clergymen signed the petition, but one 'inveterate' enemy of dissent attempted to use technical arguments against any signatures from across the county line. Without such pressure, it was claimed, the Woburn petition would have been a quarter to a third larger (Richard How to James Phillips, 26 March 1792, in Bedfordshire Record Office, How Papers, HW87/451). A letter to the *Morning Herald*, 27 April 1792 sounded a note of implicit danger which was to dominate the rest of the decade:

> the tender feeling of that virtuous majority who would vote away a lucrative branch of the national commerce cannot be too much applauded by every enthusiast for universal freedom, and the Rights

of Men. . . . Immortal be the fame of those amiable Sectaries, who set their marks to such a torrent of addresses for the Abolition of the Slave Trade, as stifled all opposition, and hold forth hope to every friend of innovation that time will shortly bring about Revolutions more important and more adequate to their wishes.

If the convicts of Africa should not be transported by British ships, what, asked the writer, could be said of Botany Bay, the flogging of soldiers, the pressing of seamen, of all exploitive labour for manufactured goods? See also the *Morning Herald*, 30 April 1792: 'reforming Sectaries seem to have objects in contemplation of much greater extent. . . .' Abolition of the slave trade was the 'engine of the *Rights of Man*.' (Letter of a 'Friend to the Constitution', dated 21 February in the *Diary*, 11 June 1792.) On 14 June, another letter to the *Diary* branded abolition as part of a conspiracy to sap the Constitution. A 'great multitude sign without knowing' its tenor, the 'harmless and defenceless flock' being guiled by 'wolves in sheeps-clothing'. The London Abolition Committee withdrew from public agitation after 1793 and even branded radical abolitionist attacks on the supporters of the slave trade as inflamatory. See BL Add. Mss 21,256, Committee Proceedings of 12 April 1797.

66. On one occasion an MP declared that in certain cases, petitions from the lower classes 'were more respectable than those which came from the higher'. (*Morning Chronicle*, 17 February 1795.) A Bristol correspondent to the *General Evening Post* (28 February – 1 March 1792) urged every artificer, mechanic and tradesman to protest against the traffic in the human species.
67. The *Morning Chronicle* of 25 November 1795 condemned tax gatherers for going to the poor in London and Westminster and forcing them to sign petitions for the Sedition Bill. Poor women were asked to sign only with first initials, Elizabeth thus becoming Edward.
68. *Manchester Mercury*, 11, 17 December 1787.
69. In Belford and vicinity 433 persons signed, among whom were 'Ladies anxiously desiring to show their abhorrence of this abominable trade.' (*Newcastle Courant*, 3 March 1792). In Scotland several female petitions were drawn up in 1814. One at Inverkeithing obtained 200 signatures in 24 hours (*Edinburgh Evening Courant*, 21 July 1814). Gwynne E. Owen dates Welsh women's antislavery petitions from 1831. 'Welsh Anti-Slavery Sentiments 1790–1865: A Survey of Public Opinion', MA thesis, University of College of Wales, Aberystwyth, 1964, 81.
70. By 1830 abolitionist appeals were gender-inclusive ('Fathers! Mothers! Brethren! Sisters!'), calling for parallel female petitions to match every male petition. (*The Baptist Magazine for 1830*, 438.) In 1830, 3500 women signed a petition from Nottingham. (*Nottingham Review*, 7 December 1832.) The great women's petition of 1833 consisted of 179 000 names sent to the Lords and 187 000 sent to the Commons. It took several days to link and roll the sheets. The petition to the lower House was nearly half-a-mile long. Together with almost 14 000 signatures from the 'Ladies of Edinburgh' over 200 000 women's names were added to the emancipation rolls on the same day (information from a

printed broadside dated London, May 1833). On earlier female canvassing for Wilberforce, see *The Iris, or Sheffield Advertiser*, 9 June 1807. The *York Herald* hailed 'the FAIR SEX' as the best canvassers in the Yorkshire election of 1807. French women also entered politics through antislavery petitions. See *Le Semeur*, 31 March 1847, 103; *Revue Abolitioniste*, 1 (1847), 33.

71. Adam Smith, *Lectures on Jurisprudence* (Oxford, 1978), 186–7.
72. G. T. F. Raynal, *Histoire Philosophique et Politique des etablissements et du commerce des Européens dans les deux Indes* (Geneva, 1781).
73. *Morning Chronicle*, 9 August 1787.
74. See *Annals of Agriculture*, 9 (1788), 185–6. As late as the fall of 1787, the slave and sugar trade ports of Nantes and Bordeaux were the very last word in European prosperity and urban amenities for Arthur Young. Amidst all of his admiration one can not find a single admonitory word on the flawed moral basis of their exceptional wealth. See *Travels in France during the Years, 1787, 1788 and 1789*. Jeffry Kaplow (ed.) (New York, 1969), 55–9, 96–7. Young's animosity towards the French West Indian trade in was based solely upon considerations of agrarian political economy. In 1784 Young had reiterated his high valuation of the West Indies. *Annals* 1 (1784), 13. Young remained a sensitive weathervane of élite opinion. Following the St Domingue uprising and the rising fear of the French Revolution he struck a new note of caution about implementing abolition. *Annals* 17 (1792), 523–27, 'Abolition of the Slavery Trade'.
75. Davis, *Slavery in . . . Revolution*, 420–34.
76. On the prevalence of witchcraft, see PRO BT 6/9 (Privy Council hearings) ff. 304, 329, 423, 431, 440, 473, 476; BT 9/10, f. 136.
77. Pitt's determination to hold a major Privy Council Inquiry came only after Fuller reported that 'the stream of popularity runs against us' (Fuller Letterbook, I, 30 January, 6 February 1788). Thereafter Fuller made it clear that it was a case of the planters against the petitions ibid., I, 2 April, 10 May, 5 November 1788; 7 January 1789; 10 February 1789. See also the instructions to William Dickson before his visit to Scotland (Friends House Library, Papers, Temp Mss 10/14. Pitt also used the petitions of 1788 to argue for the initial consideration of the slave trade. A contemporary historian considered the Commons' swing to gradual abolition between 1791 and 1792 as the result of popular petitioning. See William Belsham, *Memoirs of the Reign of George III*, 8 vols (London, 1796), IV, 359. Opponents also described the reversal as a 'bullied compliance' to 'dictatorial petitions'. (*Public Advertiser*, 13 April 1792). In 1792 Pitt actually threatened 'to go to the country' again if the House of Commons voted to postpone abolition until 1800. (*Diary*, 24 April 1792).

5   THE IMPACT OF POPULAR MOBILIZATION IN BRITAIN AND THE CARIBBEAN

1. At the end of November 1792, an informant at Reading reported to the government that the only people still justifying reform and Paine's book

were some Quakers (PRO HO 42/22 (1792), 270, from Lancelot Aus-
twick, 23 November 1792). See also R. Anstey, *The Atlantic Slave Trade
and British Abolition, 1760–1810* (London, 1975), 277–8; James Walvin,
'The Impact of Slavery on British Radical Politics: 1787–1838',V. Rubin
and A. Tuden (eds), *Comparative Perspectives on Slavery in New World
Plantation Societies; Annals of the New York Academy of Sciences*, 292
(1977), 343–55. By early 1793 petitioning was under attack in Parliament. Edmund Burke dismissed a Parliamentary reform petition from
2500 Nottingham inhabitants in a general indictment: 'Considering the
manner in which signatures were usually procurred to Petitions, the
probability was that very few Petitioners, who had subscribed to the
present one had ever read it.' A few days later, the antiabolitionists were
attributing the vote of 1792 on the slave trade to the Commons' submis-
sion to 'clamours without doors'. In the Lords the even more vitriolic
Lord Abingdon harked back to the 'rage of petitioning that preceeded
the Grand Rebellion in the year 1640'. (*Diary*, 22, 27 February and 11
April 1793.) Reform petitions were rejected as disrespectful of the
House. See the *Diary*, 3, 7 May 1793. On the deepening crisis of
legitimacy for petitioning see also the *Parliamentary Debates* of January
and February 1795.
2. Ibid., 321–409; J. Walvin, 'The Public Campaign in England against
   Slavery, 1787–1834', in D. Eltis and J. Walvin, *The Abolition of the
   Atlantic Slave Trade* (Madison, 1981), 67.
3. In the spring of 1805 the London Abolition Committee postponed
   calling a public meeting, but sent Clarkson on another tour among the
   local affiliates. Clarkson found the same enthusiasm for abolition. The
   Committee thought that private pressure on MPs would be more advis-
   able than public meetings. See BL Add. Mss, 21, 254–21, 256, 'Proceedings of the Committee for the Abolition of the Slave Trade',
   1787–1819 (3 vols), 3, 19 March, 29 April, 9 July, 1805; 7 March, 2 June,
   30 July, 1806. On the call for grass roots pressure in 1805–7, see Friends
   House Library, London, Box H, Antislavery Tracts, open letters of
   Granville Sharp, 3 June 1805 and 30 July 1806. For 1814, see *ibid.*,
   printed letter of Clarkson, 21 June 1814, accompanying a resolution and
   the form of a petition.
4. For the West Indian evaluation of the power of 'popular opinion out of
   doors', see George Hibbert, *The Substance of Three Speeches in Parliament* (London, 1807), Preface. See also Thomas Clarke, *A Letter to Mr.
   Cobbett on his Opinions Respecting the Slave Trade* (London, 1806),
   preface, 2. By 1807, *Cowdroy's Manchester Gazette* was referring to
   General Gascoyne, MP for Liverpool, as the 'member for the *metropolis*
   of Slavery' (11 February 1807). Such observations were routine as well
   as polemic. See *Observations on the Necessity of Introducing a Sufficient
   number of Respectable Clergymen into our Colonies* (London, 1807), 4.
5. On the emergency call for the Manchester abolition petition see Clarkson to John Wadkin, 1 May 1806 (Clarkson Papers, St John's College,
   Cambridge, Box 1:2). On the result, see *Cowdroy's Manchester Gazette*,
   10 May 1806, letter of 'An old Abolitionist'; *Leeds Mercury*, 31 May
   1806; and House of Lords Record Office (Mss), Petitions on the Slave
   Trade, 13 May 1806.

6. A representative of Tewkesbury, under popular pressure, pledged himself to vote for abolition (*Diary*, 2 April 1792). In the Hereford County election of 1807, Colonel Foley campaigned on his abolitionist vote (*The Gloucester Journal*, 11 May 1807). At least some MPs switched their position in favour of abolition during the campaign. (*Northampton Mercury*, 8 November 1806, and *York Courant and Northampton Mercury*, 4 May 1807.) When the Lincoln County election was contested for the first time in 80 years, in 1807, the ultimately defeated candidate, Richard Ellison, was attacked by Major Cartwright on grounds of his sympathy for the slave trade (*Stamford Mercury*, 22 May 1807). On the issue of abolitionism in Liskeard and London, see *The Courier*, 19, 20 November 1806; at York, see the *York Courant*, 3 November 1806; at Tewkesbury, *The Hereford Journal*, 23 April 1806.

7. In the election of October 1806 the Methodists had already circularized Yorkshire to vote for Wilberforce. (P.F. Dixon, 'Politics of Emancipation', D. Phil; Oxford, 1971, 115). See also Duke University Library, Wilberforce papers, William Hey to Wilberforce, 24 October 1806. 'Might it not be said with equal propriety, that the *Country* carried the abolition, by almost generally insisting, at the late election, on a pledge from those who were about to be vested with the Country's voice?' (*Leeds Intelligencer*, 20 April 1807). The Yorkshire election of 1807 was described as more hotly contested than anything 'since the days of the REVOLUTION'. During the campaign, the West Indian Edward Lascelles pledged to vote against any move to rescind abolition (ibid., 11 May 1807); he went so far as to promise to vote for slave emancipation if a repeal measure were introduced (ibid., 18 May 1807). Even the Whig Lord Milton was tarred with his family's slave connection (*York Herald*, 6 June 1807). On the Opposition's estimate of the significance of the abolitionist vote in Yorkshire, see Dixon, 'Politics of Emancipation', 116. A letter from a Methodist at Leeds urged a vote for the two abolitionist candidates (Wilberforce and Milton) and against Lascelles, the West Indian 'Man-stealer'. (*The Iris, or Sheffield Advertiser*, 12 May 1807).

8. For the revival of popular reformism in the Manchester area see PRO HO 42/87 (1806), William Chippendale, Manchester, to Ralph Fletcher, esq., Bolton-Le-Moor, January 29, 1806, sent on to London January 31st. On the unpopularity of the slave trade's supporters, see Lord Sidmouth's speech in Parliament (*The Times*, 6 February 1807). For a private Antiabolitionist assessment of public opinion, see PRO T 70/1585, S. Cook to Lord Howick on the Slave Bill, February 13, 1807.

9. Naomi C. Miller, 'John Cartwright and radical Parliamentary reform, 1808–1819', *English Historical Review*, 83,329 (October 1968), 705–28; John Cartwright, *Reasons for Reformation* (London, 1809), 24. For 1814, see Bedfordshire Record Office, Samuel Whitbread Mss, Correspondence on the Slave Trade, no. 4169, John Cartwright to Whitbread, 30 August 1814.

10. S. Drescher, 'Public Opinion and the destruction of British Colonial Slavery', in J. Walvin (ed.) *Slavery and British Society*, 24ff.

11. Principally, Lords Castlereagh and Liverpool, hard core antiabolitionists in 1807.

12. Drescher, *Econocide*, chapter 9; Betty Fladeland, 'Abolitionist Pressures on the Concert of Europe, 1814–1822', *Journal of Modern History* 38 (1966), 355–73. *The Morning Chronicle*, 11 August 1814, reported the number of petitions to the Commons as 861 and the number of signatures as 755 000. If there were any complaints it was about the insufficient number of places set aside for signatures. Bedfordshire Record Office. Whitbread Mss, Correspondence, no. 4162, Joseph Brown, MD, to Whitbread, Islington, 21 June 1814.

13. Dixon, 'Politics of Emancipation', 144–6. By 1814 British commanders were refusing to force American slaves who fled on board their ships to return to American owners, although the latter were allowed to interview their ex-slaves on deck (*Gloucester Journal*, 27 June 1814). In French cartoons the British were portrayed as Negrophiles, burning Washington and freeing slaves. In the 1814 campaign the abolitionists moved Britain directly and permanently against one principle of the new international system which favoured their nation's interests. A cornerstone of that system was to be the insulation of the Continental politics from colonial, maritime and commercial competition beyond Europe. The British government's initial recognition of the foreign slave trade was one means of pacifying post-Napoleonic France, and of demonstrating of the 'liberality' of British overseas hegemony. As soon as British policy became actively abolitionist and tightened the screws on the slave trade, it had to reveal more of the iron fist than the velvet glove of the 'Pax Britannica'.

14. *Parliamentary Papers*, 83 (1852–3), 104–5, 'Return of the number of Petitions Presented in each of five years ending 1788–9, 1804–5, 1814–15', etc.

15. AN C2425 (session of 1844) 233, 'Ouvriers de Paris demandant l'abolition de l'esclavage'. In the 1844 petition, 7126 signed in Paris and 1704 in Lyons, for a total of 8130. A great number of Lyons' workers, including women, designated themselves as 'Proletaires'. On the psychological impact of the working-class petitioners in Paris, see *Le Semeur*, 8 May 1844, 147. The petition was reproduced in the Juste-Milieu *Journal des Debats* and *Constitutionnel*; the radical *Réforme*, the religious *Semeur*, *L'Univers*, *Réformateur Religieuse* and *Archives Israelites*, and a few provincial newspapers. Only the *Globe*, heavily subsidized by the colonial councils, took a hostile position. Within a month the Minister of Marine and Colonies introduced a Bill to simplify the terms of private manumission. The French abolitionist society expanded its terse reports into a somewhat more popular format. The total number of petitions to the Chamber of Deputies between 1836 and 1846 was 7704 (*Le Siècle*, 18 March 1847). The number of British emancipation petitions of 1830 and 1833 were therefore each equal to more than seven years of petitions in France.

16. AN SO-M, SA 197 (1489), petitions of 1847.

17. The increase of 'notable' petitioning from French Departmental Councils after the petitions of 1847 may be seen from the table below. However, the 21 departments of 1847 still represented only one-fifth of the total.

Resolutions in favour of emancipation presented by Conseils Généraux of French Departments, 1835–47

Date	Number	Number from new Departments
1835	5	5
1836	6	1
1837	5	3
1838	10	2
1839	11	1
1840	6	1
1841	7	1
1842	4	0
1843	4	0
1844	3	0
1845	3	0
1846	4	1
1847	21	13

SOURCE AN SO–M., 156 (1301), 'Voeux des Conseils–Généraux pour l'abolition, 1835–1847'.

18. The government was forced to discuss the petitions of 1847 because of the growing strength of abolitionism outside the Chambers. See BN NA 3631, Schoelcher Papers, Jabrun, delegate of Guadeloupe, to the president of the Council of Martinique, 14 September 1847. Jabrun was particularly struck by the spread of abolitionism to the provinces. The question had moved beyond containment through subventions of the Paris press. By the spring of 1847 the delegate for Martinique also concluded that 'public opinion is turning against us'. The first two newspapers identified as favouring the petition of 1847 were '*l'Univers*, religious newspaper of the clergy, and *l'Atelier*, newspaper of the workers'. (ibid., Jollivet to Martinique, 13 February 1847.) The Legitimist newspapers which had hitherto opposed action against slavery were also no longer willing to defend the colonies (ibid., 29 April 1847). By the end of the year an abolitionist coalition seemed to be forming between the abolitionist society, members of the Catholic clergy, 'men of colour' and radicals in Paris. Abolitionists began to tear down Parisian wall notices of slaves for sale in the colonies (*Le Semeur*, 17 November 1847, 9 February 1848). Early in 1848 a new set of emancipation petitions arrived from several departments. See AN C2429, no. 93, and AN CC475 (645). Eleven petitions, bearing more than 2000 signatures, had reached the Chamber of Deputies by the outbreak of the February Revolution.

19. During the 1840s the major reason given for rejection of immediate emancipation by the French government was France's financial situation. Guizot emphasized the requirement of a 'sacrifice' of 250 to 300 million francs to the planters. See BN NA 3631, Schoelcher Papers, letter of Jollivet to the Council of Martinique, 28 June 1843. See also

S. Drescher (ed.), *Tocqueville and Beaumont on Social Reform* (New York, 1968), 172. While the colonists were advised to brace themselves for further piecemeal moves against slavery (BN NA 3631, Schoelcher Papers, Jollivet to Martinique, 14 February 1848), their strongest line of defence remained the indemnification of '250 millions'. (See ibid., Dupin to Martinique, 29 April 1847; and the *Siècle*, 30 July 1847.) There was still no mention of colonial slavery at the opening of the 1848 legislative session either in the Address from the Throne or in the discussion of the Chambers' reply. (See *Le Semeur*, 29 December 1847, 408.)

20. Drescher, 'Public Opinion', 43–5. A year before British emancipation an address was presented to the British King on Parliamentary reform. Each of the 236 000 signatures was accompanied by an identifying address. Twenty committees spent three weeks alphabetically transcribing the names from 2000 sheets of parchment. The mile-long document was moved on rollers nine feet in diameter (*Le Semeur*, 18 April 1832). It was in such a context that British abolitionism had to compete. See ibid., 7 August 1833, 12 March, 1 August 1834, 21 December 1836, etc. (On the 270 000 women's signatures for emancipation in 1833, see *Cobbett's Weekly Political Register 85* (16 August 1834), 401.)

21. Drescher, 'Public Opinion', 47. There were obviously enough positive results among targets of public petitioning to encourage its rapid general growth as a political instrument. In rallying nonconformity to the abolitionist petition of 1814, *The West Briton and Cornwall Advertiser* (1 July) pointed to the examples of the defeated Sidmouth Bill and of the rejected modification of the Corn Laws. See also, *inter alia, Votes and Proceedings of the House of Commons* (1823), Appendix no. 441, 351, 2 May; *Glasgow Advertiser*, no. 650, 13–17 February 1792, 107; *Wheeler's Manchester Chronicle*, 10 August 1833.

22. C. Duncan Rice, 'Literary Sources and the Revolution in British Attitudes to Slavery', in C. Bolt and S. Drescher (eds), *Anti-Slavery, Religion, and Reform* (Folkestone, Kent/Hamden, Conn., 1980), 319–34, esp. 326–7. The dramatic impact of the abolition campaign in the reordering of priorities may be seen in S. J. Pratt's lengthy poem, *Humanity, or the Rights of Nature* (London, 1788). The preface announced that African slavery had been moved up to the leading position in the poem because of the 'emulative Benevolence' now coursing through the Empire. Pratt also reversed the standard sequence of British libertarian poetry. Usually the muse of liberty or of civilization was traced from antiquity to the present in a series of begats, passing from people to people and reaching its apotheosis in Britain. *Humanity* followed the spread of slavery from Egypt to Greece, to Rome, to Portugal, to Spain and to the Americas, until 'Humanity' began to radiate from Britain. Pratt's case is merely illustrative. A more detailed analysis would be necessary to demonstrate the longer-term literary shift away from the assumed inevitability of tropical slavery in British creative writing. At the very least, Rice correctly asserts that a definitive change had occurred by the time of the defeat of Napoleon. (On Equiano's response to Pratt's poem, see Shyllon, *Black People*, 233, 257–8.)

23. Drescher, *Econocide*, 107, 111. Anstey, *Atlantic Slave Trade*, 326–9; Dale H. Porter, *The Abolition of the Slave Trade in England, 1784–1807* (Hamden, Conn., 1970), 97–9.

24. 'Britannicus,' *A Letter to the Right Hon. William Pitt, Containing some new arguments against the Abolition of the Slave Trade* (London, 1804), 7.

25. Hansard, *Parliamentary Debates*, 28 (1814), 448, speech of George Canning, 29 June 1814.

26. Mary Turner, *Slaves and Missionaries: The Disintegration of Jamaican Slave Society, 1787–1834* (Urbana, Ill. 1982), 105. Manchester was clearly a case where art imitated political life. The petitioning was well underway when *Oroonoko* opened at Manchester's theatre. When the existing versions of the play were deemed insufficiently abolitionist, it was rewritten to conform to Manchester's new militancy. *Oroonoko* was still playing in February 1788 (*Manchester Mercury*, 27 November 1787, 18 February 1788). See John Ferriar, *The Prince of Angola: a tragedy altered from the play of Oroonoko* (Manchester, 1788), preface). All degrading references to the black hero were removed. Newspapers also noted the increase in performances of Oroonoko elsewhere: *World*, 16 January 1788.

27. *Flower's Political Review*, I (1807), xxxv, xlvi; *Cobbett's Political Register* 11 (7 March 1807), 364; also 85 (16 August 1834), 403; *Poor Man's Guardian*, 21 October 1833, 346; 30 May 1835, 546.

28. Drescher, 'Public Opinion,' 32. Just before the mass mobilization of 1823, Clarkson's first 'emancipation' tour was countered by a planter counter-propaganda campaign (Huntington Library, Thomas Clarkson Papers, CN33, 113).

29. G. M. Ditchfield, 'Repeal, Abolition, and Reform: A Study in the interaction of reforming movements in the Parliament of 1790–6', in Bolt and Drescher, *Anti-Slavery*, 101–18.

30. See, above all, C. L. R. James, *The Black Jacobins* (London, 1938); Sidney Mintz and Douglas Hall, 'The Origins of the Jamaican Internal Marketing System', *Yale University Publications in Anthropology*, 57 (1960), 1–26; Michael Craton, *Testing the Chains: Slave Rebellions in the British West Indies, 1629–1832* (Ithaca, New York, 1982), 242–323; J. Walvin (ed.), 'Introduction', *Slavery*, 16; M. Craton, 'Slave Culture, Resistance and the Achievement of Emancipation in the British West Indies, 1783–1838', ibid., 100–22, esp. 102.

31. Craton, *Testing*, Chapter 19.

32. B. W. Higman, *Slave Populations of the British Caribbean, 1807–1834* (Baltimore and London, 1984), 394.

33. See the letter of 'Civis' in the *Morning Chronicle*, 5 February 1788, 'On the Slavery of the Blacks'.

34. James Stephen anticipated a long historiographical tradition with his notion that slave systems existed primarily on the basis of psychological terror, akin to a superstitious belief in ghosts. This mentality supposedly disappeared forever with the St Domingue Revolution (*The Crisis of the Sugar Colonies* (London, 1802) 27 and 72–5). Henry Brougham took immediate exception to Stephen's psychological theory of slave sub-

servience in *The Edinburgh Review*, 1 (October 1802), 224. On this point see also David Geggus, 'British opinion and the emergence of Haiti', in Walvin, *Slavery*, 122–49. The impact of Haitian independence on the pace of British abolition was ephemeral. See ibid., 149, and Geggus, 'Haiti and the Abolitionists: Opinion, Propaganda and International Politics in Britain and France, 1804–1838', forthcoming in David Richardson (ed.), *Abolition and its Aftermath in the West Indies*, vol. 1, *The Historical Context, 1790–1870* (London, 1985).

35. On the role of black slaves in saving and expanding British slavery see Roger N. Buckley, *Slaves in Redcoats: The British West India Regiments, 1795–1815* (New Haven, Conn., 1979), esp. 140–4; Drescher, *Econocide*, 167–70; Craton, *Testing*, 165. The impact of the St Domingue Revolution on metropolitan attitudes is equivocal in both the short and long run. It was the West Indians who took the lead in tying the St Domingue uprising to the abolitionist movement (*Morning Chronicle*, 3, 16, 23, 27 February 1792). William Dickson's diary indicates that in Scotland it was the also antiabolitionists who first availed themselves of the 'St. Domingo affair' and the danger of metropolitan agitation. (Diary, Perth, 5 February 1792.) The abolitionist response to the uprising was defensive. One tactic was to publish accounts of British West Indian tranquillity and safety from insurrection. (*Public Advertiser*, 5 March, 9 April 1792.) Later historical assumptions about St. Domingue's role in bolstering Parliamentary support for abolition have never been very closely argued or empirically based. On the contrary, Henry Dundas, moving in 1792 for gradual abolition in 1800 reasoned that one could proceed cautiously with British abolition. It 'had nothing to do with the disorders in Saint Domingo'. As the responsible Minister, his official information was 'that our islands were in a state of the most perfect tranquility'. (*Diary*, 24 April 1792). In voting to postpone abolition for at least three years the House of Commons apparently agreed that immediate abolition was not imperative.

36. Drescher, *Econocide*, 153–4; Geggus, 'Haiti and the Abolitionists'.

37. *Parliamentary Debates*, 3rd ser., vol. 17, 1218 (14 May 1833). On the economic embarrassment of Haiti to the abolitionists, see Huntington Library, MY 146, Clarkson to Z. Macaulay, 5 December 1827.

38. E. D. Genovese, *From Rebellion to Revolution: Afro-American Slave Revolts in the Making of the Modern World* (Baton Rouge/London, 1979), Chapters 2 and 3. 'After 1807 marronage became increasingly individualistic, and rebellion took on creolized forms' (Higman, *Slave Populations*, 393).

39. Genovese, *From Rebellion*, esp. Chapter 3; Craton, *Testing*, Parts II, III.

40. Craton, *Testing*, 335–9: 'Chronology of Resistance'. These, and all my calculations on slave resistance, are based upon data from the 75 events listed in Craton's chronology. I have not included independently discovered incidents from newspaper accounts. My own research did not cover or sample newspaper accounts for the entire two centuries between the 1630s and 1830s. It is unlikely that metropolitan coverage of plots and incidents would have been as good during the seventeenth as during the

eighteenth century. For examples of data not recorded in Craton's chronology, see the *London Chronicle*, 1–14 July 1787, reporting a plot in Antigua; the *Morning Chronicle*, 24 June 1788, reporting restiveness in Jamaica; the *Middlesex Journal*, 1–3 June 1769, reporting a large plot in Jamaica. To avoid distortion by choice of periods, periodization was varied to test the general reliability of trends. On this see also S. Drescher, 'Paradigms Tossed: The Decline Thesis of British Slavery since the Mid-Seventies', Table I, (forthcoming, in *Caribbean Slavery and British Capitalism*, B. Solow and S. Engerman (eds).)

41. Higman, *Slave Populations*, 121. For chronological purposes Higman assigns the British Caribbean colonies to three phases: those acquired and developed by 1750; those obtained in 1763; and those obtained after 1792 (*Slave Populations*, 67). For his economic context, however, Higman analytically combines second– and third–phase sugar colonies into the category 'new sugar colonies'. Jamaica and the non-sugar colonies are placed in sets of their own. When using the term 'old colonies' below, without further qualification I mean, as does Higman, those acquired and developed by 1750.

42. In global estimates I have included slave resistance in all the colonies. The general trends described in the following table also hold for the sugar colonies alone.

    Some trends are, of course, almost completely obscured if one simply combines all the British West Indian colonies without regard to their stage of economic and demographic development. As a totality the chronology reveals one instance of active resistance in about every *six* years for both 1650–1700 and 1700–90. Acts and plots combined also occurred on a average of once every *3.6* years for both the above periods. Looking at the rate of aborted plots, the percentage was 43 before 1700 and 40 from 1700–90. Without analytically distinguishing between developed and developing colonies, the resistance rate appears to be constant and the relationship between slave resistance and development in the 140 years before the era of abolitionism is invisible. Regarding plots, historians sometimes too casually attribute their appearance to planter 'paranoia'. This attribution seems to beg some important questions. It is still necessary to account for why 'paranoia' varied so much from one colony to another and from one slave–holding generation to another.

43. *The Public Advertiser* of 22 July 1760 carried an account of the 'free Negroes' bringing in 17 pairs of ears, and two heads of rebelling Jamaican slaves. Before 1790 Jamaica's maroon 'slave catchers' were regarded in Britain as part of 'the strength of that island'. See [John Campbell], *Candid and Impartial Considerations on the Nature of the Slave Trade*, etc. (London, 1763), 105.

44. Craton, *Testing*, Chapter 8; Genovese, *From Rebellion*, 54–5.

45. Compare Walvin, 'Introduction' to *Slavery*, 10; Craton, *Searching for the Invisible Man* (Cambridge, Mass., 1978), 142–9, 172; Barry Higman, *Slave Population and Economy in Jamaica* (Cambridge, Mass., 1978), 231–2.

Sugar colony resistance rates, with
average number of years between incidents*
(including plots and actions 1649–1832

Period	(1) 'old' colonies	(2) Jamaica	(1+2)	(3) 'new' colonies	(2+3)
1649–99	7	10	4	—	—
1700–60	15	15	10	—	—
1760–90	30	10	8	5	3
1700–90	18	13	8	—	—
1760–1815	55	7	6	4	2
1791–1815	+	5	8	2	2
1791–1832	21	5	4	3	2
1816–32	8	4	3	16	3

* *The larger* the number the *lower* the rate.
† no plots or resistance recorded during this period in the old islands.

SOURCE   Craton, *Testing the Chairs*, Chronology.

46. See Walvin, 'Introduction' to *Slavery*, 10, citing M. Craton *Searching for the Invisible Man: Slaves and Plantation Life in Jamaica* (Cambridge, Mass., 1978), and *Testing*, 163, 267; B. W. Higman, *Slave Population and Economy in Jamaica, 1807–1834* (Cambridge, Mass., 1976). On the shift to sugar, see Higman, *Slave Populations*, 71, Table 3.9; on the reduction of labour, see ibid., 187; and on abolition of the trade as the decisive variable, ibid., 394.

47. On the preponderance of free foreign blacks in the British Caribbean rebellions of the 1790s see the *Morning Chronicle*, 4 May, 2, 29 June, 1, 6 July, 2, 28 August 1795. See also note 51 below. In Dominica, maroons often raided the plantations, burning slave quarters along with estates, and causing slaves to fight alongside their masters. (*London Chronicle*, 31 January–2 February 1786; *Public Advertiser*, 6 February 1786.) To some extent this pattern carried over into the French Revolutionary period in the Caribbean.

48. Craton, *Testing*, Chapter 17. See also *The Star*, 1–3 February 1792. On slave reactions to abolition debates, see Craton, *Testing*, 253, and Turner *Slaves and Missionaries*, Chapter 5.

49. See Duke University Library, Wilberforce Mss, Granville Sharp to Wilberforce, 4 June 1795.

50. *Parliamentary Debates*, 8 (1806–7), 952.

51. For their own reasons abolitionists usually accepted, and even seized upon, the idea that Africans were more rebellious than Creoles. See 'Africanus', Letter XI, *Norwich Mercury*, 13 November 1787. West Indian MPs claimed that Grenada and St. Vincent were saved by the

loyalty of British colonial blacks. (*Morning Chronicle*, 19 February 1796.) See also Craton, *Testing*, 165–6, and Edward L. Cox, *Free Coloreds in the Slave Societies of St. Kitts and Grenada, 1763–1833* (Knoxville, Tenn. 1984), 80–90.

52. On creolization as a biocultural process, see Craton, *Testing*, 15–16, 48–51, 241–53. The fundamental distinction is a demographic one between African and Caribbean-born. (Higman, *Slave Populations*, 121–35.)

53. On the wide demographic divergence of slave populations, see Higman, *Slave Populations*, esp. Chapters 5, 9. Michael Craton places the greatest causal weight on the "proto-peasant" characteristics developed among the slaves. "Proto-peasant Revolts? The late slave rebellions in the British West Indies 1816–1832," *Past and Present* 85 (1979), 99–125. The difficulty is that such characteristics had been evident generations before the late slave rebellions.

54. Craton, *Testing*, 291; Turner, *Slaves and Missionaries*, 163; Higman, *Slave Populations*, 181–8. On the suspension of governmental action on slavery during the Reform Bill crisis, see Hansard, *Parliamentary Debates* (3rd ser.); 4, 372, Lord Howick (27 June 1831).

55. Turner, *Slaves and Missionaries*, 162–3; Mary Record, 'The Jamaica Slave Rebellion of 1831', *Past and Present* 40 (1968), 108–25.

56. Craton, 'Slave Culture', 121: 'The news from Jamaica in 1832, though, overwhelmed the remaining opposition to emancipation.' See also William A. Green, *British Slave Emancipation: The Sugar Colonies and the Great Experiment 1830–1865* (Oxford, 1976), 112. On the other hand see the more negative assessments of Dixon, 'Politics of Emancipation', 203, and Anstey, unpublished third chapter of his manuscript on British emancipation (page 21).

57. Dixon, 'Politics of Emancipation', 304, ff. The King himself opposed emancipation (ibid., 305, Letter to Goderich, 5 June 1832).

58. *Aris's Birmingham Gazette*, 27 February 1832. The convergence of Anglo–Caribbean antislavery agitation was abundantly clear during the campaigns against colonial apprenticeship. See Alex Tyrell, 'The "Moral Radical Party" and the Anglo-Jamaican campaign for the abolition of the Negro apprenticeship system', *English Historical Review*, 99; 392 (July, 1984), 481–502.

6 GOD'S WORK: ANTISLAVERY AND RELIGIOUS MOBILIZATION

1. E. Williams, *Capitalism and Slavery* (Chapel Hill, 1944), 178, quoting R. Coupland, *The Empire in These Days* (London, 1935), 264.

2. R. Anstey, *Atlantic Slave Trade and British Abolition, 1760–1810* (London, 1975), Part II.

3. D. B. Davis, *Slavery and Human Progress* (New York, 1984), Chapter 5.

4. Mary Turner, *Slaves and Missionaries: The Disintegration of Jamaican Slave Society, 1787–1834* (Urbana, Ill., 1982), 10–11.

5. Alan D. Gilbert, *Religion and Society in Industrial England: Church, Chapel and Social Change, 1740–1914* (London, 1976), Chapter 1. A letter (by 'Lucy Grant') to the *Gazetteer* of 9 September 1767 casually began, 'I am just arrived from one of his Majesty's West India islands, so that it is almost needless to tell you that I have not much religion in me.'

6. See J. Harry Bennett, Jr, *Bondsmen and Bishops: Slavery and Apprenticeship on the Codrington Plantation of Barbados, 1710–1838* (Berkeley, California, 1958), 3–5, 82–5; D. B. Davis, *The Problem of Slavery in Western Culture* (Ithaca, New York, 1966), 219–222. SPG expenditures in the 30 years after 1777 fell below those for the period before. C. F. Pascoe, *Two Hundred Years of the S.P.G.: An Historical Account of the Society for the Propagation of the Gospel in Foreign Parts* (London, 1901), 822–32. As late as 1830 the SPG voted against a motion that West Indian slavery was contrary to the Christian religion (*The Record*, 21 October 1830). Apologists, of course, could also refer to the Society as an example of Christian practical sanction (see PRO BT 9/11, Privy Council hearings).

7. On the eve of slave emancipation, the Superior of the Congregation de Saint-Esprit, which supplied French missionaries to the colonies, still took a stance of neutrality. Freedom would be welcome 'at the earliest possible moment', on condition that it neither 'hurt the legitimate interests of the masters nor exposed them to evils which would be still more dire than slavery' (*Le Semeur*, 1846, 368). On the extraordinary degree to which the French clergy in the colonies remained 'creolized', see the letter of Prefect Apostolique Castelli to Baron Mackau, 10 juillet 1841. (AN, Archives Privées, 156 (Fonds Mackau), 1 (46).) The French hierarchy did not protest colonial demands for the reassignment of priests who were too enthusiastic about preaching the gospel. (RHASSP G/103, France, Isambert to Scoble, 19 January 1843.) On the doctrine of the legitimacy of slavery in the seminary of Saint-Esprit, see Victor Schoelcher, *Histoire de l'esclavage pendant les deux dernières années*, 2 vols (Paris, 1847), 1, 186–196. In 1842 the British Antislavery Society appealed directly to the Archbishop of Paris to launch an antislavery campaign among the French clergy. The response on the French side was to emphasize the dangers of immediate emancipation, and the necessity instead for more missionaries. (See Archevêché de Paris, Archives historique, Direction Des Oeuvres, 4KII, Dossier: 'Pour l'abolition de l'esclavage', letter of Richard Madden to Msgr Affre, Archbishop of Paris, 17 March 1842, with a comment by M. Teste.)

The progress of abolitionism did provoke extensive discussion within Catholic circles during the July Monarchy. However, it revolved more around the role of Christianity in ending European than overseas slavery. See Frank Paul Bowman, *Le Christ Romantique* (Genève, 1973), Chapter 4. For the same discussion among Anglo-American abolitionists, see Davis, *Slavery and Human Progress*, Part II, Chapter 4.

8. Since thousands of Africans were annually supplied to the Spanish and French islands by British slavers with official encouragement, it is not surprising that recruitment into the true faith was not incorporated into

English mercantile guides. See *The Merchant's Dayly Companion* (London, 1684), 373, and subsequent merchant manuals. As late as the 1780s black slaves were brought to Spain in English vessels (letter from Seville in *The Morning Chronicle*, 24 September 1788).

9. John Oldmixon, *The British Empire in America* (London, 1741 edn), 418: 'The Clergy trouble themselves little, and the Church doors are seldom opened.' Patrick Gordon's *Geography Anatomiz'd*, 20th edn (London, 1754), 390, stated that Negroes had no religion, 'for Slaves all over *America* hate the People who buy and sell them, and consequently hate all their modes of Worship, which demonstrate a Religion only external'. *The Gentleman's Magazine*, 10 (1740), 341, regarded it as beyond dispute that 'the Countries they [Africans] go to have less of true Virtue and Religion than their own'. On the eve of abolitionism there was still only one clergyman to 12 000 Carribean inhabitants (*Public Advertiser*, 14 May 1787).

10. According to *The History and Present State of the British Islands*, 2 vols (London, 1743), 1, 268, ministers claimed that the great planters refused Christian instruction to slaves for fear of consequent demands for 'better usage'.

11. Turner, *Slaves and Missionaries*, 52–9; P.D. Curtin, *Two Jamaicas: The Role of Ideas in A Tropical Colony, 1830–65* (Cambridge, Mass., 1958), 31; Orlando Patterson, *The Sociology of Slavery: An Analysis of the Origins, Development and Structure of Negro Slave Society in Jamaica* (London, 1967), 185–202; Monica Schuler, 'Afro-American Slave Culture', in M. Craton (ed.) *Roots and Branches: Current Directions in Slave Studies* (Toronto, 1979), 121–37. For the early period see Morgan Godwyn, *A Supplement to the Negro's and Indians Advocate* (London, 1681), 3. One hundred years later the failure of conversion among the slaves was taken for granted in a sermon by the Bishop of Chester (*Morning Chronicle*, 29 August 1783).

12. Turner, *Slaves and Missionaries*, 168 ff.

13. H. O. Dwight, H. A. Tupper and E. M. Bliss (eds), *The Encyclopedia of Missions* (New York, 1904), appendices II and VI.

14. S. Drescher, 'Two Variants of Anti-Slavery', in C. Bolt and S. Drescher, *Anti-Slavery, Religion, and Reform* (Folkestone, Kent/Hamden, Conn., 1980), 49–50; Mr S. Delacroix, *Histoire Universelle des Missions Catholiques*, 4 vols, (Paris, n.d.), 3, 14–15, Chapter 1–3.

15. Drescher, 'Two Variants', 51–2. See also *L'Univers*, 16 September, 30 October 1847. On the role of Dupanloup and the archbishop of Paris, see RHASSP C 13/111, Bissette to Scoble, 27 April 1847. Even the conservative organs of the clergy were stirred by the petition campaign of 1847. See *L'Ami de la Religion*, 133 (April, 1847), 267 ff. The colonial interest was unnerved by the activity of hitherto politically neutral lay and clerical groups. BN NA, 3631, Schoelcher Papers, Jollivet to Martinique, 29 January 1847. The usually anticlerical *La Réforme* favorably reported an abolitionist sermon at the Petite Eglise Saint–Laurent, attended by workers, Félicité de Lamennais, Edgar Quinet and Geoffroy Saint-Hilaire. (V. Schoelcher, *Histoire de l'Esclavage*, 2, 434.) See also the *Bureau de Correspondance pour l'abolition de*

l'esclavage (Paris, 19 June 1847). By 1847 abolitionists could goad their countrymen with reminders that the Swedes, the Tunisians and the Jewish Consistory of Algeria had all abolished slavery within their jurisdictions. They urged Catholic France not to allow itself to be outdistanced by Protestants, Muslims, and Jews. See *Le Semeur*, 20 May 1847, 167; 13 October 1847, 352.

16. Ira Berlin and Herbert G. Gutman, 'Natives and Immigrants, Free Men and Slaves: Urban Workingmen in the Antebellum South', *The American Historical Review*, 88, 5 (December 1983), 1175–1200. Gilbert Osofsky, 'Abolitionists, Irish immigrants and the dilemmas of Romantic Nationalism', *American Historical Review*, 80, 4 (October 1975), 889–912.

17. Osofsky, 'Abolitionists', 900–6.

18. Anstey, *Atlantic Slave Trade*, 189, 191, 192.

19. Betty Wood, *Slavery in Colonial Georgia, 1730–1775* (Athens, Ga, 1984), 65–6.

20. Davis, *Slavery in Western Culture*, 148; *Slavery in . . . Revolution* (Ithaca, New York, 1984), 203; Leland J. Bellot, 'Evangelicals and the Defense of Slavery in Britain's Old Colonial Empire', *Journal of Southern History*, 37 (1971), 19–40.

21. Davis, *Slavery in Western Culture*, 382. Significantly, Granville Sharp already took Methodist hostility to slavery for granted at the time of the Somerset decision. York Minster, Sharp Letterbook, 112, Sharp to Mr Lloyd, 31 July 1772.

22. John Wesley, *Thoughts upon Slavery* (London, 1774), 55–6.

23. Donald G. Mathews, 'Religion and Slavery – The case of the American South', in Bolt and Drescher, *Anti-Slavery*, 207–32.

24. *Morning Chronicle*, 9 August 1787; *London Chronicle*, 7–9 August 1787, 134.

25. Ibid., 212; D. G. Mathews, *Slavery and Methodism: A Chapter in American Morality 1780–1845* (Princeton, New Jersey, 1965), 295. See also Andrew E. Murray, *Presbyterians and the Negro : a History* (Philadelphia, 1966), 17; Walter Posey, *The Baptist Church in the Lower Mississippi Valley, 1776–1845*, (Lexington, Kentucky, 1957), 89–90.

26. Mathews, 'Religion and Slavery', 210–20.

27. Davis, *Slavery in . . . Revolution*, 203.

28. As late as 1823 the Jamaican Wesleyans adapted themselves quite well into the colonial hierarchy (Turner, *Slaves and Missionaries*, Chapter 1). The Methodists insisted on emphasizing secular obedience abroad and abolitionist mobilization at home as emancipation agitation increased. *Wesleyan Methodist Conferences*, 6 (1825), 51.

29. *A Journal of the Reverend Dr. Coke's Visit to Jamaica* (London, 1789); Thomas Coke, *A History of the West Indies, containing the Natural, Civil and Ecclesiastical History of Each Island*. 3 vols (Liverpool, 1808–11), 1, 415–17.

30. On the Moravians, see Davis, *Slavery in . . . Revolution*, 193; Turner *Slaves and Missionaries*, 9, 117.

31. Turner, *Slaves and Missionaries*, 14–16.

32. Ibid., Chapter 5.

33. Ibid., *Slaves and Missionaries*, 11.
34. Coke, *A History*, 1, 417–19.
35. Turner, *Slaves and Missionaries*, 9–27.
36. Ibid., 27–9, 109–11.
37. Ibid., Chapter 3. In 1791 Coke estimated the total evangelical population in the West Indies at 50 000 (*Chester Chronicle*, 9 September 1791).
38. Turner, *Slaves and Missionaries*, 80–1.
39. Ibid., 115.
40. Ibid., 105–6, 118–19. Richard Watson claimed that with rare exceptions, the colonial Anglican clergy never baptized Africans: *A Defence of the Wesleyan Methodist Missions in the West Indies* (London, 1817), 47–52.
41. C. Duncan Rice, 'The Missionary Context of the British Anti-Slavery Movement', in J. Walvin (ed.), *Slavery*, 150–63. By 1830 newspapers with abolitionist sympathies had headlines like: 'PRAYING PUNISHED BY FLOGGING!' (*Sheffield Iris*, 16 July 1830).
42. W. R. Ward, *Religion and Society in England, 1790–1850* (London, 1972), Chapter 1. The popular antisaccharite crusade of the early 1790s had relatively little recourse to Christian symbolism. It appealed to the 'law of nature, that individual felicity keep a fixed pace with the well-being of the aggregate of the species', *Morning Chronicle*, 23 March 1792.
43. G. M. Ditchfield emphasizes the comparative religious harmony in Lancashire and Cheshire before 1787, and the lack of deep religious antagonism before 1789. 'The Campaign in Lancashire and Cheshire for the Repeal of the Test and Corporation Acts, 1787–1790', *Transactions of the Historic Society of Lancashire and Cheshire*, 126 (1977), 109–38, esp. Section IV. F. C. Mather speaks of a unity between the intellectuals and reformers *c.* 1790, never regained thereafter: *Chartism and Society: An Anthology of Documents* (London, 1980), 37.
44. J. Walvin, 'The Public Campaign in England against Slavery, 1787–1834', in D. Eltis and J. Walvin (eds), *The Abolition of the Atlantic Slave Trade* (Madison, 1981), 63–79, esp. 65–6. On the non-denominational pattern of the Sunday School movement in the late 1780s, see Ward, *Religion and Society*, 14–16; also Thomas Laqueur, *The Sunday School Movement*, 27–9. One of the significant features of the first abolitionist mobilizations was that its opponents found it difficult to agree on its specific social political or religious profile. See *General Evening Post*, 2–5 February 1788, letter from a Bristol Merchant.
45. J. Walvin, 'The Impact of Slavery on British Radical Politics: 1787–1838', in V. Rubin and A. Tuden (eds), *Comparative Prespectives on Slavery in New World Plantation Societies; Annals of the New York Academy of Sciences*, 292 (1977), 343–55, esp. 345; P. Fryer, *Staying Power: The History of Black People in Britain*, (London and Sydney, 1984), 106–7.
46. *Norwich Mercury*, 18 February 1792.
47. Salop Record Office, Plymly Diaries, 103 (11 May–21 July 1814). Fuller reported to Jamaica that 'all the dissenters in the House of Commons are with Wilberforce' (Letterbook, 2, 1 August 1791).

48. For some examples from many such accusations, see letters in the *Public Advertiser*, 4 February 1788; *Diary*, 29 June 1789; for rebuttals, see *Public Advertiser*, 4, 7, 22 February 1788. After the Quakers, the Baptists were apparently the first to give denominational support to the London Abolitionist Society. See BL Add. Mss 21, 255, 'Proceedings of the Committee for the abolition of the Slave Trade, 1787–1819', 9 December 1787. By then Wesley had already offered his personal endorsement.
49. G. M. Ditchfield, 'Repeal, Abolition and Reform', in Bolt and Drescher, *Anti-Slavery*, 101–18. By 1830 letters calling on ministers to petition both Houses of Parliament went to each Baptist and Wesleyan clergyman. See *The Baptist Magazine*, 22 (1830), 342–3.
50. Gilbert, *Religion and Society*, 27–8.
51. Ibid., 125–7. The transatlantic impact of Anglican-Methodist antagonism was visible as early as the mobilization against the Sidmouth Anti-itinerancy Bill of 1811. See Ward, *Religion and Society*, 57. (On the particular appeal of antislavery to Methodists in Wales, see G. E. Owen, *Welsh Anti-Slavery*, 11.)
52. P. F. Dixon, 'The Politics of Emancipation', 95. On Anglican fear of a Whig/Dissenter alliance see *The Record*, 8, 22 October 1832; on radical contamination, ibid., 16, 23 May, 4 July 1833 and *The Cumberland Paquet*, 28 August 1832. *The Record* was attacked at a Leeds public meeting for its scriptural apology for slavery. (*Halifax and Huddersfield Express*, 25 May 1833.) The *Christian Observer* (May,1833), 314, was equally dismayed at the support of antisectarian and pro-slave Jamaicans by Anglican publications and religious societies.
53. S. Drescher, 'Cart Whip and Bill Roller: Antislavery and reform symbolism in industrializing Britain', *Journal of Social History*, 15, 1 (1982), 10.
54. *Preston Pilot*, 22 September 1832. *Cumberland Paquet*, 28 August 1832, 'West India Slavery'. In 1788–92, ministers of the established clergy, including Scotland, sponsored between 14 and 22 per cent of abolitionist petitions, the Scottish clergy making their decisive contribution in 1792.
55. The 'Rights of Man' was completely legitimized in Methodist antislavery rhetoric. (*Liverpool Courier*, 15 October 1832). See also R. Anstey, 'Parliamentary Reform, Methodism and Anti-Slavery Politics, 1829–1833', in *Slavery and Abolition* 2:3 (1981), 220–223 (posthumous) D. B. Davis, ed.
56. See *The Record*, 16 May, 4 July 1833.
57. See Davis, *Slavery in . . . Revolution*, Chapters 8, 9; Anstey, *Atlantic Slave Trade*, Chapters 7–9.
58. See, *inter alia*: E. Hurwitz, *Politics and the Public Conscience*, 48, 79 and 81 (although there is a later statement that all strata supported emancipation); Davis, *Slavery in . . . Revolution*, 357, 361–5, 385, 421 and 450; Dixon, 'Politics of Emancipation', 208–11; Williams, *Capitalism and Slavery*, 181; Patricia Hollis, 'Anti-slavery and British working-class radicalism', in Bolt and Drescher, *Anti-Slavery*, 294–313. T. Haskell, 'Capitalism and the Origins of the Humanitarian Sensibility', in *The American Historical Review*, 90, 2 (June 1985); H. Temperley 'The

Ideology of Antislavery', in Eltis and Walvin, *The Abolition*, 28. Howard Temperley, following E. M. Hunt, remarks that the constituency of popular abolitionism, in the early period at least, 'drew its support from a broad range of social classes'; see his 'Anti-Slavery', in P. Hollis (ed.), *Pressure from Without*, 33. For emphasis on a broader social base, see also Walvin, 'The Public Campaign in England', 63–79; Drescher, 'Two Variants', 57–9; and 'Cart Whip', 3–24.

59. Drescher, 'Two Variants', 48, 58, Tables 2 and 3.
60. *Chester Chronicle*, 23 December 1791, 9 March 1792.
61. Drescher, 'Two Variants', 48; Dixon, 'Politics of Emancipation', 118. On the important role of the Methodists in the campaign of 1814, see Huntington Library, Macaulay Papers, MY 143, Clarkson to Z. Macaulay, 8 June 1823.
62. According to A. D. Gilbert, 1787–8, 1791–2, 1806–7, 1814, 1822–3, 1830–1, 1832–3, were years of rapid Methodist expansion. High growth cycles of nonconformity in general occurred in 1783–9, 1804–16, 1820–4, 1832–40. See Gilbert, 'The Growth and Decline of Non-Conformity in England and Wales, with special reference to the period before 1850', D. Phil, University of Oxford, 124, Table 3. Schisms occurred after the abolitionist campaigns of 1792, 1814, and 1833. Between 1787 and 1833 all years of abolitionist campaigns, except 1792, were also peak recruitment years among the New Connexion Baptists. Cf. *Statistics of the New Connexion Baptists 1770–1843* (Leicester, 1844), 76. Until the late 1820s periods of political polarization and economic depression were relatively unfavorable to nonconformity.
63. It seems unlikely that the 'new' Dissenters were higher on the social ladder in the late eighteenth century than in 1830. Data on Keighley Round, West Riding, for 1763, sets the percentage of 'manufacturers' at 65.1 (i.e. excluding labourers and agriculturalists on the one hand and merchants and professionals on the other). From Charles Isaac Wallace, 'Religion and Society in Eighteenth Century England: Geographic, Demographic and Occupational patterns of Dissent in the West Riding of Yorkshire, 1715–1801', PhD dissertation, Duke University, 1973, 219. The Quakers were also still two-thirds artisanal in the last quarter of the eighteenth century. (Ibid., 235–6.) The Methodist leaders were quite self-conscious about their heavily collier-miner-mechanic constituency in dealing with the government (Ward, *Religion and Society*, 62).
64. This is derived from a list of advertisements and descriptions of 33 separate meetings in 1788 and 78 meetings in 1792. One may, of course, emphasize that the artisanry had more affinity to the small tradesmen than to the unskilled labourers of the early industrial revolution. But one should not arbitrarily assign the artisans to the 'middle class' for purposes of writing the history of abolitionism and then reassign them to the world of labourers for the purposes of writing the history of the working class.
65. Thomas Hardy, like Tom Paine, came out of eighteenth-century dissent. *The Memoirs of Thomas Hardy* (London, 1832), 4. Equiano wrote his memoirs at Hardy's house in 1792 and the London Corresponding Society made its public appearance on the very day of the Parliamentary debate on the slave trade (ibid., 15–16).

66. Gilbert, *Religion and Society*, 60–8.
67. John Iliffe, *The Emergence of African Capitalism* (London, 1983), 33–4.
68. A miner or manufacturing worker of the eighteenth century was more likely than a farm labourer or small farmer to be a Methodist or dissenter. John Rule, *The Experience of Labour in the Eighteenth Century* (London, 1981), 208. See also Iain McCalman, 'Anti-Slavery and Ultra-Radicalism in Early Nineteenth-Century England: The Case of Robert Wedderburn', Mss given at the Nantes international colloquium on the slave trade, 1985.
69. For E. P. Thompson the ideological break with paternalism dates from the 1790s, following a path from middle-class dissenters to urban artisans. 'Eighteenth-century English society: class struggle without class?', *Social History*, 3: 2 (May 1978), 163–4. Abolitionism calls our attention to a break with paternalism which preceeded the 1790s and originated in the dissenting urban artisanry. John Wesley's victories in Cornwall were due to the fact that he was regarded as an insurgent against traditional institutions. John Rowe, *Cornwall in the Age of the Industrial Revolution* (Liverpool, 1953), 32. Dissent entered a critical period of mass mobilization at the end of the 1780s. It reflected a crisis (especially in the West Riding and Lancashire) created by an Anglican clergy which was literally rising into the gentry class. 'The Methodists might put on displays of loyalty; but they were plainly severing the natural links between the upper and the lower orders at a time when everything else seemed to be conspiring in the same direction.' Ward, *Religion and Society*, 50–3. See also W. R. Ward, 'The Tithe Question in England in the Early Nineteenth Century', *Journal of Ecclesiastical History*, 16:1 (April 1965), 72ff. The Bishop of Chester estimated that the tract from Manchester through Yorkshire to Richmond might already have had a majority of dissenters full of the 'democratic spirit', before the end of the French wars (Ward, *Religion and Society*, 54). Among rural immigrants to northern industrial towns, religious antagonism was especially sharpened by social distance. At least in the first two decades of abolitionism 'the Methodist flock had been so much on one side of the social divide as to leave the preachers no real option but to follow them' against the wealthier trustees. W. R. Ward, 'Popular religion and the problem of control', in C. J. Cumeng and Derek Baker (eds), *Popular Belief and Practice* (New York, 1972), 242–3. In some areas, such as Cornwall, class tension remained relatively muted until after the age of popular abolitionism. Michael Flinn stresses the upward trend of real wages and the standard of living for colliers until 1830: *The History of the British Coal Industry*, vol. 2, *The Industrial Revolution 1700–1830*, 395, 440–1. Cornish miners seem to have become active abolitionists in the early 1790s, following the revival of the copper industry. Rowe, *Cornwall in the Age of the Industrial Revolution*, 91.
70. On working-class respectability and its distance from the casual labourer, the unemployed and the pauper, see E. P. Thompson, *The Making of the English Working Class* (London, 1968), 266–7; Rule, *The Experience of Labour*, 204–6; Roydon Harrison (ed.), *Independent Collier: The Coal Miner as Archetypical Proletarian Reconsidered* (New York, 1978), 2–6, 61–2, 68–71; and Gareth Stedman Jones, *Outcast*

London (London, 1971), 338–9. In 1792, a reported meeting of 'Mechanics and Inhabitants' at Warrington near Manchester spoke strongly in favour of political rights for yeomen, farmers, manufacturers, artisans and labourers. They saw society as divided into '*Gentry*, the *industrious Poor* and the *lazy Poor*', with the industrious poor supporting the whole. (Meeting of 3 November 1792, reported in the *Manchester Herald* and sent on to the Home Office PRO HO 42/22, 1792, f. 197.) Sean Wilentz emphasizes the suppleness of the concept of 'labour' in the early nineteenth century. A broad definition might include merchants, professionals, and bankers as productive citizens; a narrow one might exclude all but those who actually worked with their hands. See *Chants Democratic: New York City and the Rise of the American Working Class* (New York, 1984), 158. The flexibility of the term reflected the ideological penumbra between productive capitalism and free labour which emphasized a far wider chasm between free and chattel labour. On the general prosperity of the artisanal base of nonconformity in the late eighteenth century, see also Ian R. Christie, *Stress and Stability in Late Eighteenth-Century Britain: Reflections on the British Avoidance of Revolution* (Oxford, 1984), 204–9.

71. Cecil Driver, *Tory Radical: The Life of Richard Oastler* (New York, 1946), 17–18.

72. Iorwerth Prothero, *Artisans and Politics in Early Nineteenth Century London* (Folkestone, 1979). Nonconformist religious culture in the growth period was particularly hospitable to the circumstances of artisans. Gilbert, 'The Growth and Decline of Non-Conformity', 190.

73. It was the Manchester Methodists who established a 'Stranger's Friend Society', early in 1792 (*Sheffield Advertiser*, 6 January 1792).

74. In his relation to his tools and his product the artisan was a capitalist. In his relation to his apprentices he was a master of his craft, a relationship akin to a professor with his students. See Karl Marx, *Capital*, trans. Ben Fowkes (London, 1976), 1, 1029. The radical society of Sheffield in 1792 was founded by 'mechanics', with the leaven of 'a few Quakers' and 'a number of Methodists'. (C. Wyvill, *Political Papers*, 5, 47–48, letter of May 1792.)

75. See Chapter 3, note 19. In 1844 the presenting Deputy emphasized that the petition had come from the workers without external prompting. AN SO–M Généralités, 171 (1379), letter of Isambert, Paris, 14 February 1844. The first petitions came from printing shops, from which well over a thousand names were gathered. The signatories also included carpenters, cabinet makers, mechanics, clock makers, tailors, sculptors, jewellers, rope makers, foundry workers, laundresses, dressmakers, milliners, housepainters, marble workers, sawyers, artists, engravers, lithographers, etc. AN C2425 (1844), 233, 'Ouvriers de Paris demandant l'abolition de l'esclavage'. The faubourg St Antoine was very heavily represented.

76. *L'Union, Bulletin des Ouvriers*, II, 7 June 1844.

77. Drescher, 'Two Variants', 63n.

78. John B. Jentz, 'Artisans, Evangelicals, and the City: A Social History of the Labor and Abolitionist Movements in Jacksonian New York' PhD dissertation, City University of New York, 1977, 208 and 217.

79. Edward Magdol, 'A Window on the Abolitionist Constituency: Anti-slavery Petitions, 1836–1839'. Typescript kindly supplied by the author. Wilentz provides an occupational breakdown of New York Methodists in 1812 as shown in the following table:

| *New York City Methodists* | |
Occupation	Percentage
(1) Merchants and professionals	9.4
(2) Shopkeepers and retail	10.9
(3) Master craftsmen	14.1
(4) Small masters and journeymen	48.4
(5) Unskilled labourers	17.2

SOURCE   Wilentz, *Chants Democratic:* 81n. The 'artisonal' categories (3 and 4) together constitute 62.5 per cent of the New York Methodist membership, compared with 62.7 per cent in Gilbert's sample for all England in 1800–37. Gilbert's artisans also include men who were independent craftsmen (*Religion and Society*, 63).

80. Berlin and Guttman, 'Natives and Immigrants', esp. 1198–2000. See also Fred Seigel, 'Artisans and Immigrants in late Ante-Bellum Virginia and South Carolina: The Politics of an Anomaly', 36–57 (typescript kindly furnished by the author).

81. John B. Jentz, 'The Antislavery Constituency in Jacksonian New York City', in *Civil War History*, 27, 2 (June 1981), 101–22.

82. As early as 1708, Oldmixon also concluded that black slaves worked much less than day labourers in England: *The British Empire in America* (London, 1708), 289. Although opponents of slavery maintained that free persons ordinarily worked harder than slaves, one merchant, writing of colonial conditions in a more neutral context, claimed that 'no *White* servant in *Jamaica*, works near so hard as many of our Husbandmen in this Country, or doth much more than half the work of a Black'. There, 'no planter in his wits' would keep more than the legally required minimum of whites. *The Case of John Wilmore Truly and Impartially Related, or a Looking-Glass for all Merchants and Planters that are concerned in the American Plantations* (London, 1682), 3.

83. Temperley, 'The Ideology of Antislavery', 21–35, esp. 28; D. Eltis, 'Abolitionist Perceptions of Society after Slavery', in Walvin, *Slavery*, 195–213, esp. 213. See also H. Temperley, Abolition and the National Interest', in *Out of Slavery: Abolition and After*, J. E. S. Hayward (ed.) (London, 1985). For Davis, *Slavery in . . . Revolution*, 450, British abolitionism was predominantly a middle-class articulation which 'filtered down' by the 1820s to dissenting and improving working men.

84. Adam Smith argued that the cost of maintaing slave labour was everywhere greater than that of maintaining free labour: *An Inquiry into the Nature and Causes of the Wealth of Nations* (New York, 1937), 80. He also treated slavery in the tobacco and sugar colonies as 'exceptional,' in

that European demand enabled the British colonists in those areas not only to bear the extra cost of slave management, but 'to dispose of their produce to buyers for more than what was sufficient to pay the whole rent, profit and wages necessary for preparing it and bringing it to market'. In this general statement Smith never mentioned the reduced cost of 'wear and tear' created by the African slave trade, where the function of 'replacing or repairing' was not managed by 'a negligent master or careless overseer', but by a competitive enterprise for buying, transporting and selling stolen people. Smith's second premise was that slave labour was the dearest of all because universal experience showed that labour could be 'squeezed' out of a slave only by violence (ibid., 365). But for Smith at least one system, the French slave colonies, also proved that slaves could be managed so that 'the slave was rendered not only more faithful, but more intelligent and therefore upon a double account more useful'. (Ibid., 554.) There, 'the slave approaches more to the condition of a free servant and may possess some degree of integrity and attachment to his master's interest, virtues which frequently belong to free servants, but which never can belong to a slave, who is treated as slaves commonly are in countries where the master is perfectly free and secure.' (Ibid., 554.) The same phenomenon occurred in British North America, where masters worked alongside slaves and treated them almost as 'friends and partners'. (*Lectures on Jurisprudence*, 185.) Thus the universal rule was sufficiently malleable in certain environments to drastically reduce the motivational difference between free and slave labor. The slave/free dichotomy seemed less clearcut in the fields of the Americas than in the mines of Europe. Smith never actually broached the question of whether well-managed slaves on transatlantic sugar plantations, fed by an efficient slave trade, were in the end cheaper for a master than production by freemen. However, his abolitionist users, if not all of his disciples, were more than satisfied by his unequivocal general statement. On citations of the free-labour argument in early abolitionism, see *Morning Chronicle*, 3 April, 8 November, 27 November 1788; *Public Advertiser*, 19 February 1788; *Diary*, 26 March 1792. The free-labour ideology did not depend on Smith. Compulsion was regarded as a source of inefficiency primarily because of actual metropolitan experience. 'The fruitlessness of compulsive labour' was proved every day in 'every workhouse in the kingdom. There is in proof too, the felons in the hulks, who produce not a fourth part of the ballast which is raised by the adjoining barges, where the men are working on their own account.' *Morning Chronicle*, 15 September 1785. See also ibid., 3 October 1785; *London Chronicle*, 29 September–1 October and 1–4 October 1785. Usually the more radical the abolitionist, the more sanguine was his faith in the exportability of the free-labour principle. An unqualified version of the free-labour ideology was propounded by the early socialist, William Thompson, in *An Inquiry into the Principles of the Distribution of Wealth* (London, 1824, reprinted 1963), 44–5, 174.

The problem was always whether this 'law' was transferable beyond the line. In the early 1790s Sierra Leone was considered to be the first test case for 'free' tropical staple agriculture. Clarkson anticipated that sugar would be the most profitable crop of the new colony, and regarded the experiment as a straightforward test of freemen versus slaves. (Huntington Library, Clarkson Papers, CN54 (1702), 17.) He anticipated that each hundredweight of sugar from Sierra Leone would be two-thirds cheaper than from the slave islands. The rate of profit 'will be precisely one hundred per cent'. (Ibid., 19.) Joseph Priestly's *A Sermon on the Slave Trade* (Birmingham, 1788), 28, note, also assumed that African sugar could be raised at half the cost of the West Indian product. On the other hand, just prior to the Sierra Leone venture, the more conservative William Paley stated that free labor would cost the British planters about one-twelfth more than slavery (from 6d to 6½d per pound). See *Principles of Moral and Political Philosophy* (London, 1787), Book III, Pt. 2, Chapter 3. In 1792 Arthur Young called for competitive experimentation before deciding on abolition. *Annals of Agriculture* 17 (1792), 524. After Sierra Leone's failure as a staple exporter, attention moved toward the Caribbean. During the abolition debates there were calls to use undeveloped Trinidad as an experimental area for Adam Smith's assumption that 'slave labour was the dearest of all'. Wilberforce was almost drawn into supporting such an experiment. He was warned off by James Stephen, who believed that the very opposite was the case in the colonial situation. (Duke University Library, William Smith papers, William Wilberforce to William Smith, 18 August and 5 September 1806.) James Stephen fought against all free labour experiments. He anonymously denounced the Chinese free labour experiment in Trinidad as 'preposterous,' in *The Dangers of the Country* (London, 1807), 205. Stephen had already stated his belief in the decisive advantage of slave labor for sugar production. *The Crisis of the Sugar Colonies* (London, 1803), 191. (See also S. Drescher, *Econocide*, 156–7). He openly re-iterated this opinion in Parliament, in opposing a motion for a government-sponsored free labor experiment. Stephen cited the Chinese experiment as proof that 'while slavery existed in the West Indies, it was impossible that free labour could succeed in competition with it'. *Parliamentary Debates*, 19 (4 April 1811), 710. Governor Picton of Trinidad agreed with Stephen. Sugar could not be 'advantageously cultivated or manufactured' without slaves. (PRO CO 295/2, Trinidad, April 12, 1802.) The Dutch were still unable to make Java competitive with the American sugar colonies at the end of the eighteenth century, despite record prices for sugar and the fact that the daily price of common labour in Java was between one-third and one-half that of hired slaves in the West Indies. (PRO CO 295/2, Trinidad, 16 July 1802.)

On the ambivalence of British political economists right down to slave emancipation itself, see S. Drescher, 'Cart Whip', 5–6. Doubts were not confined to British political economists. J. B. Say, referring to Steuart, Turgot and Smith as free labourites, cautioned: 'I fear that these respectable writers wanted to justify by reason, an opinion which was inspired by humanity.' J. B. Say, *Traité d'Economie politique* 2 vols (Paris, 1814), I, 283. For Say it was *unsupervised* free labour which was more efficient when done by free men. A German translation of James

Steuart's *Political Economy* restricted the advantage of free labor to manufacturing enterprises. Say, *Traité* 5th edn (Paris, 1826), 357. For Say, the issue of relative profitability was settled by the master's choice, but he drew a distinction between long term development and profitability. See Say's reply to Adam Hodgson's *A Letter to M. Jean Baptiste Say on the Comparative Expense of Free and Slave Labour*, 2nd edn (London, 1823), 60. Charles Ganilh's *An Inquiry into the Various Systems of Political Economy*, trans. D. Boileau (London, 1812), 150, cautioned against inferring 'that at all times, in all places, and under all circumstances, the labour of the free man ought to be substituted for that of the slave'. 'Although it appears demonstrated that the labour of the free man is more advantageous than that of the slave, it is perhaps equally true, that, in the present colonial system, the labour of the slave is more advantageous than that of the free man.' In *La Théorie de l'economie politique fondu sur les faits résultans des statistiques de la France et de l'Angleterre* 2 vols (Paris, 1815), I, 278, 284–90, Ganilh offered perhaps the most elaborate analysis of free versus slave labour before British emancipation. He estimated that the annual yield on metropolitan agricultural capital was only 8 per cent, compared with 12 per cent in the islands. Because of the higher cost of colonial capital, however, Ganilh found the difference in profitability to be only $3\frac{1}{2}$ per cent in favour of slave agriculture. The superiority of slave production was due to causes extrinsic to the efficiency of slave labour, but those causes did make slavery more profitable in the colonies. (ibid., 288).

West Indians were even more adamant about the distinction between making 'a negro, a free-man', and making him a 'labourer'. See J. R. Gosset, *Remarks on West India Affairs* (London, 1824), 76. 'Who would not wish,' said Jon Braithwaite to the Privy Council in 1788, 'to have labour performed freely rather than on compulsion', but the free blacks of Barbados would not 'work for pay, but be idle and vicious'. No medium existed between compulsion and idleness. (PRO BT 6/9, Evidence before the Privy Council, f. 31.) The distinction between the cost of labour in the metropolis and in the colonies was just as relative for Eric Williams as it had been for planters and political economists. Williams took issue not with Adam Smith's general premise, but with Smith's failure to distinguish between early and late stages of colonial development. Slave labour was necessary during the 'rise' of British slavery, even though 'other things being equal', free men would be preferred. (Williams, *Capitalism and Slavery*, 6, also noted in S. L. Engerman and David Eltis, 'Economic aspects of the abolition debate', in Bolt and Drescher, *Anti-Slavery*, 277. The continuance of the frontier situation for British slavery casts doubt on whether 'other things' were 'equal' even by 1833.)

85. On Adam Smith's testimony the servile Scottish collier earned 50 per cent more than the free collier of Newcastle. The amenities of liberty were therefore worth at least one-third of their incomes to the independent colliers of eighteenth-century England. How much more or less the Scottish chattel owner made on each ton of coal is unclear. See Roydon Harrison, *Independent Collier*, 2.

H. Temperley, 'Capitalism, Slavery and Ideology', 107–18.
The decisive shift in attitude was in the outlook of the working, not the entrepreneurial, sector. When Britain was creating its overseas slave system, 'only the vanguard of entrepreneurs operated as economic rationalists'. Only in the next century did such rationalism become internalized by workers, as well as by investors, both as *consumers* and as *producers* (Joyce Appleby, 'Ideology and Theory: The Tension between Political and Economic Liberalism in Seventeenth-Century England', *The American Historical Review*, 81:3 (June 1976), 499–515. Ironically, just when such 'rationalism' had been internalized by workers they rejected the immorality of the market-rationalized slave trade. The necessary catalysts were, as always, particularly sensitized individuals, whether Anstey's men of the gospel, or Haskell's men of the marketplace, or some combination of Davis's conservative evangelicals, ambivalent *philosophes*, and pioneering Quakers. But abolitionism as a social movement arose out of the shared experience of less exceptional people among the middle and working classes. The key question in this respect is not how abolitionism was diffused 'from above', but whether economic activity was infused with a prior ethical logic by working men and women themselves. The producers and consumers' ideologies of late eighteenth-century England were apparently easily transferred to the problem of colonial slavery: 'Labour is the most unequivocal kind of property; the labour of the negroes has not only been unpaid for, but has cost multitudes of them their lives and liberties.' (Letter by 'Common Sense' on the need to abstain from slave sugar, *Manchester Herald*, 28 April 1792). The *productivity* of labour was thus ironically less significant in the producer's ideology of metropolitan artisans than for political economists. A publication which claimed to speak for the 'better sort of mechanics', 'the men in this country whose voices loudest and longest maintain the cry against injustice', completely rejected the centrality of the low cost, free-labour argument in the emancipation debate. 'Were slave labour even ten times more productive than free labour, what of that? Would it give one man a right to take possession of his brother, and compel him to work against his will for the benefit of his oppressor?' *The Mechanics Magazine* vol. 1, 342, 24 January 1824; vol. 18, 79, 3 November 1832; and vol. 19, 416, 7 September 1833.

7 CLASS CONFLICT, HEGEMONY AND THE COST OF ANTISLAVERY

1. See, *inter alia*, R. Coupland, *Wilberforce* (London, 1923, 1945), and *The British Anti-Slavery Movement*, (London, 1935); E. Williams, *Capitalism and Slavery* (Chapel Hill, 1944), Chapter 12; E. M. Howse, *Saints in Politics* (Toronto, 1952).
2. For the Colonies, M. Craton, *Testing the Chains* (Ithaca, New York, 1982), 323–325; and M. Craton *Searching for the Invisible Man: Slaves and Plantation Life in Jamaica* (Cambridge, Mass., 1978), 380–94;

H. Tinker, *A New System of Slavery: The Export of Indian Labour Overseas 1830–1920* (London/New York, 1974); Johnson U. J. Asiegbu, *Slavery and the Politics of Liberation 1787–1861: A Study of Liberated African Emigration and British Anti-Slavery Policy* (New York, 1969); Monica Schuler, *'Alas, Alas, Kongo': A Social History of Indentured African Immigration into Jamaica, 1841–1865* (Baltimore/London, 1980). For emphasis on the early correlation of metropolitan exploitation and overseas antislavery, see D. B. Davis, *Slavery in . . . Revolution* (Ithaca, New York, 1984), 358 ff. and for the later period, P. Hollis, 'Anti-Slavery and British Working Class Radicalism', in C. Bolt and S. Drescher (eds), *Anti-Slavery, Religion, and Reform* (Folkestone, Kent/ Hamden, Conn., 1980), 303–8. Abolition was referred to among some contemporary working-class radicals as 'humbugging us under the name of emancipation, yet making our chains the stronger' (Mr Jackson, at a meeting of the National Union of the Working Classes in London: *Poor Man's Guardian*, 22 June 1833, 199). A classic formulation of such metropolitan displacement may be found in Richard Oastler's 'Slavery in Yorkshire', in the *Leeds Intelligencer*, 24 March 1831. Variants of the theory emerged as early as the first abolitionist debate. For a critique of Davis's social control hypothesis on motivational grounds, see T. Haskell, 'Capitalism and the Origins of the Humanitarian Sensibility', in *The American Historical Review*, 90, 2 (April 1985). (April 1985).

3. Moses I. Finley, *Ancient Slavery and Modern Ideology* (New York, 1980), Chapter 4; Richard Hellie, *Slavery in Russia 1420–1725* (Chicago, 1982), 713–15.

4. William A. Green, 'Emancipation to Indenture: A Question of Imperial Morality', *Journal of British Studies*, 22, 2 (Spring, 1983), 98–121, esp. 121. For an elaboration of benefits forgone, see S. Drescher, *Econocide: British Slavery in the Era of Abolition* (Pittsburgh, 1977), Chapters 9–10, and more elaborately, David Eltis, 'Capitalism and Abolition: The Missed Opportunities of 1807–1865', typescript kindly furnished by the author, to be incorporated into his study: 'Economic Growth and Coercion'.

5. Drescher, *Econocide*, 173.

6. Engerman, "Servants to Slaves to Servants," Table II.

7. S. Drescher, 'The Historical Context of British Abolition', in D. Richardson (ed.), *Abolition and its Aftermath in the West Indies* (London, 1985).

8. According to Robert W. Fogel and Stanley L. Engerman, 'Philanthropy at Bargain Prices: Notes on the Economics of Gradual Emancipation', *Journal of Legal Studies*, 3, 2 (1974), 377–401, compensation and apprenticeship gave the planters (or their creditors) upwards of 96 per cent of the value of their slaves. J. R. Ward reduces the estimated planter compensation to about three quarters of the value of their slaves. ('The Profitability and viability of British West Indian Plantation Slavery, 1807–1834', unpublished paper presented to the Institute of Commonwealth Studies, 1979.)

9. B. R. Mitchell and P. Deane, *Abstract of British Historical Statistics* (Cambridge, 1962), 396.

10. *Poor Man's Guardian*, 29 June 1833, 215.
11. S. Drescher, 'Public Opinion and the Destruction of British Colonial Slavery', in J. Walvin (ed.), *Slavery and British Society* (1982), 44–5.
12. Eltis, 'Economic Growth and Coercion', Chapter 6.
13. Davis, *Slavery in . . . Revolution*, 348–9 ff. and esp. 466–7.
14. *London Chronicle*, 31 March–2 April, 25–8 July 1787.
15. S. Drescher, 'Two Variants of Anti-Slavery', in Bolt and Drescher, *Anti-Slavery*, 58.
16. House of Lords Record Office, Mss, 13 May 1806, Petitions on the slave trade.
17. See Davis, *Slavery in . . . Revolution*, 349–50, 361–2, 384–5, 403, for the second proposition, and *Slavery and Human Progress* (New York, 1984), 109, for the first. In the latter work Davis has modified his capitalist-oriented causal nexus. A causal explanation would in his view, still have to relate antislavery sensibility to the 'triumphant hegemony of a capitalist worldview and particularly to capitalist views of labor'. It would, however, avoid 'any temptation to reduce the rise of abolitionism to the interests of an entrepreneurial class – a class that for the most part detested abolitionists' (ibid.). Whether this general characterization of most entrepreneurs towards abolitionists holds for the *British* case is an open question. As early as 1788 the *Morning Chronicle* (14 February) counted 'even the majority of the merchants' in favour of abolition. From the unending denunciations of Northern factory capitalists for their hypocritical support of emancipation, at least a substantial proportion must have actively supported the abolitionist movement when not linked to factory legislation. For an alternative view of the relationship between capitalism and labour in British antislavery, see S. Drescher, 'Cart Whip and Billy Roller: Antislavery and reform symbolism in industrializing Britain', *Journal Of Social History* 15, 1 (1982), 3–24.
18. Davis, *Slavery in . . . Revolution*, 362–3, 383–4, 421.
19. 'The friends of this country have to thank heaven, and the wisdom of Government, that the *downfall and ruin of our Empire* are no longer topics to which attention is paid.' (*Morning Chronicle*, 19 July 1787; also ibid., 29, 31 July, 1, 17 August 1786; *Public Advertiser*, 10 August and especially 15 August 1786.) On the tranquillity of both Indies, see *Morning Chronicle*, 7 September 1786.
20. 'Our East India and West India ships and others are pouring in from all quarters of the globe somewhat prosperously and richly laden with the produce of all lands and all seas!' (from 'Retrospect of Commerce', in *Felix Farley's Bristol Journal*, 11 August 1787. See also *London Chronicle* 1–3, 3–6 March, 1–3, 3–5 May, 19–21 June, 20–2 September 1787; *Morning Chronicle*, 6 March, 28 April, 5 May, 21 September 1787. Crops of sugar were much greater in 1787 than 1786 in most British islands and the planters looked forward to making 'ample amends' for losses sustained in the previous hurricane year. (*General Advertiser*, 26 October 1787.) In comparison, Guadeloupe's plantations were almost destroyed by a hurricane, and pestilence broke out at St Lucia. *Morning Chronicle*, 6 March; *London Chronicle*, 3–5 May 1787, 426. The increase of West Indian trade was given principal credit for the trade boom in the summer of 1787 (*Morning Chronicle*, 23 June 1787). With an improved West Indian crop

and consequently rising governmental revenue in 1787, the administration was expected to run a budgetary surplus. (*London Packet*, 23–5 April, *Morning Chronicle*, 28 April 1787.) For 1788, see *Morning Chronicle*, 8 July, 13 August 1788. Five years later it was not the distress but the affluence of the planters which Pitt premised in favour of the timeliness of abolition. No planter 'was in a great state of want, and many were in a great state of prosperity', *Diary*, 28 April 1792.

The African trade shared in the rising tide of prosperity on the eve of abolitionism:

> It appears that the number of ships now employed in the East and West India trade never was greater at any period of English history than it is in the current year . . . [our] ships [in] the African trade are quite sufficient to convey from Africa the negroes wanted in our islands, together with all the articles of traffic that can be found among the Africans. *Morning Chronicle*, 24 April 1786.

21. See *inter alia, Manchester Mercury*, 24 July 1787; *General Evening Post*, 8–10 January 1788; *Morning Chronicle*, 7 July, 14 December 1787, 25 January 1788; *Edinburgh Advertiser*, 1–2 May 1788 (letter from Glasgow); *Leeds Mercury*, 19 February 1788; *The Country Chronicle and Weekly Advertiser for Essex, Herts, Kent, Surrey, Middlesex*, etc., 5 January 1788.

22. *Morning Chronicle*, 25 August 1787, 9 May 1788; *Public Advertiser*, 11 September 1787. The *General Evening Post* reported on 19–22 January 1788, that 1787 had given Britain 200 days without a drop of rain. 'Let us compare this blessing with the earthquakes, the inundations, the storms and tempests, of the nations around us.' The next month the newspaper noted Necker's observation on the progressiveness of English agriculture, philosophy, manufacturing and enterprising genius (2–5 February 1788). The harvests for the years just preceding the abolitionist petitions of 1788 and 1792, ranged from 'good' to 'halcyon'. T. S. Ashton, *Economic Fluctuations in England 1700–1800* (Oxford, 1959), 24. The good trade years were part of a boom which lasted until 1792 (ibid., 61).

23. *Public Advertiser*, 11 May 1787; *Morning Chronicle*, 25 January 1788. British cotton manufacturers were fully employed, while the silk manufacturers of Lyons were reported to be begging in the streets (*Gloucester Journal*, 14 January 1788).

24. G. N. Von Tunzelman estimates that there was little overall trend in real wages for Britain as a whole between 1768 and 1788–92, but the North and Scotland did show an upward trend. Lancashire labourers' wages in particular rose 64 per cent and craftsmen's 40 per cent. 'Trends in Real Wages, 1750–1850, Revisited', *Economic History Review*, 22, 1 (1979), 33–49. See also *The Use of Machines in the Cotton Manufacture* (1780), 14–15.

25. See *Morning Chronicle*, 23 February 1787, 8, 12 January, 24 April, 27 September 1787, 8 July 1788; *World*, 8 January, 10 May 1787; *Morning Herald*, 2, 3, 20 March 1786; *Manchester Mercury*, 10 July 1787.

26. In 1787 the principal concern of the government appear
    overcrowding in places of incarceration. See PRO HO 42/
    in the King's speech opening the Parliamentary session (*Morning Chronicle*, 23 January 1787). Significantly, between January and June 1788
    the most alarming item in the Home Office papers was the Jamaican
    agent's warning on the possibility of violent consequences arising from
    English abolition. PRO HO 42/13 (1788), f. 5, Stephen Fuller to Lord
    Hawkesbury, 20 January 1788, passed along to Lord Sydney at the
    Home Office.

27. Christopher Wyvill, *Political Papers*, 4 vols (London, 1794–6), 4, 32–3,
    Wyvill to Pitt, 29 July 1787.

28. *The Morning Post* summarized a host of commentaries at the turn of
    1788: Britain's enemies were weaker, her allies stronger; India was
    reformed and 'enjoying the rights of men and citizens'

    > If you turn to the West Indies and America, there you will find that
    > trade has been improved by opening several free ports, and that those
    > valuable colonies are about to be effectually secured to the kingdom,
    > by improving their fortifications, and augmenting their garrisons. In
    > Ireland we find a proud, and often discontented and turbulent people,
    > not only hushed into peace, but pleased and gratified beyond what they
    > could have expected. And in our native island, we perceive and we
    > enjoy – more extensive and valuable manufactures – more commerce,
    > both domestic and foreign – greater returns not only on the balance of
    > exchange, but on that of trade – a more productive revenue – a more
    > expanded credit – and a growing national importance already admired, and envied by every power in Europe. (7 January 1788)

    Four days later an 'Ode to the Old Year' spoke wealth, place, honour
    and balance 'held with a steady hand'. For similar assessments see, *inter
    alia*, *Morning Chronicle*, 14, 17, 20, 31 December 1787, 9 January, 24
    September 1788; *London Chronicle*, 23–6 February, 28 February–1
    March 1788; *Liverpool General Advertiser*, 21 February 1788; *County
    Chronicle and Weekly Advertiser*, 8, 22 February 1788; *General Evening
    Post*, 27–31 May 1788. The last Jacobite pretender died almost unnoticed while the newspapers looked forward to the forthcoming jubilee of
    the Revolution of 1688: 'and there is no instance of a people enjoying a
    century of such civil and religious liberty as the British nation has done
    since. Let the period be indelibly fixed on the mind of everyone who has
    the happiness to be born a Briton.' *General Evening Post*, 15, 17 January
    1788; and *Public Advertiser*, 20 January 1788.

29. 1791–2 and 1814 were also periods of self-congratulatory and exhuberant prosperity. See e.g. *York Chronicle*, 3 February 1792; *Diary*, 1
    January, 13 February 1792; *York Chronicle*, 30 June 1814.

30. From the summer of 1791 the growth of popular disaffection in Manchester was linked to the prosperity of its trade, high wages and the
    influx of 'estranged, unconnected' persons. There was 'also now a very

general Spirit of Combination amongst all sorts of labourers and artisans'. Report of Thomas B. Bayley and Henry Norris to the Home
Office, 19 July 1791 (PRO HO 42/19, f. 175). For early links of abolitionism with animal rights, *Diary*, 29 December 1789; with game and
penal laws, *Morning Chronicle*, 16 February 1788. The expansive ideological implications of slave-trade abolitionism were manifest at a Glasgow public dinner in 1791. Among the toasted were Granville Sharp and
the London Abolition Committee, their counterparts in Paris, the Sierra
Leone Company, the African Prince of Robana, and finally, 'liberty to
all mankind without distinction of colour, country or sect' (*Diary*, 2
December 1791). In 1792 the commemoration of the French Revolution
by the Society for Constitutional Information at Sheffield toasted the
abolition of 'every species of the Slave Trade, at home and abroad'. The
city of Belfast's procession commemorating the fall of the Bastille
carried the banner: 'Can the African Slave Trade, though morally
wrong, be politically right?' (*Manchester Herald*, 28 June 1792.) On
Equiano's abolitionist work in Belfast, see P. Fryer, *Staying Power: The
History of Black People in Britain* (London and Sydney, 1984),
110–12. The Universal Liberty Club, holding its first meeting in Scotland
on 30 January 1792, called for the abolition of the slave trade (*York
Courant*, 28 February 1792). The slave trade offered an opportunity to
compare the 'manly stile' of abolitionist petitioning with the narrow
corporation spirit that characterized 'courtly sycophants'. *The Patriot; or
Political, Moral, and Philosophical Repository*, 3 vols (London, 1792),
1: 3, 5, 7, 32, 38–9; 2: 215; 3: 162. The petition campaign also gave
Parliamentary reformers a chance to jibe at those who represented small
electorates (*Diary*, 4 May 1792). In 1792 antiabolitionists regarded the
'active spirit of liberty' in Britain and France as analogous (*Dorchester
and Sherbourne Journal*, 20 January 1792, 'A Retrospective view of
1791'). The radicalization of the 1792 campaign among even the Friends
was noted in a public letter from Joel Sandys 'to the people called
Quakers' (*Diary*, 28 March 1792, and reply, ibid., 30 March 1792).

31. For Clarkson, in the fall of 1791, the two most promising areas in the
world were Sierra Leone and France. (Salop Record Office, Katherine
Plymly Diaries, 1, October 20–1, 1791.) Clarkson, who found general
approval of the French Revolution during his tour of 1791, was soon
accused of being a revolutionist. Wilberforce warned him that the
French connection was harming their cause. (See ibid., 9–24 February
1792, and Friends House Library, William Dickson Diary, 17 January, 4
February 1792.) As late as November 1793 Clarkson secretly visited the
Manchester radical Thomas Walker on the eve of the latter's trial for
sedition. See B. Jerrold (ed.), *The Original*, 2 vols (London, 1874), 1,
53.

32. S. Bradburn, *An Address to the People called Methodists* (Manchester,
1792), 20–1. Davis cites Bradburn's *Address* as an instance of the
dissenting public's sense of powerlessness (*Slavery in . . . Revolution*,
381). It seems rather to be infused with the new sense of popular power
that welled up in Britain before the reaction of late 1792.

33. Less than a week before the Parliamentary discussion of April 1792 squibs appeared designating abolitionism as a stalking horse for the Opposition and for repealers of the Test Act (*Diary*, 29 March 1792). A more sustained counter-attack began about a week after the abolition debates. See *Morning Herald*, 9–14, 18, 20, 21 April 1792; *The World*, 12, 13, 14 April 1792. The link was clearly illustrated in the headline 'CA IRA CLUB – HIC NIGER' which continued: 'CHIMNEY SWEEP-ERS trample (in idea) over LORDS and LADIES; they kick down DUKES, and relegate the concerns of mighty EMPIRES!' (ibid., 13 April). The *Morning Herald* quickly extended its sneers to meetings of manufacturers in Sheffield, weavers in Manchester and 'the *sons of Levi*' in London (20 March 1792). See also *Morning Chronicle*, 13 April 1792; *The Oracle*, 3 May 1792; *Morning Herald*, 30 April; *Star*, 25 April 1792. The *World*, 14 April 1792, referred to meetings of 'the *Soot* Club of Democrats'. Antiabolitionists and abolitionists alike linked the liberation of Africa, Europe, America and Asia. Major Crewe, *A Very New Pamphlet Indeed! . . . containing some strictures on the English Jacobins and evidence . . . respecting the Slave Trade* (London, 1792); *The British Tocsin; or, Proofs of National Ruin* (London, 1792), 49; *Political Dictionary* (London, 1792), 131. An 'Essay on the Slave Trade' exposed the general 'fallacy' of Priestly, Paine and other modern reformers (*Diary*, 29 November 1792). Bentham did not publish his work on the political emancipation of the French Colonies, fearing that he would be taken for a Republican (HO 42/25 (1793), f. 391, Jeremy Bentham to Henry Dundas, 20 May 1793).

34. 1807 was also 'a year of low social tension'. See W. R. Ward, 'Popular religion and the problem of control', in C. J. Cuming and Derek Baker (eds), *Popular Belief and Practice* (London, 1972), 238–57, esp. 239. In less turbulent times abolitionists were more sympathetic to radical labels. The abolitionist *The Philanthropist*, 2 (1816), 292–327, took the position that 'Jacobin' was nine times out of ten applied to things that were worthwhile. (On the long-term continuity of ultra-radical abolitionism see McCalman, 'Anti-Slavery' (Mss).)

35. Hansard, *Parliamentary Debates*, 3rd ser., 3 (1831) 1137–40; 4 (1831), 372.

36. See Drescher, 'Cart Whip', 8–17.

37. See ibid.; also Patricia Hollis, 'Anti-slavery and British Working–Class Radicalism', 294–313.

38. For the connection of slavery with child labour see *The Poor Man's Advocate*, 4 February, 4 August, 1 December 1832; *The Poor Man's Guardian*, 12, 20 January, 2 March 1833; *Carpenter's Monthly Political Magazine*, 1–2 (June 1832), 398–403; *The British Labourer's Protector and Factory Child's Friend* (25 January 1833), 48. The rhetorical cross-over took place before 1830. As soon as the popular abolitionist campaign heated up in 1823 *The Black Dwarf* entitled an essay 'WHITE SLAVE TRADE-FLOGGING OF WORKMEN' (11 (3 September 1823), 335–49). A month earlier a correspondent had begun another essay on flogging: 'At a time when we are called upon to unite our

endeavors in behalf of the West India slaves', etc. (ibid., 11 (6 August 1823), 212). On the public linkage between the factory children and colonial slaves see *The Manchester Courier*, 2 March, 13, 20 April, 27 July 1833. For a detailed illustration of the use of abolitionist arguments in the metropolis, see *Society for the Improvement of the Condition of the Factory Children* (London, 1833), 2–15. *The Christian Observer* (November 1832), 729, also supported both Sadler's Factory Bill and the anti-Truck Bill on grounds that children or adults were placed in a condition similar to those of slaves.

39. The radical *Examiner* emphasized the cross-class nature of abolitionist petitioning in 1814: 'it is of little importance amongst what class, or when, or how the sentiments of the People are to be collected – it is quite sufficient to establish what no one can hardly deny, that there are circumstances in which a feeling exists so generally, as to be recognized for that of the Public at large' ('Vox Populi', 12 June 1814). Ideological extension came as easily to the *Examiner* on social issues like military flogging as on foreign policy issues like the forced union of Norway and Sweden (ibid., 3 July 1814; 28 August 1814). If there was any class-edged opposition to the petition campaign in 1814, it came from hostility toward the masses. In August 1814 the *Examiner* attacked *The Times* for sneering at abolition speeches by the 'lean, unwashed artificers' of England (7 August 1814).

40. Patricia Hollis, 'Anti-slavery and British Working-Class Radicalism', 294–313. A Bolton meeting in 1833 on slavery was disrupted by men who contended that slaves were better off than Lancashire weavers: *Wheeler's Manchester Chronicle*, 13 April 1833. See also *The Poor Man's Advocate*, 4 February 1832, 23; *Poor Man's Guardian*, 22 June 1833. The 'well fed Negro' remained a staple image for *The Poor Man's Guardian* throughout the emancipation and apprenticeship period. See ibid., 6 September 1834, 245; and 23 May 1835, 540–1.

41. For Cobbett the abolitionists were 'the hypocritical sect of negro-loving philanthropists'. *Letters to the Right Honorable Lord Hawkesbury and . . . Henry Addington* (London, January 1802), 150, and *Cowdroy's Manchester Gazette*, 21 June 1806.

42. *Manchester Guardian*, 8 September 1832. Cobbett gave a similar speech at Hulme. At Manchester Cobbett singled out 'two objects of special interest to this community', the Factory Bill and the colonial slave question. *The Poor Man's Advocate* (Manchester), 15 December 1832, reporting Cobbett's speech, did not question the popularity of emancipation in Manchester.

43. *Manchester Courier*, 16 December 1832. Cobbett actually voted against all abolitionist Amendments to the Emancipation Bill and against the Bill itself, on grounds that he was pledged only to vote for emancipation, not for any new debts or for apprenticeship. *Political Register* 80 (June 15, 1833), 674, "The Negro Affair." Cobbett was also pleased when Americans rejected British abolitionist agents ibid., 85 (16 August 1834), 403–4.

44. Our source for the Oldham election is R. A. Sykes, 'Some Aspects of Working Class Consciousness in Oldham 1830–42', *Historical Journal*,

23 (1980), 167–79. My thanks to James Esptein for bringing this essay to my attention. At Oldham in 1832, 'the really crucial factor was the incompetence of both Whig and Tory parties . . . and, above all, the fact that both their eventual candidates were hopelessly tainted by involvement with negro slavery'. John Fielden, running with Cobbett at Oldham, explicitly demand immediate emmancipation with no compensation to 'loud applause from the Radical and anti-slavery preachers'. (*Manchester Courier*, 15 December 1832.) Those who cast less than 25 per cent of their total votes for the Tory and Whig candidates were the weavers (5 per cent), shoemakers (0 per cent), tailors (0 per cent), miners (21 per cent), shopkeepers (11 per cent), butchers (21 per cent), and farmers (8 per cent). Those casting more than 75 per cent of their votes for the same candidates were cotton manufacturers (86 per cent), and clergy (100 per cent). (From Sykes, 'Working class consciousness', 174–5, Table 2.) See also table below.

Share of votes cast at Oldham for the Whig and Tory candidates condemnéd by the Anti-Slavery Society, 1832*

Occupation	Votes cast for Bright and/or Burge	% cast for the same
Weavers	2	5
Cotton spinners	30	38
Total textiles	44	30
Shoemakers	0	0
Total crafts	17	23
Retailers	24	17

* 25 or more total votes cast.

The *Christian Observer* of January 1833, 57, claimed that Oldham radicals 'had done themselves the signal honour' to elect the pro–emancipation Mr Cobbett, while Preston had 'the good sense' to reject the 'unrepentant' Mr. Hunt. The intensification of class conflict took many forms, and Oldham workers were class conscious in a democratic more than a socialist sense. See Gareth Stedman Jones 'Class Struggle and the Industrial Revolution', in *Language of Class: Studies in English working class history 1832–1982* (Cambridge, 1983), 60. Soon after emancipation the Manchester Wesleyans did split along class lines. See David Gowland, 'Methodist Secessions and Social Conflict in South Lancashire 1830–1857', PhD dissertation, University of Manchester, 1966.

45. *Voice of the West Riding*, 4, 1 (29 June 1833), 29. *The British Labourers' Protector and Factory Children's Friend*, 25 January 1833, 48, emphasized the positive impact of the libertarian tradition on metropolitan reform. See its closing issue, 19 April 1833, 250, 'Coercion in England and Scotland'. *The Working Man's Friend*, 16 March 1833, 100, listed

the emancipation petition among the six 'numerously' signed petitions sent by Oldham ('Cobbett's Town') to Parliament early in 1833. Like Cobbett, even the most hostile of radical working-class papers begrudgingly conceded the overwhelming support for abolition with phrases like 'even admitting them [the people of England] to be unanimous on the subject' (*The Poor Man's Guardian*, 15 June 1833, 189). Others, like *Carpenter's Monthly Political Magazine* and *The Crisis*, were proabolitionist.

46. Drescher, 'Cart Whip', 11–12.
47. On Owen's admiration for Wilberforce, see P. F. Dixon, 'Politics of Emancipation', 100; also *Crisis*, 1, 167 (22 December 1832), 49–50 (19 October 1833); 1, 201 (15 February 1834). The putative insensitivity created by antislavery sensibility towards wage labour is not borne out in the case of Britain's most famous early socialist. Owen, despite his enthusiasm for slave emancipation, had no qualms about declaring that the British working classes were in 'a state of misery and degradation worse than that of any slaves in America or the West Indies'. (Lecture at Manchester, reported in the *Manchester Courier*, 27 July 1833.) See also Drescher, 'Cart Whip', *passim*.
48. House of Commons, *Select Committee on Petitions*, appendix, 191.
49. Drescher, 'Cart Whip', 11–16. The concern with child labour by abolitionists was not entirely new in 1830. John Fothergill, one of Britain's earliest abolitionists, was also among the first to emphasize the debilitating effects of lace and gauze manufactures on women and children. They 'already appear like another race of people; that vigour and strength which distinguished the labouring poor of this kingdom from those of every other, is sunk down to pallid debility'. (See John Lettsom, *Some Account of the late John Fothergill, M.D.* (London, 1783), clxxvi.) The first popular campaign against slavery itself, in 1823, elicited a comparison between factory children and slaves by the journeymen cotton–spinners of Rochdale. (See Drescher, 'Cart Whip', 8.) What was novel after 1830 was the emergence of a mass factory-reform movement and its intensified ideological reliance on antislavery.
50. Cobbett's *Political Register* 81 (3 August 1833), 257; *Poor Man's Guardian*, 15 June, 10 August 1833. Compensation was not assumed at the popular level. At a meeting in Halifax a speaker mentioned the need for compensation. The response was: 'no, no, from all parts of the meeting'. The *Halifax and Huddersfield Express* (23 February 1833.) A Bradford meeting of 2000 was told that the issue at hand was immediate emancipation. As for compensation, the speaker taunted, manufacturers would also like it for the hours they would lose under the Factory Bill. It simply would not be granted. (Ibid., 13 April 1833. See also note 42.) On the subsequent outrage over the financial terms of the Emancipation Bill, see *Wheeler's Manchester Chronicle*, 14 May 1833; *Leicester Chronicle*, 22 May 1833. *The Birmingham Journal*, 15 June 1833, was astonished that Parliament could offer £20 million to the planters when free labour was cheaper than slave. The Blackburn Political Union, the Norwich Political Union, and the National Union of the Working Classes in London denounced the terms of the Emancipation Bill (*Poor Man's*

Guardian, 15 June 1833, 196; 22 June 1833, 199, 203. See also *Voice of the West Riding*, 1, 27 (20 July 1833), 56–7).

51. It was the abolitionists who embraced, and the MPs who rejected, the full logic of the *immediate* superiority of free over slave labour. See *House of Commons, Select Committee on Public Petitions. Reports*, 1 (1833), 1120–3, 'Petition of the undersigned Electors of Representatives, in various parts of the United Kingdom'; see also *Voice of the West Riding*, 1, 8 (27 July 1833), 63.
52. *Select Committee on Petitions*, appendix, 1609.
53. *Poor Man's Guardian*, 22 June 1833, 199.
54. 'V.C.L.', 15 May 1833, *The Crisis* (1833), 250–1. Socialists as well as capitalists and evangelicals absorbed abolitionism into a progressive philosophy of history. *The Crisis* observed that emancipation was but the second stage of three. The first ended *'feudal slavery'*. The second abolished *'legal slavery'* (with some credit allotted to the role of the Christian religion). There remained only the 'last blot', the *'social slavery of men . . .* the fluctuating value put upon his labour'. Other Clarksons and other Wilberforces would soon arise, 'to arouse the minds and hearts of men to a perception of the last blot' (*The Crisis*, 23 November 1833) 101. See also the *Pioneer*, 13 (30 November 1833).
55. The *Northern Star*, 11 and 25 August 1838. The launching of Scottish Chartism also evoked the abolitionist pattern. *Birmingham Journal*, 26 May 1838. 'Public opinion is the great controller of human actions', was *The New Moral World's* judgement on abolitionist agitation: (183, 28 April 1838). *McDouall's Chartist and Republican Journal*, I, 3 April 1841, 5, also considered emancipation a victory for public opinion 'over tyrannical wealth and ambitious usurpation', and put its hope in a similar 'stream of opinion', ultimately rising above 'the roar of machines'. The *Northern Star* prophesied that the same power which broke the chains of slavery could rescue the children of Britain. (28 May 1842, 5).
56. Brian Harrison, 'A Geneology of Reform in Modern Britain', in Bolt and Drescher, *Anti-Slavery*, 122.
57. D. B. Davis, 'The Crime of Reform', *New York Review of Books*, 26 June 1980, 27 (II), 14; and *Slavery in . . . Revolution*, 357; see also Hollis, 'Anti-slavery and British Working-Class Radicalism', 303. In *Slavery and Human Progress*, 340, note, Davis again joins the social base of antislavery and the New Poor Law: 'both [measures] appealed for different reasons to reformers, administrators, and aristocratic landlords'. My own impression is that the principal reformers behind the New Poor Law, above all the political economists, were not very forward in supporting abolition. The aristocratic landlords were significantly overrepresented as protectors of the slave–owners in the House of Lords. The abolitionists, on the other hand, were overrepresented among the number of opponents to the 'indoor' relief provision of the New Poor Law in the House of Commons. See 'Cart Whip', 23, 24. The Parliamentary record still leaves open the question of popular support. Hollis assumes that both measures appealed to the same class base of support. ('Anti-slavery', 302–3.) This is an extension of Davis's hypothesis that abolitionist ideology was closely tied to the unconscious interests

of the English middle class, with its 'highly selective response to labor
exploitation' (*Slavery in . . . Revolution*, 241–54, 358–61, 455–62).
Davis sees another point of connection in the coincidence between
Joseph Townsend's 'famous' attack on the Old Poor Law in 1786
(favouring instead the spur of hunger for the poor) and the publication
of Clarkson's prize-winning *Essay on Slavery* the same year. Yet Townsend was one of the less likely candidates for a pro-hunger/antislavery
ideological coalition. Townsend lavishly *approved* of slavery in the
Spanish colonies:

> The treatment of the negroes in the Spanish settlements is so humane,
> so wise, so just, and so perfectly agreeable to the principles of
> political economy, that I rejoice in the opportunity of giving to their
> government the praise which is so peculiarly its due . . . Is not this
> regulation more beneficial to the whole community, than if all the
> slaves indiscriminately were restored to freedom? *A Journey Through
> Spain in the Years 1786 and 1787*, 3 vols (London, 1791), 2, 381–2.

Townsend condemned Spanish galley slavery only for its pampering
inefficiency, but not the English-run Spanish slave trade (ibid., 2, 381,
and 3, 125). Elite British approval of the labour discipline of the
workhouse should not be taken for granted for most of the early
abolitionist era. In 1787 the 'great objection' against workhouses 'among
all humane gentlemen' was that 'this imprisonment, especially to grown
up persons, is generally for life'. (Letter to the *Norwich Mercury*, 30
June 1787.) The free-labour ideology may have united some abolitionists and Poor Law reformers but incarceration was an obstacle, not an
incentive, to convergence.

58. At the moment when the 'Speenhamland' extension of the poor-law
system was taking shape, Whitbread, an abolitionist MP, pressed for the
expansion of the Poor Law for the newly distressed labourers. (See
Morning Chronicle, 19 November 1795.) The actions of 1795 repre-
sented a strengthening of customary obligations under the old Poor
Law. See Peter Dunkley, 'Whigs and Paupers: The Reform of the
English Poor Laws 1830–1834', *Journal of British Studies*, 20, 2 (Spring
1981), 124–49, esp. 126; also E. P. Thompson, *The Making of the
English Working Class* (rev. edn London, 1968), 73; and Raymond G.
Cowherd, *Political Economists and the English Poor Laws* (Athens,
Ohio, 1977), Chapter 1. Whitbread introduced another Poor Law re-
form motion while the slave-trade Abolition Bill of 1807 was moving
through the Commons. His measure provided for the *abolition* of
already existing workhouses. (*Substance of a Bill for Promoting and
Encouraging Industry Amongst the Labouring Classes of the Community*
(London, 1807), 25.)

For another ideological transference of antislavery to the poor see
J. N. Brewer, *Some Thoughts on the Present State of the English Peasantry;
Written in Consequence of Mr. Whitbread's motion in the House of
Commons February 19, 1807, Relative to the Poor Laws*, 24. Brewer
spoke of the suffering 'of those [poor] who herd together beneath one
low roof, within almost as few square feet as are allowed to the victims

on board an African slave ship'. One simply cannot attribute a 'distractive' function to abolitionism without systematic attention to the full range of analogical uses, their frequency, timing and context.

59. Sidney and Beatrice Webb, *English Poor Law History* 3 vols (London, 1927–29), II, 90–100. Historians assume that political economists were aligned with abolitionism. Contemporary workers thought differently in 1832. A Bolton political rally, with 5000 workers in procession, carried the following banners: 'The victims of the Political Economists'; 'Success to the Loom'; 'Better wages to the weavers'; 'No monopolies'; 'Abolition of Slavery'; 'Tax the rich relieve the poor'; etc. *Manchester Courier*, 8 December 1832.

60. Steven B. Webb, 'Saints or Cynics: A Statistical Analysis of Parliament's Decision for Emancipation in 1833', Table 3 (forthcoming essay, kindly sent by the author).

61. Drescher, 'Cart Whip', 17–18. For another view see Davis, *Slavery and Human Progress*, 340, note 26, and for a slightly different perspective, D. Eltis, 'Economic development', Chapter 5. Some abolitionists who were sympathetic to domestic welfare were even inclined to extend the English welfare system to the aged and the young ex-slaves in the West Indies (*Leeds Intelligencer*, 24 January 1833).

62. A year *before* emancipation was implemented (August 1833), the *Christian Observer* declared that the Emancipation Bill was insufficient. See also Drescher, 'Cart Whip', 23–4, note 69. George Stephen, the organizer of the popular campaign, anticipated and denounced the Whig government's postponement of full emancipation for five to seven years. He considered the Whigs untrustworthy 'rogues'. (See Stephen to Lord Suffield, 18 January 1833 and Stephen to Powell, 9 July 1833, from the George Stephen papers discovered by David Brion Davis at the Hull Museums and kindly sent to me.) Deep suspicion of the government's past record on antislavery action was a hallmark of Stephen's correspondence.

63. Drescher, 'Two Variants', 57–8; 'Public Opinion', 37–9. 'The 1790s were perhaps the high point of both radical and artisan cultures in England', while the early 1830s also marked another high point, this time of more class-conscious political activity. See Craig Calhoun, *The Question of Class Struggle: The Social Foundations of Popular Radicalism during the Industrial Revolution* (Chicago, 1982), 14. On the growing social gulf in the textile areas from the 1830s, see Anthony Howe, *The Cotton Masters 1830–1860* (Oxford, 1984), 306.

64. A. D. Gilbert, *Religion and Society in Industrial England* (London, 1976), 59–68, 147–8, 158–160.

65. William A. Green, 'Emancipation to Indenture: A Question of Imperial Morality', *Journal of British Studies* 22, 2 (Spring 1983), 98–121, esp. 108–9. For a similar French perspective see A. de Tocqueville, 'On the Emancipation of Slaves', in S. Drescher (ed.), *Tocqueville and Beaumont on Social Reform* (New York, 1968), 142.

66. Mitchell and Deane, *Abstract*, 355. The long-term rate of cotton expansion began to decline in 1837–42, and the depression of 1846–9 universalized workhouses in Lancashire where *per capita* poor rates had ranked among the lowest in the nation. D. A. Farnie, *The English Cotton, Industry and the World Market 1815–1896* (Oxford, 1979), 43, 63.

67. *McDouall's Chartist and Republican Journal* was indifferent to the laissez-faire attack on the sugar duties. It was 'the next humbug'. 'What is that to the handloom weaver? What boon is it to any trade in this great nation?' (29 May 1841, 65). *McDouall's* also asked why Parliamentarians spent £20 000 000 to make sugar dearer for the sake of emancipating slaves and 'now ask us to eat Cuba and Brazil sugar grown by slaves?' 29 May 1841, 1. On the coverage given to Parliamentary comparisons of Jamaican and British workers, see ibid., 12 June 1841, 82–4. *The Northern Star*, 15 May 1841, 5, also considered the sugar debate a humbug.

68. Evidence before the Select Committee on the West India Colonies, *Parliamentary Papers*, 12 (1842), 479, 6158, 6275 (cited in Green, 'Emancipation to Indenture', 109, note).

69. First published in *Fraser's Magazine*, 60 (December, 1849), 670–9.

70. R. J. M. Blackett, *Building an Antislavery Wall: Black Americans in the Atlantic Abolitionist Movement 1830–1860* (Baton Rouge, 1983), 18–25, 199–203.

71. See Green, 'Emancipation to Indenture', 109; Tocqueville, 'On the Emancipation of Slaves', 169.

72. Drescher, 'Cart Whip', 18; H. Temperley, *British Anti-Slavery 1833–1870* (London, 1972), Chapters 8, 11.

73. Thompson, *The Making of the English Working Class*, Preface and Postscript.

74. Compare Davis, *Slavery in . . .* Revolution, esp. 366–73, 461–2, with Betty Fladeland, *Abolitionists and Working-Class Problems in the Age of Industrialization* (London, 1984), Chapters 1, 3. Davis also implies that Sharp's radicalism, always 'backward looking', became less radical and increasingly obsessed with 'social discipline' after the beginning of the Sierra Leone experiment (*Slavery . . . in Revolution*, 394–5, note). Davis may have relied too much on a West Indian accusation that Sharp urged Londoners to withold charity from the black poor to force them all to embark for Africa in 1788. At least 23 of the 440 who were boarded by February 1787 were discharged for 'mutinous' behaviour before sailing. In the second sailing, Sharp himself reduced the number of passengers by 30 per cent to eliminate crowding. See letter of Sharp to Dr John Coakney, 13 October 1788, in Huntington Library, Clarkson Papers, CN147. Sharp later favoured the extension of London parish relief to all the poor, regardless of origin. (*The Star*, 9 February 1792.) This would have obviously relieved the black poor of London as well. Far from moderating his position on abolition, Granville Sharp proposed general emancipation in the British colonies as the proper response to the French revolutionary strategy in the Caribbean. (Duke University Library, Wilberforce Papers, Sharp to Wilberforce, 4 June 1795.) When Capel Lofft rejoiced at Fox's achievement in accelerating the abolition of the slave trade, Sharp emphasized that neither Fox 'nor any other person in Parliament has yet urged the indispensable necessity of abolishing Slavery itself in the British colonies' (Gloucestershire Record Office, Hardwicke Court Muniments, papers of Sharp, Box 28–F, Slave Trade, etc., Sharp to Lofft, 21 October 1806). For Sharp's

continued equation of the poor and the slaves, see also his *Extract of a Letter to a Gentlemen in Maryland* (London, 1793), 10. No one could have accused Sharp of creating a pretty picture of the English labourer. In his first tract on slavery he wrote: 'If the English labourer is not able, with hard work, to earn more than what will barely provide him his necessary food and coarse or ragged clothing, what more can his employer reasonably desire of him, even if he were a slave?' *A Representation of the Dangerous Tendency of Tolerating Slavery* (London, 1769), 75. Since the whole tenor of Sharp's writings and behaviour was identification with the powerless, identifying him as an accessory to social discipline would seem to require a far more cogent analysis to establish this counter-intuitive proposition. On Sharp's reforming activities, see copies of his letters at York Minster Library: 17 May 1768 on the apprehension of blacks in London; 4 August 1768 on the Florida Indians; 12 September 1769 on indentured servants in Virignia; 21 August 1772 on slaves and the slave trade in the colonies; 21 July 1772 on the immigrant poor in America; 18 February 1772 on the plight of Negroes, Indians and white servants in the colonies; 31 July 1772 on West Indian Slavery; 10 October 1772 on the natives of St Vincent; 21 December 1772 on the colliers and salters of Scotland; 18 November 1774 on the European slave trade; and some time in 1785 on the gleaning rights of English agricultural labourers. In short, Sharp added a new antislavery dimension to domestic radicalism and made himself the centre of a nascent network for the protection of one unfavored group after another. See also *The Black Dwarf*, 9 (4 September 1822) 343. Even at the peak of the anti-French reaction, Sharp denounced the enormous burden of war taxes ('Barley . . . is taxed to the amount of *at least 7 times the landlord's Rent*') and the 'illegal compulsion of *Seaman*'. There was 'no safety but in a *Constitutional Reformation*' (Bodleian Library, Wilberforce Ms, d. 15, f. 52).

75. R. Anstey, *The Atlantic Slave Trade and British Abolition, 1760–1810* (London, 1975), 181, Fladeland, *Abolitionists*, ix. For early radical pledges of support for abolition, see Huntington library, Clarkson Papers, Box 1, 1787–1818, CN123, letter of John Cartwright to Granville Sharp, 15 October 1787; Capel Lofft to S. Hoare, 23 December 1787. On Parliamentary abolitionists as reformers see Ian Campbell Bradley, 'The Politics of Godliness: Evangelicals in Parliament, 1784–1832', D. Phil, Oxford University, 1974, iv.

76. Drescher, 'Cart Whip', 1–18.

77. See, *inter alia, Ipswich Journal*, 5 April 1788; *Chester Chronicle*, 2 December 1791, 17, 24 February, 9, 16, 23, 30 March, 6, 27 April 1792; *Northampton Mercury*, 4 February 1792; *Edinburgh Advertiser*, 31 December 1791, 10 January 1792; *The Bee, or Literary Weekly Intelligencer*, 1, 9 February 1791, 228; *Glasgow Advertiser*, 23, 26 March, 18–21 May 1792; *Manchester Herald*, 14, 21, 28 April, 12 May, 9 June, 13 October 1792; *Diary*, 13 June, 29 December 1789; *Morning Chronicle*, 31 August 1790, 20 July 1791, 13 February, 12 March, 2 April 1792; *General Evening Post*, 9–11 February 1792. The *Derby Mercury* (16 February 1792) published adjacent ads for Mary Wollstonecraft's *The*

Rights of Woman, a Birmingham antislavery meeting, a long list of abolition petitions, a suggestion for a separate ladies' petition, and a report of lower sugar sales. In ibid., 1 March, there were advertisements for free sugar, Paine's *The Rights of Man*, Parliamentary Reform, and a petition of Chesterfield inhabitants for abolition. During the mobilization for the Manchester petition of 1792 a citizen of Broughton called for the relief of certain 'fellow citizens (parish apprentices) . . . who are . . . suffering under the hands of as cruel task masters as in the West Indies' (letter of 30 January 1792, in *Manchester Mercury*, 31 January 1792); an inquiry was in fact launched. *Northampton Mercury*, 4 February 1792).

In Ireland the *Dublin Post* noted that all were unanimous for 'an abolition of slavery in our West India possessions – why not begin at home' with oaths of allegience and supremacy? (25 March 1788.) And while the British were giving liberty to the Africans, the Irish 'must seize their own'. (ibid., 3 May 1792.) See also Belfast's *Northern Star*, 28 January–1 February 1792. A patriotic meeting in Ireland toasted 'the cause of all those who are persecuted because they are *black*, and *blackened* because they are *persecuted!*' (*Diary*, 14 April 1792.) Thomas Spence's *Pig's Meat*, 3 vols (London, 1793–5), 1, 268–72, compared Africans with the 'Celtic slaves' in the Hebrides; William Godwin compared West Indian slaves and English servants in *The Enquirer: Reflections on Education, Manners, and Literature* (London, 1797), 211. The first of John Thelwall's *Political Lectures* (London, 1795), referred to impressment as *'that European slave–trade!'*, and he joined the inhabitants of Gallia and the 'sooty African' in claiming rights as 'a MAN and a BROTHER!' (ibid.). See also J. Thelwall, *The Tribune*, 3 (London, 1796), no. 35, 47; *The British Crisis, or the Disorder of the State at its Height* (London, 1797), 35, and Thomas Somerville's *Discourse on the Slave Trade at Jedburgh* (Kelso, 1792), 28–9: 'Every little domestic tyrant, who domineers among his relations and dependents, and treats them like slaves – parents, who, by severe usage, *provoke their children to wrath* – husbands who are *bitter against their wives* – masters who make their servants *serve with rigour*, and make their lives grivious *with hard bondage* . . . – landlords who are oppressive to their tenants'; all these had been brought 'into view by investigating the history of the slave trade'.

The symbolic transference of slavery to female subservience also became a permanent feature of the age of abolition. 'All women are slaves', Mary Wollstonecraft's fictional heroine Marie declared in 1798. Similar linkages by William Thompson and Owenite women in the 1830s and 1840s were part of a continuous rhetorical tradition. See Barbara Taylor, *Eve and the New Jerusalem: Socialism and Feminism in the Nineteenth Century* (New York, 1983), 32–5. Thomas Spence claimed that property in land or the funds depended on the same arguments as the slave trade: Spence, *The Important Trial of Thomas Spence on May 27, 1801* (London, 1807), preface, 15–16. A handbill was circulating among the soldiers in 1792; 'O Soldiers . . . reflect how cruelly you are used worse by far than Negroes in our transatlantic possessions. How are you flogged, how are you tormented, how are you punished and above all starving upon a sixpence a day' (PRO HO 42/23). On the 'unity' of popular liberties, see M. E. Happs, 'The Sheffield Newspapers', 28.

78. Davis rests his case for displacement in 1807 largely on the impact of J. Stephen's *The Dangers of the Country* (London, 1807). (See Davis, *Slavery in . . . Revolution*, 366–7, 465–6.) However, in the same issue that Benjamin Flower hailed the '*triumph of humanity* in the *abolition of the slave trade*', he condemned the government for 'the massacre and slaughter committed at VELLORE in the East Indies', and 'the union of the *saints* and the *contractors*' at Sierra Leone (*Flower's Political Register*, 1 (1807), xvi, xxxv, 220). Referring specifically to Stephen's *Dangers of the Country*, Flower noted that it overlooked the country's *real* dangers, executive influence, Parliamentary corruption, and arrogant domination of the seas. Flower emphasized that Stephen's call for national reformation called for only one reform: abolition. (Ibid., 1, 3 (March 1807), xlii–xliv); Compare with Davis, *Slavery in . . . Revolution*, 365–8. For good reasons, Tory political pamphlets after 1807 made only the briefest mention of the passage of abolition without editorial comment. See *A True History of a Late Short Administration* (London, 1807), 2. For the impact of Parliamentary abolition on Manchester's mobilization for relief in 1811–12, see Clive Emsley, *British Society and the French Wars, 1793–1815* (London, 1979), 155. See also *Cowdroy's Manchester Gazette*, 14 December 1816 for the rhetoric of 'African slavery' in the Spa Fields Riot.

79. Drescher, *Econocide*, 152–61; 'Two Variants', 59; J. Walvin, 'The Public Campaign in England against Slavery, 1787–1834', in D. Eltis and J. Walvin (eds), *The Abolition of the Atlantic Slave Trade* (Madison, 1981), 67–8; *Gloucester Journal*, 27 June, 11 July 1814.

80. Betty Fladeland, 'Abolitionist Pressures on the Concert of Europe, 1814–1822', *Journal of Modern History*, 38 (1966), 355–73. For scenes of the enchained Africans at victory celebrations see *Manchester Exchange Herald*, 12 July 1814. The progovernmental *Courier* in 1814 denounced the slave-trade petitioners for dampening the enjoyment of victory (ibid., 5 July, 5 August 1814).

81. *The Black Dwarf*, 4 (23 February 1820), 228. In 1814 Canning reminded Parliament and the country that all but two members of the Cabinet which was in office when the King signed the Bill of 1807 were among 'the commonest opposers of the Abolition'. (*Morning Chronicle*, 30 June 1814; *Examiner*, 7 August 1814, 503.)

82. Contemporaries had no difficulty in making distinctions and combinations. The Opposition deeply resented Wilberforce's insinuation that because York's 1792 slavery petition was more numerously signed than the Sedition Bills petition of 1795–6, the county was less favourably disposed toward of the latter (*Morning Chronicle*. 7 December 1795). The West Indians could only push their *tu quoque* just so far. Despite Pitt's opposition to the slave trade the West Indian MPs knew that their best hope lay with the conservatives (see *Morning Chronicle*, 2 December 1795). Benjamin Flower attacked the hypocrisy of Pitt and Grenville, and 'our *evangelical* Wilberforces and Thorntons' as early as 1796.

See *National Sins Considered, in two Letters to the Reverend Thomas Robinson* (Cambridge, 1796), 24–5, 48–9. A cartoon entitled 'The Victorious Procession to St. Paul' (British Museum Prints and Drawings no. 9046, 1797), shows Wilberforce holding a Common Prayer book in one hand, a paper marked 'slave trade' in his pocket, a pistol held behind him and a Negro in livery. See also *The British Crisis* (London, 1797), 34; *A Letter to William Wilberforce,* (London, 1797); John Gale Jones, *Sketch of a Political Tour through Rochester, Chatham* etc. (London, 1796), 62–3; *Exposition of the Principles of the English Jacobins* (Norwich, 1796), 31; *The Speeches of John Horne Tooke* (1796), 32; Anthony Pasquin, *Legislative Biography* (London, 1795), 19–20; *Considerations on the French War . . . by a British Merchant* (London, 1794).

Benjamin Flower hailed the passage of abolition while accusing Pitt and Grenville of having hatched a systematic plan 'for subduing the old British spirit', and while denouncing Cobbett as the one advocate of the slave trade 'among the people at large'. *Flower's Political Review*, 1 (1807), first essay, vii, xxxv, xliv, xlvi. A 'Freeholder' attacked Wilberforce in his Yorkshire stronghold for thinking of peace for Africa alone, and for not relieving his own society by lowering the tax burdens on his constituents (*York Herald*, 30 May 1807). In 1814 Wilberforce was accused of voting for 'the starvation of the brave and innocent Norwegians into subjection' (*Cowdroy's Manchester Gazette*, 4 June 1814). In 1818 T. J. Woller's *The Black Dwarf* wrote an open letter to Wilberforce:

> You saw the negro in chains, you raised your voice in his behalf, and effected a *partial redemption* from his bonds. But you paused. It was dangerous to offend the *sons of power* too far; and you had obtained all the popularity, from the friends of liberty, that they could bestow. [You helped] your friends to fasten the shackles of tyranny upon every hand at home, and make whites the successors of blacks in the manacles of bondage.

Granville Sharp, on the other hand, was always recognized as a fellow reformer (ibid., 2 (18 March 1818), 165–7; 3 (24 November 1819), 771).

83. *The Black Dwarf*, 21 (11 March 1824), 328–9, emphasized that the key question was *not* who assailed a grievance, but whether it existed. The journal would have welcomed West Indian support on Ireland, and pointedly recalled how severe some of the Saints had been with 'the sufferings of the people'.
84. Davis, *Slavery and Human Progress*, 123.
85. *The Abolitionist*, 1 (1834), 25, 26, 58, 66.
86. Ibid., 50. For the formal abolitionist protest against West Indian claims to compensation and apprenticeship, see *House of Commons, Select Committee on Public Petitions* 1833, 1, petition 9178, appendix 1009.
87. It is also possible to cite a fraction of the epistolary evidence: the English poor, *World*, 31 January 1788; *Morning Chronicle*, 17 March, 9 July, 8 November 1788; day labourers, maids of all work, the poor, seamen, and soldiers, *St James's Chronicle*, 18–20 March, 29 March–1 April, 18–21 October, 17–18 November 1788; impressment, bull baiting, and

chimney sweeps, *Bristol Journal*, 16 February 1788, and the *Gazetteer*, 5 March 1788, 15 May 1789; poor laws, debtor laws, impressment, religious intolerance, *The Repository*, 4 (16 February 1788), 95–6; mechanics and day labourers, *Chelmsford Chronicle*, 22 March 1788; British workers and soldiers, *Whitehall Evening Post*, 22–4, 29–30 January, 27–9 March, 19–21 June 1788; the miners of Cornwall, the Scottish Highlanders, and the Irish poor, *Public Advertiser*, 13 May 1788; schoolboys, *The Argus of the Constitution*, 29 February 1792; prize fighters, ibid., 20 February 1788, *Morning Chronicle*, 13 April 1792; animal cruelty, *Diary*, 14 January 1792; deportees in Botany Bay, convicts, prostitutes, white slaves in Canada, and plundering in India, ibid., 18 April 1791, 24 January 1792. See also Jesse Foot, *A Defence of the Planters in the West Indies* (London, 1792), and *An Appeal to the Candour and Justice of the People of England* (London, 1792), *passim*; an antiabolitionist MPs rejoinder to John Gale Jones in *Sketch of a Political Tour through Rochester*, etc. (London, 1792), 62–3. For specific assertions that West Indian slaves were better off than other groups, especially the workers of Europe, see: *Bristol Journal*, 16 February 1788; *Public Advertiser*, 10 March 1788, 2 April 1792; *Morning Chronicle*, 27 June, 19 September 1788; *St. James's Chronicle*, 18–20 March, 29 March–1 April, 19–23 April, 18–21 October, 17–18 November 1788; *Diary*, 24, 28 April, 25, 26 June, 21 July 1789; 28 April 1792. Antiabolitionists also shifted the analogy between colonial slaves and European peasants to a comparison between the manufacturing towns of Britain and the 'manufactories' of the West Indies. See *Letters Concerning the Abolition of the Slave Trade* (London, 1807), 7.

Such comparisons appear to have been quite reflexive. Instances of the British labour/colonial slave analogies occurred even before 1788, whenever stimulated by discussions of slavery. See, for example, [John Newbery] Tom Telescope, *The Newtonian System of Philosophy adapted to . . . Young Gentlemen and Ladies* (London, 1761), 121 and an anti-Somerset letter in the *Gazetteer* of 15 July 1772. In the very first deliberations of the Edinburgh abolition committee in 1792 an opponent of immediate abolition favourably compared the slaves with the British poor. (See Dickson, *Diary*, Edinburgh, 17 January 1792.) Comparisons continued right through and beyond emancipation. Slaves were 'more comfortably settled than the working classes in Ireland', and it was inconsistent with both justice and Christianity 'that a child of a British labourer should be subject to longer toil than a convicted felon or an adult slave'. *House of Commons Select Committee on Public Petitions* 1833, 963, 1222–3, 1325. For Cobden's analogy see BL Add Mss 50131 ff. 38–9, Cobden to Sturge, 20 July 1841.

88. See William L. Garrison (ed.), *Lectures of George Thompson, with a full report of the discussion between Mr. Thompson and Mr. Borthwick, the pro-slavery agent* (Boston, 1836), 90–4. It was difficult for those who regularly flogged soldiers not to think of them as slaves.

But such a set of wanton idle Knaves!
You're forced by G-d! to treat them all as Slaves.
(From *The Military Adventures of Johnny Newcome* (London, 1816,

reprinted 1904), 146–7, kindly furnished by Roger N. Buckley from his forthcoming *'Treat Them Like Slaves:' Crime and Punishment in the British Army 1796–1824*).

89. The routine scenes on a 'Slave Ship could not be matched by any spectacles of misery and cruelty exhibited in this country'. *Diary*, 1 June 1793, letter of 'S. M. P.'

90. *Leeds Intelligencer*, 18 May 1833. The power of such comparisons was provided by a correspondent to *The Poor Man's Advocate* on 'British Colonial Slavery *versus* British Domestic Slavery' (3 August 1832), 228–9. The writer was moved by the lectures of Thompson and Reverend William Knibb. But he was also moved to reflection when Knibb observed that the clothes he was wearing 'were made by a slave who was obliged to pay his master no less than *thirteen shillings and fourpence per week for leave to work*'. Was there any British mechanic, as industrious as Mr Knibb's slave, who could maintain himself and also accumulate such high weekly premiums 'for any purpose whatever?'

91. As late as the autumn of 1793 one of the principal Jacobin charges against Brissot de Warville was his provocation of the ruin of the colonies. In 1848 the radical *Club des Amis des Noirs* was swept aside in the general reaction. The élite French abolitionists also became inactive. See AN SO-M, Généralités, 153 (1276), Dutrone to Schoelcher, 23 March 1848. The absence of abolitionist movements certainly did not coincide with otherwise high levels of metropolitan reform movements or radical agitation in the Netherlands, Denmark or Sweden.

92. On labour in America, see Eric Foner, *Free Soil, Free Labor, Free Men: The Ideology of the Republican Party before the Civil War* (London/New York, 1970), 29–39, 46–51, 58–61; I. Berlin and H. G. Gutman, 'Natives and Immigrants, Free Men and Slaves', *The American Historical Review*, 85, 5 (December 1983), 1194–9. On the contrary, in Southern cities with a large white labour force elements of the local élite were seeking to *disenfranchise* the working class on the eve of the American Civil War. See Fred Siegel, 'Artisans and Immigrants in the Politics of Late Ante-Bellum Georgia', *Civil War History*, 27, 3 (Fall 1981), 221–30; and 'Artisans and Immigrants in Late Ante-Bellum Virginia and South Carolina: The Politics of an anomaly' (Mss kindly sent by the author). On the social and ideological links between British antislavery and social movements for the poor, workers, women, animals, etc., see Brian Harrison, *Peaceable Kingdom: Stability and Social Change in Modern Britain* (Oxford, 1982). As John Bohstedt concludes: 'if the English people were not inclined towards insurrection, that is no proof of the "hegemony" of their rulers or of the primacy of ideological rather than political and economic domination' (*Riots and Community Politics in England* (Cambridge, Mass., 1983), 222). For a regional example of *convergent* mobilizations, see Frank W. Munger, Jr 'Contentious Gatherings in Lancashire England 1759–1830', in Louise A. Tilly and Charles Tilly (eds), *Class Conflict and Collective Action* (London/Los Angeles, 1981), 73–109.

93. See Davis, *Slavery in . . . Revolution*, 363–421.

8 ANTISLAVERY AND CAPITALISM

1. For the most recent historical analysis of the abolition debate in Britain in relation to labour discipline see David Eltis, 'Abolitionist Perceptions of Society after Slavery', in J. Walvin (ed.), *Slavery*, 195–213, extended with great subtlety in 'Economic Growth and Coercion', Chapters 5–7. The debate over the cheapness of free versus slave labour was not always assumed to be settled even among avowed abolitionists: 'The time is not, perhaps, yet come, when this question can meet with a fair discussion.' (See James Anderson's *The Bee*, 6, 86 (16 November 1791) and above, Chapter 6, note 84. Social engineering plans by the more conservative abolitionists usually allowed for special legislation to limit the alternatives for ex-slaves. For Britain, see Eltis, 'Abolitionist Perceptions of Society after Slavery', 195–213; for France, S. Drescher, *Dilemmas of Democracy: Tocqueville and Modernization* (Pittsburgh, 1968), Chapter 6. All abolitionists did not, however, assume that the continuity of plantation production was a *sine qua non* of post-emancipation economies. In 1827, an extended essay in the *Edinburgh Review* by T. B. Macaulay demonstrated how the free-labour ideology could undermine arguments for restrictions on labour mobility after emancipation. Responding to protests that free blacks in the British colonies never worked the fields, the essayist replied:

It by no means follows that a man feels an insurmountable dislike to the business of setting canes, because he will not set canes for six-pence a day, when he can earn a shilling by making baskets. . . . We will grant that the free blacks do not work so steadily as the slaves, or as the labourers in other countries . . . To us it appears to be the universal effect of an advance in wages, an effect not confined to tropical countries, . . . [It is] an unsteadiness which cannot surprise any person who has ever talked with an English manufacturer, or ever heard the name of Saint Monday . . . [The] great general principle is the same in all [countries]. All will work extremely hard rather than miss the comforts to which they have been habituated; and all, when they find it possible to obtain their accustomed labour, will not work so hard as they formerly worked, merely to increase them . . . ; for the Chinese peasant would work as irregularly as the Englishman, and the Englishman as irregularly as the negro, if this could be done without any diminution of comforts. Now it does not appear from any passage in the whole Report, that the free blacks are retrograding in their mode of living. It appears, on the contrary, that their work, however irregular, does in fact enable them to live more comfortably than they ever did as slaves. The unsteadiness, therefore, of which they are accused . . . is equally an argument for coercing the spinners of Manchester and the grinders of Sheffield. . . . We never denied, that of two kinds of coercion, the more severe is likely to be the more efficient. Men can be induced to work only by two motives, hope and fear. . . . We hold that, in the long run, hope will answer best. 'Major Moody's *Report*', in *The Edinburgh Review*, 45 (March 1827), 399–410).

The ideological shift to the 'longer run' superiority of free labour was so complete that even for colonies the necessity of forced labour was now a *new* philosophy. (Ibid., 394–5.) See also Howard Temperley, 'Antislavery as Cultural Imperialism' in C. Bolt and S. Drescher (eds), *Anti-Slavery, Religion, and Reform* (Folkestone, Kent/Hamden, Conn., 1980), 335–50. The most important point, however, is not the argument over economic efficiency but how *peripheral* this whole argument was to popular antislavery rhetoric. See George Thompson's speech as the agent for the antislavery society in the great electoral campaign of 1832. (See *Speech on British Colonial Slavery, delivered at the Wesleyan Methodist Chapel, Irwell-Street, Salford, Manchester*, Monday, 13 August 1832.) Thompson met the question of possibly reduced export production head on. If Haitian exports were down by two–thirds, so what? If the West Indies decreased its consumption of British exports this was simply irrelevant. Would Ireland be any worse off if she exported less, ' "if instead of so much pork, she were to keep it for home consumption?" (*Loud Cheers*).'

2. What was at issue was probably best summed up by the cutlers of Sheffield. When the slave interest attempted to line up economic and political support against abolition in their abortive counter-mobilization of 1789, the cutlers formulated their response in a petition to the House of Commons. Their position was honed as sharply as their blades:

> Humble Petition of Several of the Freemen of the Corporation
> of Cutlers, in Hallamshire in the County of York
>
> That your petitioners being informed that the African Slave Trade is shortly expected to become a subject of consideration in this Honorable House and the cutlery wares made by the freeman of the said corporation, being sent in considerable quantities to the Coast of Africa, and disposed of, in part, as the price of Slaves – your petitioners may be supposed to be prejudiced in their interests if the said trade in Slaves should be abolished. But your petitioners having always understood that the natives of Africa have the greatest aversion to foreign Slavery, and defend themselves to the utmost of their power, against being sent away from their native country, and frequently perish in numbers, in their attempts to escape from what they deem so great an evil,
>
> Your petitioners therefore humbly represent to this Honorable House, that the obligations they are under, to consider the case of the nations of Africa as their own, is so much greater than any inducements of interest they can have in a trade, so much the aversion and dread of the people who are carried away by it, that your petitioners think themselves called upon to request this Honorable House, that as far as their interest may be deemed a part of the national policy of continuing the said trade, the same may be laid out of the question, unless it should appear that any other trade may be opened to Africa than that which brings away the people of the country (as the returns of our exports) as much against their inclinations as, it appears to your

petitioners, it would be against their own to be carried away in the same manner.

[24 April 1789, Signed by 769 FREEMEN CUTLERS; *Diary* 11 July 1789.]

3. Historiographical concern with the 'problem' of labour in the Atlantic economies has obscured some of the anthropological roots of hostility to Afro-American slavery. Thomas Clarkson established his abolitionist credentials with an essay, *On the Slavery and Commerce of the Human Species*. It was the corruption of the market mechanism which bore the first brunt of the antislavery onslaught. Just as the definition of slaves does not reside primarily in their deprivation of the means of production, so the ideology of freedom does not reside in the transformation of a special form of extra-economic coercion. See Muhammad A. Dandamaev, *Slavery in Babylonia from Nabopallassar to Alexander The Great (626–331 B.C.)*, rev. edn transl. by V. A. Powell et al., (De Kalb, Ill., 1984), 73–4, citing the work of K. K. Zel'in, *Formy Zavisimosti v vostochnom Sredizemnomor'e ellinisticheskogo perioda* (Moscow, 1969), 6f., 23.

4. D. B. Davis, *Slavery in . . . Revolution* (Ithaca, New York, 1984), 381–2. Early abolitionism overwhelmingly focused on slaving as a capitalist enterprise rather than a 'feudal' or seigneurial system.

5. The abolitionists' collection of principal documentary evidence for the campaign of 1792 was a structural clone of Clarkson's *Essay on the Slavery and Commerce of the Human Species*. The testimony was drawn from the Parliamentary hearings on the slave trade, but the topical breakdown and the titles themselves were derived from Clarkson. Thus the shape of the abolitionist argument pre-dated the whole systematic collection of governmental data and policy questions. The only substantive additions to Clarkson's essay were two chapters on the mortality and the treatment of white sailors, both independently documented by Clarkson in his own early investigations. The slave trade was *'a libel on the character of Commerce'*, because it entailed indiscriminate exile, the loss of family, place and posterity. See Letter of 'Leo Africanus', *Diary*, 16 April 1790.

6. J. Bohstedt, *Riots and Community Politics in England* (Cambridge, Mass., 1983), Chapter 3.

7. For early examples see Newbery, *The Newtonian System*, 121 as well as letters and petition advertisements: *General Evening Post*, 10–13, 13–15 November, 25–7 December, 1787; *Morning Chronicle*, 2, 4, 7, 14, 16 February, 12 May, 9, 11 July, 3 October, 11 November 1788; *Public Advertiser*, 29 January, 4, 14, 29 February 1788; *Leeds Mercury*, 23 October, 18 December 1787; 24 January 1788; *Chelmsford Chronicle*, 22 February 1788; *Lincoln, Stamford and Rutland Mercury*, 30 December 1791; *York Chronicle*, 13, 27 January 1792; *York Courant*, 21 February 1792; *Sheffield Advertiser*, 22 February 1792; *Manchester Herald*, 12 May 1792; *Food for National Penitence, or a Discourse intended for the Approaching Fast Day* (London, 1792), 10; Charles Pigott, *Political*

Dictionary, Explaining the True Meaning of Words (London, 1795), 131; Thomas Hall, *Achmet to Selim, or, the Dying Negro* (Liverpool, 1792), 5–10; S. Bradburn, *An Address to the People called Methodists* (Manchester, 1792), 2–3; *The Horrors of the Negro Slavery existing in our West Indian Islands* (London, 1805), 32 (the principal propaganda pamphlet of the abolitionist campaign of 1805–1806); *Cowdroy's Manchester Gazette*, 16 March 1805; Robert Aspland, *Divine Judgements on Guilty Nations* (Cambridge, 1804), 22; *Speech of the Bishop of St. Asaph, June 24, 1806* (London, 1806) 3. For similar arguments towards the end of the abolitionist era see the petitions to Parliament and organizational literature such as *The Wesleyan Preacher*, 3 vols (1832–3), 2, 175 ff.

8. The London abolitionists clearly felt that their fundamental strength lay in avoiding the *policy* of the question: Friends House Library, Dickson Diary, 'instructions'.

9. In terms of historiographical tradition, it might be noted that the abolitionist position, that man does not live by bread, or remuneration for labour, alone, is analogous to the position taken by many recent working–class historians in the 'standard of living' controversy during the English industrial revolution. The 'pessimists' insistence on comparing a broader range of amenities is similar to the abolitionist insistence on a more humanistic basis of similar comparisons. In this respect the abolitionists of the age of the industrial revolution are the forebears of recent Marxian historians.

10. For a contrary view, see D. B. Davis, *Slavery and Human Progress* (New York, 1984), 109–10, 249. Too much emphasis has been placed upon the government's 'handling' of the issue of emancipation in 1832–3 (or in 1788–92). What appears to emerge from a process that dragged out for a year after the summer of 1832 was the government's utter bewilderment under cross-pressure: it feared to approach the problem in the face of a public mobilization that would not go away and thirty or forty million in slave capital that could not go away. See Izhak Gross, 'The Abolition of Negro Slavery and British Parliamentary Politics 1832–3', *The Historical Journal*, 23, 1 (1980), 63–85, esp. 81–5; and 'Parliament and the Abolition of Negro Apprenticeship 1835–1838', *English Historical Review*, 96, 380 (July 1981), 560–76.

11. Davis, *Slavery and Human Progress*, 222.

12. Ibid., 351, note, 171; see also Lawrence Stone, 'Madness', *New York Review of Books*, 16 December 1982, 28–36.

13. Britain was not assumed to be immune from the cycle of rise and fall. Europe might someday sink while Africa picked up the torch of liberty and commerce: 'Let us not, therefore, vainly arrogate to ourselves a superiority of endless duration. Let us respect human creatures where ever we meet them, as being capable of rising to the highest exaltation of which finite existence can boast.' *The Bee*, 6, 350 (21 December 1791). It was the Earl of Westmoreland, an antiabolitionist who, on the eve of the new century, sarcastically called abolitionists 'these emperors of the world'. The epithet was ironic in more ways than Westmoreland intended.

Bibliography

MANUSCRIPT SOURCES

France

I. Archives des Affaires Etrangères

Etats Unis. Correspondance
Politique. vols. 96–100, 1840–44.

II. Archives Nationales

Archives privées, Fonds Mackau, 156 API
Marine et Outre-mer, série K1 and K2 (1848–49).
Chambre des Deputés et des Pairs petitions.
C2425, C2429 (93), CC475 (645),
C2425.
Assemblée Nationale
C942, Enquête sur les evenements de mai et juin 1848, dr. 4, 'Club des
  Amis des Noirs'
Section Outre-Mer.
Généralités, 153 (1275), Généralités, 153 (1276).
Généralités, 156 (1301), 'Voeux des Conseils-Generaux pour l'abolition'
SA 197 (1489), petitions of 1847, in 48 cashiers.

III. Achevêché de Paris

Archives Historiques. Direction des Oeuvres 4KII, dr: 'Pour l'abolition de
  l'esclavage'.

IV. Bibliothèque Nationale

Nouvelles Acquisitions 23,769, Isambert Papers, 3629–31, Schoelcher Papers.

V. Chateau de Presler

Abbé Gregoria and Hippolyte Carnot Papers.

Belgium

V. *Archives du Royaume, Brussels*

Archives du Comité du Commerce maritime.
180. 2150–3. (Trade of Habsburg subjects with Africa and the French Islands, 1783).

Great Britain and the USA

VI. *Bedfordshire County Record Office.*

How Family Papers, 1788–90.
Whitbread MSS. Correspondence of Samuel Whitbread on the Slave Trade.

VII. *Bodleian Library, Oxford*

Wilberforce Papers.

VIII. *British Library* (formerly *British Museum*)

Add MSS 21,254–56 London Abolition Committee Minute Books, 1787–1819.
Add MSS 27,808 Francis Place Papers
Add MSS 43,845, 50,131, Sturge Papers.

IX. *Friends House Library, London*

Minutes of Meeting for Sufferings, Committee on the Slave Trade, Box F.
Box H Antislavery Tracts
Temp. MSS Box 10/14 William Dickson, 'Diary of a Visit to Scotland, 5th January–19th March, 1792, on behalf of the Committee for the Abolition of the Slave Trade'.

X. *Gloucester Record Office*, Hardwicke Court Muniments, Granville Sharp Papers.

XI. Henry E. Huntington Library, San Marino, California BR
Box 12 (21), Philadelphia anti-slave trade petition, 1773.
CN 42, Thomas Clarkson Papers.
MY 146, Macaulay Papers.

XII. House of Lords Record Office MSS

Petitions on the Slave Trade, May 13, 1806.

XIII. Hull Museums

George Stephen Letters (identified by David Brion Davis).

XIV. Liverpool Public Library Record Office

92–ROS, Roscoe Papers.

XV. Minster Library, York

Granville Sharp Letterbook.

XVI. Perkins Library, Duke University

Stephen Fuller Letterbook.
Wilberforce MSS.

XVII. Public Record Office, London (PRO)

AO 12/99 Loyalist Claims
(BT) 9/11 Board of Trade.
CO 294/2 (Trinidad).
HO 35 series (1785).
HO 42 series (1786–1806).
T 70/1585.
T 630/1000–647/1572, Minutes for the Relief of the Black Poor.
TS 11,961/3507, Society for Constitutional Information Papers.

XVIII.   Rhodes House Anti-Slavery Society Papers (RHASSP)

Foreign correspondence of the Anti-Slavery Society.

XIX.   St John's College, Cambridge

Clarkson Papers

XX.   Salop County Record Office

Katherine Plymly Diaries (1791–1814).

OFFICIAL AND SEMIOFFICIAL DOCUMENTS

Note: the place of publication is London unless otherwise stated.

Parliamentary papers,

AP 1777, LIX (9), General State of the Trade to Africa.
PP 1842, XII (479); 1852–3, III (83), 104–5, 'Return of the number of Petitions Presented. . .'
Cobbett, William (ed.)
  The Parliamentary History of England from the Earliest Times to the year 1803.
  Stockdale's *Parliamentary Debates.*
Cobbett, William (subsequently Hansard, T. C.)(ed.)
  The Parliamentary Debates from the Year 1803.
Calendar of State Papers. Colonial America and the West Indies. 1677–80.
House of Commons. Report of the Select Committee on Public Petitions, 1833.
Votes and Proceedings of the House of Commons. 1830–31.

NEWSPAPERS AND PERIODICALS (only years cited)

L'Abolitioniste francais, 1844–47.
L'Ami de la Religion, 1847.
Annals of Agriculture, 1784–1806.
Anti-Slavery Reporter, 1841, 1842, 1858.

Argus of the Constitution, 1792.
Aris's Birmingham Gazette, 1832.
L'Atelier, 1844.
Baldwin's London Weekly Journal, 1772.
Baptist Magazine for 1830.
Bee, or Literary Weekly Intelligencer, 1791.
Birmingham Journal, 1830–3, 1838.
Black Dwarf, 1818, 1820–4.
Bristol Gazette and Public Advertiser, 1788.
Bristol Journal, 1788, 1789.
British Labourer's Protector, 1833.
Carpenter's Monthly Political Magazine, 1832.
Chelmsford Chronicle, 1788.
Chester Chronicle, 1791, 1792.
Christian Observer, 1832, 1833.
Le Constitutionnel, 1844.
County Chronicle and Weekly Advertiser for Essex, Herts, Kent, Surrey, Middlesex, etc. 1788.
Courier, 1806, 1814.
Cowdroy's Manchester Gazette, 1805–7, 1814, 1816.
The Craftsman, or Say's Weekly Journal, 1772.
Crisis, 1832–4.
Cumberland Paquet, 1832.
Daily Advertiser, 1772, 1773, 1775, 1783, 1785.
Daily Journal, 1728.
Daily Universal Register, 1785.
Derby Mercury, 1792.
Diary, 1789–93.
Dorchester and Sherbourne Journal, 1792.
Dublin Evening Post, 1788, 1792.
Edinburgh Advertiser, 1791, 1792.
Edinburgh Evening Courant, 1788, 1792, 1814.
Edinburgh Review, 1802, 1827, 1899.
Examiner, 1810, 1814.
Felix Farley's Bristol Journal, 1787.
Flower's Political Review, 1807.
Gazetteer, 1767, 1769, 1771, 1772, 1788, 1789, 1792.
General Advertiser, 1786, 1787.
General Evening Post, 1772, 1787, 1788, 1792.
Gentleman's Magazine, 1740, 1741, 1763, 1767, 1783, 1788.
Glasgow Advertiser, 1792
Le Globe, 1844.
Gloucester Journal, 1788, 1792, 1807, 1814.
Gore's General Advertiser, 1788.
Halifax and Huddersfield Express, 1833.
Hereford Journal, 1806.
Ipswich Journal, 1788, 1792.
Journal des Debats, 1844.
Leeds Intelligencer, 1807, 1831, 1833.

Leeds Mercury, 1787, 1788, 1806.
Leicester Chronicle, 1833.
Leicester Journal, 1792.
Lincoln, Rutland and Stamford Mercury, 1788, 1791, 1792.
Liverpool Chronicle and Commercial Advertiser, 1805, 1806.
Liverpool Courier, 1832.
Liverpool General Advertiser, 1782, 1788.
Lloyd's Evening Post, 1760, 1762, 1767, 1769.
London Chronicle, 1764–66, 1785–8.
London Courant, 1710.
London Evening Post, 1772.
London Gazette, 1788.
London Packet, 1787.
McDouall's Chartist and Republican Journal, 1841.
Manchester Courier, 1832, 1833.
Manchester Exchange Herald, 1814.
Manchester Herald, 1792.
Manchester Mercury, 1771, 1772, 1787, 1788, 1792.
Mechanics Magazine, 1824, 1832, 1833.
Middlesex Journal, 1769.
Morning Chronicle, 1772, 1783, 1785–6, 1814.
Morning Herald, 1785–88, 1792, 1810.
Morning Post, 1788.
New Moral World, 1838.
Newcastle Courant, 1788, 1792.
Norfolk Chronicle, 1791, 1792.
Northampton Mercury, 1788, 1791, 1792, 1806, 1807.
Northern Star, 1838, 1841, 1842.
Northern Star (Belfast), 1792.
Norwich Mercury, 1787, 1792.
Nottingham Journal, 1788.
Nottingham Review, 1832.
Patriot: or Political, Moral and Philosophical Repository, 3 vols. 1792.
Philanthropist, 1816.
Pioneer, 1833.
Poor Man's Advocate, 1832.
Poor Man's Guardian, 1833, 1834, 1835.
Post–Man, 1706.
Preston Pilot, 1832.
Public Advertiser, 1760, 1769–72, 1785–88, 1792.
Record, 1830, 1832, 1833.
La Reforme, 1844.
Repository, 1788.
Revue Abolitioniste, 1847.
St James's Chronicle, 1764, 1765, 1788.
Salisbury and Winchester Journal, 1788.
Le Semeur, 1838, 1842, 1844, 1846, 1847, 1848.
Sheffield Iris, 1807, 1830.
Sheffield Register, 1788, 1791.

Shrewsbury Chronicle, 1791, 1792.
Le Siècle, 1839, 1840, 1847.
Stamford Mercury, 1807.
Star, 1792.
Times, 1787, 1807, 1814.
L'Union, 1844.
L'Univers, 1847, 1848, 1858.
Voice of the West Riding, 1833.
Wesleyan Methodist Conference, 1825.
West Briton and Cornwall Advertiser, 1814.
Westminster Journal and London Political Miscellany, 1771, 1772.
Wheeler's Manchester Chronicle, 1814, 1833.
Whitehall Evening Post, 1788.
Williamson's General Advertiser and Marine Intelligencer, 1792.
Williamson's Liverpool Advertiser, 1783.
Working Man's Friend, 1833.
World, 1787, 1788, 1792.
York Herald, 1807.
York Chronicle, 1788, 1792, 1814.
York Courant, 1787, 1792, 1806, 1807.

INDIVIDUAL WORKS

An Abridgement of the Laws of England in Force and Use in Her Majesty's Plantations, 1704.
Abstract of the Evidence . . . before . . . the House of Commons . . . 1790 and 1791, on . . . the abolition of the slave trade. 1791, reprinted Cincinnati, 1969.
Adamson, Alan H. *Sugar without Slaves: The Political Economy of British Guiana, 1838–1904*. New Haven, 1972.
Anstey, Roger T. *the Atlantic Slave Trade and British Abolition, 1769–1810*. 1975.
———— and P. E. H. Hair (eds) *Liverpool, The African Slave Trade and Abolition*. Liverpool, 1976.
———— 'Parliamentary Reform, Methodism and Anti-Slavery Politics, 1829–1833'. *Slavery and Abolition* 2:3 (1981) 209–26. Postumously edited by David Brion Davis).
———— 'The Profitability of the Slave Trade in the 1840's'. *Comparative Perspectives on Slavery in New World Plantation Societies*. V. Rubin and A. Tuden (eds), New York, 1977, 84–93.
An Appeal to the Candour and Justice of the People of England in Behalf of the West India Merchants and Planters . . . 1792.
Appleby, Joyce 'Ideology and Theory: The Tension between Political and Economic Liberalism in Seventeenth-Century England'. *American Historical Review* 81:3 (1976), 499–515.
Ashton, T. S. *Economic Fluctuations in England 1700–1800*. Oxford, 1959.
Asiegbu, Johnson U. J. *Slavery and the Politics of Liberation 1787–1861: A*

Study of Liberated African Emigration and British Anti-Slavery Policy. New York, 1969.

Aspland, Robert *Divine Judgements on Guilty Nations*. Cambridge, 1804.

Atiyah, P. S. *The Rise and Fall of Freedom of Contract*. Oxford, 1979.

Aufruf zur Bildung eines Deutschen Nationalvereins für Abschaffung der Sklaveri. Heidelberg, 1848.

Bagwell, Richard *Ireland under the Stuarts and During the Interregnum* 3 vols 1909–16.

Bailyn, Bernard 'The Challenge of Modern Historiography'. *American Historical Review* 87:1 (1982), 1–24.

Barber, Anthony J. *The African Link: British Attitudes to the Negro in the Era of the Atlantic Slave Trade, 1550–1807*. 1978.

Bauer, Carol P. 'Law, Slavery and Sommerset's Case'. PhD dissertation, New York University, 1976.

Baxter, Richard *Chapters from a Christian Directory, or a Summ of Practical Theology and Cases of Conscience*. J. Tawney (ed), 1925 reprinted edition of 1673.

The Beauties of Nature and Art Displayed, in a Tour throughout the World. 13 vols 1763–4.

Becker, Robert A. *Revolution, Reform and the Politics of American Taxation 1763–1783*. Baton Rouge, 1980.

Beckles, Hilary M. 'The Economic Origins of Black Slavery in the British West Indies, 1640–1680: A Tentative Analysis of the Barbados Model'. *Journal of Caribbean History* 16 (1982), 36–56.

——'White Labour in Black Slave Plantation Society and Economy: A Case Study of Indentured Labour in Seventeenth-Century Barbados'. PhD dissertation, University of Hull, 1980.

Bellot, Leland J. 'Evangelicals and the Defense of Slavery in Britain's Old Colonial Empire'. *Journal of Southern History* 37 (1971) 19–40.

Belsham, William *Memoirs of the Reign of George III*, 6 vols 1796.

Bennett, J. Harry *Bondsmen and Bishops: Slavery and Apprenticeship on the Codrington Plantations of Barbados, 1719–1838*. Berkeley, 1958.

Berlin, Ira and Herbert C. Gutman 'Natives and Immigrants, Free Men and Slaves: Urban Workingmen in the Antebellum South'. *American Historical Review* 88:5 (1983), 1175–1200.

Berlin, Ira 'Time, Space and the Evolution of Afro-American Society on British Mainland North America'. *American Historical Review* 85:1 (1980), 44–78.

Bethell, Leslie M. *The Abolition of the Brazilian Slave Trade: Britain, Brazil and the Slave Trade Question, 1807–1869*. Cambridge, 1970.

Bird, James Barry *The Laws respecting Masters and Servants: Articles, Clerks, Apprentices, . . .* 1795.

Blizard, William *Desultory reflections on police: with an essay on the means of preventing crimes*. 1785.

Bohstedt, John *Riots and Community Politics in England*. Cambridge, Mass., 1983.

Bolt, Christine, and Seymour Drescher (eds) *Anti-Slavery, Religion and Reform: Essays in Memory of Roger Anstey*. Folkstone and Hamden, 1980.

Bowen, E. A. *A Complete System of Geography* 2 vols, 1747.

Bowman, Frank Paul *Le Christ romantique*. Geneva, 1973.

Bradley, Ian Campbell 'The Politics of Godliness: Evangelicals in Parliament, 1784–1832'. DPhil. dissertation, Oxford University, 1974.

Bradburn, Samuel. *An Address to the people called Methodists*. Manchester, 1792.

Braidwood, Stephen J. 'Initiatives and Organization of the Black Poor'. *Slavery and Abolition* 3:3 (1982), 211–27.

Brewer, J. N. *Some Thoughts on the present State of the English Peasantry. Written in consequence of Mr. Whitbread's motion in the House of Commons, February 19, 1807, relative to . . . the Poor Laws*. 1807.

Brewer, John *Party Ideology and Popular Politics at the Accession of George III*. Cambridge, 1976.

Britannicus. *A Letter to the Right Hon. William Pitt, Containing some new arguments against the abolition of the Slave Trade*. 1804.

The British Crisis, or, the Disorder of the State at its Height. 1797.

The British Merchant: A Collection of Papers Relating to the Trade and Commerce of Great Britain and Ireland. 2nd. edition, 3 vols, 1743.

The British Tocsin, or, Proof of National Ruin. 1795.

[Broglie, duc de] *Commission instituée . . . 26 mai 1840, pour l'examen des questions relatives a l'esclavage . . .* Paris, 1843.

Brooks, George E. 'A Nhara of the Guinea-Bissau Region: Mae Aurelia Correia', in Clare C. Robertson and Martin A. Klein (eds) *Women and Slavery in Africa*. Madison, 1983.

Browne, Patrick *The Civil and Natural History of Jamaica*. 1756.

Buckley, Roger N. *Slaves in Red Coats: The British West India Regiments, 1795–1815*. New Haven, 1979.

———'*Treat them like Slaves': Crime and Punishment in the British Army 1796–1824* (forthcoming).

Bureau de Correspondance pour l'abolition de l'esclavage. Paris, 1847.

Bynkershoek, Cornelius van *Questionum Juris Publici Libri Duo* 2 vols, Tenny Frank, transl. vol. 2, Oxford, 1930.

Calhoun, Craig *The Question of Class Struggle: the Social Foundations of Popular Radicalism during the Industrial Revolution*. Chicago, 1982.

[Campbell, John] *Candid and Impartial Considerations on the Nature of the Sugar trade . . .* 1763.

Carey, John *An Essay on the State of England in relation to its Trade . . .* Bristol, and London, 1695.

Carlyle, Thomas 'Occasional Discourse on the Nigger Question'. *Fraser's Magazine* 40 (1849), 670–79.

Carrington, S. H. H. 'Econocide' – Myth or Reality? – The Question of West Indian Decline, 1783–1806'. *Boletin de estudios latinoamericanos y del Caribe* 36 (1984), 13–48.

[Carter, S] *Legal Provisions for the Poor*. 1710.

Cartwright, John *Reasons for Reformation*, 1809.

Carver, Jonathan *The New Universal Traveller*. 1779.

The Case of the Sugar Colonies. 1792.

Catterall, Helen T. (ed) *Judicial Cases Concerning American Slavery and the Negro*. 5 vols. Washington, 1926–37.

Chamberlayne, Edward *Angliae Notitia*. 1669. Later published as *Magnae Britanniae Notitia*. 1708.

Child, Josiah *A New Discourse of Trade*. 1698.

Christie, Ian R. *Stress and Stability in Late Eighteenth-Century Britain: Reflections on the British Avoidance of Revolution*. Oxford, 1984.

Clarke, Thomas *A letter to Mr. Cobbett on his opinions Respecting the Slave Trade*. 1806.

Clarkson, Thomas *An Essay on the Slavery and Commerce of the Human Species, particularly the African*. 1786.

———— *The History of the Rise, Progress and Accomplishment of the Abolition of the African Slave Trade by the British Parliament*. 2 vols. 1808.

Cobbett, William *Letters to the Right Honorable Lord Hawkesbury and . . . Henry Addington . . .* 1802.

————*Political Register*. 1804, 1805, 1807, 1814, 1823, 1832–4.

Cohen William B. *The French Encounter with Africans: White Response to Blacks 1530–1880*. Bloomington, Indiana, 1980.

Coke, Thomas *A History of the West Indies, containing the Natural, Civil and Ecclesiastical History of Eash Island*. Liverpool, 1807–11.

————*A Journal of the Reverend Dr. Coke's Visit to Jamaica*. 1789.

Colman, George *Inkle and Yariko*. 1787.

Considerations on the French War . . . by a British Merchant. 1794.

Cooper, Thomas *Supplement to Mr. Cooper's Letters on the Slave Trade*. Manchester, 1787.

Corner, B. C. and C. C. Booth (eds) *Chain of Friendship: Selected Letters of Dr. John Fothergill of London, 1735–1780*. Cambridge, Mass. 1971.

Coupland, Reginald *Wilberforce*. 1923, 1945.

————*The British Anti-Slavery Movement*. 1933.

Cowherd, Raymond G. *Political Economists and the English Poor Laws*. Athens, Ohio, 1977.

Cox, Edward L. *Free Coloreds in the Slave Societies of St. Kitts and Grenada 1763–1833*. Knoxville, 1984.

Craton, Michael 'Proto-Peasant Revolts? The late Slave Rebellions in the British West Indies 1816–1832'. *Past and Present* 85 (1979), 99–125.

————(ed) *Roots and Branches: Current Direction in Slave Studies*. Toronto, 1979.

———— *Searching for the Invisible Man: Slaves and Plantation Life in Jamaica*. Cambridge, Mass. 1978.

————*Testing the Chains: Slave Rebellions in the British West Indies, 1629–1832*. Ithaca, 1982.

Crewe, Major *A Very New Pamphlet Indeed! . . . containing some strictures on the English Jacobins and . . . evidence . . . [on] the Slave Trade*. 1792.

Cugoano, Ottabah *Thoughts and Sentiments on the Evil . . . of Slavery*. 1787.

Cumeng, C. J. and Derek Baker (eds) *Popular Belief and Practice*. New York, 1972.

Cunha de Azeredo Coutinho, Joseph Joachim da. *Analyze sur la Justice du Commerce du Rachat des Esclaves sur la Côte d'Afrique*. 1798.

Curtin, Philip D. *The Atlantic Slave Trade: A Census*. Madison, 1969.

———— *Economic Change in Pre-Colonial Africa: Senegambia in the Era of the Slave Trade*. 2 vols. Madison, 1975.

—— *The Image of Africa: British Ideas and Action, 1780–1850.* Madison, 1964.

—— *Two Jamaicas: The Role of Ideas in a Tropical Colony, 1830–65.* Cambridge, Mass., 1958.

Dandamaev, Muhammed A. *Slavery in Babylonia from Nabolpallassar to Alexander the Great (626–331 B.C.)* rev. edition transl. V. A. Powell *et al.* DeKalb, Ill. 1984.

Davies, C. S. L. 'Slavery and Protector Somerset: The Vagrancy Act of 1547'. *Economic History Review* 1–3 (1966), 533–49.

Davies, K. G. *The North Atlantic World in the Seventeenth Century.* Minneapolis, 1974.

Davis, David Brion 'The Crime of Reform'. *New York Review of Books* 27:2, June 26, 1980, 14.

——*The Problem of Slavery in the Age of Revolution, 1770–1823.* Ithaca, NY 1975.

——*The Problem of Slavery in Western Culture.* Ithaca, NY 1966.

—— *Slavery and Human Progress.* New York, 1984.

Davis, Ralph *The Rise of the Atlantic Economies.* 1973.

Debbasch, Yvan *Couleur et liberté.* Paris, 1967.

Debien, Gabriel *Les Colons de Saint-Domingue et la Revolution: Essai sur le club Massiac.* Paris, 1953.

Deerr, Noel *The History of Sugar.* 2 vols. 1949–50.

[Defoe, Daniel] *A Plan of the English Commerce.* 1728.

Delacroix, S. *Histoire Universelle des Missions Catholiques.* 4 vols. Paris, n.d.

Ditchfield, G. M. 'The Campaign in Lancashire and Cheshire for the Repeal of the Test and Corporation Acts, 1787–1790'. *Transactions of the Historic Society of Lancashire and Cheshire* 126 (1977), 109–38.

—— 'Manchester College and Anti-Slavery' (MSS)

Dixon, Peter F. 'The Politics of Emancipation: The Movement for the Abolition of Slavery in the British West Indies, 1807–1833'. D Phil. Oxford, 1971.

Donnan, Elizabeth *Documents Illustrative of the Slave Trade to America.* 4 vols. Washington, D.C. 1933.

Drescher, Seymour 'Cart Whip and Billy Roller: Antislavery and Reform Symbolism in Industrializing Britain'. *Journal of Social History* 15:1 (1981) 3–24.

——*Dilemmas of Democracy: Tocqueville and Modernization.* Pittsburgh, 1968.

——*Econocide: British Slavery in the Era of Abolition.* Pittsburgh, 1977.

—— 'Econocide, Capitalism and Slavery: a commentary'. *Boletin de estudios latinoamericanos y del Caribe* 36 (1984), 49–65.

——'The Historical Context of British Abolition', in *Abolition and its aftermath in the West Indies, vol. 1. The Historical Context, 1790–1870,* David Richardson (ed.). 1985.

——'Paradigms tossed: The Decline Thesis of British Slavery Slavery since the mid-seventies'. In *Caribbean Slavery and British Capitalism* B. Solow and S. Engerman (eds) (forthcoming).

——'The Slaving capital of the world: Liverpool and national opinion in the age of abolition'. (MSS)

———(ed) *Tocqueville and Beaumont on Social Reform.* New York, 1968.
Driver, Cecil *Tory Radical: The Life of Richard Oastler.* New York, 1946.
Duckham, Baron F. *A History of the Scottish Coal Industry.* 2 vols. Newton Abbot, 1970.
Dunkley, Peter 'Whigs and Paupers: The Reform of the English Poor Laws 1830–1834'. *Journal of British Studies* 20:2 (1981), 124–49.
Dunn, Richard S. *Sugar and Slaves: The Rise of the Planter Class in the English West Indies, 1624–1713.* Chapel Hill, 1972.
Dutton, M. *The Law of Masters and Servants in Ireland . . .* 1723.
The Duty and Character of a National Soldier. 1779.
The Duty of Abstaining from the Use of West India Produce. A Speech delivered at Coach-Makers' Hall. January 12, 1792.
Dwight, H. D. *et al.* (eds) *The Encyclopedia of Missions.* New York, 1904.
Edwards, Paul and James Walvin (eds) *Black Personalities in the Era of the Slave Trade.* Baton Rouge, 1983.
Ehrman, John *The Younger Pitt: The Years of Acclaim.* New York, 1969.
Eltis, David and James Walvin (eds) *The Abolition of the Atlantic Slave Trade: Origins and Effects in Europe, Africa and the Americas.* Madison, 1981.
Eltis, D. 'Economic Growth and Coercion: The Ending of the Atlantic Slave Trade'. (forthcoming)
———'Free and Coerced Transatlantic Migrations: Some Comparisons'. *American Historical Review* 88:2 (April, 1983), 251–80.
Emmer, P. C. 'Anti-Slavery and the Dutch: Abolition without Reform'. *Anti-Slavery, Religion and Reform.* C. Bolt and S. Drescher (eds) Folkestone and Hamden, 1980.
Emsley, Clive *British Society and the French Wars 1793–1815.* 1979.
Encyclopédie, ou dictionnaire raisonée des sciences, des arts et des metiers. . . Geneva, 1776–9.
Engerman, Stanley 'Contract Labor, Sugar and Technology in the Nineteenth Century'. *Journal of Economic History* 43:3 (1983), 635–59.
———, 'Slavery and Emancipation in Comparative Perspective: a look at some recent debates', MS.
——— and Eugene D. Genovese (eds) *Race and Slavery in the Western Hemisphere: Quantitative Studies.* Princeton, 1975.
Engerman, S. and D. Eltis 'Economic aspects of the abolition debate'. *Antislavery, Religion and Reform.* C. Bolt and S. Drescher (eds) Folkestone, Hamden, 1980, 272–93.
Equiano, Olaudah *The Interesting Narrative of the Life of Olaudah Equiano or Gustavus Vasa, written by himself.* 2 vols. 1789.
An Essay upon Plantership. 1765, 1773, 1787.
Estwick, Samuel *Considerations on the Negro Cause, commonly so called, addressed to the Right Honorable Lord Mansfield . . . 2nd. edition 1773.*
Exposition of the Principles of English Jacobinism, Norwich, 1796.
Farnie, D. A. *The English Cotton Industry and the World Market 1815–1896.* Oxford, 1979.
Farther Reasons of a country gentlemen for voting against Mr. Wilberforce's motion. 1792.
Fenning, Daniel and J. Collyer, revised by Frederick Hervey *A New System of Geography.* 2 vols 1785.

Ferriar, John *The Prince of Angola, A tragedy altered from the play of Oroonoko*. Manchester, 1788.

Finley, Moses *Ancient Slavery and Modern Ideology*. 1982.

Fladeland, Betty 'Abolitionist Pressures on the Concert of Europe, 1814–1822'. *Journal of Modern History* 38 (1966) 355–73.

_____ *Abolitionists and Working-Class Problems in the Age of Industrialization*. 1984.

Floud, R. and D. McClosky (eds), *The Economic History of Britain Since 1700*. Cambridge, 1981.

Flower, Benjamin *National Sins Considered, in Two Letters to Reverend Thomas Robinson*, 1796.

Fogel, Robert W. and Stanley L. Engerman 'Philanthropy at Bargain Prices: Notes on the Economics of Gradual Emancipation'. *Journal of Legal Studies* 3:2 (1974), 377–401.

Fogel, Robert William *Without Consent or Contract: The Rise and Fall of American Slavery* (forthcoming).

Foner, Eric *Free Soil, Free Labor, Free Men: The Ideology of the Republican Party Before the Civil War*. New York, London, 1970.

Foner, Philip S. 'Alexander von Humboldt on Slavery in America'. *Science and Society*. 47:3 (1983), 330–42.

Food for National Penitence, or a Discourse intended for the Approaching Fast Day. 1792.

Foot, Jesse *A Defense of the Planters in the West Indies*. 1792.

Foster, Samuel *A Digest of all the laws relating to Customs, to Trade and Navigation*. 1727.

Fox-Genovese, Elizabeth and Eugene Genovese *Fruits of Merchant Capital: Slavery and Bourgeois Property in the Rise and Expansion of Capitalism*. New York, 1983.

Freyer, Peter *Staying Power: The History of Black People in Great Britain*. 1984.

Furneaux, Robin *William Wilberforce*. 1974.

Fyfe, Christopher *A History of Sierra Leone*. Oxford, 1962.

Galenson, David W. *White Servitude in Colonial America: An Economic Analysis*. New York, 1981.

Ganilh, Charles *An Inquiry into the Various Systems of Political Economy*. trans. D. Boileau. 1812.

_____ *La Théorie de l'economie politique fondu sur les faits resultans des statistiques de la France et de l'Angleterre . . .* 2 vols. Paris, 1815.

Garrison, William L. (ed) *Lectures of George Thompson, with a full report of the Discussion between Mr. Thompson and Mr. Borthwick, the Pro-slavery agent*. Boston, 1836.

Geggus, David 'British opinion and the emergence of Haiti'. In *Slavery*. J. Walvin (ed) 122–49.

_____ 'Haiti and the Abolitionists: Opinion, Propaganda and International Politics in Britain and France, 1804–1838' In *Abolition and its Aftermath* I, *The Historical Context*. D. Richardson (ed) 1985.

Gemery, Henry and Jan Hogendorn 'The Atlantic Slave Trade: A Tentative Economic Model'. *Journal of African History* 15 (1974):223–46.

_____ (eds) *The Uncommon Market: Essays on the Economic History of the Transatlantic Slave Trade*. New York, 1979.

Genovese, Eugene D. *From Rebellion to Revolution: Afro-American Slave Revolts in the Making of the Modern World*. 1979.

_____*The World the Slaveholders Made: Two Essays in Interpretation*. New York, 1969.

Geography Epitomized. Philadelphia and London. 1786.

Geography for Youth. 1790.

Geography made easy for Children. 1793.

George, M. D. (ed) *Catalogue of Political and Personal Satires in the . . . British Museum* 11 vols. 1978.

Gilbert, Alan D. 'The Growth and Decline of Non-Conformity in England and Wales, with special reference to the period before 1850'. DPhil. dissertation, Oxford University, 1973.

_____*Religion and Society in Industrial England: Church, Chapel and Social Change 1740–1914*. 1976.

Godwin, William *The Enquirer: Reflections on Education, Manners and Literature*. 1797.

Godwyn, Morgan. *The Negro's and Indians Advocate, Suing for their Admission into the Church . . . 1680*.

_____*A Supplement to the Negro's and Indians Advocate*. 1681.

_____*Trade Preferr'd Before Religion, and Christ Made to Give Place to Mammon . . . 1685*.

Gordon, Patrick *Geography Anatomized*. 1693, 20th edition 1754.

Gossett, J. R. *Remarks on West India Affairs*. 1824.

Gowland, David 'Methodist Secession and Social Conflict in South Lancashire 1830–1857'. PhD dissertation, University of Manchester, 1966.

Green, William. *British Slave Emancipation: The Sugar Colonies and the Great Experiment 1830–1865*. Oxford, 1976.

_____'Emancipation to Indenture: A Question of Imperial Morality'. *Journal of British Studies* 22:2 (1983), 98–121.

Green-Pedersen, Svend E. 'The Scope and Structure of the Danish Negro Slave Trade'. *Scandinavian Economic History Review* 19:2 (1971) 194–7.

Gross, Izhak 'The Abolition of Negro slavery and British Parliamentary politics'. *The Historical Journal* 23:1 (1980), 63–85.

_____ 'Parliament and the Abolition of Negro Apprenticeship 1835–1838'. *English Historical Review* 96–380 (1981), 560–76.

Gunn. J. A. W. *Beyond Liberty and Property: The Process of Self-Recognition in Eighteenth-Century Political Thought*. Kingston and Montreal, 1983.

Guthrie, William *A New Geographical, Historical and Commercial Grammar*. 1771, 1779, 1787, 1790, 1795, 1806, 1808, 1819, 1843.

Hall, Thomas *Achmet to Selim, or, the Dying Negro*, Liverpool, 1792.

Halley, Edmund *Atlas Maritimus and Commercialis*. 1728.

Hanway, Jonas *Distributive Justice and Mercy*. 1781.

Hardy, Thomas *The Memoirs of Thomas Hardy*. 1832.

Harrison, Brion *Peaceable Kingdom: Stability and Social Change in Modern Britain*. Oxford, 1982.

Harrison, Royden (ed) *Independent Colliers: The Coal Miner as Archetypical Proletarian Reconsidered*. New York, 1978.

Happs, M. E. 'The Sheffield Newspaper Press and Parliamentary Reform, 1787–1832'. B. Litt. thesis, Oxford University, 1973.

Harvey, A. D. *Britain in the Early Nineteenth Century*. New York, 1978.

Haskell, Thomas 'Capitalism and the origins of the Humanitarian Sensibility: Some Analytical Considerations'. *American Historical Review* 90:2 and 3 (April and June 1985), 339–61 and 547–66.

Hellie, Richard *Slavery in Russia 1429–1725*. Chicago, 1982.

Hibbert, George *The Substance of Three Speeches in Parliament*. 1807.

Higman, B. W. *Slave Populations of the British Caribbean, 1807–1834*. Baltimore and London, 1984.

Hill, Anthony *Afer Baptizatus: or, the Negro Turn'd Christian*. London, 1702.

Hill, Sir Richard *Letter of Sir Richard Hill to Reverend J. Plymly, chairman of the Abolitionist Society of Salop, a portion of his undelivered speech in the Commons*. 1792.

Hirschman, Albert O. *The Passions and the Interests: Political Arguments for Capitalism Before its Triumph*. Princeton, 1977.

The History of the Present State of the British Islands. 2 vols. 1743.

Hoare, Prince *Memoirs of Granville Sharp*. 1820.

Hochstetter, Franz *Die wirtschaftichen und politischen Motive für die Abschaffung des britischen Sklavenhandels im Jahre 1806–1807*. Leipzig, 1905.

Hodgson, Adam *A Letter to M. Jean Baptiste Say on the Comparative Expense of Free and Slave Labour*. 2nd. edition 1823.

Hollis, Patricia (ed) *Pressure from Without in Early Victorian England*. 1974.

The Horrors of the Negro Slavery existing in our West India Islands. 1805.

Howe, Anthony *The Cotton Masters, 1839–1860*. Oxford, 1984.

Howell's *State Trials*. 33 vols. 1814.

Howse, E. M. *Saints in Politics: The Clapham Sect and the Growth of Freedom*. Toronto, 1952.

Hunt, E. M. 'The North of England Agitation for the Abolition of the Slave Trade, 1780–1800'. M. A. thesis, University of Manchester, 1959.

Hurwitz, Edith F. *Politics and the Public Conscience: Slave Emancipation and the Abolitionist Movement in Britain*. 1973.

Illife, John *The Emergence of African Capitalism*. 1983.

James, C. L. R. *The Black Jacobins: Toussaint L'Ouverture and the San Domingo Revolution*. 1938.

James, Francis Godwin *Ireland in the Empire 1688–1770*. Cambridge, Mass. 1976.

Jennings, Lawrence C. 'The French Press and Great Britain's campaign against the slave trade, 1830–1848'. *Revue Française d'Histoire d'Outre-Mer* 67:246–7 (1980), 5–24.

Jentz, John B. 'The Antislavery Constitutency in Jacksonian New York City'. *Civil War History* 27:2 (1981), 101–22.

_____'Artisans, Evangelicals and the City: A Social History of the Labor and Abolitionist Movements in Jacksonian New York'. PhD dissertion, City University of New York, 1977.

Jerrold, Blanchard *The Original* 2 vols. 1874.

Jones, John Gale *Sketch of a Political Tour Through Rochester, Chatham, etc.* 1796.

Jones, Gareth Stedman *Language of Class: Studies in English working class history, 1832–1982*. 1983.

Journal of Commisioners for Trade and Plantations from January 1776 to May 1782. 1938.

Jus Imperij . . . et Servitutis, or the Law Concerning Masters, Apprentices, Bayliffs, Receivers, Stewards . . . 1707.

Knox, William *Three Tracts Respecting Conversion.* 1767, 1780.

Laqueur, Thomas Walter. *Religion and Respectability: Sunday Schools and Working Class Culture.* New Haven, 1976.

Latimer, John *The Annals of Bristol in the Eighteenth Century.* 1893.

Leslie, Charles *A New History of Jamaica . . . in Thirteen Letters.* 1740.

A Letter to William Wilberforce. 1797.

Letters concerning the abolition of the Slave Trade. 1807.

Lettsom, John *Some account of the late John Fothergill, M.D.* 1783.

Lilywhite, Bryant *London Coffee Houses: A Reference Book.* 1963.

Lipscomb, Patrick C. 'William Pitt and the Abolition of the Slave Trade'. PhD dissertation, University of Texas, 1960.

Litwack, Leon F. *North of Slavery: the Negro in the Free States 1790–1860.* Chicago, 1961.

Lloyd, Evan *A Plain System of Geography.* Edinburgh, 1797.

Locke, John *Two Treatises of Government. A Critical Edition with an Introduction and Apparatus Criticus, by Peter Laslett.* Cambridge, 1960.

London Unmask'd or the New Town Spy. 1783.

Long, Edward *Candid Reflections upon the Judgement . . . in Westminster-Hall, on what is commonly called the Negro-Cause, by a Planter.* 1772.

Lovejoy, Paul E. *Transformations in Slavery: A History of Slavery in Africa.* Cambridge, 1983.

Lysons, Daniel (compiler). *Collectanea: or, a Collection of Advertisements and Paragraphs from the Newspapers relating to Various Subjects.* 5 vols. n.d. British Library Press-mark, 1889. e. 5.

McCloy, Shelby *The Negro in France.* Lexington, Ky. 1961.

McKendrick, Neil, John Brewer and J. H. Plumb *The Birth of a Consumer Society: The Commercialization of Eighteenth-Century England.* Bloomington, 1982.

McNeill, William H. 'Slavery as a Moral Ambiguity'. *Washington Post National Weekly Edition*, November 5, 1984. 34.

Mackrell, J. Q. C. *The Attack on 'Feudalism' in Eighteenth-century France.* 1973.

Magalhaes, Jose Calvet de. *Historia do Pensamento Economico em Portugal: Da Idade-media ao mercantilismo.* Coimbra, 1967.

Magdol, Edward 'A Window on the Abolitionist Constituency: Antislavery Petitions, 1836–1839'. (MSS)

Mair, John *A Brief Survey of the Terraquous Globe.* Edinburgh, 1762.

Malcolmson, Robert W. *Life and Labour in England 1700–1780.* Hutchinson, 1981.

Manning, Patrick 'Contours of Slavery and Social Change in Africa'. *American Historical Review* 88:4 (October, 1983), 835–57.

Marshall, Herbert and Mildred Stock *Ira Aldridge: The Negro Tragedian.* 1958.

Marshall, Peter J. and Gwynn Williams *The Great Map of Mankind: Perceptions of New Worlds in the Age of the Enlightenment* Cambridge, Mass. 1982.

Marshall, Peter. *The Impeachment of Warren Hastings.* 1965.

_____'The Moral Swing to the East: British Humanitarianism, India and the West Indies'. (MSS)

Marshall, Samuel *A Treatise on the Law of Insurance*. 2 vols. Boston, 1805.

Martyn, William Frederick *The Geographical Magazine*. 2 vols, 1785.

Marx, Karl *Capital*. trans. Ben Fowkes. 1976.

Mather, F. C. (ed) *Chartism and Society: An Anthology of Documents*. 1980.

Mathews, Donald *Slavery and Methodism: a Chapter in American Morality 1780–1845*. Princeton, 1965.

Meirs, Suzanne and Igor Kopytoff *Slavery in Africa: Historical and Anthropological Perspectives*. Madison, 1977.

[Meriton, George.] *A Guide for Constables, Church-wardens and Overseers of the Poor . . .* 1682.

The Merchants' Dayly Companion. 1684.

Miller, Naomi C 'John Cartwright and radical Parliamentary reform, 1808–1819'. *English Historical Review* 83:239 (1968), 705–28.

The Military Adventures of Johnny Newcome. 1816, reprinted 1904.

Mintz, Sidney and Douglas Hall 'The Origins of the Jamaican Internal Marketing System'. *Yale University Publications in Anthropology* LVII (1960), 1–26.

Mintz, Sidney W. *Sweetness and Power: The Place of Sugar in Modern History*. New York, 1985.

Mitchell, B. R. and P. Deane *Abstract of British Historical Statistics*. Cambridge, 1962.

Moll, Herman *A System of Geography*. 1701.

Molloy, Charles *De Jure Maritimo et Navali; or, a Treatise of Affairs and of Commerce*. 1676. 3rd edition 1682.

Moody, T. W. *et al. A New History of Ireland*. Vol. 3 *Early Modern Ireland 1534–1691*. Oxford, 1976.

Moore, John Hamilton *New and Complete Collection of Voyages and Travels*. 2 vols. 1780.

Morden, Robert *Geography Rectified*. 1688.

Munger, Frank W. 'Contentious Gatherings in Lancashire England, 1759–1830'. *Class Conflict and Collective Action*. ed. L. and C. Tilly 1981, 73–109.

Murray, Andrew E. *Presbyterians and the Negro – A History*. Philadelphia, 1966.

Murray, David R. *Odious Commerce: Britain, Spain and the Abolition of the Cuban Slave Trade*. Cambridge, 1980.

Nash, Gary B. 'Slaves and Slaveowners in Colonial Philadelphia'. *William and Mary Quarterly*. 30 (1973), 226–52.

Necheles, Ruth F. *The Abbé Grégoire 1788–1831: The Odyssey of an Egalitarian*. Westport, Conn., 1971.

Newbery, John (ed) *Circle of the Sciences*. 7 vols. 1748.

_____Tom Telescope. *The Newtonian System of Philosophy adapted to the capacities of young Gentlemen and Ladies . . .* 1761.

Norton, Mary Beth *The British Americans: The Loyalist Exiles in England 1774–1789*. Constable, 1974.

Observations on the Necessity of Introducing a Sufficient number of Respectable Clergymen into our Colonies. 1806.

Oldmixon, John *The British Empire in America*. 1708, 1741.

Osofsky, Gilbert 'Abolitionists, Irish Immigrants and the dilemmas of Romantic Nationalism'. *American Historical Review* 80:4 (1975) 889–912.

Owen, Gwynne E. 'Welsh Anti-Slavery Sentiments 1790–1865: A Survey of Public Opinion'. M A thesis, University College of Wales, Aberystwyth, 1964.

Paley, William *Principles of Moral and Political Philosophy*. 1787.

Palmer, Colin A. *Slaves of the White God: Blacks in Mexico 1570–1650*. Cambridge, Mass., 1976.

Parker, *Evidence of Our Transactions in the East Indies . . . with an Enquiry into our National Conduct*. 1782.

Pascoe, C. F. *Two Hundred Years of the S. P. G.: An Historical Account of the Society for the Propagation of the Gospel in Foreign Parts*. 1901.

Pasquin, Anthony *Legislative Biography*. 1795.

Patterson, Orlando *Slavery and Social Death*. Cambridge, Mass., 1982.

———*The Sociology of Slavery: An Analysis of the Origins, Development and Structure of Negro Slave Society in Jamaica*. 1967.

Phillips, John A. *Electoral Behavior in Unreformed England: Plumpers, Splitters and Straights*. Princeton, 1982.

Pigott, Charles *A Political Dictionary, explaining the true meaning of words*. 1795.

Pinchard, George *Notes on the West Indies*. 3 vols. 1806.

Playfair, William *The Commercial and Political Atlas: Representing By Means of Stained Copper Plate Charts, the Exports, Imports, and General Trade of England*. London, 1786.

Poem Upon the Undertaking of the Royal Company of Scotland . . . Trading to Africa and the Indies. Edinburgh, 1697.

A Poetical Epistle, from the Island of Jamaica. Kingston, Jamaica, 1776.

The Political Progress of Britain. 1792.

Pollock, John *Wilberforce*. New York, 1977.

Porter, Dale H. *The Abolition of the Slave Trade in England, 1784–1807*. Hamden, Conn., 1970.

Porter, Roy *English Society in the Eighteenth Century*. 1982.

Posey, Walter *The Baptist Church in the Lower Mississippi Valley 1776–1845*. Lexington, 1957.

Postlethwayt, Malachy *The African Trade, the Great Pillar and Support of the Plantation Trade in General*. 1745.

———*The National and Private Advantages of the African Trade Considered . . .* 1746, 1772.

Pratt, Samuel Jackson. *Humanity, or the Rights of Nature*. 1788.

The Present State of the West Indies, including all Possessions. 1788.

Priestly, Joseph *A Sermon on the Slave Trade*. Birmingham, 1788.

Prothero, Iorwerth *Artisans and Politics in Early Nineteenth Century London*. Folkestone, 1979.

Puckrein, Gary A. *Little England: Plantation Society and Anglo-Barbadian Politics 1627–1700*. New York, 1984.

Quinney, Valerie 'The Committee on Colonies of the French Constituent Assembly, 1789–1791'. PhD dissertation, University of Wisconsin, 1967.

Ragatz, Lowell *A Guide for the Study of British Caribbean History 1763–1834*. Washington, DC, 1932.

Raynal, G. T. F. *Histoire Philosophique et Politique des établissemens et du commerce des Européens dans les deux Indes*. Geneva, 1781.

Record, Mary 'The Jamaica Slave Rebellion of 1831'. *Past and Present* 40 (1968), 108–25.

Reid, Anthony (ed) *Slavery, Bondage and Dependency in Southeast Asia*. St Lucia, Queensland, 1983.

Reilley, William *William Pitt the Younger*. New York, 1979.

A Report from the Committee of Warehouses of the United East India Co. Relative to the Culture of Sugar. London, 1792.

Resnick, Daniel P. 'Political Economy and French Antislavery: The Case of J. B. Say'. *'Proceedings of the third Annual Meeting of the Western Society for French History*. 1976.

———'The *Société des Amis des Noirs* and the abolition of Slavery'. *French Historical Studies* 7:4 (1972), 558–69.

Richardson, David (ed) *Abolition and its aftermath in the West Indies: The Historical Context, 1790-1870*. 1985.

Ripley, C. Peter, *et al.* (eds). *The Black Abolitionist Papers, I, The British Isles, 1839–1865*. Chapel Hill, 1985.

Robertson, Claire C. and Martin A. Klein (eds) *Women and Slavery in Africa*. Madison, 1983.

Roberts, Lewis *The Merchants' Map of Commerce*. 1677.

Robinson, Robert *A Sermon*. 1788.

Rogers, Nicholas 'London politics from Walpole to Pitt: patriotism and independency in an era of commercial imperialism, 1738–63'. PhD thesis, University of Toronto, 1974.

Rowe, John. *Cornwall in the Age of the Industrial Revolution*. Liverpool, 1953.

Rubin, Vera and Arthus Tuden (eds) *Comparative Perspectives on Slavery in New World Plantation Societies* vol. 292 of *Annals of the New York Academy of Sciences*. New York, 1977.

Rudé George *The Crowd in the French Revolution*. Oxford, 1959.

———*Wilkes and Liberty*. Oxford, 1962.

Rule, John *The Experience of Labour in the Eighteenth Century*. 1981.

Ruth, John Towhill (ed) *Diary of Thomas Burton esq*. 4 vols. 1828.

Saunders, A. C. DE C. M. *A Social History of Black Slaves and Freedmen in Portugal 1441–1555*. Cambridge, 1982.

Savary des Bruslons, Jacques. *Le Parfait Negociant, ou instruction générale pour ce qui regarde le Commerce de toute sorte de Marchandises*. Geneva, 1676.

———*Universal Dictionary of Trade*. transl. and supplemented by M. Postlethwayt. 1774.

Say, Jean-Baptiste *Traité d 'Économie Politique*. 2 vols. Paris, 1814, 1826.

Schoelcher, Victor *Histoire de l'esclavage pendant les deux dernières années*. 2 vols. Paris, 1847.

Schuler, Monica *Alas, Alas Kongo: A Social History of Indentured African Immigration into Jamaica, 1841–1865*. Baltimore and London, 1980.

Schwartz, Stuart B. 'Indian Labor and New World Plantations: European Demands and Indian Responses in Northeastern Brazil'. *American Historical Review* 83:I (1978), 43–79.

Sharp, Granville *Extract of a Letter to a Gentleman in Maryland*. 1793.

————*The Just Limitation of Slavery in the Laws of God, compared with the unbounded claims of the African Traders and British American Slaveholders*. 1776.

————*A Representation of the . . . Dangerous tendency of slavery*. 1769.

————*Short Sketch of Temporary Regulations . . . for the Intended Settlement . . . near Sierra Leone*. 1786.

Shyllon, Folarin *Black People in Britain 1555–1833*. 1977.

————*Black Slaves in Britain*. 1974.

Siegel, Fred 'Artisans and Immigrants in late Ante-Bellum Virginia and South Carolina: The Politics of an Anomaly'. (MSS)

————'Artisans and Immigrants in the Politics of Late Ante-Bellum Georgia'. *Civil War History* 27:3 (1981), 221–30.

Smith, Adam *An Inquiry into the Nature and Causes of the Wealth of Nations*. 1776, reprinted New York 1937.

———— *Lectures on Jurisprudence*. R. L. Meek *et al.* (ed) Oxford, 1978.

————*The Theory of Moral Sentiments*. D. D. Rafael and A. L. Macfie (eds). Oxford, 1976.

Smith, Thomas *The Commonwealth of England, and manner of government thereof . . .* 1601.

Smollet, Tobias *Present State of All Nations*. 8 vols. 1768.

Soboul, Albert *La France à la vielle de la Révolution*. 2 vols. Paris, 1966.

Society for the Improvement of the Condition of the Factory Children. 1833.

Solow, Barbara and Stanley Engerman (eds) *Caribbean Slavery and British Capitalism*. (forthcoming)

Some Observations which may contribute to afford a just idea of the Nature, Importance and Settlement of our New West Indian Colonies. 1764.

Somerville, Thomas *Discourse on . . . the African Slave Trade, at Jedburgh*. Kelso, 1792.

Speech of the Bishop of St. Asaph, June 24, 1806. 1806.

Spence, Thomas *The Important Trial of Thomas Spence on May 27, 1801*. 1807.

————*Pig's Meat* 3 vols. 1793–5.

Statistics of the New Connexion Baptists 1770–1843. Leicester, 1844.

Stein, Robert Louis *The French Slave Trade in the Eighteenth Century*. Madison, 1979.

Stephen, James *Crisis of the Sugar Colonies*. 1802, reprinted New York, 1969.

————*The Dangers of the Country*. 1807.

Stone, Lawrence 'Madness'. *New York Review of Books*, December 16, 1982, 28–36.

Stuart, Charles *A Memoir of Granville Sharp*. New York, 1836.

Sykes, R. A. 'Some Aspects of Working-Class Consciousness in Oldham 1830–42'. *Historical Journal* 23 (1980) 167–79.

Taylor, Barbara *Eve and the New Jerusalem: Socialism and Feminism in the Nineteenth Century*. New York, 1983.

Temperley, Howard 'Abolition and the National Interest', in J. E. S. Hayward (ed) *Out of Slavery: Abolition and After*. 1985.
―――*British Anti-Slavery 1833–1870*. 1972.
―――'Capitalism, Slavery and Ideology'. *Past and Present* 75 (1977), 94–118.
Thelwall, John *Political Lectures*. 1795.
―――*The Tribune*. 1796.
Thesaurus Geographicus. 1695.
Thomas, Dalby. *An Historical Account of the Rise and Growth of the West India Colonies*. 1690.
Thomas, R. P. and R. N. Bean 'The Fishers of Men: The Profits of the Slave Trade'. *Journal of Economic History* 34 (1974): 885–914.
Thompson, E. P. 'Eighteenth-century English society: class struggle without class?' *Social History* 3:2 (1978), 163–4.
―――*The Making of the English Working Class*. rev. edition 1968.
Thompson, George *A Speech on British Colonial Slavery . . . delivered at the Wesleyan Methodist Chapel, Irwell Street, Salford*. Manchester, 1832.
Thompson, William *An Inquiry into the Principles of the Distribution of Wealth most conducive to human happiness* 1824, reprinted New York, 1963.
Tilly, Charles (ed) 'Britain creates the Social Movement'. *Social Conflict and the Political Order in Modern Britain*. New Brunswick, 1982, pp. 21–51.
Tinker, Hugh *A New System of Slavery: The Export of Indian Labour Overseas 1830–1920*. 1974.
Tooke, John Horne *The Speeches of John Horne Tooke*. 1796.
Townsend, Joseph *A Journey Through Spain in the Years 1786 and 1787*. 3 vols. 1791.
Trudel, Marcel *L'Esclavage au Canada Français: Histoire et conditions de l'esclavage*. Quebec, 1960.
A True History of a Late Short Administration. 1807.
Trusler, Dr John *The London Adviser and Guide, Useful also to Foreigners*. 1786.
Tryon, Thomas *Friendly Advice to the Gentlemen – Planters of the East and West Indies*. 1684.
Tudesq, André Jean *Les Grands Notables en France (1840–9): Etude historique d'une psychologie sociale*. 2 vols. Paris, 1964.
Tunzelman, G. N. von 'Trends in Real Wages, 1750–1850, Revisited'. *Economic History Review* 22:1 (1979), 33–49.
[Turnbull, Gordon] *An Apology for Negro Slavery: or the West India Planters Vindicated . . .* 1786.
Turner, Mary *Slaves and Missionaries: The Disintegration of Jamaican Slave Society, 1787–1834*. Urbana, Ill., 1982.
Tyrell, Alex 'The 'Moral 'Radical Party' and the Anglo-Jamaican campaign for the abolition of the Negro–apprenticeship system'. *English Historical Review* 99:392 (1984) 481–502.
The Use of Machines in the Cotton Manufacture. Manchester, 1780.
Veitia-Linage, Joseph de *The Spanish Rule of Trade to the West Indies*. 1702.
Verlinden, Charles *The Beginnings of Modern Colonization: Eleven Essays with an Introduction*. transl. Yvonne Freccero. Ithaca, New York, 1970.
―――*L'Esclavage dans l'Europe médiévale: t. première: Péninsule Ibérique, France*. Brugge, 1955.

Vickers, John *Thomas Coke, Apostle of Methodism.* 1969.
Voyage Philosophique d' Angleterre. 1786.
Wadsworth, A. P. and J. de L. Mann *The Cotton Trade and Industrial Lancashire 1600–1780.* Manchester 1931, reprinted 1965.
Wallace, Charles Isaac 'Religion and Society in Eighteenth Century England: Geographic, Demographic and Occupational patterns of Dissent in the West Riding of Yorkshire, 1715–1801'. PhD dissertation, Duke University, 1973.
Wallace, James *A General and Descriptive History of . . . the town of Liverpool . . . together with . . . its extensive African Trade.* Liverpool, 1794.
Horace Walpole's Correspondence. New Haven. 1983.
Walvin, James *Black and White: The Negro in English Society, 1555–1945.* 1973.
——'The Public Campaign in England against Slavery, 1787–1834' in *The Abolition of the Atlantic Slave Trade.* D. Eltis and J. Walvin (eds). Madison, 1981, pp. 63–89.
——(ed) *Slavery and British Society 1776–1846.* 1982.
Ward, J.R. The Profitability and Viability of British West Indian Plantation Slavery, 1807–1834. (MSS)
Ward, W. R. *Religion and Society in England, 1790–1850.* Batsford, 1972.
——'The Tithe Question in England in the Early Nineteenth Century'. *Journal of Ecclesiastical History* 16:1 (1965), 67–81.
Warner, J. Wellman *The Wesleyan Movement and the Industrial Revolution.* New York, 1930.
A Warning to the Frequenters of Debating Clubs, being a short history of the Rise and Progress of those Clubs. 1810.
Warren, James Francis *The Sulu Zone 1768–1898: The dynamics of external trade, slavery . . .* Singapore, 1981.
Watson, Richard *A Defense of the Wesleyan Methodist Missions in the West Indies.* 1817.
——*A Sermon Preached before the University of Cambridge.* Cambridge, 1780.
Webb, Sidney and Beatrice *English Poor Law History.* 3 vols. 1927–9.
Wesley, John *Thoughts upon Slavery.* 1774.
The Wesleyan Preacher. 3 vols. 1832–3.
The West India Merchant. 1778.
Westergaard, Waldeman *The Danish West Indies under Company Rule 1671–1754.* New York, 1917.
Whitbread, Samuel *Substance of a Bill for Promoting and Encouraging Industry Amongst the Labouring Classes of the Community.* 1807.
Wilberforce, William *A Letter on the Abolition of the Slave Trade.* 1807.
Wilberforce, R. I. and Wilberforce S. *The Correspondence, of William Wilberforce.* 2 vols. London, 1840.
Wilentz, Sean *Chants Democratic: New York City and the Rise of the American Working Class.* New York, 1984.
Williams, Eric *Capitalism and Slavery,.* 1944, reprinted New York, 1966.
Wilmer, J. *The Case of John Wilmore Truly and Impartially Related, or a*

Looking-Glass for all Merchants and Planters that are concerned in the American Plantations. 1682.

Wilson, Ellen Gibson *The Loyal Blacks.* New York, 1976.

Wood, Betty *Slavery in Colonial Georgia 1730–1775.* Athens, Ga. 1984.

Wood, Thomas *A New Institute of the Imperial or Civil Law.* 1704.

_____L. L. D. *An Institute of the Laws of England.* 2 vols. 1720, 1772.

Wood, William *A Survey of Trade, in Four Parts.* 1718.

Wright, Gordon *Between the Guillotine and Liberty: Two Centuries of the Crime Problem in France.* New York, 1983.

Wrigley, E. A. and R. S. Schofield *The Population History of England: 1541–1871 A Reconstruction.* Cambridge, 1982.

Wyvill, Christopher *Political Papers.* 4 vols. 1794–6.

Young, Arthur *Political Essays Concerning the Present State of the British Empire.* London, 1772.

_____*Travels in France during the Years 1787, 1788 and 1789.* Jeffrey Kaplow (ed). New York, 1969.

Index

Abingdon, Lord, 223 n1
Abolitionism, Anglican, 63, 123–7;
American, 48, 57–9, 184 n70; 199
n14; 210n 10, Anglo-Jamaican, 232
n58; and aristocracy, 140, 164;
black, 23, 42, 214 n44; Catholic,
115–16, 226 n18, 233 n7, 234 n15;
Clapham Sect, 61, 111; class
linkages, 128–34, 139–61, 213 n29;
Danish, 51, 200 n8; demography
and, 11, 16, 29–30; Dutch, 15, 51,
91, 199 n4; French, xiii, xiv, 52–7,
91, 132–3, 202 n19, 203 n21, 23,
216 n49, 234 n14; German, xiv, 50,
198 n1; and industrialization, 2, 3,
10, 11, 58, 131–4, 153; Irish, 12,
46–7, 116, 250 n30; in literature,
94; middle-class, 132–3, 153–4;
Northern England, 67–73, 155, 160,
163, 211 n19, 217 n53; propaganda,
62–4, 66, 71, 78, 80, 94–5, 147–8,
156–9, 204 n27, 206 n42, 43, 47,
217–18 n55, 267 n5; Quaker, xiii,
59, 61–4 (see also Quakers); and
radicals, 124, 142–9, 164, 250 n30,
257 n63; and reform, 91, 96, 124,
142, 144–53, 164, 209 n8; 249–50
n30, 251 n33, 253 n45, 259 n74, 260
n77; Scottish, 76, 77, 80, 124, 217
n54; 220 n69, 237 n54; Spanish, 52,
199 n4 and Tories, 125, 140, 148,
261 n78; and Whigs, 257 n62;
women in, 78–9, 85, 149, 151, 215
n44–5, 219 n58, 221 n69–70, 225
n15; and working-class movements,
145–51, 159–60, 201 n14, 203 n21,
225 n15
Abolitionist, The, 157
Africa, and abolitionism, 6, 44, 214 n44;
popular images, 6, 18, 19, 156, 179
n48, 51, 205 n34; Portuguese, 52;
slave trade, 4, 5, 15, 18, 62, 65, 87–
8, 91, 138, 156, 170 n24, 183 n67,
201 n14, 248 n20

African merchants, 23, 64, 86–7
African Institution, 44, 45, 196 n61
America, Civil War, 59, 98;
Revolutionary War, 66, 68, 115
Amis des Noirs, 53–5
Anglican Church, and slavery, 39, 112–
14, 236 n40, 237 n52
Animal rights, 156, 160
Anstey, Roger, 1, 2, 21, 62, 63, 111,
114, 116, 155, 166, 245 n87
Antiabolitionism, 20, 71, 81, 83, 89–90,
95–6, 125, 126, 156–8, 202 n19, 203
n21, 204 n24, 207 n50, 211 n20, 213
n31, 214–17 n42, 44–7, 220 n65, 236
n42, 245 n87, 262–3 n87
Antisaccharites, 78–81, 131, 143, 214
n42
Apprenticeship, see indentured labour
Artisans, and abolitionism, 128–34, 146,
153, 245 n87, 252 n39; and
radicalism, 143, 225 n15, 249–50
n30, 251 n34, 253 n44
Atlantic Slave Trade and British
Abolition, 1
Austrian Netherlands, 170 n24

Baartman, Saartjie, 43–5, 48
Baptist War, 105, 108–9, 120
Baptism, and freedom, 32–5, 178 n44,
188 n24
Baptists, and slavery, 94, 119, 120, 124,
237 n51
Barker, Anthony, 6, 19
Bailyn, Bernard, 26
Barbados, 16, 18, 103, 105, 106–7, 112,
174 n36, 219–20 n62
Barton, John, 212 n23
Baxter, Richard, 182 n65
Beckford, William, 178–9 n47
Bedford, 77
Belfast, 250 n30
Belize (British Honduras), 101
Belgrade, 177 n42
Benezet, Anthony, 40, 63, 117

Bengal, 65
Bentham, Jeremy, 251 *n*33
Bible, and slavery, 20, 127
Birmingham, 75, 78, 150–1
Bissette, Cyril Charles Auguste, 202
  *n*20, 203 *n*21
Black Caribs, 65, 102, 103, 104, 106
Black Dwarf, 156
Blacks, Loyalists, 43; poor, 35–41, 60–1,
  72, 157, 191 *n*33, 195 *n*54, 205 *n*34,
  258 *n*74; population, 14, 27–30, 61,
  185 *n*10, 189 *n*25; Society, of
  London, 195 *n*60; transported from
  England, 34–5, 60, 191 *n*30; unpaid
  service, 34–41, 198 *n*75
Blackburn, 254 *n*50
Blackstone, William, 40
Blake, William, frontispiece, 155
Bloch, Marc, 49
Blome, Richard, 6
Bolton, 218 *n*56
Bordeaux, 222 *n*74
Bowling, Yorkshire, 148–9
Bradburn, Samuel, 143
Bradford, 254 *n*50
Braidwood, Stephen, 28
Braithwaite, John, 244 *n*83
Brazil, 8, 52, 258 *n*67
Bright, John, 4, 168 *n*9
Brissot de Warville, 55, 264 *n*91
Bristol, 23, 41, 71, 75, 77, 79, 86, 174
  *n*34, 186 *n*16, 195 *n*61, 211 *n*20
Brougham, Henry, 238 *n*34
Bugeaud, Marshal, 203 *n*23
Burke, Edmund, 182 *n*65, 223 *n*1
Buxton, Thomas Fowell, 147, 157

Cahiers de doléance (1789), 53–4
Cambridge University, 64
Capitalism and Slavery, 1
capitalism, and antislavery, 19–24
Carlyle, Thomas, 154
Carolina, Constitution, 24
Cartwright, John, 224 *n*6
Castlereagh, Lord, 91, 156
Catholic Emancipation Act (1829), 144
Catholicism, and missions, 115; and
  slavery, 115–16, 226 *n*18
Chartism and abolitionism, 150–1, 160
Chesapeake, 7, 119
Child labour, 147–8, 156, 157, 159, 160,
  174 *n*34, 252 *n*38, 254 *n*49, 260 *n*77,
  263 *n*87
Children's literature, 174 *n*34
Chimney sweeps, 43, 46–7, 157

Christianity, and slave resistance, 108
Clarkson, Thomas, x, 23, 33, 42, 55, 64,
  65, 67, 72, 78, 79, 81, 82, 86, 117,
  142, 163, 164, 166, 169 *n*13, 206
  *n*43, 218 *n*55, 223 *n*3–5, 228 *n*28,
  242–3 *n*84, 250 *n*31, 256 *n*57, 267
  *n*3–5
Class, and abolitionism, 39, 128–33,
  140–3, 145–54, 202 *n*20, 213 *n*29,
  238 *n*64, 241 *n*83, 252 *n*39, 255 *n*57
Clergy, creolization, 113–4, 233 *n*7
Club des amis des Noirs (1848), 264 *n*91
Cobbett, William, 34, 95, 145–6, 149,
  150, 151, 190 *n*27, 252–4 *n*41–5, 262
  *n*82
Cobden, Richard, 168 *n*9
Coke, Thomas, 119, 120, 121
Colonial trade, British and French,
  138–9
Compensation, 46–7, 93, 136, 149, 226
  *n*19, 254 *n*50, 258 *n*67, 262 *n*86
Condorcet, Marquis de, 55
Congress of Vienna, 91, 156
Conscription and impressment, 156, 259
  *n*74, 260 *n*77
Contract, and slavery, 38, 41
Corn Laws, 154, 227 *n*21
Cornwall, 79, 81, 131, 141, 219 *n*56, 238
  *n*69
Cotton, 7, 68–9; 141, 170 *n*18, 216–17
  *n*47; manufacturers, 68–9, 141, 212
  *n*25, 247 *n*17, 257 *n*66
Coupland, Reginald, 111
Cowper, William, 81, 155
Craton, Michael, 100, 101, 102, 239 *n*40
Creolization, and slave emancipation,
  97, 101, 102, 103, 107, 114, 121–2,
  238 *n*38, 231 *n*51, 232 *n*53
Crisis, The, 148, 150, 255 *n*54
Cuba, 8, 137, 258 *n*67
Cugoano, Ottabah, 205 *n*34
Curtin, Philip D., 21, 205 *n*34

Davis, David Brion, 1, 2, 14, 59, 62, 63,
  87, 111, 112, 118, 133, 138–40, 155–
  60, 166, 171 *n*27, 173 *n*31, 182 *n*66,
  245·*n*87, 247 *n*17, 255 *n*57, 257 *n*61,
  62, 258 *n*74, 261 *n*78, 268 *n*10
Demerara, 103, 107–8
Democracy, and abolition, 55, 155–8,
  253 *n*44, 264 *n*92
Denmark, 51
Demography, and abolitionism, 11, 16,
  29, 93, 173 *n*31, 201 *n*15
Decline, British colonial, 8–10

Defoe, Daniel, 181 *n*61
Dickson, William, 217 *n*54, 222 *n*77
Dissent, *see* Non-conformity
Ditchfield, G. M., 96, 124
Dolben, Sir William, 76
Dominica, 104, 105, 231 *n*47
Dundas, Henry, 238 *n*35
Dunning, John, 40, 190 *n*28
Dupanloup, Abbé, 115

East Indies, 19, 33
Edinburgh, 77, 79, 81, 83, 212 *n*23, 218 *n*56, 220 *n*70
Elections, French, 56–7, 203 *n*21, British, 90, 145–7, 224 *n*6–7
Eltis, David, 2, 4, 133, 134, 138, 244 *n*84, 246 *n*4, 257 *n*61
Emmer, Pieter, 52
Encyclopédie, 179 *n*48
Engerman, Stanley, 244 *n*84, 246 *n*8
England, black population, 15, 27–30, 60–1, 185 *n*10; 'free soil', 26, 29, 32, 37, 38, 42–5, 47–9, 177 *n*42, 185 *n*7, 187 *n*19, 192 *n*34, 196 *n*63, 197 *n*67, 69, 70, 197 *n*72; liberation of children, 45; magistrates and slaves, 27, 63, 73, 189 *n*25; minorities in, 15, 30–1, 186 *n*18; slave market, 29, 30, 42; slave advertisements, 25, 28–30, 43, 45, 190 *n*28, 191 *n*34, 192, *n*43, 195 *n*60, 61; slaves, 15, 16, 25–49
Equiano, Olaudah, 23, 34, 35, 169 *n*13, 182 *n*64, 190 *n*26, 250 *n*30
Erskine, Thomas, 205 *n*34
Essay on the Slavery and Commerce of the Human Species, 163
Estwick, Samuel, 86, 193 *n*45
Evangelicals, and slavery, 59, 116–30
Examiner, The, 95, 252 *n*39
Exeter, 75
Exeter, Hall, 147

Factory labour, 134, 145–9, 159, 252 *n*38
Falmouth, 75, 77
Felice, G. de, 202 *n*20
Ferriar, John, 228 *n*28
Fielden, John, 253 *n*44
Fielding, Sir John, 189 *n*25, 192 *n*34
Fifth Monarchy men, 125
Finley, Moses, 136
Fladeland, Betty, 155, 159
Flanders, 172 *n*28

Flogging, 251 *n*38, 263 *n*88
Flower, Benjamin, 261 *n*78, 82
Fogel, Robert, 182 *n*66, 246 *n*8
Fox, Charles James, 61, 65, 68, 74, 84, 124, 212 *n*25, 258 *n*74
Fox-Genovese, Elizabeth, 13
France, Algerian slavery, 57, 203 *n*23; artisans and anti-slavery, 56, 132–3; Constituent Assembly, 1848, 53; Departmental and Colonial Councils, 201 *n*23, 225 *n*17; electoral propaganda, 56–7; emancipation, 52–7, 92–3, 200 *n*12; galley slaves, 17, 41, 54, 195 *n*57, 201–2 *n*15; July Monarchy, 56, 92, 159, 201 *n*14, 202 *n*19, 225 *n*15, 233 *n*7; Napoleonic Wars, 9, 53, 94, 97, 125; petitions, 53–6; Restoration, 55, 56; Revolutionary Wars, 52–5, 97–9, 104–5, 119; Second Empire, 53, 55, 201 *n*14; second slavery, 11, 52, 56, 119, 160, 201 *n*13; slaves in, 15, 173 *n*33, 189 *n*25; war scare, 56–7, 202 *n*19, 203 *n*21
Free labour, Chinese experiment, 243 *n*83; and free trade, 154; ideology, 133–4, 152–3, 162, 241–5, 254 *n*50, 255 *n*51, 265–6; and slave labour, 14, 22, 85–6, 133–4, 146, 148, 149, 154, 157–9, 182 *n*62, 204 *n*27, 240 *n*70, 241–5, 254 *n*47–9, 259 *n*74, 262–3 *n*87, 264 *n*90; and slave emancipation, 135, 136, 138, 151–3, 258 *n*67
Free trade, and free labour, 73; and slavery, 69, 181 *n*61
Freyer, Peter, 42, 45, 188 *n*24, 197 *n*69
Fuller, Stephen, 213 *n*38
Fustian campaign, 68–9

Galley slaves, French, 17, 41, 54, 173 *n*33, 195 *n*57, 201–2 *n*15; Spanish 256 *n*57
Ganilh, Charles, 244 *n*83
Gazetteer, 45
Geggus, David, 98
Gemery, Henry S., 3
Genovese, Eugene, 13, 99
Geographers, 17–19, 169 *n*14, 175–9
George III, 29, 67, 156, 261 *n*81
Georgia, 117, 179 *n*49
Gilbert, A. D., 131, 133
Glasgow, 218 *n*57, 250 *n*30
Godwin, William, 260 *n*77

Godwyn, Morgan, 33, 39, 188 n24
Gordon riots, (1780), 83, 84, 142, 220
    n63
Gosset, J. R., 244 n83
Great Britain, abolition of 1806–07, xiii,
    89–90, 91, 105, 119, 156; abolition
    policy, xiii, 2, 4, 50, 51, 57, 58, 61,
    91, 121, 138, 140, 156, 203 n23, 225
    n; agriculture, 141, 156, 248 n22,
    259 n74; Anglican Church, 13, 62,
    112–14, 125–7; Catholic
    Emancipation (1829), 96, 144;
    cotton industry, 68–9, 71–2, 210
    n12, 212 n25, 247 n17, 248 n23, 257
    n66; Factory Movement, 145–9;
    General Chamber of Manufactures,
    69; Northern England, 67–73, 145–
    7; Poor Law Amendment Act
    (1834), 151; Reform Act (1832),
    92, 96, 108, 126, 144; slave colony
    trade, 9, 10, 141, 183 n66;
    emancipation, *see* slave
    emancipation; slave resistance, 33,
    35, 45, 97–110; sugar absention,
    78–9, 104; Sunday School
    Movement, 124, 142, 236 n44, West
    India Regiments, 98, 229 n35
Green-Pedersen, Svend E., 51
Gegoire, Abbé, 55
Grenada, 47, 104, 105, 106, 109, 231
    n51
Guadeloupe, 98, 105, 109, 226 n18, 247
    n20
Guizot, François, 203 n23
Gunn, J. A. W., 68
Guthrie, William, 169 n13–4

Habeas Corpus, 37, 41, 42, 195 n57
Haiti, xiii, 10; *see also* St Domingue
Hampden Clubs, 144
Hardwicke, Lord (Sir Philip Yorke), 31,
    32, 34, 191 n30
Hardy, Thomas, 124, 238 n65
Harrison, Brian, 151
Haskell, Thomas, 181 n59, 198 n1, 245
    n87
Hastings, Warren, 66
Hawkesbury, Lord, later Lord
    Liverpool, 76–7
Hegemony, and abolitionism, 135–40,
    225 n13, 246 n2, 247 n17, 164 n92
Heine, Heinrich, 52
Hellie, Richard, 136
Henley, Lord Chancellor, 35, 40

Hill, Richard, 218 n56
Higman, Barry, 97, 230 n41
Hirschman, Albert, 183 n
Hoare, Samuel, 205 n34
Hogendorn, Jan, 3
Hodgson, Adam, 244 n83
Holt, John, 32, 40
'Hottentot Venus' affair, *see* Baartman,
    Saartjie,
How, Richard, 199 n5
Howick, Lord, 105
Humanity, or the Rights of Nature, 227
    n22
Humboldt, Alexander von, 50
'Hungry forties', 153–4
Hunt, E. M. 67
Hunt, Henry, 253n, 44
Hurwitz, Edith, 114
Hylas, John, 191 n30

Indentured labour, 10, 16, 18, 41, 135,
    137, 149, 151–2, 157, 195 n57, 206
    n34, 259 n74
India, 10, 65–6, 68, 109, 141, 208 n53,
    208 n58, 247 n20
Industrialization, and abolitionism, 2, 3,
    10, 11, 58, 71–2, 131–4, 153, 155,
    162
Intermarriage, racial, 34, 190 n26
Ipswich, 79, 81
Ireland, 46–7, 69, 79, 96, 109, 116, 142,
    156, 174 n34, 194 n52, 260 n77, 262
    n83
Isambert, F. A., 202 n19, 203 n21
Italy, 12, 115, 170

Jacobinism, 84, 89, 144, 217 n49, 251
    n34, 264 n91
Jamaica, 8, 15, 18, 33, 76, 89, 100, 101,
    107, 108, 113, 151, 171 n24, 178
    n44, 185 n10, 208 n53, 258 n67;
    Baptist War, 105, 108–09; slave
    resistance, 100–5, 107–8, 120, 177
    n42
James, C. L. R., 1, 97
Java, 175 n39, 243 n83
Jews, 30, 187 n18, 235 n15
Jentz, John, 133
Johnson, Samuel, 178 n44
Jollivet, Thomas, 203 n21, 226 n18
Judicial cases, Butts v. Penny 185 n2
    Cay v. Crichton, 194 n52,
    Chamberline v. Harvey, 188 n24;
    Grace decision, 37, King v. Thames

Ditton, 195 *n*54, Pearne, *v*. Lisle, 32, Smith *v*. Gould, 185 *n*7

Kendal, 77
King, Henry, 191 *n*34
Knibb, Rev. William, 154, 264 *n*90

Lagos, 14
Lamennais, Felicité de, 234 *n*15
Lancashire, 30, 68–9, 89, 147, 156, 174 *n*34, 210 *n*12, 239 *n*69, 248 *n*24, 257 *n*63
Las Casas, Bartolomé de, 19, 23
Lascelles, Edward, 224 *n*7
Law of nations, 24, 163, 184 *n*69
Leeds, 75
Leghorn, 170 *n*24
Leicester, 125, 148, 218 *n*56
Lewes, 76
Liberty, ideology of, 17, 24, 43, 73, 175–6 *n*40, 197 *n*69, 267 *n*3; localized, x, 14, 16–9, 172 *n*28, 173 *n*31; and slavery, 17
Lille, 201 *n*14
Lisbon, 14
Literature, and abolitionism, 94
Liverpool, 21, 58, 64, 71, 79, 81, 89, 181 *n*59, 192 *n*40, 211 *n*20, 212 *n*25, 213 *n*27, 216 *n*47, 223 *n*4; slave sales, 46, 174 *n*34, 195 *n*61; slaves liberated, 197 *n*68
Livingstone, David, 201 *n*14
Locke, John, 23, 184 *n*69
Lofft, Capel, 258 *n*74
London, 21, 28, 31, 33, 35, 39, 41, 43, 44, 46, 56, 58, 59, 60–1, 68, 71, 76, 80, 82, 89, 145, 157, 174 *n*34, 194 *n*54, 205 *n*34, 258 *n*74
London Abolition Society, 59, 62, 65, 66, 70, 78, 89, 95, 210 *n*17, 212 *n*23, 221 *n*65, 223 *n*3, 268 *n*8
Long, Edward, 20, 28, 191 *n*34, 193 *n*45
L'Ouverture, Toussaint, 136
Lyons, 133, 160, 225 *n*15, 248 *n*23

McNeill, Williams, 11
Madeira, xiii, 173 *n*31, 177 *n*42
Magdol, Edward, 133
Maidstone, 76
Manchester, 67–75, 76, 77, 80, 82–3, 85, 86, 90, 93, 125, 140, 145–6, 157, 163–4, 210 *n*13, 17, 212 *n*23, 213 *n*26, 27, 228 *n*26, 241 *n*41, 42, 253 *n*44, 261 *n*78

Manning, Patrick, 5
Mansfield James, Counsel for Somerset, 32, 197 *n*72
Mansfield, Chief Justice, xiii, 15, 32, 36–43, 59, 60, 185 *n*10, 192 *n*37, 39, 41, 42, 193 *n*45, 48, 51, 194 *n*52, 53, 54, 195 *n*57, 196 *n*63, 197 *n*66, 204 *n*30, 205*n*31
Marshall, Peter, 65
Martinique, 203 *n*23, 226 *n*18
Marx, Karl, 155, 164
Massachusetts, xiii, 13
Matthews, Theobald, 116
Mercantilism, 4, 23, 76-7
Methodism, and slavery, 85, 86, 116, 124–30, 143, 164, 224 *n*7, 237 *n*51, 238 *n*61; English, 86, 116, 124, 143, 149, 239 *n*69; social composition, 128–30, 149, 238 *n*62–4, 239 *n*69, 241 *n*79; Southern, 118–21; West Indian, 113, 117–20, 235 *n*28, 236 *n*37; Manchester, 117, 143, 253 *n*44
Middleburg, 15
Mill, John Stuart, 164
Milton, Lord, 224 *n*7
Missionaries, 115–20, 153, 154, 233 *n*7; martyrs, 123
Monmouth, 220 *n*65
Montagu, Duke of, 205 *n*34
Moravians, 113, 120
Morning Chronicle, 43–4
Morning Herald, 45
Mulhouse, 133

Nantes, 222 *n*74
Napoleon I, xiii, 9, 55, 97, 119, 160, 201 *n*13
National Union of the Working Classes, 254 *n*50
Nazi Germany, 11
New Poor Law, *see* Poor Law
New Jersey, xiii, 14
New York, xiii, 14
Newspapers, and abolition, 40, 65, 70, 192 *n*40, 42, 196 *n*62, 212 *n*23, 213 *n*29, 213 *n*34; black advertisements, 28, 29
Nonconformity, and abolitionism, 111, 118–31, 227 *n*21; and Anglicanism, 120–6; and artisans, 128–34, 153; and British industrialization, 128–32, 153, 238–40
North, Lord, 62, 72, 74, 84, 217 *n*54
North Africa, 17, 41

Northampton, 75, 76, 81, 213 *n*34
Northern Star, 151, 255 *n*55
Norwich, 68, 74, 76, 77, 85, 219 *n*58
Nottingham, 75, 81, 125, 213 *n*25, 218
    *n*56, 220 *n*64, 223 *n*1

Oastler, Richard, 132, 147
'Occasional Discourse on the Nigger
    Question', 154
O'Connel, Daniel, 116
Oglethorpe, James, 177 *n*43
Oldham, 146, 149, 252-4 *n*44-5
Olney, 77, 81
Oroonoko, 228 *n*28
Ostend, 170 *n*24
Owen, Robert, 148, 150, 254 *n*47
Oxford University, 76, 125

Packwood, George, 30
Paine, Tom, 123, 130, 143, 155, 251 *n*33
Paley, William, 155, 243 *n*83
Papacy, xiv, 115
Paris, 15, 55, 92, 132-3, 160, 200 *n*12,
    201 *n*23, 217 *n*49, 225 *n*15, 240 *n*75
Parish apprentices, *see* child labour
Patterson, Orlando, 26
Paupers, 84-5, 156, 174 *n*34
Peace of Paris (1814), 91, 261 *n*80
Peace of Versailles (1783), 65-6, 170
    *n*24, 206 *n*41, 207 *n*48
Peel, Robert, 73, 90
Pennsylvania, xiii, 13, 18, 62, 210 *n*10
Petitions, of 1787-8, 3, 53, 58, 70-8,
    91-2, 93, 124, 210-14; of 1792, 80-
    4, 93, 124, 143, 218-9 *n*56-8; of
    1806, 90; of 1814, 58, 92, 93-4,
    156; of 1823-24, 58; of 1830-31, 58,
    92, 144; of 1833, 58, 92, 94, 144; of
    1838, 3, 58; American, 133;
    Birmingham, 75, 212 *n*25;
    challenged, 81-2, 84, 211 *n*20, 21,
    218 *n*56; French, 53-6, 92-3, 202
    *n*20, 225 *n*15-18, 240 *n*75; signers,
    80-85, 218-19 *n*56-8, 221 *n*66, 69;
    Liverpool, 71, 211 *n*20;
    Manchester, 70-5, 90, 140, 210 *n*12,
    13, 211 *n*20, 21, 212 *n*23, 25, 213
    *n*26, 218 *n*56, 223 *n*5; numbers, 58-
    9, 70-6, 80, 82-3, 85, 91-4, 210
    *n*13, 17, 213 *n*35, 218-19 *n*56-61,
    221 *n*69-70, 225 *n*12, 15, 227 *n*20;
    and Parliament, 62, 74, 76, 77, 80,
    84, 85, 92-3, 220 *n*64, 222 *n*77, 250
    *n*30; Pennsylvania, 210 *n*10; and

    violence, 84; Virginia, 210 *n*10;
    women's 78-9, 85, 149, 151; and
    workingmen, 56, 81, 128-34, 212
    *n*25, 214 *n*41
Phillips, John A., 76
Pinney, John, 83
Pitt, William (the Elder), 177 *n*43
Pitt, William (the younger), 59, 61, 65,
    68, 82, 84, 142, 205 *n*34, 206 *n*38,
    222 *n*77, 248 *n*48, 261-2 *n*82
Planters, 10, 33, 52, 248 *n*20
Playfair, William, 19
Plymouth, 77
Political economists, 19, 242-4 *n*84-5,
    256 *n*57
Poor Law, and abolitionism, 151-3,
    255-7 *n*57-61, 256 *n*57, 257 *n*66;
    and blacks, 35, 38, 41, 60, 191 *n*33,
    195 *n*54, 258 *n*74; Speenhamland
    system, 152, 256 *n*58
Popular violence, 84, 96-109, 141-2,
    220 *n*63, 249 *n*26
Portugal, 14, 52, 197 *n*69
Poverty, and abolitionism, 43, 149, 256-
    9, 260 *n*77, 261 *n*78
Pratt, Samuel J., 227 *n*22
Preston Pilot, 126
Priestley, Joseph, 123, 243 *n*83, 251 *n*33
Prince, Mary, 197 *n*70
Prince of Angola, 228 *n*28
Privy Council, 61, 77, 88
Prussia, 50
Public Advertiser, 66

Quakers, xiii, 21, 23, 59, 61-4, 65-8,
    71-3, 113, 123, 125, 128, 150, 195
    *n*61, 206 *n*43, 47, 212 *n*23, 223 *n*1,
    250 *n*30; petition, 59, 62, 204 *n*30,
    206 *n*42
Quinet, Edgar, 234 *n*15

Race, and slavery, 19, 20, 27, 34, 48,
    143, 154, 173 *n*33, 252 *n*41, 260 *n*77
Racism, 154, 165, 205 *n*34, 251 *n*33
Radicals, 84-5, 124, 138, 142-9, 200
    *n*12, 216 *n*49, 226 *n*18, 252-4 *n*44-
    5, 257 *n*63
Ramsay, James, 42, 65
Raynal, Abbé, 86
Record, The, 127
Revolutions, Great French, xiii, 53-5,
    115, 142-4, 200 *n*12, 201 *n*15, 217
    *n*49, 250 *n*30, 258 *n*74; of 1848, 93,
    115, 159, 201 *n*14, 203 *n*21

Rhode Island, xiii, 14
Rice, Duncan, 94
Rights of Man, 143, 221 n65
Right of Search, Quintuple Treaty, xiv
Rio de la Plata, 7
Roman Catholic Relief Act, (1829), 126
Roscoe, William, 197 n68
Royal Addresses (1787–8), 70, 142
Royal African Company, 23, 26
Rule, John, 131
Russia, 35, 63, 141

St Bartholomew, 51, 171 n24
St Domingue, 8, 10, 55, 79, 97–9, 105, 119, 136, 217 n49, 222 n74, 229 n35, 266 n1 (*see also* Haiti)
St George's Parish, London, 28
St Helena, 33
St Lucia, 104, 109, 247, n20
St Vincent, 104–6, 109, 231 n51, 259, n74
Saint-Hilaire, Geoffroy, 234 n15
'Saints', abolitionist, 1, 59, 61, 111, 128, 135, 261 n78
Sansum, Henry, 150–1
Say, Jean-Baptiste, 243–4 n83
Schoelcher, Victor, 53, 98, 201 n14
Schofield, R. S., 11
Scotland, 76, 77, 79, 80, 85, 102, 131, 156, 157, 175 n39, 217 n54, 259 n74
Sedition Bills, 74, 82–3, 219 n61, 221 n67, 261 n82
Semeur, Le, 201 n13 and 14
Sepúlveda, Juan Gines de, 19
Serfdom, 51–2, 54, 115, 136, 173 n31, 200 n8, 201 n15
Seven Years War, 102, 141
Sharp, Granville, 32, 39, 41, 43, 59, 60, 64, 105, 155, 175 n38, 189 n25, 191 n29, 192 n61, 204 n30, 205 n34, 235 n28, 258 n74, 262 n82
Sharpe, Sam, 108
Sheffield, 75, 76, 82, 262–3 n2
Shrewsbury, 75
Shropshire, 75
Shyllon, Folarin, 28, 42, 197 n70
Sidmouth Bill, 237 n51
Sierra Leone, 6, 60–1, 169 n13, 205 n34, 242 n84, 250 n31, 258 n74, 261 n78
Slave emancipation, America, xiv, 58; Brazil, xiv, 5; British colonies, xiv, 4, 25, 46, 57, 60, 144, 257 n62; Cape Colony, 57; compensation, 46–7, 93, 136–8; Cuba, xiv, 5; Danish, xiv, 51; Dutch, xiv, 52–3;

French, xiii, xiv, 11, 52–7, 136, 137–8, 159, 200 n12, 233 n7; Pennsylvania, xiii, 62; Thirteenth Amendment, xiv, 15
Slave labour, and free, 14, 22, 85–6, 133–4, 146, 148–9, 154, 157–9, 182 n62, 204 n27, 244 n85, 259 n74, 262–4 n87–8
Slave prices, 36,42, 194 n54
Slave regiments, 98, 229 n35
Slave resistance, and abolitionism, 97–110; American, 98, 154, 186 n16; British, 45, 97–110, 154, 186 n16, 189 n25, 229–32; Barbados, 103, 106–7; and christianization, 108, 110, 121–3; and creolization, 97, 101, 103, 231 n51, 232 n53; Danish, 98; Demerara, 103, 107–8; Dominica, 104, 231 n47; French, 10, 53, 97–8, 102; Grenada, 104–6, 231 n51; Guadeloupe, 98, 105, 109; Jamaica, 100, 103, 177 n42, 229 n43, 249 n46; Maroon, 99–100, 104, 231 n47; Martinique, 98; old colonies, 99–101; plots, 101–4; post-Napoleonic, 102–4, 106–10; St Domingue, 10, 53, 97–9, 105; St Lucia, 98, 104; St Vincent, 104, 109, 231 n51
Slave trade, African, 4, 6, 170 n24; Brazil, 4; British abolition, xiii, 4, 65; British foreign, 140, 233 n8; French, 52–3, 56, 91, 170 n24, 201 n14; insurance, 204 n31; and Napoleon III, 53, 201 n14; North African, 17, 141, 177 n42; Russian, 177 n42
Slavery, African, 52, 177 n40; Algerian, 141, 177 n42, 203 n23, 235 n15; ancient, 12, 136; Asian, 171 n24, 27; Cape Colony, 44; Caucasian, 17, 176 n40, 177 n42; Christian, 12, 16, 17, 27, 32, 62, 111–23, 128–30, 143, 175 n39, 233 n7, 234 n9; Dutch, 15; in England, 16, 25–49; French, 15, 113, 173 n33, 189 n25, 201 n15, 233 n7, 242 n84; French Restoration, xiii, 11; and the French Revolution, 52–5; and Judaism, 111, 235 n15; Latin American, 137, 200 n11; Mediterranean, 12, 13, 15, 111, 172 n31; Moslem, 12, 111, 235 n15; North American, 242 n84; Polish,

17, 176 *n*40; Portuguese, 14, 45, 115, 172 *n*30; Roman, 12, 136, 138, 166; Russian, 17, 35, 136, 138, 166, 176 *n*40; Scottish, 173 *n*31, 175 *n*39, 186 *n*16, 189 *n*24, 191 *n*30, 244 *n*85, 259 *n*74; Spanish, 13, 14, 115, 172 *n*28, 234 *n*8, 256 *n*57; Tartar, 177 *n*40; Turkish, 12, 17, 175 *n*39, 40

Smith, Adam, x, 17, 18, 85, 133–4, 173 *n*31, 191 *n*30, 241–2 *n*84

Smith, William, 217 *n*53

Société Française pour l'abolition de l'esclavage, 55, 201 *n*14, 202 *n*19, 20, 225 *n*15

Society for Constitutional Information, 206 *n*43, 250 *n*30

Society for the Propagation of the Gospel, 112, 207 *n*48, 233 *n*6

Somerset case (1772), 15, 28, 36–43, 59, 60, 117, 177 *n*41, 184 *n*70, 190 *n*26, 192 *n*41, 193 *n*44, 45, 194 *n*52, 195 *n*57, 196 *n*62, 63, 198 *n*75, 77, 204 *n*27

Somerville, Thomas, 260 *n*77

Sonthonax, Léger-Félicité, 55

South Shields, 214 *n*25

Southampton, 77

Soviet Union, 11

Spa Fields riots, 156

Spain, 13, 14, 115, 172 *n*28, 30, 234 *n*8, 256 *n*57

Speenhamland system, 152, 256 *n*58

Spence, Thomas, 174 *n*34, 260 *n*77

Staffordshire, 78

Stamford, 77

Stanley, Edward, 99

Stephen, George, 257 *n*62

Stephen, James, 126, 155, 228 *n*34, 243 *n*83, 261 *n*78

Steuart, James, 243–4 *n*83

Strong, Jonathan, 189 *n*25

Stuart, Charles, 193 *n*45

Sturge, Joseph, 155

Sugar, 7, 8, 78–9, 104, 137, 138, 153–4, 169, *n*19, 208 *n*53, 215–17, *n*45–9, 241–3 *n*84, 245 *n*87, 247 *n*20, 258 *n*67; and St Domingue, 79, 217 *n*49, 266 *n*1; world production, 8, 9

Sunday schools, 124, 142

Swansea, 77

Talbot, Charles, *see* Yorke-Talbot opinion

Tarleton, Banastre, 81, 218 *n*56

Temperley, Howard, 2, 28, 133, 134

Test and Corporation Acts, 67, 124, 126, 144

Texas, 203 *n*23

Tewkesbury, 224 *n*6

Thelwall, John, 260 *n*77

Thomas, Dalby, 181 *n*61

Thompson, E. P., 131–2, 155

Thompson, George, 264 *n*90, 266 *n*1

Thompson, William, 242 *n*84, 260 *n*77

Three Months in Jamaica, in 1832, 147

Times, The, 207 *n*50–1

Tobago, 170 *n*24

Tocqueville, Alexis de, 16, 57, 155, 164, 202 *n*20

Townsend, Joseph, 256 *n*57

Trinidad, 94, 243 *n*83

Tunisia, 235 *n*15

Turgot, Anne Robert Jacques, 243 *n*83

Turner, Mary, 108, 122

Tuscany, 170 *n*24

Univers, L', 115, 201 *n*14

Valladolid, 19

Vassa (or Vasa), Gustavus, *see* Equiano

Verlinden, Charles, 12–13

Veuillot, Louis, 201 *n*14

Villeinage, 47, 185 *n*7

Virginia, 14, 120, 177 *n*42

Voice of the West Riding, 146–7, 149

Wages, 31, 33, 35–8, 41, 43, 153–4, 181 *n*62, 189 *n*25, 193 *n*46, 194 *n*52, 54, 195 *n*57, 196 *n*61, 198 *n*75, 239 *n*69, 244 *n*85, 248 *n*24, 249 *n*30, 264 *n*90

Wales, 77, 79

Walker, Thomas, 69, 205 *n*34, 212 *n*25, 250 *n*31

Walpole, Robert, 177 *n*43

Walvin, James, 2, 31, 38, 41, 42, 124

Ward, J. R., 10, 246 *n*8

Warrington, 68, 240 *n*70

Waterford, Ireland, 46–7

Watson, Richard, 64

Wealth of Nations, 133–4, 241–2 *n*84

Wedgwood, Josiah, 69, 77, 78

Wellington, Duke of, 156

Wesley, John, 64, 78, 86, 117, 119, 123

West Indians, 18–9, 34, 36–9, 42, 56, 58, 83, 84, 90, 95, 103, 105, 106, 150, 193 *n*45, 198 *n*75, 203 *n*23, 204 *n*27, 204 *n*30, 208 *n*53, 213 *n*29, 223 *n*4, 261 *n*82

West Indies, 19, 65, 87, 95, 97–110,
　　112–23, 137, 138, 140, 141, 153–4,
　　157, 178 n45, 179 n49, 201 n23, 207
　　n48, 229–32, 233 n5, 234 n9–10, 247
　　n20, 258 n67
West Riding, of Yorkshire, 131, 146,
　　238 n63, 239 n69
Westmoreland, Earl, 180 n57, 268 n13
Whitbread, Samuel, 141, 256 n58
Whitefield, George, 116–17
Whitely, Henry, 147
Whydah, 179 n51
Wife sales, 175 n36, 190 n27
Wilberforce, William, 59, 64, 65, 80, 84,
　　90, 124, 126, 155, 156, 205 n34, 222
　　n70, 224 n7, 243 n83, 261 n82
Wilentz, Sean, 240 n70
Williams, Eric, 1, 2, 4, 10, 166, 244 n83
Williamson's Liverpool Advertiser, 64
Wilkes, John, 68, 74, 210 n9
Woller, T. J., 262 n82
Wollstonecraft, Mary, 259–60 n77
Worcester, 77
Workingmen, and abolitionism, 72, 92,
　　145 ff; 213 n41, 216–17 n47–54, 218
　　n56, 225 n15, 239–40, 245 n87, 258
　　n67, 259 n74
Wrigley, E. A., 11

York, 75, 82
Yorke, Sir Philip, *see* Hardwicke
Yorke-Talbot opinion, 31–7, 187 n19,
　　190 n28, 191 n30
Yorkshire, 68, 77, 85, 89, 90, 131, 145,
　　147, 224 n7, 238 n63, 271 n82, 266
　　n2
Young, Arthur, 17, 86, 184 n70, 222
　　n74, 243 n83

Zong case, 59, 60, 204 n30